Encyclopedia of Home Care for the Elderly

ENCYCLOPEDIA
OF HOME CARE
FOR THE ELDERLY

Edited by ADA ROMAINE-DAVIS,
JENNIFER BOONDAS,
and AYELIFFE LENIHAN

Foreword by Robert N. Butler

Greenwood Press
Westport, Connecticut • London

Library of Congress Cataloging-in-Publication Data

Encyclopedia of home care for the elderly / edited by Ada Romaine-
   Davis, Jennifer Boondas, and Ayeliffe Lenihan ; foreword by Robert
   N. Butler.
       p.   cm.
   Includes bibliographical references and index.
   ISBN 0–313–28532–2 (alk. paper)
     1. Aged—Home care—United States.   2. Aged—United States.
   I. Romaine-Davis, Ada.   II. Boondas, Jennifer.   III. Lenihan,
   Ayeliffe A.
   HV1461.E5   1995
   362.6—dc20   94–17989

British Library Cataloguing in Publication Data is available.

Library of Congress Catalog Card Number: 94–17989
ISBN: 0–313–28532–2

First published in 1995

Greenwood Press, 88 Post Road West, Westport, CT 06881
An imprint of Greenwood Publishing Group, Inc.

Printed in the United States of America

The paper used in this book complies with the
Permanent Paper Standard issued by the National
Information Standards Organization (Z39.48–1984).

10 9 8 7 6 5 4 3 2

Contents

List of Entries

Foreword

In recent years, there has been a steady movement away from deinstitutionalization toward community and home care for people of all ages, including older persons. In the process, home care has become an industry, spawning profit-making, publically owned companies that employ thousands of workers. Home care has also become an important element in the debate over national health care reforms, especially in the provision of long-term care. In short, home care has reached the big time, and it is here to stay.

The publication of the *Encyclopedia of Home Care for the Elderly* is therefore not only timely, but also valuable, for it covers a wide range of topics relating to this multidisciplinary field, encompassing issues relevant to the practice of geriatrics and gerontology, social work, nursing, psychiatry, occupational therapy, and other disciplines. Consequently, this fine reference book will meet many needs with its broad array of up-to-date articles written by some of the best practitioners and researchers in the country.

As we move into the twenty-first century, home care and community care are likely to become even more desirable and useful to the American public. For decades we have talked about the continuing spectrum of care, which is essential to match the changing needs of older persons over time. But for too long this concept has been more an aspiration than a reality. Now the public and health professionals are in tune. They are speaking with one voice, clamoring for affordable, high-quality care in the home, where most of us wish to remain for as long as possible.

Robert N. Butler, MD

Introduction

The President's Health Care Reform plan emphasizes the need for and the importance of home health care. While there seems to be general agreement that reform will be incremental, the restructuring of the nation's health care system embodies the concepts of consumer access to health care services, consumer responsibility for self-care and informed decision making, and consumer utilization of cost-effective quality care.

Home care as a component of the total health care delivery system is defined as an array of preventive, therapeutic, and supportive services provided to patients in their homes because of illness and disability. From the standpoint of the elderly, this care option is appealing because it enables them to live in the familiar surroundings of their own homes. From the standpoint of policy makers, many believe that home care, rather than institutional care, can provide the elderly with varying levels of care at a significant savings when compared with the cost of institutional care.

Today there are more than 6,000 home health agencies in the United States. These may be for-profit proprietary agencies, hospital-based programs, nonprofit voluntary agencies, or part of state or local health departments. The home care provided by voluntary agencies is coordinated by a visiting nurse. Home health aides, similar to nursing aides in the hospital setting, provide a large proportion of in-home personal care. In recent years, because patients receiving home care are substantially more acutely ill than in the past, nurse practitioners are becoming members of home care agency staffs to provide the more complex care that is required. Besides nursing care, other services provided include physical, occupational, and speech therapy, and counseling related to nutrition, clinical pharmacology, and social work needs. Many agencies also provide the nursing portion of hospice care or operate full-fledged hospice programs certified by Medicare for reimbursement. Hospice care is provided to terminally ill patients projected to be in the last six months of life, when the patient can no longer be cared for in the home.

Any patient or family may purchase home care from an agency. Under Medicare, patients who meet certain criteria are eligible for reimbursement of these costs. The criteria are that (1) the patient is under the care of a physician and is largely homebound, and (2) the patient has an active medical problem that requires skilled nursing or other skilled professional services, such as physical or occupational therapy. Because of the criterion that the patient must have an active medical problem requiring skilled care, payment for the services of a home health aide is often denied when the active problem becomes stable, even when the home health aide's services are important to maintain the patient's health. At this point, caregivers become the patient's spouse or family members, many of whom must provide care over many months, even years.

The most common problems referred to home care agencies are postsurgical wound care, congestive heart failure, hypertension, orthopedic problems requiring rehabilitation, diabetes, incurable cancer, AIDS, stroke and other incapacitating neurological problems, decubitus and stasis ulcers, dementia, and chronic obstructive pulmonary disease (emphysema).

Home care is a fast-growing and complex industry. Contributing to this reality are several factors. The number of elderly, particularly the oldest old, is increasing more rapidly than other age groups in the total population. Although the majority of older persons enjoy good health, many exhibit physical and mental impairments, frailty, poor health practices, or an inability to care for themselves. Also, many elderly are vulnerable to injury, and both acute and chronic illnesses. All of these tax the inner strength and resources of them and their families. Early hospital discharges are resulting in referrals to home care for continuity of care. Improved technology has dramatically changed the nature of care that is provided at home even for those who require sophisticated medical equipment.

The compelling intent behind this encyclopedia is the relevance of home health care, and the interest and concern it generates. Because of Health Care Reform, home care is more than ever at the threshold of further expansion and revision. As the term implies, this encyclopedia is designed to comprehensively address the subject. The articles represent a wide range of topics and are arranged alphabetically by subject for easy reference for consumers and providers. It is the goal of the editors to afford deeper insights and new perspectives regarding the complexity of home health care.

The Encyclopedia is oriented toward trends, issues, and facts, as well as characteristics of the aged who present distinctive needs in a period of their lives when their physical and mental capabilities are diminishing and their resources are declining.

The editors firmly believe that care provided outside the hospital should involve a multidisciplinary team and, based on this premise, sought contributions for this encyclopedia from as many disciplines as possible. Contributors therefore represent medicine, nursing, social work, administration, policy analysis, physical therapy, and others who play key roles in restoring the patient to optimal health and mobility.

The Encyclopedia could not have been possible without the thoughtful contributions of all the authors who in their own way clearly demonstrate their expertise and commitment to home health care with a gerontological focus. The editors wish to express their gratitude to each of the authors. Special thanks are given to the editors at Greenwood Press, George F. Butler, PhD, and Mildred Vasan, who have provided insightful and valuable guidance throughout the development of this project.

Encyclopedia of Home Care for the Elderly

A

Abuse of the Elderly: Kinds of Abuse

INTRODUCTION

Despite promotion of our national health and the disease prevention objectives for a longer and healthier life, the incidence and prevalence of comorbidities in older people will remain considerably higher than in younger people. The baby boomers of 1946–1964 will be senior boomers by 2010–2030; of these, 25 percent will have no children, and 20 percent will have only one child. Yet more and more health care will be needed. The universal bottleneck into nursing homes in the latter part of the twentieth century will only become more narrow. With ongoing dehumanization in institutional living, and an increased emphasis on home health care, the ever increasing numbers of frail dependent elderly are at high risk for maltreatment.

Though most family caregivers are heroic and committed in their caregiver efforts, there will be fewer of them in the future and many of these may be depressed, anxious, overstressed, with insufficient supports and time for attention to personal well-being or for personal growth and development beyond the caregiving commitment. Elderly who require care are at high risk for verbal abuse by depressed and anxious caregivers, and for physical abuse and financial exploitation by caregivers who are substance abusers. Developmentally, mentally, or physically disabled persons who have required the care of parents in the past cannot become caregivers of dependent elderly. Such a home situation can lead to severe abuse.

DEFINITION

The definition of elder maltreatment can be divided into physical, psychological, material, and active and passive neglect.

Physical maltreatment is defined as the infliction of physical pain or injury, physical coercion, confinement against one's will, being slapped, bruised, sexually molested, cut, burned, or physically restrained.

Psychological abuse is the infliction of mental anguish, being called names, treated as a child, frightened, humiliated, intimidated, threatened, isolated, etc.

Material maltreatment is the illegal or improper exploitation and/or use of funds or other resources.

Active neglect is the refusal or failure to fulfill a caretaking obligation including a conscious and intentional attempt to inflict physical or emotional distress on the elderly such as deliberate abandonment or deliberate denial of food or health related services.

Passive neglect is the refusal or failure to fulfill a caretaking obligation excluding a conscious or intentional attempt to inflict physical or emotional distress on the elderly such as abandonment, denial of food or health related services because of inadequate knowledge, laziness, infirmity, or disagreement of the value of the prescribed services.

HISTORY

Historically, child abuse first received wide attention in the 1960s with ever stronger advocacy, knowledge base, financial support, avenues of prevention, reporting, and useful interventions. Subsequently, spouse abuse received similar attention in the 1970s. Elder maltreatment only began to get attention in the 1987 amendment to the Older Americans Act of 1965, followed by congressional appropriations to the states in 1991 and establishment of a National Institute for Elder Abuse. Although all 50 states have had reporting laws since the 1980s, public health departments had little knowledge of them, and many providers of care did not use them. Resources for prevention, intervention, and follow-up were minimal. The 1980s have become known as "the Decade of Shame and Inaction" in regard to elder maltreatment.

SURVEYS AND CLINICAL OBSERVATIONS

Research initiatives have been sparse in this area. Disparities exist between the prevalence and incidence of elder abuse. In random samples in Massachusetts, researchers reported a prevalence of elder abuse of 32 and incidence of 26 per 1,000 respectively, while reported cases during that same time were only

1.8 per 1,000. Underreporting is due to the generally held misconception that maltreatment is rare, does not occur in what appear to be normal relationships, that it is a private matter within the family, and that victims are responsible for their abuse. Primary providers of care of the elderly often have psychological defenses similar to those of the abusers: denial, rationalization, and minimization. Inadequate response to reporting by Adult Protective Services (APS) was another factor in underreporting. APS had inadequate funding and many lacked well-trained multidisciplinary teams to be involved in prevention, identification, intervention, and follow-up.

The federal government mandated, and states implemented, the Ombudsmen reporting system in long-term care facilities. Although potentially effective, these programs have many limitations because of a dearth of well-informed families and a high proportion of residents in long-term care facilities who do not have families or advocates. Ombudsmen are volunteers and their training varies from region to region. The purpose of an Ombudsman is to resolve problems within the institution and to report to the state only if the problem cannot be resolved. A late 1980s survey by Pillemer and Finklehor of 677 staff members in 31 nursing homes (ranging in size from 19 to 300 beds) found that substantial abusive behaviors occurred, especially from staff who were considering quitting and who perceived the elderly as children.

Analysis of case vignettes reveals that comprehensive assessment followed by psychotherapy for both frail dependent elder and caregiver is often indicated, but not available. Resistance to necessary interventions are seldom approached in a manner that could lead to acceptance of practical, protective, and supportive interventions. A review of reporting laws reveals that providers of care need to be well versed in their state's reporting laws, which differ from state to state, in terms of the nature of abuses that require reporting, how soon after identification of maltreatment reporting must take place, whether and what kind of penalties there are for failure to report, and how soon after reporting must an investigation occur. There are no mandates for follow-up or for interventions following investigation. Follow-up depends primarily on the discipline, level of training and expertise, and the availability of staff and consultants to Adult Protective Services. Only in criminal cases is it appropriate to have the Justice Department deal with the situation and institute punitive action.

Profiles of victims indicate that most are aged 75 and older, and that 64.2 percent are women. Victimized parents often fear not being believed, reprisal, abandonment, and institutionalization. Many of them feel ashamed to admit to their adult children's behavior towards them. In marital situations, the likelihood of a wife being abused by her husband is three times greater than husbands being abused by their wives. Abusive behaviors throughout the marriage, which become more severe and frequent as one partner becomes dependent on the other, often require different interventions than abuse that starts to occur only as one or the other or both partners become increasingly dependent.

Profiles of caregivers generally fall into the following categories: (1) those whose activities are criminal in nature, (2) those who have a marital pattern of abuse over many years' duration, (3) those that are recent in onset, and (4) those that are secondary to dysfunction such as mental disorder, mental retardation, and substance abuse. The caregivers who start out with good intentions but find themselves in unanticipated complicated life situations either because of length and complexity of care required, lack of resources, additional demands on time and energy with limited coping skills may inadvertently become abusive or neglectful.

MANIFESTATIONS OF MALTREATMENT

The spectrum of manifestation of *physical abuse* includes: bruises, welts, lacerations, punctures, fractures, evidence of excessive drugging, burns, and signs of physical restraints. Manifestations of *neglect* of elders include: malnutrition, dehydration, signs of either low degree or high degree of hearing, lack of food and water, lack of needed medications, eyeglasses, hearing aids, false teeth, prosthesis, or other aids needed for ambulation, sitting, or lying. Manifestations of *sexual abuse* include: venereal disease, HIV infection, pain or itching of the vulva or anus, bruises or bleeding of the external genitalia, vagina, or anus. Manifestations of *primary emotional abuse*, or emotional abuse secondary to physical abuse, include: resignation, ambivalence, fear, anger, cognitive impairment, depression, insomnia, substance abuse. Behaviors by caregivers *indicating emotional abuse* include: threats, insults, harassment, withholding security, harsh orders, infantilization, refusal to provide or allow travel and opportunities to visit and communicate with friends or family members, refusal of permisson to attend social and religious events, and evidence of money management that is for the benefit of the caregiver and at the expense of the elderly.

Manifestations of abuse or use of *medications* include: delirium, memory impairment, agitation, lethargy, self neglect, incoherence at times.

RECOMMENDATIONS

Elder maltreatment needs to be appropriately identified with the use of comprehensive assessment protocols, well documented by means of anecdotal records or noting physical or mental signs, followed by sensitive supports rendered with resistances for protection addressed, and followed by the necessary referrals and reporting when applicable. Advocacy for adequate reimbursement for necessary services needs to be ongoing. Research initiatives in the areas of epidemiology, assessment, and outcomes of interventions provided to dependent elderly and their caregivers need continued attention and resources. Perhaps most important of all is the need to highlight the problem in the academic and popular press, so that it receives much more attention.

References

Chairman of the Subcommittee on Health and Long Term Care. 1990. *Elder Abuse: A Decade of Shame and Inaction.* Select Committee on Aging, House of Representatives. Washington, D.C.: U.S. Government Printing Office, Comm. Pub. 101–752.

Goldstein, M.Z. 1993. Elder abuse and neglect. In *Comprehensive Textbook of Psychiatry, VI,* edited by H.I. Kaplan and B.J. Sadock. Baltimore: Williams and Wilkins.

————. Elder neglect, abuse and exploitation. In *Family Violence: Emerging Issues of a National Crisis,* edited by L.J. Dickstein and C.C. Nadleson. Washington, D.C.: American Psychiatric Press, Inc., 101–24.

Goldstein, M.Z., G. Kennedy, C. Colenda, H. Van Dooren, and W. Van Stone. 1993. *Selected Models of Practice in Geriatric Psychiatry.* APA Task Force Report. Washington, D.C.: American Psychiatric Press, Inc.

Pillemer, K.A., and D. Finklehor. 1988. The prevalence of elder abuse: a random sample survey. *The Gerontologist* 28(1):51–57.

Quinn, M.J., and S.K. Tomita. 1986. *Elder Abuse and Neglect: Causes, Diagnosis, and Intervention Strategies.* New York: Springer.

Marion Z. Goldstein

Abuse of the Elderly: Mistreatment, Assessment, and Intervention

Elder abuse is a serious and prevalent problem that is a potential threat to all older people regardless of geographic setting. It is estimated that the prevalence of abuse nationally is 32 per 1,000 elders. This number may grow as America ages. By the year 2000, 13.1 percent of the population will be 65 years of age or older. The numbers of the oldest-old (85 years and up) are also growing. The oldest-old are often those who are the least able to care for themselves and so are most dependent on others for care.

Some researchers define elder abuse as actions by the caregiver that create unmet needs in the elder. Mistreatment can be thought of as the outcome of abuse, neglect, exploitation, and abandonment.

To date, no standard ''profile'' of the elder abuse victim has emerged, but studies suggest that dependency of the elder, isolation, stress in the family, and limited resources may be parts of the whole picture.

Those who abuse the elderly are not easily categorized. Rather, it appears that the tendency to abuse cuts across gender, economic, educational, and religious lines.

Five theories have been put forth to explain elder abuse. These are:

1. Exchange Theory
2. Stressed Caregiver Theory
3. Transgenerational Violence Theory
4. Psychopathology of the Abuser
5. Impairment (Dependency) of the Elderly

Exchange Theory. The Exchange Theory proposes that the caregiver who gains a reward from abuse will continue to abuse. The reward may be psychological if the abuser sees the abuse as "evening up the score" in situations where the elder is perceived as contributing nothing to the care situation. If the abuse fails to give a reward, then the Exchange Theory says it will cease.

Stressed Caregiver Theory. The Stressed Caregiver Theory has its origins in the work done on child abuse. Within this theory, major stressors in life are seen as the cause of the abuse. Taking care of an elder, with its resultant loss of free time and mobility, is seen as a major stressor that may cause the caregiver to abuse.

Transgenerational Violence Theory. The Transgenerational Violence Theory is that violence is a learned behavior. Thus, one who was abused as a child may in turn abuse as an adult. In the case of the elder and the adult child, the abuser may be abusing the person who abused them earlier in life.

Psychopathology of the Abuser. The theory in the Psychopathology of the Abuser proposes that abusers are not psychologically normal. Rather, they have any one of a variety of problems, such as a history of alcohol or drug abuse, psychiatric illness, or subnormal intelligence, any one of which can lead to an inability to deal appropriately with the care of the elder, with subsequent abuse or neglect.

Impairment (Dependency) of the Elderly. The Impairment (Dependency) of the Elderly theory is based on the premise that the stress resulting from the dependency needs of the elder leads the caregiver to abuse. However, studies seem to indicate that it may be the dependency of the caregiver upon the elder that is problematic, a situation in which there is codependence.

TYPES OF MISTREATMENT AND THEIR INDICATORS

1. Physical abuse. Physical abuse is the most common form of reported abuse, primarily because physical abuse can actually be seen and thus provide concrete evidence. Evidence is seen in the elder with unexplained bruising, welts, or burns. A key indicator is that the injuries are often in various stages of healing, pointing to repeated injury over a period of time.

2. Psychological abuse. Many elders are abused psychologically by caregivers who yell at them, treat them as children, ignore them, or demean them in some way. Signs of depression and withdrawal can signal psychological abuse.

3. Financial abuse. Many elders are the victims of financial abuse from caregivers, financial consultants, or others who steal money and other resources. Indicators of financial abuse may include unexplained decrease in standards of living, suspicious signatures on paperwork, and evidence of threats of withdrawal of services.

4. *Neglect.* When the needs of the elder are not taken care of, a neglectful situation has occurred. Neglect can be just as serious as overt abuse, whether it is intentional or not. Malnutrition is a common sign of neglect, as are problems in personal hygiene.

With all types of abuse and neglect, it is sometimes difficult to determine whether the problem is the result of abuse or neglect, the changes of aging or disease. For example, poor hygiene can easily result from neglect but it can also be the result of weakness from the disease or loss of mobility as occurs in arthritis, which can make washing difficult.

ASSESSMENT

Assessment of elder mistreatment is difficult. The signs of mistreatment are often subtle and confounded with the results of disease symptoms and normal age-related changes. Then, too, the elderly are often reluctant to report mistreatment.

A first step in the assessment process is to query the elder regarding mistreatment. In the absence of cognitive impairment, the elderly person will be able to provide a viewpoint on mistreatment in his/her life. A thorough history may give clues to mistreatment or an outright admission of its presence.

The next steps are thorough physical and psychological assessments. The signs of disease and changes of aging must be well known so that they can be distinguished from those of mistreatment. For example, a broken bone can result from abuse, an accidental fall, or from demineralization caused by bed rest.

While time alone with the elder is essential, the health care provider should also watch the interaction of elder and caregiver. Changes in behavior in the caregiver's presence or abnormal behavior may be a signal of abuse or neglect. When abuse is suspected, it is imperative that an investigation of the suspicions be carried out by an appropriate agency. The matter should not be allowed to be dropped.

INTERVENTION

Intervention occurs at several levels. The first and most immediate action is usually at the professional level. The most effective professional intervention is multidisciplinary in nature, with nursing playing a key role. Among the common nursing interventions are care of the physical or psychological injury, consultation with multidisciplinary team members, and referrals to appropriate agencies where help can be obtained. It is also imperative that the nurse assess the potential for further harm if the patient is released from a care situation such as an emergency room. Nurses can also ensure that the appropriate education occurs with the victims, caregivers, and others involved. Intervention can also occur at the community level. Many communities have services available that directly or indirectly address the problem of abuse, examples of which are day care programs and respite care. Such services are designed to give caregivers a break from the day to day care of an elder.

Finally, intervention can occur at the legislative level. All the states now have some form of elder abuse legislation and 41 have mandatory reporting laws. However, just as there is no one definition of elder mistreatment, there is no unified national policy on the topic. Consequently, services vary tremendously from state to state.

In almost all instances, professionals are required to report abuse even if other community members do not. However, it is often difficult for professionals to know what is reportable and what is not. One study showed that decisions to report were made based on professionals' understanding of the total situation, not just the precipitating incident.

There are also ethical aspects to the decision to report mistreatment. For example, a competent elder who is mistreated may not want the incident reported, in which case the health professional has to decide how to proceed. To report the incident without permission can be seen as paternalistic, to not report the incident may lead to further mistreatment.

SUMMARY

Elder mistreatment is a serious problem that cuts across all ethnic, religious, and socioeconomic strata. The problem is estimated to affect 10 percent of all those over the age of 65. With the aging of America over the next decade, this number can be expected to rise. Nurses are often in the best position to assess mistreatment and should familiarize themselves with the signs and symptoms of its various forms, as well as with the legislation in effect in that particular locale.

When abuse is suspected, the best form of treatment is usually supplied by a multidisciplinary team. A team can help to address the manifold stresses and sequelae of mistreatment.

The community is also important in reducing mistreatment. Community services can provide an important outlet for the caregivers of the elderly along with educational and other services.

Policy regarding elder mistreatment varies from state to state. To date, there is no national policy about this important topic. Until the time when national policies are written to address this problem, elder abuse will continue to be a difficult area to be handled in a coherent and unified manner.

References

Baumhover, L., S. Beall, and R. Pieroni. 1990. Elder abuse: an overview of social and medical indicators. *Health & Human Resources Administration* 12(4):413–33.

Filinson, R., and S.R. Ingman, eds. 1989. *Elder Abuse: Practice and Policy.* New York: Human Services Press, Inc.

Fulmer, T.T., and T.A. O'Malley. 1987. *Inadequate Care of the Elderly.* New York: Springer.

Phillips, L.R., and V.F. Rempusheski. 1985. A decision-making model for diagnosing and intervening in elder abuse and neglect. *Nursing Research* 34:134–39.

Pillemer, K.A., and D. Finklehor. 1988. The prevalence of elder abuse: a random sample survey. *The Gerontologist* 28(1):51–57.

Pillemer, K.A., and R.S. Wolf, eds. 1986. *Elder Abuse: Conflict in the Family.* Dover, Mass.: Auburn House.

Anne Peirce and Terry Fulmer

Accidents: Environmental Hazards

Environmental hazards play a significant role in injury and death among the elderly. The annual cost of therapy and rehabilitation of hip fractures alone in the United States is several billion dollars. People over 65 years of age account for over two-thirds of all fatal falls. As those individuals grow older, the risk of death from accidents increases. Much can be done toward decreasing the risk of such accidents through the identification and modification of various hazards in the home environment. Such hazards may be either common to most elderly or particular to some elderly who have certain limitations in their function related to chronic health problems such as stroke, poor vision, or severe arthritis. In the latter case, remodeling of environmental structures would improve and supplement the individual's function.

INTERNAL HAZARDS

Examination of the home for environmental hazards must be thorough. It should include a search for problems that may be found in any space in the home, as well as evaluation for special hazards specific to certain areas, such as those encountered in the bathroom.

Walking surfaces throughout the house must be examined for security and safety. The bare floor should not have a slippery surface in any form. A non-skid wax is preferable to other forms of wax for either wood or linoleum. Shoes used by the resident should have soles that do not tend to slide on the floor surface. In the case of individuals with problems raising their feet, one should consider removal of saddles in doorways to reduce the risk of tripping over them. Some flooring in the home may have scatter rugs or area rugs. Since these types of rugs usually slide when placed on the floor, they cause a clear and common hazard for falls. The best solution would be their removal. The next best solution would be to place a non-skid mat, cut to size, under the rug. While the risk of sliding on the rug is decreased, the risk of tripping over the edge of the rug remains, as with the case of wood saddles in doorways. Wall-to-wall carpets may pose hazards as well if they become loose or folded.

Stairs are another general area that are hazardous; the risk of accidents may be reduced significantly through several precautions. Every effort should be made to keep the steps solid and uniform in height. They should be well lit but without glare from either interior lighting or sunshine. Such glare may make it difficult for the elderly person to see the edges of individual steps, thereby increasing the risk of falls. Glare is accentuated by cataracts. Certain geometric patterns and vivid colors used in carpets may pose hazards when used on steps, since they may cause problems with depth perception as well as with the ability to see the edge of each step. Every effort should be made to make the edge of each step easily visible, especially in descent. Hand rails should be in good repair and strong enough to support the individual.

Clutter is another hazard, especially on stairs and in hallways. Besides the hazard of falling over piles of clutter, they may cast shadows on otherwise well-lit areas and promote falls in those with decreased vision. In addition to general clutter, exposed electrical wires on floors pose added concern, not only because of the danger of tripping on them, but also because of the danger of fires. When placed under rugs, they may be walked on repetitively and break, thus exposing the rug to bare wires and further the risk of fire. Electrically controlled items of furniture or equipment should be located close to outlets to minimize electrical wires on the floor surface.

People with mobility problems may be helped significantly by installation of hand rails throughout the house, especially in bathrooms. Smoke detectors should be placed throughout the house, particularly in the kitchen and basement. Batteries in smoke detectors need to be checked regularly and replaced as needed.

The kitchen is an area used many times throughout the day, and it harbors several hazards. It is the location that often has the most cabinets for storage, many of which may require standing on a stool for access. The need for such a stool should be strongly discouraged. If it is used, the stool should be strong, stable, and have a back which can be held for safety. A better solution would be rearrangement of storage in the kitchen so that the older person need not use a stool at all. Most frequently used utensils should be arranged at a convenient level, either at countertop level or on lower shelves. Since poor balance is commonly associated with higher risk for falls, the risk is decreased if the potential problem of balance, such as standing on a stool, is eliminated or at least minimized.

The risk of burn injury in the kitchen increases as physical function and memory decline. The sources are several, and include stove flames and hot liquids such as oil, soup, and tea. Loose garments may catch fire if worn while reaching over a flame on the stove, an error which may be caused either by carelessness or dementia. Another stove hazard of fire and smoke commonly occurs when the elderly person with dementia who has access to the stove starts to prepare a meal and then leaves the kitchen with pots on lighted burners. Such individuals may be at higher risk for scald injury, either from cooking food or at times of washing and bathing. The patient with dementia is at special risk in the kitchen. Their memory and orientation decline gradually until they cannot use a stove safely. At this point the stove may be turned off or its control knobs removed.

Additional hazards in the kitchen have an impact on nutrition. Careful inspection of available foods may pinpoint someone at risk for malnutrition by noting the absence of a balanced selection of foods. If there is either inadequate food or food which is in various stages of spoilage, it would suggest a risk of malnutrition and disease, finding its origins most often in financial strain or impaired cognition.

Bathrooms commonly present several environmental hazards to the elderly. Falls may be prevented by the use of bath mats, by the installation of hand rails and grab bars at strategic places, especially next to the toilet and in the bath or shower. Grab bars provide assistance in moving about and transferring to and from the seat or bath. Those people with mobility or balance problems who take a bath alone benefit from the use of a shower chair. Transferring to and from the toilet may be assisted with the use of a raised toilet seat. The risk of falls at night may be decreased by night lights in strategic locations. The risk of burn injury from scalding in the shower may be decreased by lowering the setting of the hot water heater, if possible, to below 110°F.

Other potential causes of burns include smoking, the use of space heaters without screens, damaged electrical cords, and overloaded sockets.

As the elderly become more frail, they use the bedroom more throughout the day. Access to both telephone and lighting controls in the bedroom should be easy, as in the rest of the home. Lighting at night, such as night lights in the bedroom and bathroom, will decrease the risk of accidents because of decreased visual acuity. The bed should have a firm mattress as this will help the individual transfer from bed to chair, wheelchair, or bedside commode more easily. The mattress should be low enough for the individual's feet to touch the floor when sitting on the side of the bed. The use of space heaters should be avoided, especially in the bedroom. They pose a fire hazard with clothing or bedding, or carbon monoxide poisoning unless adequate ventilation is provided.

EXTERNAL HAZARDS

Outside the apartment or house one should identify and rectify external hazards. Pathways and halls should be kept free of clutter and gardening tools, hoses, garbage cans, leaves, and paper. Outdoor walkways should be repaired and kept free of snow and ice. Outside stairways should be inspected for irregularities and adequate lighting provided. In some cases outdoor lighting may be facilitated by the installation of automatic light-sensitive switches on the light fixtures, making them turn on automatically when daylight fades. Railings should be checked for strength and placement.

SUMMARY

Being aware of real and potential hazards in and around the home is the first step in creating and maintaining a hazard-free environment for vulnerable persons, elderly as well as children. Most hazards can be eliminated or minimized with simple solutions and a few hours of work. The hazards need to be reevaluated from time to time, based on the changing status of the person for whom they are checked.

As a final word of advice, to help in maintaining a hazard-free and safe environment in the home, one should keep a list of currently used medications, a list of phone numbers to call in case of emergency, and names of immediately available neighbors, family, and friends. The house or apartment numbers should be clearly visible from the street and well marked to assure rapid identification of the correct address by emergency teams or other providers of services to the resident at that address. Timely intervention prior to accidents is well worth the time and effort required to eliminate hazards.

References

Escher, J.E., C. O'Dell, and S.R. Gambert. 1985. Typical geriatric accidents and how to prevent them. *Geriatrics* 44:54–69.

Lipsitz, L.A. 1992. Falls in the elderly. In *Textbook of Internal Medicine*, 2d ed. Edited by W.N. Kelley. Philadelphia: Lippincott, 2420.

Marottoli, R.A., L.F. Berkman, and L.M. Cooney. 1992. Decline in physical function following hip fracture. *J Amer Geriatric Soc* 40:861–66.

Nelson, D.E., R.W. Sattin, J.A. Langlois, C.A. DeVito, and J.A. Stevens. 1992. Alcohol as a risk factor for falls. Injury events among elderly persons living in the community. *J Amer Geriatric Soc* 40:658–61.

Petro, J.A., D. Belger, C.A. Salzberg, and R.E. Salisburg. 1989. Burn accidents and the elderly: what is happening and how to prevent it. *Geriatrics*, 44:25–48.

Tinetti, M.E., and M. Speechly. 1989. Prevention of falls among the elderly. *New Engl J Med* 320(16):1055–59.

Jeffrey E. Escher

Administration of Home Care Services

DEFINITION

The types of health care services provided in a community are based on the needs of the citizens of that community. Home health care is one component of the array of health services offered in communities. Home health care is not a new type of health service—it has existed since the late 1800s—but it has changed to respond to the needs of our changing society. Home health care is dynamically evolving as a means of providing services and education for the client and the family. The types of services provided depend on the needs of the patient, family, and on the community resources and funding sources.

A formal definition of home health services as stated by Harris (1988) is:

Home health is that component of comprehensive health care whereby services are provided to individuals and families in their places of residence for the purpose of promoting, maintaining, or restoring health or minimizing the effects of illness and disability. Services appropriate to the needs of the individual patient and family are planned, coordinated, and made available by an agency or institution, organized for the delivery of health care through the use of employed staff, contractual arrangement, or a combination of administrative patterns.

GROWTH OF HOME CARE

The nature and content of home health care have changed dramatically over the past ten years. The increase in home health care and the potential for further expansion are due to many changes in our current sociopolitical situation and in economic factors that together provide the environment for health care and home care in particular. The current home care system is the result of changing patterns of disease within the population, the ever-changing economic reimbursement mechanisms, and changing social values.

The change in the distribution of disease is the first factor in the growth of home care. The availability of antibiotics, regular immunizations, and improved knowledge about diseases in general have reduced the risk of dying from certain diseases but have increased the risk of people dying from chronic diseases. Chronic diseases such as hypertension, cardiac disease, pulmonary disease, cancer, and diabetes have a long period of development leading to irreversible changes in the body and frequently permanent impairment of the person's ability to function independently. Home care has a place in being the alternative to institutionalization in meeting this need.

A second and related factor affecting the growth of home care is change in the demographics of our population. We do know that the need for assistance with activities of daily living or ADLs (bathing, grooming, meals, etc.) greatly increases with age. Only 2.6 percent of persons 65 to 74 need assistance with ADLs as compared to 32 percent of those 85 years or older (the frail elderly).

Between 1980 and 1990, the 65–74 age group grew by 14 percent. Projections for the next two decades indicate that the 75–84 age group will increase by almost 27 percent, and the over–85 by 20 percent. In fact, the 85 and over age group will increase about four times as fast as the general population.

Complicating these changes in population and the increase in scientific knowledge are the changes in the family. We have experienced changes in employment patterns, economic recession, and improved transportation, all of which have affected family life by dispersing families across the country. We know that few relatives live near each other, and more women have entered the work force, significantly reducing the number of female family members available to care for the chronically ill. Traditionally, women have been the caregivers of older family members. However, the average age of caregivers is also rising, so that today those who are in their 70s are caring for family members who are in their 90s.

Home care has responded to the changes in the increased prevalence of chronic illness by expanding rehabilitative services for those living at home who require such services. Rehabilitation is a long-term process requiring adaptation of the impaired individual as they gradually return to the home/work environment. Home health agencies have had to expand their utilization of therapies— physical, occupational, speech. Social workers' utilization and responsibilities have also expanded to help individuals to adjust to and live with chronic conditions.

Changes in reimbursement have had such a profound effect on the services provided by home care that reimbursement is now said to be setting the direction for home health care. Medicare dominates reimbursement practices and focuses on short-term intermittent interventions. Further, Medicare has made home care a profitable venture for proprietary agencies and hospitals which in turn has led to an increase in the number of agencies providing service, and increased competition.

A major change in the reimbursement system was the payment by Diagnosis Related Group (DRGs) for hospitals. Since the inception of DRGs, the level of illness of home care patients has increased, resulting in more frequent skilled visits, more time-consuming visits because of greater complexity of health problems, and more patients who are at greater risk for decompensation and rehospitalization. These cost-containment mechanisms have resulted in greater utilization of services and therefore the need for additional payment for services. Cost shifting has resulted in much higher expenses incurred by patients, including more lost income for family caregivers who must work, and other related costs. Other third party payers have followed Medicare guidelines, leading to much more managed care in all aspects of reimbursement. Managed care results in decisions about care that are based more on financial considerations than on patient care needs.

TYPES OF AGENCIES

Home care is provided through a variety of private and governmental agencies. Governmental agencies are either local or state sponsored agencies who receive funding from taxes. Health departments may provide a variety of services through their departments of nursing. These services include traditional public health nursing for maternal-child health, communicable disease investigation, health promotion, clinic care, etc. Each state decides the type of service that it will provide for their citizens. Some states and local jurisdictions support home health care that is separate from public health nursing responsibilities. A recent trend is for less involvement by local health departments in providing home care. In some states, the health department or area agency on aging act as brokers for services purchased from and provided through the private sector. Home care agencies that are owned by hospitals or other institutions are governed by the owners, and in general adhere to the philosophy and policies of the owner institution. This kind of ownership/governorship may limit the types and geographic locations of services.

Private agencies are either for-profit or not-for-profit corporations. Some of these agencies may be part of a national chain and administered through corporate headquarters, for example, Olsten Health Services. Some of these agencies are Medicare-certified and bill third party payers for services; others operate solely on a fee-for-service payment system.

Voluntary agencies are governed by a local board of directors and are established as non-profit entities. The agencies have long histories of being based in the community. Traditional visiting nurse associations or visiting nurse societies and homemaker/home health aide services are examples of voluntary organizations. Funding comes from direct fee-for-service revenues, grants, donations, and/or through the United Way.

Hospice agencies provide services for terminally ill patients with six months or less life expectancy. Care is provided under a medically supervised interdisciplinary team of professionals and volunteers. Hospice care is patterned after the hospice concept developed in Great Britain. Hospices in this country may be institution-based, for-profit, or non-profit, and may be affiliated with a home health agency.

There are other providers of support services that refer to themselves as home care agencies. These include durable medical equipment companies (DMEs), home infusion therapy (IV) companies, high technology equipment companies, and companion services. These are formed and administered through a variety of organizational structures.

SERVICES

The purpose of home care programs is to render care to the sick and/or disabled in their homes. Services are given through an array of health care professionals and paraprofessionals, with the core component being nursing care. Besides care given by physicians and nurses, other kinds of services available through home care agencies are provided by physical, occupational, and speech therapists, medical social workers, nutritionists, respiratory therapists, enterostomal specialists, intravenous infusion therapists, rehabilitation specialists, and home health aides. Part-time intermittent skilled care is the keystone for reimbursement for services, and the interpretation of these components constitutes a major area of concern in home health care today. An additional requirement for reimbursement is that the patient must be homebound and under the care of a physician. Homebound means that the patient can leave the house only with assistance; it does not mean bedbound. The interpretation of homebound can also be a source of conflict regarding reimbursement through Medicare.

Currently, Medicare reimburses at reasonable cost of service if an agency is below the federally mandated cost caps per discipline. These costs are reimbursed per visit, whereas the hospice benefit under Medicare is based on per day service with a defined maximum.

Medicaid is each state's own health insurance that is administered through state agencies. The program is designed to be a payment source for care of the poor. Each state determines its own income level and eligibility requirements. The basic services that each state must offer are nursing, home health aide, medical equipment, appliances, and supplies. Medicaid may also apply to the Federal government for waiver programs for special groups such as medically fragile children. These waivers and block grants vary by state.

Costs for home care paid by private insurance companies vary. Many follow the Medicare guidelines, or may be in lieu of institutional care. The advent of case management, as it relates to reimbursement, is the newest system of payment. The underlying intent of case management is to control costs and save money on services.

STANDARDS OF CARE

Medicare and Medicaid have defined conditions of participation and standards that must be met in order to bill these systems. These standards include policies regarding administration, management, and patient care records. An unannounced site visit by the state surveyor takes place every twelve to fifteen months. This process is called certification and is a mandatory process for Medicare/ Medicaid.

Accreditation is a voluntary process in which an agency may choose to participate. The most widely recognized accreditation bodies are the Joint Commission for Accreditation of Health Organizations (JCAHO), the National Home Caring Council, and the Community Health Accreditation Program (CHAP). All have established national standards against which an agency is measured. In August 1992, CHAP received deemed status which means that CHAP-accredited agencies do not have to be reviewed by the state surveyor for certification by Medicare. Some states have a licensure law that must be met for an agency to provide service in that state. Some state licensure laws are very restrictive and some follow Medicare conditions of participation. These laws establish operational standards that must be met at all times. In addition, many licensure laws carry criminal offenses for noncompliance.

QUALITY OF CARE

Quality should be a major concern for home health agencies and consumers. Quality encompasses all aspects of the agency including personnel, governance, management, patient care, and finance. A consumer has the right to inquire about an agency's standards of quality. This can be done by asking whether an agency is Medicare certified, state licensed, or accredited. These are some concrete measures of quality.

Quality begins with the governance of the agency, the Board of Directors, and the Chief Executive Officer. The commitment to quality care is translated down to the direct care staff and the support staff. A quality assurance or continuous quality improvement program focuses on methods to assure that quality is measured through a variety of mechanisms. Staff are a key component to high-quality care. Careful selection of personnel, helpful supervision, and ongoing education are important aspects of quality maintenance. The agency's complaint mechanism is another indicator of quality, particularly when patients, families, and health professionals are encouraged to use this and any other means to measure and assure quality.

CONCLUSION

Home health care agencies have changed over the years in response to community needs and reimbursement policies and systems. Today more services are provided along a continuum of care from very basic companion or respite care to high-tech care. The future for home care depends on the ability of agencies to provide quality care in a truly compassionate manner within required guidelines to assure cost-effectiveness.

References

Drucker, P.F. 1990. *Managing the Non-Profit Organization.* New York: HarperCollins.

Harris, M. 1988. *Home Health Care Administration.* Owings Mills, Md.: National Health Publishing.

Healthy People 2000: National Health Promotion and Disease Prevention Objectives. 1990. Washington, D.C.: U.S. Government Printing Office.

Mitchell, M., and J. Storfjell. 1989. *Standards of Excellence for Home Care Organizations.* New York: Community Health Accreditation Program, National League for Nursing.

Mundinger, M.O. 1983. *Home Care Controversy: Too Little, Too Late, Too Costly.* Rockville, Md.: Aspen.

National Hospice Organization. 1984. Conference.

Emilie M. Deady

African-Americans and Health Care

INTRODUCTION

Health in the United States is linked inexorably with social, economic, and political factors as much as with risk behaviors and genetic factors. Socioeconomic status of individuals and families impacts heavily on access to care, the timing of care, and the outcomes of care. The continuing element of racial bias plays a role in health care for minorities, particularly Blacks, with regard to policy decisions and implementations. Social problems such as unsafe environments, threat of injury by violence, toxic substances such as lead, and other components of the portrait of health care all play a role in the health status and health care of Americans.

THE EARLY YEARS

Although this reference deals primarily with the elderly, what happens in the early years influences old age. Care that is provided from birth onward often determines whether a person lives into old age.

Between 1950 and 1987, the infant mortality rate (IMR), one of the most frequently used indicators of health status among populations and, indirectly, of mothers, decreased by almost 35 percent in Blacks and 32 percent in Whites. Factors that impact on IMR, low birthweight (LBW), and preterm births include age, marital status, socioeconomic status, and educational level of the mother. Compared to White mothers, Black mothers are three times more likely to be under 18 at the time of birth of their infants, 50 percent more likely to have less than 12 years of education, four times more likely to be unmarried, more likely to be at or below the poverty level, and 25 percent more likely not to have had prenatal care in the first trimester.

While all of these factors have improved for Blacks as well as Whites over the period between 1950 and 1987, there is certainly plenty of room for future improvement. Between 1970 and 1987, the number of Black mothers under the age of 18 decreased from 14.7 percent to 10.5 percent of live births. Those with less than 12 years of education decreased from 51 percent to 31.4 percent in the same period. However, the number of unmarried Black mothers *increased* from 37.4 percent to 62.2 percent in the same period. This trend has contributed to the number of single-parent families in the United States. Culturally, Black women are strongly motivated to bear children; it is a status symbol for many. The combination of risk factors—age, education, marital status, and no prenatal care—all contribute to unfavorable birth outcomes, particularly low birth weight and preterm infants. The subsequent cost of caring for these infants has been estimated at over $300,000 each. Added to these risk factors are those related to smoking and other substance abuse, and poor or inadequate nutrition.

On the other hand, Whites have a higher incidence of congenitally malformed infants than do Blacks in 11 out of 18 common conditions.

CARE FOR OLDER BLACKS

A comparison of health care for Blacks and Whites in 1985, consisting of physician visits, general physical examinations, and screening and diagnostic tests done in the ambulatory care setting, shows that, among 14 such diagnostic or screening tests, the number of tests provided Blacks was higher than for Whites in six categories, including pelvic exam, vision acuity, urinalysis, blood assays, other laboratory tests, chest X-ray, and other diagnostic tests. Among women who reported having a Pap test within the year (1985) were 52.8 percent of Blacks and 47.9 percent of Whites, in all six age groups over age 55, with the number of Black women higher in four of the six age groups. The number of Black women receiving both the Pap test and a breast exam within the year was higher than for White women in all age groups—with 44.7 percent of White women receiving the Pap test and 49.5 percent receiving the breast exam; 52.9 percent of Black women received the Pap test, and 57 percent received a breast exam.

SUPPORT FOR HEALTH CARE OF BLACKS

While major efforts by federal, state, and local organizations and groups have been implemented over the last two decades to improve maternal and child health, in particular, and to provide diagnostic, screening, and preventive services and health education to underserved minorities, currently the mortality rates from almost all categories of chronic diseases are one-third to 2.8 times higher for Blacks than for Whites.

More than three-fourths of all deaths in the United States are caused by chronic disease, with heart disease causing 50 percent of deaths, and malignant neoplasms causing about one-third of deaths. The mortality rate from heart disease is 40 percent higher in Blacks than in Whites, although deaths caused by heart disease have declined for all population groups in the last decade, with the rate of decline of death from heart disease in both Black and White women remaining about the same over the 35 years between 1950 and 1985. Death from heart disease for Black males is, however, higher than the rate for White males.

Age-adjusted cancer incidence rates are higher for Blacks than Whites, and the percent of survivors among people with cancer is lower in Blacks than in Whites. Between 1950 and 1985, mortality rates from diabetes mellitus, chronic liver disease, and cirrhosis were higher for Blacks, especially Black males, than for Whites.

REASONS FOR DISCREPANCY BETWEEN BLACKS AND WHITES

Why the discrepancy in mortality rates between Blacks and Whites? Factors cited as reasons for these discrepancies are (1) family income differences; (2) race itself, specifically for cerebrovascular diseases such as stroke; (3) both family income and race with respect to cancer death rates; (4) high-risk cholesterol levels, which is about the same in both sexes, regardless of race; (5) high blood pressure; and (6) obesity. Both high blood pressure and obesity are more common among Blacks than Whites, particularly Black women.

Differences in mortality rates from chronic diseases in Blacks and Whites are affected by many factors. A major factor that influences higher death rates in Blacks from all chronic diseases is that Blacks often do not seek treatment for suspected or actual symptoms as early as do Whites, which delays treatment. Treatment for Blacks, once they seek care, may be less aggressive than that received by Whites, which influences the outcome of disease.

DATA SOURCES AND LIMITATIONS

Some information is not available that would help in making racial and ethnic comparisons with regard to disease incidence and the impact of disease on individuals' activity level, that is, degree of disability. These comparative measures have not been done to date.

The data do make it clear that there has been a marked decline in death rates from all chronic diseases across all races between 1950 and 1987 (with the exception of chronic obstructive pulmonary disease [COPD or emphysema], which increased by over three times, and the death rate from lung cancer which doubled in the same period). COPD is the chronic disease that is more prevalent in Whites than Blacks; one of the primary causes of COPD is cigarette smoking.

The death rate differential between Black males and White males in all chronic diseases, despite the decrease for each group separately, has widened over time. The death rate of Black females has increased for heart and cerebrovascular disease, even though the rate from these diseases has decreased overall. The death rate from breast cancer has increased among Black females.

Decreased mortality from chronic diseases has occurred across all minorities, but the decrease is more marked in Whites.

In a study of death rates by race and income level in Baltimore done between 1984–1986, data show that family income level correlated inversely with death rates to a significant degree in both Whites and Blacks (non-Whites). In each, the higher the income, the lower the mortality rate. No significant effect of race was evident when income was accounted for.

Conversely, a significant effect of race was evident in specific disease conditions, for example, cerebrovascular disease and cancer. In these conditions the data supported that race, not income, was the primary factor related to mortality. This finding therefore points to all the factors related to race, such as genetics, low income, late detection of disease, and delayed treatment.

Cancer incidence rates among Black males exceeded that of White males by 19 percent, although among Black females, the incidence of cancer is lower by 2 percent than that of White females. In specific anatomic sites of cancer, such as the breast or prostate, incidence varies between Blacks and Whites. These differences are partly explained by income level, but genetic differences also appear to play a role. More research is needed to establish specific data regarding these variables.

Cancer five-year survival rates for Whites were 45.6 percent and 32.7 percent for Blacks. Survivorship for females is higher than for males in all races.

PREVENTION OF CHRONIC DISEASE AND CANCER

Four significant risk factors associated with many, but not all, major chronic diseases and malignant neoplasms are: cigarette smoking, high blood pressure, high cholesterol, and obesity. While perhaps not directly related to all major chronic diseases and cancer, these factors undoubtedly impact heavily on overall health. In particular, cigarette smoking is seen as a cause of lung and bladder cancer. In general, Blacks are more likely than Whites to have these risk factors.

Diet also plays an important part in high blood pressure. Although salt intake for both Blacks and Whites is about the same, the diet of Blacks is thought to be deficient in calcium and potassium, both of which are implicated in high blood pressure, although the precise role of these substances is not known. The relationship between obesity and high blood pressure is well established. The prevalence of obesity, especially in Black females, is high, and is an increasing problem.

Changing these risk factors/behaviors in all populations would contribute substantially to improved death rates. Researchers concluded that the higher prevalence of these risk factors (high blood pressure and cigarette smoking) among Blacks may explain the higher death rates for heart disease and stroke.

ACCESS TO HEALTH CARE

Ideally, the health care system should provide (1) services related to early detection of disease, particularly in those diseases in which early treatment can make a difference in health outcomes; (2) effective management that helps to prevent adverse sequelae; and (3) effective treatment which decreases disability and prolongs life.

Screening to detect diseases in an early stage is essential to effective treatment and survival. Although past research indicated that disease in Blacks was often not detected early, thus delaying treatment, more recent data show that screening and early detection of cancer in Blacks are improving to some degree, especially in Black women; however, differences between races still exist and may continue for some time even while measures to improve health outcomes for Blacks and other minorities continue to be implemented.

More aggressive treatment strategies must also occur for Blacks, to equalize survival rates, particularly in such conditions as breast and prostate cancer.

OTHER CAUSES OF DEATH

Homicides, fires and burns, drownings, and pedestrian fatalities account for higher mortality in Blacks than in Whites, across all age groups. The differential between Blacks and Whites with regard to injuries as a cause of death has narrowed markedly, except with respect to Black males. Injuries often result in a considerable degree of disability, if not death, requiring long-term care.

HIV/AIDS appears to be an increasing problem among minorities. Blacks are more likely than Whites to be intravenous drug abusers, and to engage in high-risk sexual activities more than other minorities, especially Hispanics, leaving them more vulnerable to HIV infection and the development of AIDS.

This group of causes of death—injuries and HIV/AIDS—can be changed, to a large extent, by individual changes in behaviors. Making homes and communities safe places, and taking preventive actions to prohibit the spread of HIV/AIDS are important actions for individuals, families, and community groups to adopt.

CONCLUSION

While there still exist major differences in health, health care, and health outcomes between Whites and Blacks, considerable progress has been made over the last two decades, particularly with regard to infant mortality, access to care, screening for early detection of specific conditions, and follow-through to provide effective treatment. Health education plays a major role in helping individuals to understand the importance of risk behaviors and to change behaviors.

The health reform initiative will also assist in making care for all accessible and affordable, regardless of race, ethnic, and socioeconomic differences.

References

Department of Health and Human Services. 1991. *Health Status of Minorities and Low-Income Groups: Third Edition.* Public Health Service, Health Resources and Services Administration. Washington, D.C.: US Government Printing Office.

Reed, W.L. 1993. *Health and Medical Care for African-Americans.* Westport, Conn.: Auburn House.

Ada Romaine-Davis

AIDS *and the* Elderly

INTRODUCTION

Since it was first reported in 1981, the acquired immunodeficiency syndrome (AIDS) and infection with its causative agent, human immunodeficiency virus (HIV), has become a vast public health problem primarily affecting young adults. However, there is a small but finite segment of elderly people infected with HIV who go on to develop AIDS. The Centers for Disease Control reports that approximately 10 percent of AIDS occurs in people over the age of 50. Of this fraction, 25 percent occurs in those over age 60 with 4 percent occurring in people over the age of 70. It is possible that the incidence of AIDS in the elderly will increase as a result of improved surveillance by clinicians as they develop awareness as to the possibility of the diagnosis in older individuals. Accordingly, health professionals involved in the care of the elderly should be aware of the special issues regarding those patients infected with HIV.

Incidence and Prevalence

While HIV infection was initially thought to be restricted to homosexual men and individuals using intravenous drugs, it is now recognized that it can be spread by heterosexual contact. Accordingly, it has the potential to affect a broad spectrum of the populace including both sexes, all socioeconomic strata, and various ethnic groups, although the poor and minorities tend to be overrepresented. Because transmission of HIV occurs primarily through sexual contact and sharing of intravenous drug paraphernalia, AIDS has been more prevalent in younger age groups. However, smaller subsets of HIV transmission have been described in hemophiliacs and individuals receiving blood transfusions. While the risk of HIV transmission with blood transfusion continues on a very small scale, it was quite large prior to the start of large-scale HIV screening of blood components in 1985. It is in the blood transfusion segment that the incidence of HIV-related illness in those over 65 is most common.

Source of Infection

While exposure to tainted blood products is the most common source of HIV infection in individuals over age 65, other modes of transmission also occur. For example, homosexual transmission of HIV may occur in the elderly and is the most common source of transmission in those below age 65. Homosexual elders are less apt to admit their sexual preferences, primarily because they spent their younger years in a society that was less tolerant of diversity in sexual preference. Heterosexual transmission of HIV in the elderly is considered possible when based on an average reported frequency of two to four sexual encounters per month in the elderly.

Improved Treatment

Aged HIV carriers may become more numerous because of the changing nature of HIV infection. There is a growing population of aging HIV-positive homosexual men, who are living longer prior to developing symptomatic disease. In addition, those with symptomatic disease have been living longer due to improvements in disease intervention. Included in this is improved medical care in the form of antiviral agents (i.e., AZT), earlier and better treatments for related infectious diseases, and prophylactic treatment for *Pneumocystis carinii*. Apart from improvement in medical care more attention has been paid to other basic needs of HIV-infected individuals including housing, nutrition, and social interaction. These improvements in AIDS care have led to AIDS becoming a chronic illness in many infected individuals.

Risk Factors

While AIDS occurs in a finite number of older individuals, it continues to be underdiagnosed in this segment of the population because of a lack of awareness of risk factors for HIV transmission, including history of blood transfusions, multiple sexual partners, homosexuality, and past intravenous drug use. In addition, several conditions commonly associated with aging also occur with AIDS, thereby possibly masking the diagnosis of HIV infection in the elderly. Health professionals caring for this population should therefore develop an awareness of the possibility of HIV infection and AIDS in their patients, acquire an understanding of the risk factors for HIV infection, and specific issues regarding the care of older HIV-infected patients.

Course of HIV

Studies have determined that elderly HIV-infected individuals have a shorter incubation period than younger adults for developing symptomatic AIDS (5.5 versus 8 years). The elderly are also felt to have a higher risk of HIV infectivity because of preexisting immune suppression partially due to reduced numbers of T4 helper cells. This compromised immune status is manifested in aged individuals by an allergy in response to skin test of common allergens as well as increased susceptibility to several opportunistic infections and neoplastic diseases.

Associated/Opportunistic Diseases

The immune suppression of aging results in a natural risk to certain opportunistic infections in the elderly that are also commonly seen in AIDS. These include herpes zoster, Mycobacterium tuberculosis, and oropharyngeal candidiasis ("thrush"). While these infections occur in both the aged and in those infected with HIV, there are clinical differences that may suggest the underlying cause. For example, herpes zoster in the elderly is usually self-limited and responds to general supportive care, while in those with AIDS it tends to be multifocal or generalized and more commonly results in severe morbidity. Tuberculosis in those with AIDS often results in extrapulmonary sites, while in elderly individuals it is more often restricted to lung involvement and therefore easier to treat. Oropharyngeal candidiasis is occasionally seen in chronically ill, malnourished older patients and usually responds promptly to antifungal agents without recurrence. Conversely, AIDS-associated thrush commonly recurs, requires constant prophylaxis, and may become quite severe involving the esophagus. Mycobacterium avium-intracellulare (another mycobacterium), a common cause of opportunistic infection in AIDS causing chronic wasting and fever, is rarely seen in the elderly. The most common opportunistic infection associated with AIDS, pneumocystis carinii pneumonia (PCP), is also rarely seen in non-HIV infected elderly. However, PCP is just as likely to occur in an elderly patient with AIDS as any younger patient. It presents like most other acute pneumonia syndromes except for the fact that it is frequently associated with profound hypoxia (lack of oxygen).

Another consequence of immune suppression, an increased incidence of neoplastic diseases, is seen in both the elderly and those with AIDS. A prime example is Kaposi's sarcoma that was classically associated with elderly men before the emergence of HIV infection and AIDS. A major clinical difference is that Kaposi's sarcoma due to AIDS is primarily associated with sexually active homosexual men. Another neoplastic disease seen in both groups is non-Hodgkin's lymphoma; its occurrence in AIDS is associated with a poorer prognosis. AIDS occasionally presents with hematological disorders, including autoimmune thrombocytopenia purpura and pancytopenia, which also have a higher incidence in the elderly. The wasting syndrome of AIDS, primarily characterized by severe progressive weight loss, may superficially resemble weight loss that is often seen in the elderly. However, while moderate weight loss is relatively common with aging, severe weight loss in non-HIV infected elderly is usually associated with a chronic debilitating disease (cancer, emphysema, congestive heart failure, depression, etc.).

Dementia

The effect of HIV on the central nervous system is the principal example of the ability of AIDS to produce an illness that resembles a common condition of the aged. The dementia of AIDS closely resembles the cognitive dysfunction caused by several dementing conditions seen in the elderly including senile dementia of the Alzheimer type (SDAT, the condition produced by Alzheimer's Disease), multi-infarct dementia, neurosyphilis, dementias associated with vitamin B_{12} and folic acid deficiency, and others. SDAT is the most common cause of dementia of the aged and its cause is unknown. The clinical diagnosis is currently made by excluding other known causes, although the accuracy of this method has been questioned by autopsy studies. Nevertheless, an important question is whether an ELISA test for HIV should become a standard in the differential diagnosis of any new dementing condition in an older patient.

At the present time, the standard evaluation of dementia in an older patient should probably not include an ELISA test for HIV. The decision to utilize the HIV test in the evaluation of dementia in an older patient should depend on the existence of known risk factors for HIV transmission such as blood transfusion, homosexuality, or multiple sexual partners. In such cases there would be a reasonable likelihood of the diagnosis being AIDS dementia. Conversely, the use of HIV testing as a screening measure for all demented elderly individuals is problematic because of the large number of tests that would be needed to detect a very small number of cases. Consequently, an appropriate recommendation regarding the proper evaluation for AIDS as a cause of dementia in an older patient is for the evaluator to take a detailed history from the patient or friends and family for the known risk factors of HIV transmission.

From a clinical perspective, AIDS dementia contrasts significantly with SDAT and other age-associated dementias. For example, SDAT is associated with a significant nominal aphasia characterized by a loss of word finding. In contrast, AIDS dementia is rarely associated with aphasia. In addition, AIDS dementia is often accompanied by a peripheral neuropathy; other neurologic findings may include ataxia, leg weakness, and tremors. These neurologic findings are secondary to AIDS myelopathy, a spinal cord disorder resembling that seen in vitamin B_{12} deficiency. The peripheral neuropathy is characterized by parasthesias and/or dysesthesias in multiple asymmetric skin areas. Apart from pathologic changes in the nervous system caused by HIV itself, there are several opportunistic infections that may affect the central nervous system of individuals with AIDS as a result of the state of profound immunosuppression that can produce clinical syndromes resembling dementia. These include toxoplasmosis, cryptococcal meningitis, and central nervous system lymphoma (viral).

SUMMARY

The care of an elderly patient with AIDS must consider both the special problems of aging as well as those posed by HIV infection. Various issues relating to the care of the elderly and those with HIV infection overlap. It has been suggested that the model for geriatric care in the United States as it relates to long-term care and home care be applied to the AIDS population. This concept recognizes the fact that the debilitating effects of HIV infection resulting in profound functional loss often resemble that seen in many older individuals suffering from primary dementias and/or multisystem disease. Consequently, the same principles relating to the competent home care of the elderly apply to those with AIDS. Special needs of symptomatic HIV-infected elderly include the need for specific antimicrobial agents and the capacity to manage intense clinical needs. Unfortunately, persisting anxiety regarding the risk of HIV transmission (based on misinformation) may represent an obstacle toward mainstreaming the care of HIV-infected individuals into the geriatric home care industry.

References

Benjamin, A.E. 1988. Long-term care and AIDS: perspectives from experience with the elderly. *Millbank Quarterly* 66:415–43.

Boudes, P. 1991. HIV infection in the elderly. *Comprehensive Therapy* 17(9):39–42.

Fillit, H., S. Fruchtman, and L. Sell. 1989. AIDS in the elderly: a case and its implications. *Geriatrics* 44(7):65–70.

Hargreaves, M.R., G.N. Fuller, and B.G. Gazzard. 1988. Occult AIDS: pneumocystis carinii pneumonia in elderly people. *Brit Med J* 297:721–22.

Layzell, S., and M. McCarthy. 1992. Community-based health services for people with HIV/AIDS: a review from a health service perspective. *AIDS Care* 4(2):203–15.

Moss, R.J., and S.H. Miles. 1988. AIDS dementia. *Clin Geriatr Med* 4(4):889–95.

Barry M. Schultz

Alcohol and Drugs: Misuse and Dependence

Greater numbers of Americans than ever before are living longer and enjoying more years of leisure. As the threat of early death decreases, however, other risks associated with longevity emerge. For a variety of reasons, the elderly are increasingly at risk for drug and alcohol problems. Two predominant ones are the acceptance of drinking in the current elder generation and the widespread use of medication associated with ameliorative medical procedures and chronic illness extending over a longer period of life. The prevalence of alcohol consumption and drug use, special considerations associated with aging, and health care provision provide a background for identifying and understanding these problems.

PREVALENCE OF ALCOHOL AND OTHER DRUG USE

In regular drinkers, both the frequency and amount of alcohol intake tend to decrease with age. 1989 and 1990 studies on the prevalence of alcohol use in randomly chosen older populations suggest that drinking decreases significantly after age 40 in white, African-American, and Mexican persons, although men continue to have significantly higher prevalences of mild, moderate, and heavy drinking. Research on drinking behaviors in populations over forty, while limited, indicates that subjects tend to consume alcohol in light to moderate amounts, and that a smaller percentage of the population over fifty drinks heavily (6–9%) as compared to those between eighteen and fifty (20%). Approximately 52 percent of the U.S. population over fifty drinks alcohol and many older persons cease drinking altogether because of poor health. Study findings suggest that continued drinking is more common among those in good or excellent health, and those who are college educated and have a higher income.

Studies of alcohol use in older persons, however, have been conducted primarily with community-based, relatively well persons. Long-time heavy drinkers and alcoholics are unlikely to be represented in these populations because chronic consumption and its effects have resulted in their institutionalization or confinement to home or, like heavy drinkers in all age groups, they are disinclined to participate in such studies. In addition, recently published data suggest that definitions of drinking patterns may need to be modified for the elderly. While moderate drinking has been defined as no more than two drinks per day (one ounce ethanol) in dietary guidelines, physiologic changes associated with aging may result in negative cognitive and physical effects from this amount.

Research suggests that increasing age is accompanied by decreased alcohol consumption for most elderly persons; the reverse is true, however, for drug use. As persons age, they use drugs in increasing numbers. Persons over sixty may be taking as many as three prescription medications daily, and one study reports that 85 percent of the subjects were taking at least one psychoactive medication. While the elderly compose only 11 percent of the population, they account for 25 percent of prescriptions filled. In nursing homes, residents may have 8–12 prescriptions. Older persons are also consumers of large amounts of over-the-counter (OTC) drugs.

PROBLEMATIC DRUG AND ALCOHOL USE

Misuse and abuse of drugs, including alcohol, occur more commonly in the elderly than do alcohol or illicit drug dependence. Abuse and misuse of medications can be categorized in three ways:

1. intentional or accidental overuse resulting in an overdose or too high a level of medication

2. underuse as a result of forgetfulness or by choice

3. erratic use, which incorporates elements of the other two categories, that is, omitting one dose and compensating by taking two.

Abuse of alcohol or other psychoactive drugs consists of a maladaptive pattern indicated by continued use, despite knowledge of persistent or recurrent social, occupational, psychological, or physical problems caused or exacerbated by use of the substance, and/or persisting for at least one month.

The misuse of drugs among the elderly is widespread, and as the number of older persons increases, the frequency of problems around drug taking patterns increases. While the use of illicit drugs among older people is relatively rare, persistent use of heroin into late middle age continues for a small percentage of long-time addicts. This population has become more visible because of the HIV epidemic. Problems emerge in the ways in which drugs are utilized, for example, drug use while taking alcohol and overutilization of drugs in the same pharmacologic class. While alcohol use is common in the older population, for most, alcohol consumption is problematic because it is taken with other drugs, causing negative drug interaction and/or potentiating drug effect. In one study, one-half of the relatively healthy and well-educated subjects who consumed nearly five drugs a day misused the medication and alcohol in a six-month period.

Drug misuse in persons over 65 is believed to be influenced by attitudes and beliefs about medication. Older persons often retain lifelong ideas about specific remedies, both folk remedies and medically sanctioned treatment. Some clients believe that there is a drug to cure or control every ailment; this belief has been further reinforced by advertising and overutilization of physician services. Another factor appears to be a need to retain autonomy and the ability for self-care. Some clients resist the loss of control that they perceive a medical regimen imposes on them.

Over-the-counter drugs are used more frequently by the elderly than by any other group, both on a regular and ''as needed'' basis. The most commonly used and misused categories of OTC medications are analgesics, antidiarrheal medications, laxatives, vitamins, minerals, iron, antacids, cold formulas, antiemetics, emetics, hemorrhoidal, and ophthalmic and otic preparations. While these products may have significant alcohol, sodium, or sugar content, they are most important because their use reinforces notions of self-medication and a psychological dependence on drugs, rather than the appropriate utilization of dietary and exercise modifications to address alterations in body activity patterns.

Psychoactive drug abuse and dependence is believed to affect a significant number of older people, although few research studies have been conducted to explore the nature of these problems. In 1977, 58 percent of persons over 50 in one study reported use of barbiturate, sedative, or hypnotic drugs. This number also claimed to use nonbarbiturate hypnotics; 42 percent reported using minor tranquilizers, and 48 percent reported using major tranquilizers. These data exemplify the observation that elderly clients abuse and misuse anxiolytics, sedatives, analgesics, and hypnotics. Evidence of drug misuse and dependence is also seen in geriatric populations admitted to clinics and psychiatric hospitals. Reports indicate that around 20 percent of individuals admitted to these facilities are dependent on, or have misused, psychoactive drugs. Despite the fact that findings suggest that patients with psychological disorders may tend to over-medicate to seek relief from anxiety and other uncomfortable states, minor tran-quilizers are frequently prescribed for stress and transient disorders in nonpsychiatric populations.

Alcohol abuse and dependence is seen in few persons over age 50 living in the community (about 2.2%). These disorders, however, are apparent on medical wards, where at least 10 percent of the elderly have alcohol-related problems; in nursing homes, where 20 percent of residents have these problems; and in psychiatric hospitals where 28–50 percent of individuals admitted are alcohol-and/or drug-dependent. It is generally believed that the number of alcoholics in the population over age 50 is less readily detected. This may be because clini-cians do not take into consideration the impact of relatively low amounts of alcohol on an older person's function. Further, impairments in social and oc-cupational function attributable to alcoholism in younger people are less obvi-ous. The consequences of drinking problems are common correlates of aging, such as loss of a job, driver's license, and social supports which occur among older people whether they are alcoholic or not.

Alcohol dependence in the older individual has the same symptoms as de-pendence in younger people, but has more dire consequences for health. In addition to a maladaptive pattern of use, including continued use despite knowl-edge of persistent negative outcomes, dependence is evident when:

1. the use of the substance increases over time and for longer periods than is intended

2. a great deal of time is spent using the substance

3. a persistent desire or one or more unsuccessful attempts to stop using are tried

4. activities are given up or reduced, increasing isolation

5. a marked tolerance for the substance is developed (greater amounts of the substance are required to produce the desired effects)

6. characteristic withdrawal symptoms and use of the substance to relieve or avoid with-drawal symptoms occurs.

Increasing isolation and withdrawal from social and community activities are not infrequent in the older individual but may precipitate overdose, aggravate depression, and intensify suicidal ideation in the drug-dependent person. Their greater physiologic vulnerability to alcohol and other drugs also appears to place them at higher risk for complications associated with alcohol withdrawal. Pa-tients 65 and older, for example, were observed to experience a longer period of withdrawal symptoms and to require greater doses of benzodiazepines to treat these symptoms, increasing the detoxification time required prior to rehabilita-tion.

Individuals who are alcoholic after age 50 have often been described as falling into two groups. Older individuals who began drinking in young adulthood and have continued these habits into older age are viewed as early onset drinkers or survivors. Late onset alcoholics represent new cases that seem to emerge in response to the pressures of growing old, such as retirement, widowhood, or financial difficulties. Because the relationship of heavy drinking and stressful life events in the etiology of alcoholism is a tenuous one, however, such categories need further exploration to explain the onset of alcohol dependence.

VULNERABILITY TO ALCOHOL AND OTHER DRUG EFFECTS

The normal changes of aging as well as the many losses that occur with advancing age place the older person at risk for alcohol- and drug-related problems. Loneliness, the shrinking of a social network, drinking habits established earlier in life, and the loss of productive social roles are factors that influence the capacity of the individual to cope constructively. In addition, coping mechanisms previously utilized may no longer be available because of physical or financial limitations. Drugs or alcohol may then be used to assuage, or retreat from, psychological or physical pain.

The slower metabolism of the older individual results in a slower turnover of alcohol and drugs, and extends their effects. When used with other drugs, alcohol may accelerate, or inhibit, the drug metabolism. Organ sensitivity is increased in old age, and gastrointestinal and central nervous systems (CNS) are more readily affected. Diminishing changes in the brain neuronal tissues and receptor sites contribute to CNS sensitivity. Alcohol-related heart muscle disorders include arrhythmias, cardiac enlargement, and peripheral edema. With aging, adipose tissues tend to increase in proportion to lean muscle mass, decreasing the total volume of water in the body. Since ethanol is water soluble, the level of alcohol in the blood may rise because there is less water to dilute it. More marked changes are evident then, because the individual has a greater sensitivity to the drug's effects coupled with a tendency to use more drugs over a longer period of time. When taken with alcohol, for example, hypnotic drugs, central nervous system depressants, and minor tranquilizers have additive and/ or synergistic effects. Further, effects of drugs are often changed because of decreased activity, preexisting pathology, impaired drug absorption, and reduction in intestinal motility and circulatory function. Osteoporosis and vitamin deficiencies are two examples.

The interface between changes associated with aging and the effects of alcohol and drug use complicates the detection of these problems. Intellectual impairment such as recent memory loss and decreased cognitive acuity due to alcohol consumption may mimic, and be misdiagnosed as, dementia. Even social drinking has been shown to affect cognitive function in older individuals. Clinical and social effects of alcoholism such as slowed sexual functioning, that is, erectile dysfunction, and sleep disturbance such as insomnia, may not be differentiated from normal changes. The depression accompanying long-term heavy drinking is often attributed to other events or conditions rather than appropriately linked with alcohol abuse.

HEALTH CARE PROVISION

Health care providers' attitudes about, and practices of prescribing and administering, drugs influence medication use and misuse by elderly persons. The limited study of such problems, despite their current and growing prevalence, may reflect a lack of interest and a general bias toward the elderly and their health care needs. The notion that the elderly have limited time left anyway may support both the overprescription of drugs and a failure to consider the existence of drug dependence, or to intervene with the active alcoholic. Because nonpharmacologic treatments such as physical therapy and nutritional counseling may not be reimbursed through funding sources, the provider may prescribe medication instead. Practices of prescribing often do not consider special needs of the elder, resulting in miscommunication and incomplete patient education about dosage and frequency of drugs. When more than one pharmacy is used by the client/patient, misuse seems to increase and clients may attempt to save money by sharing medications with friends or hoarding previously filled prescriptions.

The following activities may reduce risks associated with prescribing, administering, and monitoring medications with the older client:

1. conduct frequent reviews of medical regimens and monitor medication schedules to reduce risks of over-medication, drug interaction, and drug misuse
2. do not prescribe or modify medication self-administration over the telephone; have personal contact
3. maintain direct communication among care providers: doctor, nurse, pharmacist, personal/family caregivers
4. monitor changes in patterns and activities of daily living to mitigate and intervene early with stress reactions
5. utilize principles of patient teaching that evaluate the client/patient's understanding of treatment, including nondrug therapy, and problems linked to alcohol use and self-medication.

Alcohol and other drug problems can be prevented and detected when the assessment of the elderly person includes special attention to drug use in the medical history and a detailed history of past and present alcohol and other (all classes) drug use. Caffeine, vitamins, and tobacco should be included. A history of past and present losses, and a review of adaptive and coping mechanisms are helpful. Clients should be evaluated independently for depression, and alcohol and other drug dependence.

Treatment for alcohol and other drug dependence should be individualized and specific to the elder's needs. About 10 percent of alcoholics in treatment are 60 years or older. Response to treatment is positive, especially when dependence has emerged late in life. Treatment approaches to these problems should include:

1. development of kinship and culturally specific community-based support groups, including "surrogate" families when family is not accessible

2. referrals to programs and providers that address the needs of the elderly in group and individual treatment

3. recognition that elders need a full range of services, including detoxification facilities, inpatient, residential, and outpatient care, alcohol education, a range of therapies, and social/recreational services

4. use of self-help resources such as Alcoholics Anonymous, Helping Hands, Seniors for Sobriety

5. development of teaching tools about prevention and intervention in these problems, including protocols for intervention and a predictive index of high-risk factors, similar to "Seven Danger Signals of Cancer"

6. efforts to expand and strengthen support systems, including economic resources, housing, and health care delivery.

SUMMARY

The growing proportion of elderly persons in society, widespread alcohol consumption, and the continued use of medications in institutions and home-based care suggest that this group will be at ongoing risk for drug and alcohol problems. The detection and management of these problems require growing expertise among practicing nurses, physicians, and other health care professionals.

References

Bernstein, L.R., S. Folkman, and R.S. Lazarus. 1989. Characterization of the use and misuse of medications by an elderly, ambulatory population. *Med Care* 27(6): 654–63.

Chenitz, W.C., S. Salisbury, and J.T. Stone. 1990. Drug misuse and abuse in the elderly. *Issues in Mental Health Nursing* 11:1–16.

Molgaard, C.A., C.M. Nakamura, E.P. Stanford, K.M. Peddecord, and D.J. Morton. 1990. Prevalence of alcohol consumption among older persons. *J Community Health* 15(4):239–51.

NIAAA. 1992. With cautions, definitions of moderate drinkers presented for elderly men and women. *Epidemiologic Report.* June–July.

Sulsky, S., P. Jacques, C. Otradovec, S. Hartz, and R. Russell. 1990. Descriptors of alcohol consumption among noninstitutionalized nonalcoholic elderly. *J Amer Coll Nutrition* 9(4):326–31.

Madeline A. Naegle

Alzheimer's Disease: Diagnosis and Care

INTRODUCTION

Alzheimer's disease (AD) affects approximately 5 percent of individuals over 65 years of age and the presence of the illness increases with age: 15 percent at 70–75; 25 percent at 80–85; and over 40 percent of Americans living to 90 will exhibit mild to moderate dementia. Additionally, another 10–15 percent of octogenarians will have some degree of cognitive impairment, commonly referred to as "benign forgetfulness." Together, the number of individuals with memory and other intellectual impairments represents a major segment of our aging society. Thus, over time, a large percentage of American families will be faced with the challenges of caring for someone with dementia, the largest percentage of whom will have AD.

The psychosocial and financial costs of this illness are staggering. In older Americans, AD is the leading cause of death after heart disease, cancer, and stroke, and current estimates are that the total yearly cost of caring for individuals with AD exceeds 60 billion dollars. It is a disease that can take whole families hostage, claiming as victims spouses, children, and grandchildren, as well as those physically affected. However, the protracted course of the illness allows time for planning. Since the course of AD may range anywhere from 2 to 20 years, families are able to prepare for the future and avoid some of the consequences of this neurodegenerative dementia.

How does one prepare for the future when a loved one is diagnosed with AD? The following information will, it is hoped, provide guidelines for such preparation.

DIAGNOSIS

Before all else, make certain that the diagnosis is dementia of the Alzheimer's type. Dementia is a general term which refers to the loss of intellectual functions. Alzheimer's disease is the most prevalent type of such impairment in individuals over 60 years of age. Senility was originally used to describe the cognitive loss occurring after the age of 65 and AD for dementia presenting before 65. Such a separation is artificial and the term AD is now used for all patients presenting with this neurodegenerative dementia. There are many causes for symptoms of dementia that can be treated and reversed. Never assume AD is present without a thorough evaluation and don't be afraid to ask for a second opinion if a physician makes a diagnosis of AD without such an examination. As a routine, a complete social, family, and medical history including past and recent medical events should be taken, and patients should receive a physical and neurological exam including full mental status testing. Occasionally, formal neuropsychological tests or a psychiatric evaluation are required to sort out the clinical difficulties. All patients require screening laboratory tests and brain imaging to rule out the many other illnesses that present as intellectual impairment. AD cannot be determined with 100 percent certainty prior to death since a definitive clinical diagnostic test does not exist. The brain must be examined after death to confirm the diagnosis. Nevertheless, reversible causes of dementia may be determined with current assessment techniques, and these must be pursued since currently there is no known treatment for AD.

CARE PLAN

Discuss openly with the physician the plans to manage the care of the family member afflicted with AD. Is the physician knowledgeable regarding long-term care issues and community resources? Will the physician be available to advise you when needs and concerns arise? What approaches are available to manage behavioral problems? Is the physician open to using medications that may require close monitoring and frequent changes? Are you comfortable sharing your fears and needs with the physician? If your physician's philosophy differs from yours, now is the time to find an area specialist in geriatrics, neurology, or psychiatry who is an expert in AD. The local chapter of the Alzheimer's Association, the county or state Office for the Aging, and the local medical society are good resources for locating such a physician.

EDUCATION

Educate yourself. The more you learn, the better you can prepare for and understand the disease and its progression. Some families will be comfortable seeking information and guidance through a support group or educational conferences and discussions offered by the local Alzheimer's Association or Office for the Aging. Interactions with other caregivers can provide invaluable experience and direction. Support groups offer an opportunity to brainstorm situations and share successful coping strategies regarding behaviors, feelings, and long-term planning. You'll be kept up to date on what resources are available in your community as well as recent research information and activities in your area. Some will be more comfortable pursuing such knowledge from other resources such as the local library or a number of current publications (see References).

PLANNING

A multitude of problems regarding clinical care issues and legal and financial planning can be avoided with early planning. Discussing sensitive issues may be difficult, but the earlier such issues are raised, the more likely patients may participate fully in these discussions. Power of attorney (POA), in particular durable POA, should be discussed with the loved one early in the illness and is a logical step to ensuring financial access for both necessary care and payment of basic bills. If not obtained, costly lawyer and court charges are incurred in the process of obtaining conservatorships to meet such needs. In many states, it is possible to appoint a health care proxy, ensuring that the physician and family will be aware of what is desired for treatment. This is extremely important and the proxy should provide substantial detail regarding the patient's wishes, because later in the course of the illness participation by the patient will be difficult, if not impossible. If health care proxy legislation does not exist, a living will should be drawn up with sufficient detail to permit physicians to understand the wishes of the patient and family. Issues to address include: a) cardiopulmonary resuscitation, b) treatment of life-threatening infections or illnesses, c) feeding tubes for nutrition and hydration.

The necessity of estate planning or financial planning to cover long-term care costs for home care and/or nursing home care should be discussed with an attorney who specializes in the field of elderlaw. The Alzheimer's Association in your area should be able to provide a list of attorneys specializing in this growing area of law. In addition to private pay mechanisms, there are now insurance programs which cover long-term care as well as public assistance through Medicaid.

COMMUNITY/HOME CARE RESOURCES

Familiarize yourself with the resources available in your community to assist in caring for patients with AD. Depending on the community, a number of health care professionals or community volunteers are available to help. Accessing the various systems is usually the most difficult part of obtaining assistance and care. Since the process can be lengthy and cumbersome, it is wise to understand how the system operates before you need to utilize it. The Alzheimer's Association, local home health agencies, and the Office for the Aging will be able to help identify what resources are available and can assist you in completing the necessary paperwork. A common error results when families procrastinate and delay these decisions only to find a sudden urgency to obtain assistance. At this point, a delay of months to even a year may occur in placing a patient in a residential care facility. Remember, you may never need to consider nursing home placement; you are simply covering all bases.

The following outline provides a brief description of services that may be available in your community.

1. Home Aide Services (provide hands-on personal care). (a) Certified Home Health Agencies (Public Health Department and Visiting Nurse Service) accept Medicare, Medicaid, third-party insurance, and private pay reimbursement; (b) Licensed Health

Care Agencies establish private contracts with families. Reimbursement is generally via private pay mechanisms although some third-party insurances cover the cost; (c) Private contracts made by aides/nurses directly employed by the family.

2. Companion Services (no personal care). Patient supervision, meal preparation, light housekeeping, chores, or errands, etc., are performed by the assistant.

3. Day Programs. (a) Social day care programs that may include supervision, some personal care, meals, and activities appropriate for each individual's level of functioning; (b) Adult day health care programs are affiliated with a nursing home or hospital, and are licensed by the Department of Health. Professional staff such as nurses, physical, occupational, and recreational therapists, social workers, and nutritionists provide a broader range of health and social services including case management, nursing supervision and personal care, meals, transportation, and recreational activities.

4. Volunteer Respite Programs. Home visitations are usually available through the Office for the Aging, Alzheimer's Association, or local compeer organizations.

5. Nursing Homes. These facilities may require state mandated assessment of patients with AD and a screening instrument may be utilized. A nurse from one of the nursing agencies who is trained and licensed can complete these forms for you. The assessment is usually updated every three months in order for subjects to remain active on a waiting list.

CARE FOR THE CAREGIVER

Finally, and perhaps most important of all, take time for yourself. AD takes many victims other than the patient. It causes spouses to withdraw and become isolated while caring for their loved one. It is important to meet your needs by maintaining social contacts and using the above services to allow for needed respite so you can continue to be an effective, healthy caregiver. You will need time alone; you will need rest; you will need support. This illness is difficult and results in prolonged demands on caregivers. Without caring for oneself, the burden of caring may exceed the capacity to care. You are not being selfish when you take time out; indeed, you are ensuring even better care of your loved one because you will have more to give.

In coping with Alzheimer's disease, as in coping with life itself, be sure to plan for the worst, hope for the best, and live each day to the fullest.

References

Cohen, D., and C. Eisendorfer. 1986. *The Loss of Self.* New York: Norton.

Gruetzner, H. 1988. *Alzheimer's: A Caregiver's Guide and Sourcebook.* New York: Wiley.

Mace, N.L., and P.V. Rabins. 1991. *The 36-Hour Day: A Family Guide to Caring for Persons with Alzheimer's Disease, Related Dementing Illnesses, and Memory Loss in Later Life,* 2d ed. Baltimore: Johns Hopkins University Press.

Noyes, L. 1982. *What's Wrong with My Grandma?* Available from Northern Virginia

Alzheimer's Association, Yorktown, 50 Building, Suite 401, 8316 Arlington
    Boulevard, Fairfax, Va. 22031. (703) 207–7044.
Robinson, A., B. Spencer, and L. White. 1989. *Understanding Difficult Behaviors: Some
    Practical Suggestions for Coping with Alzheimer's Disease and Related Illnesses.*
    Ypsilanti, Mich.: Eastern Michigan University.

Jane Swinton, Marguerite Nickel, and Robert W. Hamill

Alzheimer's Disease: Eating Behaviors

INTRODUCTION

Eating behaviors and habits are frequently altered in individuals with Alzheimer's disease (AD). The issue of eating is important since proper nutrition is needed to reduce complications associated with poor dietary intake and to help the person remain at home for as long as possible. As AD progresses, the person may eventually refuse or be unable to eat or drink altogether. Consequently, it is important for caregivers to keep the person as well nourished for as long a time as possible.

From the time the person is first diagnosed as having AD, it is important to discuss the individual's personal wishes regarding health care choices with family and members of the health care team, while such decisions can still be made. It may seem frightening to discuss these issues while the patient is still relatively well, but if feeding problems or other health problems occur later, as they undoubtedly will, it is necessary and comforting to know the individual's wishes beforehand. This process assures that personal desires will be carried out in the event the person is eventually unable to make decisions regarding his or her own care. A statement that no heroics, that is, respiratory and cardiopulmonary resuscitation, etc., be carried out is not sufficient. The subject of artificial feeding and hydration also needs to be specifically addressed. Mechanisms are in place in most states to formally document an individual's instructions regarding artificial feeding through a stomach tube along with other health care decisions that must be made during a serious or final illness. Information regarding such forms for documenting family and individual wishes about health care can be obtained from private physicians or from local and state health departments. Requirements for advance directives vary from state to state.

BACKGROUND

Changes in eating habits include either an increase or decrease in food intake. As AD progresses, the amount of food and drink consumed may periodically fluctuate. Specific alterations in behaviors include: (a) forgetting how to chew or swallow; (b) inability to open the mouth; (c) dislike of food; (d) failure to recognize edible objects as food; (e) consumption of nonfood items; and (f) loss of sense of taste, hunger, and thirst. Siebens et al. (1986) also identified other behaviors including spitting, drooling, overstuffing the mouth, and nasal regurgitation. Along with eating aberrations, cognitive impairment also results in such behaviors as inability to use utensils, failure to remember to eat or to recognize the need to eat, and inability to sit at the table to finish a meal.

These problems may be due to one or more underlying causes, such as: cognitive and behavioral changes, decreased attention span, apraxia (inability of fingers and hands to perform familiar tasks), insufficient caregiving, metabolic or neurochemical imbalances (which may or may not be related to the dementia), depression, social withdrawal, or medication side effects. Other causes may include disease-related disruptions within particular brain regions that control food intake, weight, and the sense of taste and smell.

EVALUATION

The challenge for the caregiver is to find creative ways to keep the person eating once the disease begins to interfere with normal eating habits. The first consideration is to try and determine why the person is experiencing a change in appetite or eating behavior. Specific questions to explore are: Is there a change in overall health or comfort? Is vision adequate? Is there an underlying infection? Are there dental problems, such as ill-fitting dentures? Is it related to new or long-standing prescription drug therapy? If all of these possibilities have been evaluated and treated, and the changed behavior persists, then the change may be the result of disease progression. A final conclusion may require medical review by the physician or nurse practitioner.

MANAGEMENT

There are numerous strategies that can be used that will assist in improving the person's appetite and thus food and fluid intake. The recommended approaches are summarized within the following categories: (a) comfort and support, (b) vision, (c) timing, (d) flexibility, (e) nutrition and preferences, (f) medical/nursing interventions, (g) mechanics, and (h) public dining.

Comfort and Support

A calm and stress-free environment before and during mealtime is conducive to optimal eating behaviors. The person should be seated comfortably, neither too warm nor too cold, and wearing clothing that is not restrictive (such as a collar or belt that is too tight). The caregiver should encourage the AD person to participate in meal preparation, perhaps by setting the table or arranging placement of chairs, etc. Other activities can be suggested based on the ability of the individual to perform them. If possible, the caregiver should sit at the table and eat with the individual.

Visual

Adequate non-glare lighting and protection from direct bright sunlight should be provided. Facing away from distracting influences such as windows through which traffic movement and sounds are heard, or groups of noisy children, will enable the AD individual to concentrate on what is needed at the moment— eating, reading, taking medications, etc. To enhance visual perception, color contrast should be used to distinguish between dishes and tablecloth, or papers and books from background (desk, table, etc.).

Timing

Everything should be in order and in place before seating the patient at the table or desk. The meal should be ready to serve. Meals and other activities should be arranged within a carefully followed time plan, since disruption in routine is often upsetting for AD persons. Change should occur only when absolutely necessary.

Flexibility

Despite adherence to fixed routines, sufficient time should be allowed for meals. The person with AD may need time for pacing or other activity that interrupts the meal. The caregiver must, above all, show unlimited patience with these individuals, so long as the behavior is not worrisome to either the caregiver or the individual. For example, if the AD person insists on having a sandwich for breakfast, rather than a more traditional menu, these whims should be satisfied as far as possible. The important element is the overall nutritional status, not particular foods at particular times of the day. Many AD persons wander, pace, or are otherwise hyperactive; they need extra calories to match the amount of energy expended in these activities. Finger foods that they can eat while pacing may be one answer, or small, frequent meals throughout the day. Flexibility is the key to caring for individuals with AD.

Nutrition and Preferences

Food should be attractively presented and served at the proper temperature. AD persons frequently exhibit changes in food and taste preferences. Ask before food is prepared, to avoid uncomfortable situations and wasted food. It may be possible for the caregiver to acquire additional help in food selection and preparation from a nutritionist, local agencies which provide food in the home, or from home delivery of cooked meals. Local restaurants and cookbooks may also help in finding new ways to meet the nutritional needs of AD patients when the usual kinds of food and preparation are no longer acceptable. Previously refused menu items may later be enjoyed again. The caregiver also needs to be aware that AD persons often hoard (hide) food; they need to be protected from eating spoiled food.

If the person is not eating well and if there are no dietary restrictions, serve high-nutrient foods such as high-protein milkshakes, eggs, cheese, and cream soups. Sugary foods may be appealing and satisfy hunger, but calories from these foods are quickly used up. As with all people, a balanced diet of fresh fruits, vegetables, grain products, and assorted kinds of high-protein foods is best. Snacks between meals are fine, as long as they do not interfere with meal-time intake of important foods.

On the other hand, if the person is overweight or has dietary restrictions, the choice of low-calorie foods is obviously necessary, with greater emphasis on fruits, vegetables, whole-grain foods, and low-fat dairy products. If overstuffing cannot easily be controlled, distraction during eating may be needed by sug-gesting a walk, watching a particular television program, or simply taking the food off the table and ending the meal.

Medical and Nursing Interventions

In circumstances such as the AD person refusing to eat for two days or longer, exhibiting a 10 percent weight loss, refusing to take medications normally as-sociated with meal times, or if other problems arise, the caregiver needs to notify the physician or nurse. The decision may be to hospitalize the patient for di-agnostic testing to determine the cause for the changed behavior or new problem.

Mechanics

An individual may have the desire to eat, but may be unable to manage the usual silverware and dinnerware. A creative approach may be needed. One so-lution may be the use of finger foods exclusively, or the introduction of me-chanical devices that assist people with physical disabilities. A bowl, rather than a plate, may be better for scooping up food. An undersurface of plastic or other material to keep utensils from sliding may be helpful. If the person is over-whelmed by too many choices, providing only one food item at a time may be best. The caregiver can give verbal cues and assist as needed, perhaps even feeding the person.

One problem may be consistency of the food, where soft or pureed foods may be preferable and easier to manage than foods that need to be chewed. If swallowing is a problem, the caregiver must be alert to choking and either remove food from the mouth or apply the Heimlich maneuver. All caregivers of AD persons should be trained in first aid techniques, including use of the Heimlich maneuver.

Public Dining

Having AD does not automatically mean that the person must avoid a previously enjoyable social activity such as eating in a favorite restaurant. All that may be required are some simple adjustments to the restaurant routine. Eating at an off-peak time may be easier for everyone. The caregiver may need to discreetly inform the server that the AD person has a memory impairment. This can be done either by calling ahead or by using preprinted cards. It may be helpful to order certain foods for the AD person and for the caregiver to order alternative foods known to be favorites of the AD person. Ask the server to remove unnecessary items from the table such as extra silverware or glassware. In this situation, too, flexibility is necessary to deal with unexpected situations. Having the company and assistance of a third person will often be helpful.

SUMMARY

The person with AD undergoes almost continual changes in eating and other behaviors. Changes, and the rate of change, vary considerably from one individual to another, and are often unpredictable. The essential part of care is to provide sufficient food and fluids for the maintenance of health, weight, and physical and psychological needs. Eating disorders are a multifaceted problem. Strategies for dealing with inadequate and inappropriate eating have been presented. The goal is to provide the best possible nutrition within a comfortable and supportive environment for as long as the person is able to participate in eating.

References

Hellen, C.R. 1990. Eating: an Alzheimer's activity. *Amer J Alzheimer's Care and Related Disorders and Research* 5(2):5–9.

Mace, N.L., ed. 1990. *Dementia Care: Patient, Family, and Community.* Baltimore: Johns Hopkins University Press.

Morris, C.H., R.A. Hope, and C.G. Fairburn. 1989. Eating habits in dementia: a descriptive study. *British J of Psychiatry* 154:801–6.

Robinson, A., B. Spencer, and L. White. 1989. *Understanding Difficult Behaviors: Some Practical Suggestions for Coping with Alzheimer's Disease and Related Illnesses.* Ypsilanti, Mich.: Eastern Michigan University.

Siebens, H., E. Trupe, A. Siebens, F. Cook, S. Anshen, R. Hanauer, and G. Oster. 1986. Correlates and consequences of eating dependency in institutionalized elderly. *J Amer Geriatric Society*, 34:192–98.

Volicer, L., B. Seltzer, Y. Rheaume, J. Karner, M. Glennon, and M.E. Riley. 1989. Eating difficulties in patients with probable dementia of the Alzheimer's type. *J of Geriatric Psychiatry and Neurology* 2:188–95.

Eileen M. Johnson, Mary E. McCarthy, and Robert W. Hamill

Alzheimer's Disease: Social Work Intervention

A complete assessment of individuals with Alzheimer's disease and their care-givers results in both a more comprehensive plan of care and improved accep-tance of the recommendations by the recipients. To give care successfully often means that family members must struggle with increased responsibilities, inter-pret and adapt to the varied and worsening symptoms of Alzheimer's disease, and cope with the disruption of the family lifestyle, while attempting to avoid premature nursing home placement. The social worker, through the use of cre-ative and sensitive interventions, can improve caregiving within the family when a member is afflicted with Alzheimer's disease.

PROGRESSION OF THE DISEASE

Alzheimer's disease usually involves a long, slow decline, as the victim pro-gressively worsens, and family support systems become physically, emotionally, and financially strained. The likelihood of developing the disease increases with age. In light of the increased longevity of Americans, the age-related prevalence of Alzheimer's disease will be a continuing area of research and concern to health care providers and policymakers.

The diagnosis is made by a careful history, physical examination, and cog-nitive screening. A reliable independent history is invaluable. Currently, no di-agnostic test exists to make the diagnosis of Alzheimer's disease with absolute certainty unless pathologic evaluation of brain tissue is performed. The disease, often referred to as dementia, has a characteristically gradual onset. Family members frequently do not recognize the subtle memory and behavioral changes until several years after the initial symptoms begin. This may unfortunately prevent informed decisionmaking while the affected individual is able to partic-ipate in their own future plans.

The progressive nature of the disease may be generally subdivided into three stages. The first stage shows a decline in memory, judgment, orientation, and in the ability to follow through with routine work patterns. The second stage involves increasing difficulty in caring for one's personal self and taking re-sponsibility for bill paying and household management. In the end stage, the individual is often unable to speak intelligently, and becomes more dependent, with the final years spent being cared for in a nursing home or by a caregiver in the individual's home.

SOCIAL WORK INTERVENTION

The term "caregiver" includes the spouse, children, siblings, grandchildren, nieces, nephews, or friends. In some cases, caregivers may believe that no one else can or will perform the tasks as well as they can. In other cases, the caregiving role is imposed upon a particular individual, with little support, emotionally or financially, for the burden. In these situations, counseling can be invaluable. By reviewing the family structure, the social worker discovers who is in the household, who is available to assume caregiving responsibility, and what other informal and formal services may be obtained. The social worker helps caregivers to carefully weigh the existing options that will permit the patient to remain safely in the home. The home environment is assessed by the social worker, who may suggest the addition of grab bars, smoke detectors, gates, locks, fences, additional lighting, and the removal of scatter rugs to improve the safety features. Labelling cabinets, drawers, and bathrooms with large-print signs may help the patient find his way about and to remain oriented.

In general, the relationship between the caregiver and the social worker remains intact throughout the patient's illness, facilitating the development of trust. A trusting relationship enables the caregiver to ask for help when additional help is needed, and before a crisis occurs. Some of the ways in which the social worker can assist the caregiver may be to:

- identify abuse or neglect
- initiate advance directive discussions between the caregiver and patient, with the primary provider
- assess financial status, and suggest a financial counselor who can recommend financial alternatives to prolong and protect assets
- clarify insurance claims, forms, etc.
- provide counseling regarding stress management
- provide information about community services and resources
- periodically test the patient's cognitive capabilities
- identify symptoms of depression in the patient or the caregiver
- assist in making decisions about nursing home placement, adult day care, respite care, and other forms of assistance

SOCIAL WORK RECOMMENDATIONS

Communicating with the patient is frequently one of the greatest causes of frustration for family members, because patients are often unable to articulate all of their needs and may exhibit repetitive or irrational behavior patterns that interfere with the communications process. A skilled social worker can often interpret messages or suggest possible reasons for the communications block.

Family members have legitimate thresholds for what they can learn, and how much they can adapt and sacrifice. The social worker must be flexible in the methods employed to obtain information, to assess the current family situation, and to determine what problems must be resolved immediately and what problems can be put off to another time. As an observer in the home setting, the social worker can often ascertain difficulties early, before they become major problems, and suggest alternative actions to avoid open battles. The social worker can prepare the caregiver for what is needed in all stages of the disease, each of which may be different. The caregiver's fear of change, fear of being alone, or fear of failure in this important task of caring for a loved one can be allayed to a large extent by the thoughtful, patient, and sensitive health care professional. Helping the caregiver to understand that the patient may have the same fears will often smooth the path for both.

Perhaps the social worker's most effective assistance is derived from a thorough knowledge of the external resources available to patients and families. Sharing this knowledge can help ease the burden of caregiving and provide a measure of comfort to the caregiver. This type of knowledge sharing, the trusting relationship, the ongoing assessment, the determination of immediate and future needs of both the patient and the caregiver, combine to provide the most beneficial care to patients with Alzheimer's disease and their families.

References

Bumagin, V.E., and K.F. Hirn. 1990. *Helping the Aging Family: A Guide for Professionals*. Glenview, Ill: Scott, Foresman.

Cattanach, L., and J.K. Tebes. 1991. The nature of elder impairment and its impact on family caregivers' health and psychosocial functioning. *The Gerontologist* 31(2): 246–55.

Gwyther, L.P. 1990. Clinician and family: a partnership for support. In *Dementia Care: Patient, Family, and Community*, edited by N.L. Mace. Baltimore: The Johns Hopkins University Press, 193–230.

Moore, I. 1991. Adapting to the home health care experience for Alzheimer's families: a social work perspective. *J Home Health Care Practice* 3(4):13–18.

Irene Moore

Alzheimer's Disease: Wandering Behaviors

INTRODUCTION

Wandering and pacing behaviors are common activities for persons with Alzheimer's disease (AD). Symptoms of this organic brain disease—disorientation to time and place; poor recall; and decreased ability to learn, follow directions, communicate, and judge one's surrounding space—all contribute to these motor behaviors.

Webster defines wandering as "the tendency to move about either in a seemingly aimless or disoriented fashion or in pursuit of an indefinite or unobtainable goal." Burnside felt that wandering may demonstrate a desire to search for new or to discover old experiences. Hussian (1981) reports that wandering may be to some degree under external environmental control. Mace and Rabins (1981) noted that wandering can signal a catastrophic reaction.

PROFILES AND TYPES OF WANDERERS

Monsour and Robb studied lifestyles of elderly wanderers and nonwanderers in a long-term care setting. They found that, prior to their illness, wanderers engaged in higher levels of social and leisure activities and experienced more stressful events than the nonwanderers. In addition, the wanderers previously displayed motoric reactions such as pacing and walking under stress.

A review of Alzheimer patients attending a dementia clinic described four types of wandering behaviors: (1) exit-seekers are those who attempt to leave; (2) self-stimulators manipulate the door as an activity rather than an attempt to leave; (3) akathesiacs (persons who cannot remain seated) exhibit pacing, fidgeting and restless behavior; and (4) modelers follow people around and may leave the building in an attempt to follow someone.

A study of older nursing home residents categorized wandering into three groups: (1) overtly goal-directed and searching; (2) goal-directed but industrious; and (3) simply nongoal-directed, aimlessly drawn to a stimulus. The study also found that wanderers demonstrated more problems in recent and remote memory, orientation to time and place, and ability to respond appropriately to a given topic.

Wandering behaviors can often be associated with the time of day. Increased confusion associated with late afternoon or early evening is known as Sundown syndrome. As evening approaches and there is less presence of light, persons (especially those with dementia) become agitated, restless, confused, and begin to wander. Some persons with dementia reverse their days and nights, and are found wandering at night only to fall asleep during the day. It is important, however, to remember past jobs and routines such as working the night shift or rising each day at 4 a.m. may have been the norm rather than the exception before their AD. Some persons revert back to these routines in what appears to be an attempt to put order back into their lives or because they are living in the past.

Wandering may be a coping mechanism to deal with an unmet basic need such as hunger or thirst, or fulfillment of an emotional or social need. Nighttime wandering may be an attempt to relieve a full bladder. When lighting and vision are poor and the person is disoriented, discomfort and anxiety can increase. As the anxiety increases, adrenaline levels rise, which can trigger a ''fight or flight'' behavior in an attempt to cope with a fearful situation.

Other triggers of wandering include (a) changes in temperature or weather, (b) uncomfortable or poor fitting clothing, (c) noise, (d) glare, and (e) even persons or objects in a room. Early signs of a urinary tract infection, joint stiffness, skin rash or breakdown, constipation, indigestion, or gas pains can cause such discomfort that they lead to pacing or wandering activities. Signs of cardiac distress such as angina or shortness of breath may cause the Alzheimer patient to become agitated and begin pacing in an attempt to relieve their pain or discomfort. Close observation of nonverbal clues such as grimacing, fidgeting, pacing, increased confusion, and restlessness may help in finding the cause of the behavior.

Alzheimer's disease results in changes in the brain that interrupt the normal processing of visual and auditory information, as well as the retrieval and integration of memory and thought. Accordingly, patients with AD may misinterpret their environment and their internal thoughts with resultant confusion and fear, including paranoid ideations. These latter thoughts may lead to increased agitation and wandering.

Patterns and causes of wandering are diverse, often difficult to manage and even dangerous at times. Understanding the contributing factors and profiles of wanderers helps in the development of management techniques.

MANAGEMENT

Management of wandering behaviors begins with a medical evaluation. Family observations and comments regarding past and recent medical events and social history help the physician in this evalution process. Following the assessment of possible health related causes of wandering, various interventions can minimize or even eliminate the wandering behaviors.

If the person experiences burning and frequency of urination, this increased urge to void or discomfort with incontinence may trigger increased wandering. Antibiotic therapy, fluids, and a toileting schedule will treat the urinary tract infection and eventually the behavior. Likewise, an enlarged prostate gland can cause similar discomfort.

Constipation and gas pains can lead to restless behavior and pacing as the Alzheimer's person tries to cope with the discomfort. Careful monitoring of bowel habits and plenty of fiber, fluids, and exercise can result in a regular bowel regime, increased abdominal comfort, and a more relaxed individual.

Another trigger of restless wandering is skin rash or breakdown. Keeping the skin clean and dry, avoiding the use of harsh cleaning and skin care products, providing properly fitted, manageable clothing and footwear, and checking for skin-related side effects of medications are all helpful in preventing skin breakdown or rash. The end result is a more comfortable, less restless person.

Musculoskeletal discomfort from arthritis and joint stiffness can trigger wandering behaviors. A balance of exercise and rest helps to (1) relieve the stiffness, (2) keep the joints mobile, and (3) prevent exhaustion and burning of calories that can lead to weight loss in some wanderers. The use of periodic analgesics and elevation of limbs can also increase the comfort level.

The aimless, happy wanderer often responds to diversional techniques and simple, structured activities. The activities must provide opportunities to succeed, support their highest level of functioning, and reinforce social contacts. Cooking and baking, folding laundry, and simple household chores can be effective. Music therapy in the form of exercise, singing, dancing, and playing of rhythm instruments can divert wandering energies. Pets and gardening can divert attention and stimulate happy memories. The use of soft background music can help relax the restless wanderer as well. Simple modifications of past jobs, interests, and hobbies are generally the best form of diversional activity. Some trial and error will take place before the caregiver determines those activities that are successful.

If it doesn't create a problem, allow the wandering. Treat it as an activity. A stroll down a garden path, brisk walks inside shopping malls or outdoors, or even a scenic ride in the car provide needed exercise, social stimulation, and a change of scene. Landscape architect Frederick Law Olmstead noted, ''The enjoyment of scenery employs the mind without fatigue and gives the effect of refreshing rest and reinvigoration to the whole system.''

The indoor environment must provide safety, familiarity, accessibility, and contact with the outside. Clearing pathways of throw rugs, obstructive furniture, and any dangerous objects such as light cords will help avoid falls. Loop patterns for wandering paths (instead of dead ends) involve no memory and suggest a continuous forward movement. These pathways combined with comfortable, favorite seatings (with a view to the outdoors) help to provide a balance of exercise and rest. This balance is important to avoid excess weight loss and anxious exhaustion.

Sequential thinking is very difficult for persons with AD. Thus, unsafe wandering to the outside can be avoided by the use of multiple and varied locks or latches on doors and gates. Agnosia (inability to recognize familiar objects) is common; therefore, disguising door handles and painting doors and molding to blend with the color of the walls can act as visual deterrents for the exit-seeking behavior. Fenced-in yards allow persons to explore, pace, and expend some of their energy in a secure, safe, and stimulating environment.

Area police, fire, and ambulance personnel should be given a photo and written information about the person who wanders. Local chapters of the Alzheimer's Association may have wanderer alert programs and education information for caregivers.

The use of medication to calm the anxious wanderer should be considered only if other measures fail. In situations where behavioral disorders are triggering the wandering, treatment with specific antipsychotic medications may be needed. Any use of medication should be under close medical supervision and follow-up for desired as well as adverse side effects.

The use of physical restraints such as waist, vest, or mechanical devices that tie or restrict the person's movements are strongly discouraged except for safety or vital medical treatment. Physical restraints can cause increased anxiety and are dehumanizing.

Understanding the symptoms of Alzheimer's disease, influences of environmental factors, and coexisting medical problems can help health care professionals and family members recognize the many triggers of wandering behaviors. Past coping mechanisms and social history also impact on patterns and profiles of wanderers. Close observation and a calm, open approach are critical, as persons with Alzheimer's disease often mirror those around them.

There is no single management solution for treating wandering behaviors. The causes are often multifaceted and therefore the interventions must be individualized and multiple in nature.

References

Burnside, I.M. 1980. *Psychosocial Nursing Care and the Aged*, 2d ed. New York: McGraw-Hill.

Deutsch, L.H., and B.W. Rovner. 1991. Agitation and other noncognitive abnormalities in Alzheimer's disease. *Psychiatr Clin North Amer* 14:341–51.

Evans, L.K. 1987. Sundown syndrome in institutionalized elderly. *J Amer Geriatr Society* 35:101–8.

Hirst, S.T., and B.J. Metcalf. 1989. Whys and whats of wandering. *Geriatr Nursing* 10: 237–38.

Hussian, R. 1981. *Geriatric Psychology: A Behavioral Perspective*. New York: Van Nostrand Reinhold.

Mace, N.L., and P.V. Rabins. 1981. *The 36-Hour Day: A Family Guide to Caring for Persons with Alzheimer's Disease, Related Dementing Illnesses, and Memory Loss in Later Life*, 2d ed. Baltimore: Johns Hopkins University Press.

Monsour, N. and S.S. Ross. 1982. Wandering behavior in old age: a psychosocial study. *Social Work* 27:411–15.

Randall, P., S. Burkhardt, and J. Kutcher. 1990. Exterior space for patients with Alzheimer's disease and related disorders. *Amer J of Alzheimer's Care and Related Disorders and Research* 5(4):31–37.

Mary E. McCarthy, Eileen M. Johnson, and Robert W. Hamill

American Indians

INTRODUCTION

Recognizing the role that ethnicity plays in the lives of American Indians is fundamental to understanding Indian elderly in the 1990s. A description of the diversity in American Indian communities, the status of research on elderly American Indians, and the criteria for identifying Indians are important background for that understanding.

BACKGROUND INFORMATION

Tribal/Geographic Diversity and Pantribal Identification

The cultural heritage of American Indians is widely diverse, including various lifestyles (e.g., sedentary horticulturalists and nomadic hunters), different forms of social organization (e.g., matrilineal and patrilineal descent groups), and distinct beliefs, values, and world views. Many changes have occurred in these cultural contexts, especially in the twentieth century, as Indian people have dealt with the historical reality of enforced acculturation. However, many aspects of their traditional cultures (such as social organization, religion, beliefs and values) remain strong influences in their lives in the 1990s.

Diversity for American Indians in the 1990s is also a matter of self-identity. While there are full-bloods and many degrees of "breeds," the choice of whether to identify as Indian, and to what extent, is an individual decision. It is a choice that those who live in urban areas are especially free to exercise.

People who choose to identify as Indian today frequently do so in the context of intertribal events. Even a tribal celebration usually includes members from other tribes either as participants in the event or as visiting friends. Political associations such as the National Congress of American Indians and the National Indian Council on Aging (NICOA) are by nature composed of Indians from many different tribes and geographic locations.

No longer predominantly rural, 52 percent of American Indians live in urban centers, both large (e.g., Los Angeles) and small (e.g., Ponca City, Oklahoma). Those who remain in their tribal communities live in rural areas on small reservations (e.g., Taos Pueblo, New Mexico) and large reservations (e.g., Navajo Reservation). Indian people also live in rural non-reservation areas, as in Oklahoma where reservations no longer exist.

Indians prefer to identify themselves by tribal affiliation rather than the generic term Indian, in spite of the importance of intertribal connections and pantribal activities in their lives.

Status of Research on Indian Elderly

A number of studies since 1970 have outlined the statistical-demographic status of elderly American Indians. Although the life span for American Indians as a group has increased since World War II, it is still about seven years less than for the general population. The National Indian Council on Aging survey of older American Indians corroborates the earlier studies that identify elderly American Indians as economically deprived, with low income, poor housing and transportation, low education levels, and poor health. Indian elderly experience a higher rate of chronic ailments that afflict elderly people; these ailments are manifested at an earlier age.

In addition, the NICOA survey underscores the uncertainty and lack of documentation about exact numbers and locations of Indian/Alaskan Native elderly. This lack of information creates additional problems in providing services.

In spite of the difficulties that elderly Indians face, there are several studies that indicate that Indian ethnicity provides a supportive context for Indian elderly in many communities.

Functional Definition of Age

NICOA suggests the use of a "functional" definition of age to identify elderly Indians rather than a formal (chronological) definition. Studies show that the characteristics of impairment exhibited at ages 45–55 by American Indians are comparable to the characteristics of impairment exhibited by non-Indians in the 60–65 age range. Chronological age is not a good predictor of need for aging Indians.

The functional definition of Indian elderly also includes a "positive" dimension. Older individuals who have lived their lives according to the norms and cultural prescriptions of their communities, who are knowledgeable and exhibit wisdom, are revered as the elders of the tribe. They are respected as the preservers of tribal history and cultural patterns. There is no set chronological age for a person to reach the stage of tribal elder; historical and cultural circumstances and personal life trajectories are the determinants.

CULTURAL CHARACTERISTICS OF AMERICAN INDIAN ELDERLY

Many American Indian elderly live within familial, tribal, and intertribal contexts in which they often have important statuses and perform important roles. Basic to the values and lifestyle of American Indians and their elderly is intergenerational, interdependent interaction between the generations. Events are generally non-age–segregated. Such intergenerational activities can be observed at Fifth Sunday Sings that take place at the Brighter Day Baptist Church in Los Angeles or at the yearly four-day encampment of the Otoe-Missouria tribe in north central Oklahoma.

The relationship between grandparents and grandchildren has traditionally been one of great affection and interaction, and is an example of reciprocity between generations. Several contemporary styles of grandparenting have been noted and echo traditional patterns in which grandparents were responsible for the rearing of children while the parents were involved in the hunt or in tending the horticultural gardens. Orphaned children were and are usually the responsibility of grandparents.

The elders are a source of strength in Indian families as they act to unify the family and guard the rights of children. It is through this strong association between grandparents and grandchildren that cultural traditions and values are transmitted. Interdependence and reciprocity are grounded in the web of relationships that surround Indian elders and their family members. As examples, grandparents initiate grandchildren into the dance arena; and grandchildren provide transportation for grandparents who can no longer drive.

Fictive kinship in the form of adoptions and special friends extends the obligations/responsibilities and privileges of family, as when an elder adopts a younger person after his or her parent dies. This adoption may be between members of the same tribe or different tribes.

Sharing is a fundamental value among American Indians and is frequently expressed at public events. Sharing may include food or the giving of gifts of goods or money at a giveaway. Elderly people are often honored simply because they are elders and have accumulated honor and prestige because of their long lives and past contributions. The giveaway is representative of a longstanding tradition of sharing and exchange that may take different forms in different tribal communities, but which constitutes a basic value and practice of Indian people.

Whether based on Christianity, native religion, or the tenets of the Native American Church, spirituality is intrinsic to the world view of American Indians. Transmitting spirituality to the young continues to be a function of the elders.

Prestige and value are accorded the old when those individuals have followed the precepts of their ethnic communities or have in other ways achieved a successful life. Even those who do not follow cultural norms are often considered with compassion and understanding by community members. Since the 1960s, Indians have become more willing to identify as Indian; this renaissance of Indian culture and the desire to hold on to traditions has served to enhance the status of tribal elders.

Intercultural Variation

The cultural characteristics described are functional for those Indians who are able and willing to participate in the Indian community. There are elderly Indians who, because of economic and/or health problems, lack of immediate family, geographic isolation, or because of personal choice, do not participate in the social exchanges. The generally deplorable status of the social, economic, and health characteristics of American Indian elders is real and should be recognized. It is appropriate and imperative, however, to also acknowledge the supporting role that ethnicity plays in the lives of elderly American Indians.

CONCLUSIONS

In spite of the attempts by the Federal government to foster the assimilation of American Indians into the mainstream of America, and in spite of the fact that nearly half (48% in 1980) of Indian elderly live in urban areas and away from their tribal communities, those who are elders today continue to be Indian in outlook, values, and behavior.

Sensitivity to Indian perspectives, culture, history, and present-day needs is a primary concern of the elderly as they try to use state and Federal service programs. Cultural sensitivity should be a primary concern of policy planners and service providers.

References

John, R. 1988. *American Indian Aging. A Selective Annotated Bibliography for Gerontology Instruction.* Washington, D.C.: Association for Gerontology in Higher Education.

Schweitzer, M.M. 1987. The elders: cultural dimensions of aging in two American Indian communities. In *Growing Old in Different Societies, Cross-Cultural Perspectives,* edited by J. Sokolovsky. Acton, Mass.: Copley Press, 168–78.

Weibel-Orlando, J. 1989. Well-being in Indian old age. *American Indian Culture and Research Journal* 13(3 & 4):149–70.

———. 1991. Grandparenting styles: Native American perspectives. In *The Cultural Context of Aging: Worldwide Perspectives,* edited by J. Sokolovsky. Westport, Conn.: Bergin and Garvey, 109–25.

Williams, G.C. 1980. Warriors no more: a study of the American Indian elderly. In *Aging in Culture and Society. Comparative Viewpoints and Strategies,* edited by C. Fry. Brooklyn, N.Y.: J.F. Bergin, 101–11.

Marjorie M. Schweitzer

Amputee Rehabilitation

Major scientific advances provided by a highly technological society have successfully resulted in the prolongation of life expectancy in the United States. But in turn, increased longevity has created a number of problems for the health care system, one of which is care of the patient with amputation of the lower extremity as a result of peripheral vascular disease.

Despite the tremendous improvement in the care of the amputee, the patient still faces a severe, sometimes catastrophic, trauma that strikes not only the body, but the mind and the emotions as well. To the patient, amputation signifies a painful venture into the frightening unknown.

When faced with the reality of amputation, the patient must successfully adapt to the situation by living life as normally as possible despite the disability and its attendant consequences. According to Crate, successful adaptation is "the ability of the person with a chronic illness to live comfortably or resignedly within himself as a person who has this specific condition." The patient must realize that changes are required in order to function within the limitations resulting from the amputation. The limitations are at first unknown to the person; the primary need is to test these limitations.

In order to meet the demands placed on the individual's physical and emotional state, the patient attempts to adapt to the rehabilitation process by making the required changes within the self, in the lifestyle, and within the immediate family.

Admittedly, this is a highly mobile society in which we live, one that admires the independent achiever, not the dependent disabled individual. The importance of physical attractiveness is continually presented in every form of media as being the most essential element for survival in a modern competitive world. The body beautiful is held as the ideal.

Since the values associated with appearance are important, when an individual does not meet this most critical of requirements, he/she is regarded as "different." From this dilemma, problems arise.

The physical problems of an amputee involving the loss of a lower extremity include: physical disfigurement, the loss of locomotion, and decreased endurance for all activity.

A person's psychological responses to amputation are numerous and can range from anxiety, anger, fear, and frustration, to depression and nonacceptance of a prosthesis. These defense mechanisms are used by the amputee to counteract the threats to his life and self-esteem.

In addition, the impact exerts changes within the family. Family support is greatly needed to enable the patient to make his adaptation to an altered state of wellness. The presence of long-term stressors requires that changes occur in the traditional roles. The inability to cope and adjust to changes can lead to a high incidence of family disruption and breakdown, which may ultimately lead to disruption in the total rehabilitation process.

Therefore, an amputation of the lower extremity signifies much more than simply the loss of a limb. The effects are more far-reaching and more complex than the immediate mechanical problem. To the amputee, it symbolizes the end of mobility and the destruction of a satisfying self-image, the loss of a whole, intact body forever.

Clearly, the success of rehabilitation requires the patient to develop compromises within the self, the environment, and the way of life. Fears and anxieties must be overcome to secure a level of functioning that is appropriate for the altered physical state. Cognitively, the individual must accept this new level of functioning and learn to live and work within these new parameters. A tall order for even the most confident person.

The basic needs for air, food, shelter, safety, and sex must be satisfied before the higher-level needs for belongingness, self-esteem, and self-actualization can emerge.

For the majority of disabled persons, particularly amputees, the goal of rehabilitation is to achieve at least 90 percent independence with the use of a prosthesis. The time to achieve maximum rehabilitation goals, as reported by researchers, varies over a wide range according or relative to the number of hospitalization days, from 40 to 400 days. However, most studies confirm that a 4- to 5-month period is required before the amputee is able to return to his preamputation level in society.

Consequently, adapting to an amputation is an individual, ongoing process for the duration of the rehabilitation period. The individual must call upon a reservoir of coping mechanisms and develop new mechanisms in an attempt to function as in the pre-crisis life. The rehabilitation process must focus first on the physical disability and then address the immediate psychologic trauma, and as soon as possible move on to developing new behaviors, roles, and coping styles.

Such matters as age, physical status, condition of the stump, occupation, body weight, motivation, acceptance, the realization of one's expectations, and the individual's support systems must all be considered.

Many amputees do not or cannot openly express their fears and frustrations, and the caregiver must be aware of the diversity of needs and the varying intensity of needs that must be satisfied in order for the person to maintain progress toward adjustment. These needs may be biogenic or sociogenic in nature. Biogenic needs evolve from the biology of the organism and relate to such things as hunger, thirst, and avoidance of pain. Sociogenic needs relate to the person's self-esteem and self-image. These conflicts can be modified, can be somewhat compromised, but they cannot be negated. The role of the caregiver becomes one of assisting the individual to incorporate the new limitations into the person's life patterns to assure minimal interference with the activities of daily living.

The overall literature review demonstrates that an amputation of a lower extremity constitutes a major lifestyle adjustment, particularly in the elderly. The goal, regardless of the age of the patient, is to return the individual to a useful life within the family and community, as a well-established, functional, independent human being.

The rehabilitation process is said to be completed when the patient's physical and psychological adjustments are no longer considered a focal point. It is when the patient uses the prosthesis automatically, or at least subconsciously, the patient's awareness of being physically limited and "different" becomes less threatening, and the use of the prosthesis becomes a minimal source of interference in one's daily living activities. Only then can one say that the elements of a successful rehabilitation have been achieved.

References

Cotton, L.T. 1991. *Limb Amputation: From Aetiology to Rehabilitation*. London, New York: Chapman and Hall.

Crate, A.L. 1965. Nursing function in adaptation to chronic illness. *Amer J Nursing* 65: 287.

Griffin, S. 1992. We let this patient down. *RN* 55(3):49–51.

Roinseville, C. 1992. Phantom limb pain: the ghost that haunts the amputee. *Orthopedic Nursing* 11(2):67–71.

Sanders, G.T. 1986. *Lower Limb Amputations: A Guide to Rehabilitation.* Philadelphia: F.A. Davis.

Varni, J.W. 1991. Effects of stress, social support, and self-esteem on depression in children with limb deficiencies. *Arch of Physical Med & Rehab* 72(13):1053–58.

Williamson, V.C. 1992. Amputation of the lower extremity: an overview. *Orthopedic Nursing* 11(2):55–65.

Joan A. Panchal

Anticoagulation Therapy (Oral) and Monitoring

INTRODUCTION

Following discharge from the hospital, many patients are on continuous oral anticoagulant therapy. Often, patients are referred to home care for anticoagulation teaching and monitoring. The following information provides guidelines for teaching and monitoring anticoagulation therapy for patients living in the community.

WARFARIN SODIUM

Tablet Identification

The overwhelming majority of patients on oral anticoagulation receive warfarin sodium (Coumadin, DuPont brand). Coumadin tablets are available in six different strengths, which can be identified by the color of the tablet: 1 mg (hot pink), 2 mg (lavender), 2.5 mg (green), 5 mg (peach), 7.5 mg (yellow), and 10 mg (white). On one side of the tablet is the word "Coumadin" and the number of milligrams, and on the other side is the word "DuPont." Patients should be instructed to always verify that they have the correct brand and strength coumadin tablet when they get a new prescription filled. In addition, it is usually easier to have patients take fractions or multiples of the same strength tablet, rather than juggle two different strength tablets. For example, a patient may be instructed to take one 5 mg tablet on Monday, Wednesday, and Friday, and half of a 5 mg tablet on the other days, rather than using both 5 mg and 2.5 mg tablets.

Action of Warfarin Sodium

Warfarin helps to prevent clot formation by inhibiting the formation of "Vitamin K-dependent" clotting factors (II, VII, IX, X). While some refer to warfarin as a "blood thinner," this is not entirely correct, as the drug does not thin the blood; it prolongs the time of clot formation, and in this fashion prevents new clot formation.

Indication for Therapy

The patient should be made aware of why they are taking warfarin specifically, not just that it is a "blood thinner" or that it prevents clot formation. The care provider should also try to find out how long the patient is to stay on warfarin, which can be three months post-deep venous thrombosis (DVT), or lifetime for chronic atrial fibrillation. Other important information for the patient and the care provider to keep in mind is the date when anticoagulant therapy began.

Importance of Compliance

The nurse and other caregivers must stress the importance of taking warfarin as prescribed. Since warfarin has a narrow therapeutic index, often the patient will be on a seemingly complex warfarin regimen. Frequently, very small dosage changes will have a significant impact on the prothrombin time. Therefore, it is vital that the patient not miss doses or take extra tablets. Generally, the medication regimen is formulated according to results of blood studies that show the clotting or prothrombin time (PT). DuPont provides plastic "strip packs" with a compartment for each day that the patient is to take the drug, making it easier for the patient to remember to take the drug, and when. The patient is advised to take the Coumadin at the same time every day; actual time doesn't matter, so long as it is the same time.

Prothrombin Test

The prothrombin time test is a measure of how long it takes the patient's blood to clot. These results are used in determining the patient's warfarin dose. The most recently published standards for anticoagulation therapy take it one step further: the prothrombin time is determined by adding calcium and thromboplastin to citrated plasma. The sensitivity of thromboplastin varies from lab to lab, and to compensate for this variability, laboratories are encouraged to report INRs (International Normalized Ratios), which is the prothrombin time ratio (PT patient divided by PT control), raised to the power of the ISI (International Sensitivity Index). The ISI is a reflection of how sensitive the thromboplastin is that is used by the lab. The PT is dependent on three different ISI values (1.8, 2.3, and 2.8).

Potential Drug Interactions

Warfarin interacts with many different medications, causing either an elevated or blunted response to warfarin. Because of this, the care provider should consult with the pharmacist about other medications that the patient may be taking. The patient and caregiver should tell all providers that the patient is taking warfarin. When warfarin is taken, the patient should avoid taking aspirin, and aspirin-containing products, because aspirin interacts with warfarin and may increase the risk of bleeding. The patient's pharmacist should be kept informed of the fact that the patient is taking warfarin, particularly when the patient requests any over-the-counter (OTC) drugs that may contain aspirin.

Alcohol also interacts with warfarin. Chronic use of alcohol increases the metabolism of warfarin, which requires that patients take higher than usual maintenance dosages. Acute alcohol ingestion decreases the metabolism of warfarin, leading to an exaggerated response to warfarin and an elevated prothrombin time. Aside from the interaction, the use of alcohol is discouraged because of the risk of increased bleeding.

Dietary Factors

As mentioned, warfarin acts by inhibiting the synthesis of Vitamin K-dependent clotting factors. If the patient does not eat a diet that is consistent in Vitamin K content, the prothrombin time will not be stable. The patient should avoid excessive amounts of food that are high in Vitamin K, such as leafy vegetables, including collards, turnip greens, spinach, asparagus, and broccoli, as well as green tea, fish, and fish or sardine oil. The key is consistency; the same diet should be eaten regularly.

Informing Other Health Care Providers

All of the patient's health care providers should be aware that the patient is taking warfarin. Optimally, the patient would carry a list of all medications (prescription and nonprescription) to share with all providers.

Informing Physician Before Changing Medications or Procedures

The patient should tell all physicians and other providers such as dentists, podiatrists, ophthalmologists, and other specialists that they are taking warfarin. Prescribers need to know this to avoid drug interactions. In addition, before undergoing any treatment, surgery, or dental work, the health care professional should be informed that the patient is taking warfarin. In some situations, the patient may have to stop the drug before a procedure can be performed.

Importance of Regular Follow-up

The patient who is taking warfarin needs to be followed closely by the physician or other primary provider. If the patient is to remain on warfarin, it is necessary to regularly check the prothrombin time and assess the patient for adverse effects.

Signs of Toxicity

The most common adverse effect associated with warfarin therapy is bleeding, usually related to the intensity of anticoagulation. Bleeding is much more likely to occur when the PT is more than 2.5 times control. The patient should be taught to check for any signs of bleeding: smokey urine, dark tarry stools, bleeding from any site, bruising, or abdominal pain. Any such sign or symptom should be followed closely. Rarely, warfarin can cause skin necrosis, "purple toe" syndrome, nausea, and vomiting.

Signs or Symptoms of Thrombus or Embolus

The patient must understand how a repeat or initial embolus would clinically manifest itself. The thrombus or embolus may be from a deep venous thrombosis, with accompanying swelling, redness, warmth, pain, numbness, pallor, or increase in leg diameter; cerebrovascular accident or transient ischemic attack, with accompanying blackouts, dizziness, blurred speech or vision, or personality changes; mesenteric embolus, with side or abdominal pain; or valvular dysfunction, with accompanying chest pain, fatigue, syncope, dizziness, or difficulty in breathing. The patient needs to know that, if any of these signs or symptoms occur, they are to contact a physician or other care provider immediately.

Use of Emergency Identification

When a patient is taking warfarin, they should be instructed to wear a MedicAlert bracelet or necklace to convey that information to others in case of emergency. The patient should also at all times carry a wallet card with that information.

Provide Written Materials

In addition to educating the patient and caregivers about warfarin, and all the consequences and possible problems that might occur in a patient who is required to take warfarin, the provider should also give written materials so that the patient can review from time to time the most recent information and instructions. DuPont provides an excellent patient teaching packet, and the home care agency may also have similar written materials. The caregiver should make certain that the patient can read and understand the materials.

By following a teaching checklist, and documenting patient education that is given and understood, the home care nurse can contribute greatly toward optimizing the therapeutic outcomes for the patient on anticoagulant therapy. The number of patients being anticoagulated at home will continue to increase as more indications are added. This increase in the number of home care patients on warfarin will result in a greater role for the home health care provider.

Reference

Dalen, J.E., and J. Hirsh, eds. 1992. Third ACCP Consensus Conference on antithrombotic therapy. *Chest* 102(4): 3035–45.

Mary Lynn McPherson

Arthritis

INTRODUCTION

Arthritis is the most common disease condition present in elderly persons. Forty-seven percent of persons over the age of 65 years are affected by arthritis. In 1984, the National Center for Health Statistics ranked arthritis first among the top ten chronic health problems.

The accumulation of chronic non-life–threatening illness, chiefly arthritis, is a major factor in limiting physical activity. Seventeen percent of persons over the age of 65 cannot carry out daily activities such as housework or jobs. Forty-five percent of those over the age of 65 have some activity limitation, increasing to 60 percent of those over 75. In contrast, only 8 percent of the population under 65 has activity limitations.

For homebound elderly persons, arthritis is the most common limiting factor. Indeed, arthritis may be the chief contributing factor toward becoming homebound. The continuing pain and functional limitations associated with arthritis critically affect the quality of life for older persons. Loss of functional ability results in dependence on others to carry out basic activities of daily living.

When those confined to institutions are excluded, about 14 percent of non-institutionalized elderly persons have limits in physical mobility. Two percent of these elderly persons are bedbound, 5 percent are housebound, and 7 percent go outdoors only with difficulty. These factors greatly impede the ability of elders to care for themselves, interact with friends and community, and maintain independence.

OVERVIEW

Arthritis literally means inflammation of the joint. Several distinct types of arthritis can be described, each with differing cause and rate of progression.

Osteoarthritis

Among the types of arthritis, osteoarthritis is the most common. Osteoarthritis is not a usual characteristic of aging. Normal aging does produce observable changes in the articular cartilage and bone; however, these changes are distinct from the changes that are seen in osteoarthritis. The theory that osteoarthritis is a normal result of aging has been abandoned. Normal aging may somehow predispose one to the development of this type of arthritis, but osteoarthritis is now clearly recognized as a disease.

Osteoarthritis typically involves the last and next to last joints of the hands, the base of the thumb and great toe, the hips, the knees, and the spine. The wrist, elbow, shoulder, and ankle are usually spared, for reasons that are not clear. Trauma to these joints may predispose the development of osteoarthritis. Involvement of the knee, perhaps the most common manifestation of osteoarthritis, results in transfer limitations.

Symptoms include stiffness, particularly early in the morning or after inactivity. Pain is present with active movement and with passive motion. Effusion, or swelling in the joint, is common. With time, joint deformities occur. Disease in the joint can lead to pinching of the nerves passing close to the joint. This nerve compression may lead to pain, numbness, and tingling in the hands or legs.

There are no characteristic laboratory abnormalities in osteoarthritis. Radiographs do show characteristic degenerative changes in the bones. Treatment must be individualized. Physical therapy, such as exercise or splints, combined with anti-inflammatory or analgesic drugs, help to alleviate the symptoms.

Rheumatoid Arthritis

Rheumatoid arthritis is the most common chronic inflammatory type of arthritis, affecting about three percent of the adult population. The peak onset is between the thirty-fifth and forty-fifth year. Few new cases occur in elderly populations. However, since the disease is chronic, the number of persons suffering from rheumatoid arthritis steadily increases with age. Many persons who develop this progressive disease carry the burden of disability into geriatric age.

The cause of rheumatoid arthritis is unknown. Some unknown initiating agent induces an immunological reaction in the joints. The disease develops only in the presence of a certain individual genetic makeup. Apparently, only individuals with this certain type of genetic makeup respond to the initiating agent. The result is a symmetrical inflammation, or synovitis, of the small joints of the hands, feet, wrists, and knees. Painful swelling occurs in these joints. Prolonged early morning stiffness is prominent. Joint deformity and destruction may follow.

The course of rheumatoid arthritis can be roughly divided into thirds. One-third develop an acute illness with severe short-term symptoms but a benign course. One-third will develop a chronic, indolent arthritis. In another third, the disease proceeds to an inactive state. Rheumatoid arthritis that first begins in elderly persons tends to be a milder form.

Specific laboratory abnormalities and characteristic radiological findings help diagnose the illness. Treatment options depend on the severity of the disease. In addition to physical therapy measures, several drug treatment options exist. Therapy begins with simple analgesics and progresses through anti-inflammatory drugs, heavy metals, and immunological suppressant drugs. There is evidence that early treatment with several agents may prevent later joint deformities.

Crystal Deposition Arthritis

Deposition of crystals in the joint space can result in arthritis. Two common types of crystals are associated with arthritis. The most common is urate crystals, the cause of gout. Deposition of calcium pyrophosphate crystals produces a more uncommon type of crystal disease.

Gout results from the deposition of urate crystals in the lining of the joint. This causes severe inflammation with abrupt onset of symptoms. In the elderly, the disease is common but is atypical in clinical symptoms. More than one joint tends to be involved, and the pattern may differ from that in younger persons.

The diagnosis of gout is established by finding crystals in the joint fluid by microscopy. A typical presentation of disease may not require joint aspiration. The uric acid level in the blood is a poor guide to diagnosis in the elderly. Treatment is aimed at control of inflammation. In chronic or frequently occurring cases, treatment aimed at blocking the production or increasing excretion of uric acid may be used.

Polymyalgia Rheumatica

Several other arthritic conditions are much rarer, but still important in their impact. One of these is polymyalgia rheumatica. This condition occurs almost exclusively in individuals over age 50. Women are affected more than men. Symptoms include aching in the large muscles of the shoulders, thighs, and upper arms. About half of patients affected with polymyalgia rheumatica develop inflammation in larger arteries, termed giant cell arteritis. This inflammation may lead to occlusion of blood vessels, particularly in the eye, causing sudden blindness.

Diagnosis is confirmed by biopsy and suggested by striking elevation in the sedimentation rate of blood cells. Treatment with corticosteroids is very successful, resulting in resolution of symptoms within 24 to 48 hours.

CONCLUSIONS

Arthritis of various types frequently leads to pain, immobility, and functional impairment. In the homebound elderly, therapeutic options focus on issues of safety, prevention of falls, and increasing activity level. Physical therapy measures, both taught to the family and supervised by the therapist, are important to improve mobility. The ability to maintain function depends on adequate pain relief. Planning therapy for arthritis patients depends on an adequate knowledge of arthritis differential diagnosis.

References

Olshansky, S.J. 1985. Pursuing longevity: delay versus elimination of degenerative diseases. *Amer J Publ Health* 75:754–56.

Pinals, R.S. 1992. Management of chronic inflammatory and degenerative joint disease. In *Textbook of Internal Medicine*, 2d ed. Edited by W.N. Kelley. Philadelphia: Lippincott, 1020–28.

U.S. Department of Health and Human Services. 1978. Current estimates from the Health Interview Survey: United States 1978. *Vital and Health Statistics*, Series 10, No. 130. (Pub. No. 80–1551, November). Washington, D.C.: Government Printing Office.

David R. Thomas

Assessment (Functional)

Functional assessment is a process that entails measurement of an individual's ability to perform basic and higher level activities required in daily life. Most functional assessment approaches incorporate the use of objective, standardized criteria for measurement of the functions that influence, directly or indirectly, the individual's ability to perform daily activities effectively, appropriately, and safely. Physical performance, cognitive ability, emotional status, behavioral appropriateness, and social support are some of the aspects of function that may be measured either singularly or as part of a comprehensive package of functional measures.

Measures of physical function usually focus on a series of daily tasks called Activities of Daily Living (ADLs). These include such activities as eating, bathing, toileting, dressing, grooming, transfer, and mobility. Instrumental Activities of Daily Living (IADLs), which tend to be more complex activities, may also be measured. IADLs include such activities as meal preparation, laundry, housekeeping, money management, and use of the telephone. Cognitive, psychological, and social aspects of functioning are often measured as separate spheres, but are integrally connected to physical functioning.

USE OF FUNCTIONAL ASSESSMENT

Functional assessment is an important component in the care of older persons, as well as younger persons, with functional impairments. The uses of functional assessment are numerous, and the intended use will often dictate the instrument and type of measurement criteria selected.

At the most basic level, functional measures have been incorporated into needs assessments of population groups. The scales used for this purpose are usually abbreviated, and the measurement categories tend to be quite broad. The information gained from such measures tends to be rather general and largely descriptive, but it is useful for planning service systems and guiding health and social services policy.

Functional assessment is becoming increasingly common in the long-term care field for guiding decisions about the allocation of resources. Limitations of both monetary and manpower resources make it necessary to target available resources to those most in need. Functional measures are utilized to determine eligibility for services and serve as guidelines for the types and amounts of services needed.

At the individual level, functional assessment has proven useful for early detection of physiological abnormalities and illness in the elderly. Acute illnesses, electrolyte or metabolic imbalances, nutritional deficiencies, and complications from trauma may first be manifest by changes in functional abilities. When sensitive, standardized measurement criteria and definitions are employed, repeated measurement of an individual's function over time can provide important indicators of the need for further evaluation and treatment. Early detection and treatment increases the likelihood of positive treatment outcomes.

Functional assessment also plays a prominent role in the determination of an individual's needs for long-term care and the planning of services to meet those needs. Functional measures provide critical information regarding an individual's ability to fulfill daily self-care tasks and tasks necessary for maintaining one's living environment. Measurements reflecting the types, the degree, and the regularity of limitations provide valuable guides for planning and implementing care that are appropriate to the needs of the individual.

In addition to determining need for care, repeated functional measures provide data necessary to evaluate the effectiveness of both the plan of care and the provider of care. For example, when recuperative and rehabilitative care is provided, one expects improvement in one or more areas of function. If improvements do not occur or are slower than anticipated, changes in the plan of care or the way in which the plan is implemented may be indicated. Similarly, declines in function may indicate a change in the individual's condition, an inappropriate plan of care, or failure of the provider to carry out the plan of care.

When declines in function are anticipated and unavoidable, functional assessment provides measurements for monitoring both the decline of specific functions and the severity of changes. This information is useful in plotting rates of decline and predicting the future course of an individual's condition. Such predictions allow earlier planning and preparation for service needs.

Functional assessment, used as a measurement of outcomes of care, is providing important knowledge for clinical interventions. Much remains to be learned about the effectiveness and efficacy of various plans of care and service approaches, given different types, levels, and causes of functional impairment. The systematic monitoring and recording of functional changes in relation to a plan of care adds to our body of knowledge about the effectiveness of specific interventions and service strategies.

INSTRUMENTS FOR FUNCTIONAL ASSESSMENT

There is a wide range of instruments available for functional assessment. Some measure one aspect of function, while others measure a range of functional characteristics. Instruments measuring a range of functional characteristics tend to be divided into sections, with each focusing on a different aspect of function. For example, one section will examine physical functioning, while another section will contain questions designed to evaluate cognitive abilities.

Functional instruments vary from the specific to the very general. The purpose of the assessment will tend to dictate the particular instrument chosen. In the least sophisticated forms, questions are asked about either the ability to perform or the need for assistance with a series of routine daily activities. Response categories may be mere "yes" or "no" responses or a slightly more specific "none of the time," "some of the time," or "all of the time." This type of measurement approach is useful for screening tools and for descriptive studies of large populations, particularly where the instrument is self-administered.

Much more sophisticated measurement strategies are needed in clinical situations where eligibility determinations are made, individualized plans of care are developed, resources are allocated to meet the needs of an individual, and changes in function are monitored to determine the effectiveness of a plan of care. In these cases, measurements of function related to specific tasks are often made along a several-point scale. Each point of the scale represents a change in performance level. Some scales measure only observed performance of a task, while others incorporate timeframes in which the task is accomplished, regularity and effectiveness in performance of the task over a period of time, and whether the task is performed appropriately and safely.

In some instruments, physical function and cognitive ability are incorporated in the same scale. Others measure each area separately and provide a combined score or leave it to the professional to deduce the relevance of the two measures. The same is found with social and behavioral measures.

Our attempts to combine functional measures tend to be rudimentary. Although conceptually it is difficult to separate physical, cognitive, behavioral, social, and environmental factors in measuring performance, it is also difficult to incorporate two or more of these variables into one measure.

The design and definition of scales also pose a serious limitation in many functional assessment measures. In all measurements incorporating scales, the measurement criteria for each level of the scale need to be clearly specified. The reliability and validity of functional measurement scales depend on their clarity and lack of ambiguity. Many of the scales available today lack these basic features.

FACTORS INFLUENCING FUNCTIONAL MEASURES

Functional assessment must be combined with other diagnostic procedures to attain a clear understanding of the nature of functional impairments. Medical conditions can cause or exacerbate functional impairments. In such cases, treatment or management of the underlying condition may resolve or reduce the impairment, thereby eliminating the need for further assistive services.

A number of other factors can also influence the ability and/or willingness of an individual to perform activities. Social support from family, friends, or others can either enhance or compromise an individual's functional abilities. Supportive assistance which complements functional strengths and enhances individual capabilities reduces the impact of impairments. On the other hand, over-protective support persons can create unnecessary dependency that artificially masks functional capabilities. Measurement strategies that reflect capabilities rather than behavior are important under these circumstances.

The physical environment also plays a significant role in function. Environments that are adapted to facilitate independent function of disabled persons can greatly enhance performance and decrease the need for assistive services. Likewise, adaptive devices can enhance performance capabilities. The living environment of the person must be considered in measuring functional performance and determining need for assistance. However, consideration should always be given to ways the person can be more functionally independent through adaptations in the environment and the use of adaptive appliances rather than reliance on human assistance.

SUMMARY

Functional assessment is becoming a standard part of comprehensive assessment of older and disabled persons. It is receiving increasing attention as a strategy for determining long-term care service needs and allocating resources. In many states, eligibility for publicly funded long-term care services is based on functional criteria. Plans of care in long-term care facilities are developed, in part, around functional measures. Third-party reimbursement for long-term care relies heavily on functional criteria.

While functional assessment tools are plentiful, there is much work still to be done in identifying the most important factors to be measured and the best measurement approaches. How are physical, psychological, social, and environmental components of function interrelated? Can we predict difficulties with specific areas of task performance by measuring cognitive ability alone? In what ways do emotional disturbances affect function and how do we separate their effect from other factors? How does motivation and coping ability influence function and how can these best be measured? These and many other questions await reasoned answers based on sound research.

References

Applegate, W. 1987. Use of assessment instruments in clinical settings. *J Am Geriatr Soc* 35:45–50.

Duke University Center for the Study of Aging and Human Development. 1978. *Multidimensional Functional Assessment, The OARS Methodology.* Durham, N.C.: Duke University.

Fillenbaum, G. 1985. Screening the elderly. A brief instrumental activities of daily living measure. *J Am Geriatr Soc* 33:698.

Finucane, T.E., and J.R. Burton. 1991. Geriatric medicine: special considerations. Functional assessment. In *Principles of Ambulatory Medicine,* edited by L.R. Barker, J.R. Burton, and P.D. Zieve. Baltimore: Williams & Wilkins, 67.

Ham, R.J. 1989. Functional assessment of the elderly patient. In *Clinical Aspects of Aging,* 3rd ed. Edited by W. Reichel. Baltimore: Williams & Wilkins, 26–40.

Kane, R., and R. Kane. 1981. *Assessing the Elderly: A Practical Guide to Measurement.* Lexington, Mass.: D.C. Heath.

Linda J. Redford

Assistive Technology

INTRODUCTION

The increased availability of homecare services and the growth of assistive technology have made it possible even for persons with severe impairments to remain at home. Properly used, assistive technology devices (ATDs) can enhance function, promote independence, postpone or avoid institutionalization, and reduce the burden of disability for the patient and caregiver.

The majority of elderly persons live at home, but with advancing age, the proportion of those requiring assistance increases dramatically. While 12 percent of men and 16 percent of women 65 or older living at home need assistance in daily activities, for those 85 or older, help is required by 31 percent of men and

37 percent of women. Since the elderly, especially those 85 and above, are the fastest growing segment of the U.S. population, the need for ATDs can be expected to increase exponentially in the next several decades.

With advancing age comes an increasing number of chronic health conditions that can result in psychological, physiological, and anatomic abnormalities or "impairments." Impairments may or *may not* affect a person's ability to function independently. A person is said to have a "disability" when an impairment causes loss of function. For example, arthritis causes joint abnormalities (impairment) that may lead to difficulty in climbing stairs (disability). A "handicap" results when there are no provisions for persons with disabilities to fulfill their normal roles. Thus, a person who cannot climb stairs and is therefore unable to use a library, is handicapped *because* no ramp has been provided. The role of assistive technology is to improve or overcome disabilities and handicaps through the use of personal adaptive aids and environmental modifications.

ATDs may be high or low technology devices. High technology devices include such things as computer-assisted speech synthesizers, ventilators for in-home use, and telemonitoring computers that measure a patient's vital signs and communicate directly with the physician's office. The most commonly used devices are low technology products designed to help with physical functioning, mobility, and hygiene.

ASSESSMENT

Effective prescription of ATDs requires careful assessment of the underlying impairment(s) and resultant disability or handicap. ATDs are best used as part of a multidimensional treatment plan including evaluation and treatment of the underlying problem, assessment of the patient's ability and/or willingness to use the device prescribed, and investigation of other options such as increased social support. These tasks are best accomplished by an interdisciplinary team. Team composition may differ depending on the issues to be addressed. Most often, evaluation of problems requiring the use of ATDs is performed by a physician, nurse, physical or kinesiotherapist (PT or KT), occupational therapist (OT), and social worker. In some cases, it may be helpful to obtain additional input from a speech pathologist, pharmacist, dietician, optometrist, audiologist, psychologist or psychiatrist. Efficient team function requires common goals, team planning, and regular review of the patient's progress.

ROLE OF THE PHYSICIAN

There are many potentially treatable causes of functional decline in the elderly, such as hidden infection, depression, and adverse drug effects. For example, arthritis pain causing decreased mobility may be improved by medication, joint injection, or joint replacement. The physician's role as a member of the health care team is to perform a thorough evaluation and treat any reversible or re-mediable conditions.

In addition to a complete history with special attention to medications and a physical examination, the evaluation should include assessment of functional, cognitive, psychological, and social domains. Lachs et al. (1990) have developed a brief, multidimensional assessment for the elderly patient that can be per-formed in an office visit. This instrument quickly screens for problems in vision, hearing, activities of daily living, urinary incontinence, nutrition, mental status, depression, home environment, and social support. In addition, substance abuse is a relatively common problem among elderly men seeking medical care, and screening for this problem should be part of the assessment. If abnormalities are uncovered in the screening assessment, more in-depth evaluation may be per-formed by the appropriate team member.

ROLE OF THE PHYSICAL THERAPIST AND KINESIOTHERAPIST

In addition to providing detailed assessment of physical capabilities, PTs and/or KTs design therapeutic exercise programs to improve physical fitness, func-tional mobility, and independence in gross motor activities such as ambulation, transfers, wheelchair skills, driving, and community re-entry. PTs also use phys-ical treatment modalities such as heat and ultrasound to improve or maintain functional abilities. PTs and KTs can help patients select appropriate adaptive equipment for mobility such as wheelchairs, canes, and walkers.

ROLE OF THE OCCUPATIONAL THERAPIST

OTs assess and treat functional impairments in basic and instrumental activ-ities of daily living (ADL & IADL) such as eating, dressing, transferring, home-making tasks, money management, and safety. OTs can help with the selection of adaptive equipment such as reachers, modified eating utensils, and shower chairs to help accomplish these tasks.

HOME EVALUATION

Home evaluation performed by the OT, KT, or PT provides valuable infor-mation in determining appropriate prescriptions of ATDs, as well as an assess-ment of the patient's and caregiver's skills in the home setting.

There are usually several "stations," including bedside, living area, and din-ing room, where the patient spends the majority of his/her time. At each station the lighting, use of the telephone, and availability of supplies should be ana-lyzed. For example, is the lighting adequate to reveal hazards?

During the home evaluation, the patient should be asked to demonstrate safe entry into the house, transfers to all surfaces, bathroom accessibility, and bed mobility. If the patient is not ambulatory, the entry, doorway, and all rooms in the house should be checked for wheelchair accessibility. The caregiver should be given appropriate training to assist with transfers, ambulation, and ADLs.

Home evaluation includes not only accessibility but safety. Falls are a leading cause of morbidity and mortality in the elderly, and the majority of falls occur in the home. The average household is full of hazards that could cause a fall. It is important to remove as many hazards as possible. Interventions to minimize common hazards include installing grab bars and raised toilet seats, removing clutter and throw rugs, and providing adequate lighting. Many elderly persons fear they will not be able to get up off the floor after a fall. In these cases, practicing fall recovery techniques may help build confidence.

For those who live alone, an emergency plan should be set up with a neighbor, friend, or agency. This may be as simple as a daily, pre-set communication or signal that will prompt someone to check on the patient's safety.

PRESCRIPTION OF ATDS

The most careful evaluation and prescription for an ATD is useless if the equipment sits in the closet. Elderly patients may prefer not to use ATDs for a variety of reasons: (1) "Technophobia"—elderly persons have less experience than younger persons with "electronic gadgets" and may find high technology products "too confusing to worry about"; (2) Negative stereotyping—some persons may not wish to be marked with the stigma of having a disability, or may feel that ATDs make them look old; (3) Finances—Medicare covers only 80 percent of the cost of items deemed necessary by a physician. In Sweden, where ATDs are provided without charge, the utilization of aids is much higher. In prescribing ATDs it is important to set realistic, achievable goals that are meaningful to the patient in his/her own environment.

MOBILITY AIDS

Appropriate prescription of ATDs can help many people achieve safe mobility in spite of physical, psychological, and cognitive impairments. Mobility includes not only walking, but transfers (e.g., movement from bed to chair or chair to toilet), use of a wheelchair, and recovery from falls.

AMBULATION

ATDs for ambulation must be tailored to the individual's balance and function. Patients who cannot grasp a cane or walker comfortably may benefit from special grips that can be padded, triangular-in-shape, or platform style. Patients should be taught specific ambulation techniques appropriate to each device.

Ambulation on stairs, uneven surfaces, and curbs should be practiced prior to community re-entry. In ascending or descending stairs, each foot should be placed on each step. Stairs should be ascended with the stronger foot leading, and descended with the weaker foot leading. Handrails should be mounted on both sides of stairs for safety. If supervision or assistance will be needed to use an ATD, the caregiver should also be taught specific mobility techniques and safety skills.

TRANSFERS

The basic transfer is any change from one surface or position to another. Sturdy armrests are essential for safe transfers. Bathroom transfers can be improved with adaptive equipment such as a versaframe or grab bar. An electric hospital bed with siderails can improve bed mobility and transfers.

WHEELCHAIRS

Wheelchairs are available in a variety of sizes, styles, and weights. Thus, it is important to fit the wheelchair to the individual user's body composition, navigation technique, and lifestyle, for example, one-arm drive, electric chair, or lightweight folding chair. When selecting a wheelchair it is important to be sure that the overall width fits through all doorways, since interior doors are often narrower than exterior doors.

Wheelchair cushions are used for comfort and pressure relief. Since cushion depth changes seat height, the cushion should be selected when the chair is fitted. Pressure relief is an important consideration for persons who habitually use wheelchairs. It is essential that the user relieve buttock pressure by changing positions or walking short distances regularly. Pressure relief cushions of foam, air, or gel can help, but no cushion can prevent skin breakdown by itself. If continence is a problem, an easily washed cushion should be considered.

When making transfers the wheelchair should be positioned at a 35–45 degree angle to bed or toilet. After positioning the wheelchair the brakes should be set and foot pedals lifted to complete set-up for a safe transfer.

PURCHASING AN ATD

Although therapists may help with choosing appropriate ATDs, many persons buy devices directly from surgical supply stores or mail order catalogs. With the bewildering array of ATDs available, locating the appropriate device may be difficult for the consumer. Before purchasing an ATD the consumer should ask him/herself if the equipment is (1) necessary for independence, safety, or health; (2) durable and reliable; (3) safe; (4) affordable; and (5) recommended by a health professional for the disability in question. Information for consumers considering the purchase of ATDs can be obtained from groups such as the Arthritis Foundation, American Association of Retired Persons, or State Agency on Aging. Detailed product information for professionals is available from national societies, such as the Society for the Advancement of Rehabilitative and Assistive Technology, and online databases, such as Abledata.

CONCLUSION

ATDs can help maximize independence and decrease reliance on other persons and institutions. However, there is very little information available about the safety and efficacy of many products. Especially lacking is consumer-based information about which products elderly persons find to be useful and acceptable. Studies have shown that many persons who could benefit from ATDs do not have them, and many persons who have ATDs do not use them. With the aging of the population and the explosion in technology, both the need for new products and the number and type of products available are increasing rapidly. Systematic evaluation of both consumer and product is needed to assure that new ATDs are safe, effective, and fulfill the promise of increased independence for their users.

References

Allen, C.K., C.A. Erhart, and T. Blue. 1992. *Occupational Therapy Treatment Goals for the Physically and Cognitively Disabled.* Rockville, Md.: American Occupational Therapy Association.

Arthritis Foundation. 1988. *Guide to Independent Living for People with Arthritis.* Atlanta, Ga.: The Arthritis Foundation.

Lachs, M.S., A.R. Feinstein, L.M. Cooney Jr., L.M. Drickamer, R.A. Marottoli, F.C. Pannill, and M.F. Tinetti. 1990. A simple procedure for general screening for functional disability in elderly patients. *Ann Intern Med* 112:699-706.

Parker, M.G., and M. Thorslund. 1991. The use of technical aids among community-based elderly. *American Journal of Occupational Therapy* 45(8):712-18.

Straker, J.K. 1992. Communications technology and older adults: a review of the issues in technology dissemination. *Topics in Geriatric Rehabilitation* 7(4):22–35.

U.S. Consumer Product Safety Commission. 1982. *Home Safety Checklist for Older Consumers.* Washington, D.C.: U.S. Administration on Aging, Office of Human Development, U.S. Department of Health and Human Services.

Carol Joseph, Barbara Riley, and Claudia Brown

Assistive Technology Devices

All humans use technology to extend their capabilities. A can opener, for example, enables one to open a soup can, a feat that would not be possible for the human hand to achieve without the aid of the tool. Assistive technology devices are specialized tools designed to restore or enhance the capabilities of persons with physical, sensory, or cognitive impairments. Older adults often experience these impairments as a consequence of disease or aging processes. For some older adults, the impairments are so severe that their ability to perform basic activities of daily living (ADL) becomes dysfunctional. Assistive technology devices may compensate for these impairments, and thus promote functional independence or the ease, comfort, and safety of task performance.

Four common causes of ADL dysfunctions in older adults are: (1) impaired range of motion; (2) impaired dexterity; (3) impaired mobility; and (4) impaired sensation/cognition. This article discusses how these impairments may be alleviated through the use of low technology devices. The management of task dysfunctions through technology is illustrated in relation to personal self-care tasks, since these are often at risk for dysfunction in patients seen in home care. Personal self-care refers to the tasks associated with walking, feeding, bathing, hygiene and grooming, dressing, basic communication, and managing medications. In addition to compensating for impairments, assistive technology devices may also support cognitive functions and safety. These uses are also presented.

IMPAIRED RANGE OF MOTION

Problems in performing personal self-care tasks are often caused by restricted movement due to limited joint range of motion, muscle weakness, pain, or obesity. Restricted movement may make it difficult or impossible to execute a movement, such as lowering oneself to the bottom of a bathtub, or to reach a bodily part or object, such as bringing food to the mouth or picking up objects from the floor.

Assistive devices with extended (elongated) handles are designed to compensate for restricted movement. Handles are available in various lengths, and many models have wing nuts that allow the tool to be adjusted and secured at any angle. Long handles are available to assist with eating (spoons, forks), oral hygiene (toothbrushes, tooth flossers), hair care (combs, brushes), bathing (back brushes and sponges, foot brushes), and dressing (shoehorns). Back brushes and sponges are often placed on handles that are curved as well as extended to make it easier for those with minimal range of motion to wash hard-to-reach places, such as the neck, back, and shoulders.

Several specialized tools have been designed to assist with dressing. A dressing stick, which is a stick about two feet long with hooks on the ends, may be useful for pulling up pants by a belt hook, pulling up socks, or untying shoelaces. Although they are somewhat cumbersome to use, aids are available for putting on hosiery (socks, stockings, or panty hose) for those whose ability to bend over at the waist is limited. A zipper pull is another type of extension device. It is used to open and close back-opening zippers, such as those found on many women's dresses. An alternative solution is to use front-opening garments, including brassieres.

Restricted movement of the neck may make it difficult to drink since the head is usually tilted backward when drinking. A glass with a section cut out for the nose alleviates this problem, as does using a straw. If trunk movement is weak, a rope ladder may be used to come to a seated position in bed. The ladder is "climbed" by the hands or arms to lift the trunk.

Reaching objects that have fallen to the floor or are placed on shelves that are out of one's range is facilitated through reachers. Reachers vary in length, weight, handle design, gripping action (e.g., toggle level, spring mechanism), and gripping jaws (e.g., rubber or magnetized tips, automatic locking). These features influence ease of use as well as the size and weight of objects that can be comfortably picked up.

Getting into and out of a bathtub, and lowering and raising oneself to the tub bottom is difficult for persons with limited motion in the lower parts of the body—waist, hips, knees, and ankles. Use of a shower stall eliminates the need for stepping over bathtub rims and for lowering oneself into the bathtub. If a shower is not available, a chair or bench with nonskid legs may be placed inside the bathtub, so that bathing may be done while seated. A hand-held shower head can then be attached to the bathtub faucet and used to direct the flow of water over the body. If bathtub bathing is preferred, electrical or water powered equipment is available to aid in transfers and in getting to and from the tub bottom.

Standard toilet seats, which are about 15 to 17 inches high, are often too low for persons with motion limitations. Elevated (raised) toilet seats which raise seat height up to 7 inches, are designed to assist with this problem. For chairs or beds that are too low to get out of, extenders may be slipped onto the legs. Chair pads may also be used to elevate seat height. Some older adults require assistance to lift them up and out of a chair. For this problem, a seat lifter can be inserted on a chair seat, or a chair with an installed lifting mechanism can be purchased. Some people are able to raise themselves by grasping a pole that extends from floor to ceiling; this provides added leverage for pulling up to a standing position.

IMPAIRED DEXTERITY

Common causes of impaired manual dexterity are joint deformities, muscle weakness, tremors, impaired touch, and one-handedness such as that resulting from stroke or amputation. In performing manual tasks, one hand is generally used for stabilization and the other for action. When cutting meat, for example, one hand is used to stabilize the meat with a fork and the other hand is used to cut the meat with a knife. When dexterity is impaired both stabilization and action must be taken into account.

Dycem®, a nonslip material, is a versatile tool that can be used as a mat or pad to prevent objects (e.g., dinnerware, pens, telephone) from moving. Special suction bases on the bottom of tools eliminate the need for holding and are available for the following tools—dinnerware, nail brushes, nail clippers, and denture brushes.

The hand used for action must hold a tool as well as use it for the intended purpose. Older adults with hand weakness or joint involvement may find it easier to grasp tools with enlarged (built-up) handles. These are commercially available for eating utensils and shoehorns. Some have finger grips or plastic coating to promote a firm grip. Ordinary tools can be enlarged by adding foam padding or soft rubber grips. If hand grip is very weak or absent, tools can be placed in holding devices that substitute for active grip. One holding device is the universal cuff, which is fitted around the palm and back of the hand. The tool (e.g., spoon, fork, toothbrush) is inserted into a pocket on the palmar side of the cuff, freeing the hand from having to hold it. Ordinary mugs with wide handles (wide enough to accommodate 4 fingers) serve a similar function. Holder devices are available for electric shavers, glassware, and hairdryers. A speaker phone eliminates the need to hold the receiver. In general, lightweight tools are advantageous, since they put less stress on joints and lessen fatigue. Other tools that reduce the need for finger grip are a bath mitt (glove) that slips over the hand, large rings or cloth loops inserted into regular zipper tabs, and a phone rest on the receiver.

Many specialized tools have been designed to facilitate the action component of manual activities. For feeding, dishes with side rims (e.g., scoop dishes, partitioned plates) help to keep the food from sliding off the dish when one is trying to get it onto a spoon or fork. Food guards can be added to ordinary plates to provide this function. A rocker knife, which uses a rocking motion for cutting, is particularly useful for persons with one-handed disability. Oral hygiene may be facilitated through the use of an electric toothbrush as well as a flosser (dental floss inserted into a plastic device attached to a large, round handle). Toothpaste in a pump container may be used or a regular tube may be inserted into a toothpaste squeezer. The need to manipulate buttons, hooks and eyes, and even zippers can be circumvented by the use of velcro closures. Velcro can be added to garments or garments can be purchased with velcro closures already in place. A button hook, which pulls a button through the buttonhole, may be useful for those with one-handed disability. Although velcro can be added to tie shoes, many people prefer adaptations like no-bows or lace locks that secure laces without tying or shoe buttons, where a tied lace is wrapped around a button. With regard to communication, a push-button telephone with large buttons or an automatic dialing machine fosters correct dialing.

Hand tremors or shaking, caused by Parkinsonism or muscle weakness, are particularly detrimental to manual activities and are difficult to compensate for with low technology devices. Since weight may reduce the tremor and thus increase the stability of the hand, older adults experiencing tremors may profit from weighted tools. These are available for feeding and in writing utensils. Some are constructed so that the weight can be adjusted to make them heavier or lighter. To eliminate spillage when drinking liquids, a cup with an anti-splash lid can be used. Straws may also be added to glasses, and secured and positioned at the correct angle with a straw holder. One-way straws are available that keep the straw filled with liquid even after sucking has stopped; this feature is useful when sucking is weak. An electric self-feeding device is available.

IMPAIRED MOBILITY/SAFETY PROMOTION

Regardless of cause, instability in moving from place to place can be frightening, increase the risk of accidents, and reduce overall participation in activity. Mobility aids, such as canes and walkers, assist with walking. To promote safety they should be height adjusted to fit the user. When these devices are in use, the elbow should be slightly flexed (bent about 10 degrees). Quadriped (4 legs) or tripod (3 legs) canes provide more stability than one-point canes but are more cumbersome to use. Even greater stability is provided by the walker. Models are available that fold for travel or compact storage. For persons with Parkinsonism (also arthritis), a walker with wheels is usually preferable to the pickup type. The wheels allow the walker to glide so that once walking begins speed can be maintained and not disrupted by having to lift and replace the walker. However, the person must be able to control the wheeled walker, including the use of brakes. Pouches or baskets can be attached to walkers for carrying items.

Bathtub safety may be enhanced by adding grab rails to the rim of the bathtub. They provide a stable surface to hold onto when moving into and out of the bathtub, and when sitting and rising. Further protection may be given by attaching safety bars to the wall. Safety bars are available in various lengths, shapes, and colors; some are textured to enhance grip. Bars added to walls must be securely fixed to the wall to provide stability. The specific length and shape of safety rails is determined by the user's needs and the design of the bathroom. If the bottom of the bathtub or shower lacks a slip-resistant surface, a nonskid mat should be added. Slip-resistant mats should also be placed in shower stalls and outside of bathtubs and shower areas to facilitate surefootedness. Safety frames, bars, or rails may also be added to toilets to provide support for sitting and rising. For nighttime safety, a portable commode or a urinal may be placed near the bed so that the need to walk to the bathroom is avoided.

To facilitate transferring into and out of a bathtub, a tub transfer bench may be used. This allows the older adult to sit down and then slide into the tub on the bench. Chairs or benches with nonskid legs may be used when showering, so that one does not have to bathe while standing. When showering from a seated position, a hand held shower head or wall shower head that can be easily turned to any position makes it possible to direct water flow.

IMPAIRED SENSATION

Vision and hearing deficits make it difficult to receive needed information. For persons with low vision, the magnification of visual stimuli achieved from eyeglasses may be enhanced by low vision magnifiers. Some of these have lights attached so that illumination is heightened. Other common ADL aids for those with low vision include a digital thermometer with an easy to read display, a liquid level indicator that buzzes when liquid gets near the brim of a cup, an adaptor for the push-button telephone that has oversized numerals as well as large buttons, and talking clocks and watches.

The Listenaider may make it easier to communicate with those with mild hearing loss. This is an inexpensive pocket-sized sound amplifier. Often, it is used as a transition to a hearing aid. A telephone adaptor that uses a flashing light rather than an auditory signal may be needed, as well as an amplifier on the receiver.

IMPAIRED COGNITION/SUPPORT COGNITIVE FUNCTIONS

The ability to communicate basic needs, such as the desire to eat or put on a sweater or the urge to urinate, may be impaired by neurologic disorders. To assist with communication, communication boards, sheets, cards, or pictures that depict essential daily living situations may be used. Users only have to point to or touch the situation reflecting their needs.

Remembering to take medications and taking them correctly may be facilitated through the use of medication aids. The digital electronic pill reminder has a programmable alarm that may be set at intervals from 1/2 to 12 hours to remind one that it is time to take medication. Pill organizers encourage one to arrange pills for a day or week according to the time of day they are to be taken (morning, noontime, dinnertime, bedtime).

CONCLUSION

Most assistive technology devices are designed to compensate for specific motor, sensory, and cognitive impairments. Thus, the selection of a device depends on the particular impairments experienced by an older adult. To a large extent, the usefulness of a device depends on the extent to which it enhances the capabilities of the older adult so that a task may be performed more independently, easily, or safely. Devices may also be beneficial for promoting safety and supporting cognitive functions. Assistive technology devices for daily living activities are not inexpensive, and for the most part they are paid for by the individual and are not reimbursable through health insurance. Therefore, the potential user is encouraged to obtain adequate advice from a rehabilitation professional prior to purchasing any device. For some impairments, a different way of performing a task may work as well or better than an assistive device. It should also be recognized that the effective use of assistive technology often requires training and always requires practice.

References

Abledata. Newington Children's Hospital, 181 East Cedar Street, Newington, CT. 06111.
Abrams, J., and M.A. Abrams. 1990. *The First Whole Rehab Catalog*. Crozet, Va.:
    Betterway Publications, Inc.

American Association of Retired Persons. 1991. *AARP Product Report: Walkers.* Washington, D.C.: AARP.

Arthritis Foundation. 1988. *Guide to Independent Living for People with Arthritis.* Atlanta, Ga.: The Arthritis Foundation.

Friedmann, L.W., and E.S. Capulong. 1984. Specific assistive aids. In *Rehabilitation in the Aging*, edited by T.F. Williams. New York: Raven Press, 315–43.

Rogers, J.C. 1985. Low technology devices. *Generations* 10:5961–63.

Joan C. Rogers

C

Cancer Patient Care

Sixty percent of all cancers occur in the age group over 65. Therefore, those caring for the elderly will, unfortunately, need to care for many individuals with cancer. This article presents the general topic of cancer in the elderly, its natural history, the role of curative and palliative treatments using chemotherapy and radiotherapy and, finally, the role of palliative care. Much of the care will be given in an ambulatory and home setting.

CANCER IN THE ELDERLY

With regard to site specificity, cancer of the lung in men 65 to 80 years old is the single leading cause of death due to cancer. In women, breast cancer increases with age, but colorectal cancer is the leading cause of cancer deaths in people over 75. Cancer of the prostate is a disease of elderly men. Less than 1 percent of patients with this disease are under 50 years of age. The natural history and treatment of these malignancies—breast, colorectal, lung, and prostate—will be the most important cancers that the health care worker needs to understand.

The elderly are not more "susceptible" to developing cancer. Rather, as one ages, there is a higher probability that the early stages of cancer differentiation have been completed. Exposure to tobacco smoke is a good example of the multistep process of cancer development: initiation, promotion, progression, and, finally, metastases. There is no reason to approach cancer in the elderly as biologically different from cancer in younger individuals; the process is the same.

Prevention and early detection are the current keys to cancer control. Yet, for a variety of reasons, cancer control programs are not always successful in the elderly. For example, many elderly women are physically unable to perform self breast examination. Physicians are less likely to recommend screening mammography for older women. In some studies only about 5 percent of women over 65 have had a screening mammogram. Smoking cessation in this age group will lead to a decrease in the incidence of lung cancer. However, few physicians suggest to their patients that smoking cessation is a desirable goal. A new screening test for prostatic cancer is very promising, although the role of this test—the serum prostatic specific antigen (PSA) test—requires clarification.

One of the most important aspects of cancer control in the elderly is access to facilities where cancer screening occurs. The most effective factor in achieving this goal is for health care workers to suggest to older persons that cancer prevention and screening are an integral part of general health maintenance.

CARING FOR THE PATIENT RECEIVING CHEMO–AND/OR RADIOTHERAPY AT HOME

Currently, fewer than 10 percent of individuals with cancer will present at a stage where the disease can be considered "curable." When the incidence of multiple diseases and polypharmacy in the elderly is considered, even fewer elderly patients will be able to receive curative therapy. However, there is a major role for both these modalities, as well as surgery, in controlling cancer in the older person. When the elderly are receiving palliative cancer care as outpatients, the following issues must be part of the interdisciplinary care plan.

General Issues

The elderly person with cancer has many of the same social problems as the younger person but, because of many factors, these concerns can interfere with access to health care. Therefore, the following should be part of planning for cancer care at home.

1. What is the living situation? Is the patient living with an elderly companion, who might be too ill to care for the patient? Is the patient living alone or with children? Who cooks, dispenses medication, and, if required, brings the patient to the office or clinic? The use of tools such as the Katz Activities of Daily Living (ADL) and the Lawton-Brody Instrumental Activities of Daily Living (IADL) should be used in the initial evaluation of the patient.
2. What is the role of family members? Many families are not living in the same vicinity.

Who needs to know, if necessary, the health situation? Will they be involved in health care decisions or preparing advance directives?

3. Legal issues. Is the patient capable of making decisions about their medical care? Has the patient been carefully evaluated for cognitive function, using a minimental examination or neuropsychiatric evaluation? Does the patient have a will, living will, and a durable power of attorney for health care?

Medical Issues

The average older person suffers from multiple chronic illnesses for which they receive numerous medications. When deciding about choices for cancer treatment, the home health care worker must also be cognizant of the interdependent role of these two factors. For example, adriamycin, a chemotherapeutic agent used in treating breast and lung cancer, can be toxic to the heart. In the presence of heart disease, a common problem in the elderly, this drug may be contraindicated. The vinca alkaloids, useful in treating lymphomas and lung cancer, can cause constipation. The use of these agents in conjunction with an opioid for pain should always be accompanied by a bowel regimen. Other concerns include skin sensitivity to radiotherapy, build-up of metabolites of certain drugs in the bladder of men with bladder neck obstruction due to prostate enlargement, for example, cytoxan, and the alteration in physiology (decreasing creatinine clearance) that commonly occurs in the elderly, which changes drug excretion pharmacology, for example, cisplatinum. Also, any therapeutic complication such as fatigue that commonly occurs during radiotherapy, or the changes in taste and appetite that occur with chemotherapy, can diminish ADLs or IADLs. The effect of these problems, added to the underlying disease, may diminish the quality of life. Indeed, a patient with an existing mild impairment in neuromuscular function or who has lost considerable weight, can be markedly impaired. Because prevention is the best therapy in these situations, the home care professional should be as familiar as possible with the side effects of the agents their patients are receiving. The oncology staff should be asked for this information, if references are not available.

Finally, the effect of medications being used to treat the accompanying complications of antineoplastic therapy must be monitored. For example, steroids used to diminish nausea can cause a proximal myopathy or peptic ulcer activation; chlorpromazine is associated with tardive dyskinesia; and the benzodiazepines can alter sleep as well as neuromuscular function.

CARING FOR THE TERMINALLY ILL AT HOME

This section discusses the issues related to care at home for the terminally ill patient. In the palliative care setting (hospice), over 75 percent of patients will be more than 65 years old. Therefore, home care and general home care management goals as described elsewhere in this reference book are pertinent to this group.

The goals of therapy include (1) neither prolonging life nor hastening death; (2) relief from pain and other symptoms; (3) developing a support system that allows the individual to live as active a life as possible; (4) integrating all aspects of care—spiritual, emotional, and physical; and (5) attending to bereavement in family members. The medical problems to be addressed are multiple and, in the majority of patients, will occur together. In one study of terminally ill elderly, the following symptoms were noted: weakness, constipation, dry mouth, emesis, depression, confusion, insomnia, dyspnea, pain, cough, edema, headache, nausea, itching, and skin problems. Before beginning treatment, a plan of care should be developed and initiated that includes appointing a primary caregiver, if the patient is not able to take medications properly. An emergency call system must also be available and understood by all caregivers and family members involved.

The Treatment of Specific Problems

Weakness. Although people approaching death might be weak because of progression of their cancer, one should not assume that the disease process is the primary or only cause of this or any other specific complaint. Reversible etiologies of weakness include: (1) medications such as antihypertensives or hypoglycemic agents, electrolyte imbalances (amount of calcium, potassium and chlorides in the body); (2) depression; and (3) sleep disorders. The most difficult problem in this area (weakness) is the individual who, for a variety of reasons including impending death, is unable to eat or drink. Measures intended to reverse possible causes can be considered. Poor oral hygiene, taste abnormalities, early satiety, unappetizing food, nausea, and fear of vomiting are among the causes, some of which can be reversed or eliminated. Counteractions include good mouth care, giving antiemetics, preparing foods with new or different flavors, changing consistency of foods, creating a more attractive environment for meals, playing soft music to accompany meals, or even moving the person to another location for meals, such as from the bedroom to the living room. Some or all of these methods can enhance the person's desire to eat and drink. However, the issue of whose problem it is—family or patient—might be the most difficult to deal with. One needs to discuss openly with the family the issue of '' . . . eat or she'll die'' early, when the problem is first detected. As in pain management, the family might use failure to eat as a metaphor for illness, inadequate care, and death.

Constipation. This common complaint can cause a variety of other physical problems, whose common precipitating event might be overlooked. Related problems include pain, particularly rectal spasms, overflow diarrhea, mental status changes, and bladder dysfunction. In defining constipation, it is important to note not only the frequency of bowel movements (compared to normal pattern), but also consistency of the stool. A hard, dry, brittle stool or one that is composed of pellets of varying size can be a manifestation of constipation. Approaches to therapy should include all or most of the following measures. Attention to diet is foremost, particularly with regard to fiber content and amount of fluid. If the patient is on opioids or tricyclics, additional fluids are key to avoiding constipation caused by these kinds of medications. Comfort is an important factor; using the toilet or a bedside commode is more comfortable for the patient than using a bedpan. Both mobility and gravity assist in evacuation. Medications to assist bowel activity can be considered, such as senna (Senocot), bisacodyl (Ducolax), or casanthranol. In practice, combinations such as Peri-Colace or Senocot-S or their generic equivalents may be used. Start with a relatively large dose, for example, 4–6 tablets a day, and increase every other day. In fact, this type of regimen should be started any time an opioid is prescribed. The opioids are frequently the cause of constipation in older persons. If the stool is hard and dry, a small bowel flusher such as lactulose 10-ml three times a day can be added. Lactulose can cause nausea and flatulence, however. If there are no results within two days, the use of a bisacodyl suppository with an oil enema is in order.

Pain. Information about how the elderly deal with pain remains unclear. However, some general views include: (1) they tend not to report pain in order not to displease or distract the doctor or nurse from the mission of "curing" the cause of their pain; (2) they believe that one must bear pain as a part of life; and (3) they fear expressing this complaint because of past taboos, and learned stoic behaviors, for example, " ... only a weak person complains."

Pain management begins with pain assessment. In many situations, the elderly will not be forthcoming with a pain history. The health care worker should be aware of the following possibilities: (1) cognitive impairment, which prevents the individual from giving an accurate history; (2) patients who respond to questions by saying "it's just old age catching up ...''; (3) inquire about any over-the-counter or home remedies being used; (4) family members who indicate that the patient complains of pain frequently; (5) in evaluating the patient's pain, assist if necessary with descriptive words such as "sharp," "dull," "squeezing," etc.; (6) in some instances, pain is chronic and has become an accepted factor in the patient's life; (7) relate any pain with other physical symptoms such as shortness of breath, ankle edema, specific location of pain such as chest, etc.; and (8) the patient might have diminished ability to accurately feel pain. The role of depression, which is increased in the elderly with chronic illnesses, either as a modifier of pain or as a consequence of having chronic pain, is unclear in this population.

SUMMARY

Many of the diseases associated with abnormal aging are accompanied by pain. Is it any wonder that pain is often considered the "normal human experience?" However, this "normal experience" concept interferes with patients' ability to express pain and with the health care workers' response to the care of the individual with pain. How well this symptom can be controlled will greatly influence the quality of life, including enhancing the perception of people that they can die with dignity.

References

Portlock, C.S., and D.R. Goffinet, eds. 1987. *Manual of Clinical Problems in Oncology*, 2d ed. Boston: Little, Brown.

Rubin, P., ed. 1990. *Clinical Oncology: A Multidisciplinary Approach*, 7th ed. New York: American Cancer Society.

Waterbury, L., and M. Purtell. 1991. Primary care of the patient with cancer. In *Principles of Ambulatory Medicine*, 3d ed. Edited by L.R. Barker, J.R. Burton, and P.D. Zieve. Baltimore: Williams & Wilkins.

Walter B. Forman and Richard J. Roche

Cardiac Patient Care

According to the U.S. Department of Health and Human Services, more than two million people in the United States are living with cardiovascular impairment (coronary artery disease, myocardial infarction, aortic or mitral valve replacement, cardiomyopathy, angioplasty, coronary artery bypass graft, etc). This number is indeed dramatic. It is even more compelling when one closely studies the personal disruption created by such a catastrophic event as heart disease. Alterations in self-esteem, coping, activity, and sexual activity enormously disrupt patients' lives.

NEED FOR EDUCATION

Living with cardiovascular disease entails adapting to a new, often seemingly foreign, body and struggling to regain a sense of personal and social integration. Nurses care for cardiovascular disease patients at all phases of the illness continuum, from the acute and post-acute phases to rehabilitation and community reentry. Because of this continuity of nursing care throughout the recovery process, the nurse is the single most important person in planning, coordinating, and implementing educational interventions that incorporate both short- and long-term needs.

PREVENTING SUBSEQUENT CARDIAC EVENTS

The risk factors for heart disease are known. Most of these risks can be reduced through proper diet, medication, and behavioral changes, but most adults are not motivated to make changes on their own. Therefore, health care professionals need to evaluate individuals for risk factors and motivate people toward health promotion and disease prevention.

Education about cardiovascular disease is important to facilitate the patient's and family's understanding of what has occurred (the cardiac event), the treatment, and what they can do to help in caring for the patient upon discharge to home.

EFFECTIVE TEACHING/LEARNING

Educating patients and families cannot be limited to facts and figures. Recognition must be given to the values and attitudes of the patient and the family members, and to strategies to be used in influencing behavior change and overcoming fears of a possible second cardiac event. The educator should emphasize the essential need for the patient to actively participate in the learning process, to think through possible solutions to problems and dilemmas, and to find ways of coping with the treatment regimen in a way that will be of benefit to the patient and to the family. Rewards through words of support and encouragement throughout the post-event period are of critical importance for motivating the individual and the family, to ensure continuing participation and performance. Involving all family members is particularly important with respect to changing dietary intake, behaviors, and other aspects of recuperation and prevention. Both patient and family should be encouraged to verbalize ("vent") their feelings and to express their concerns, fears, anxieties, and doubts in constructive ways.

Merely providing information about risks will not reduce risk behaviors. A specific plan for the patient to follow in smoking cessation, for example, will ensure compliance with developing new attitudes and behaviors to prevent a recurrence of a cardiac event. Similarly, planning a weekly menu with the patient and family that meets requirements for calorie and fat reduction will be more acceptable than if the educator simply hands a menu to the patient and says, "Do this." The goal is for the patient to process the message and to decide to make a permanent behavior change. To accomplish this, the message must get through the maze of short-term memory and into the long-term storage memory. If possible, the patients should be made to believe that these changes are actually their ideas.

Three factors interact to support comprehension: logic, language, and experience. Patients must see that what is suggested makes sense, fits into their current life-style, can be achieved, and is worthwhile to pursue. The language used by the educator must resemble the vernacular that is familiar to the patient to obviate barriers to understanding.

CONTENT AREAS

A useful framework for education is one based on functional health patterns adapted from the North American Nursing Diagnosis Association (NANDA). In this plan, eleven major categories comprise content on assessment criteria, nursing education interventions, and patient/family outcomes: (1) health perception and health management; (2) nutritional and metabolic factors; (3) elimination; (4) activity and exercise; (5) sleep and rest; (6) cognitive and perceptual factors; (7) self-perception and self-concept; (8) role relationship; (9) sexuality and reproduction; (10) coping and stress tolerance; and (11) values and beliefs. These categories identify individual needs as well as problems or potential problems.

THE TEACHING PROCESS

Assessment is the first link in the teaching process chain. This phase includes more than the physical assessment; it includes assessing the learning characteristics of the individual such as age and developmental level, social and cultural background, level of education, level of energy, readiness to learn, and general health maintenance knowledge.

The next link is goal setting. The objective of this link is to provide a common foundation of understanding about specific aspects of the disease, and building on the patient's and family's level of knowledge, experience, and expressed needs.

Planning is the next step in the teaching process. This step requires the educator to check the available resources, consider support systems, determine content, select teaching strategies, arrange time, and adapt all factors to the patient.

The implementation and evaluation link is centered on patient teaching. A major problem that may be encountered is noncompliance. It is estimated that about only one-third of chronically ill patients adhere to therapeutic regimens; one-third adhere to a misunderstood regimen; and one-third choose to be noncompliant.

Common mistakes that occur in the teaching/learning process are: poor assessment, failure to negotiate goals, patient overload, poor timing, poor use of media, and making unfounded assumptions.

EVALUATING PROGRESS

Written behavioral objectives are used to specify and measure the patient's learning. An example of a well-formulated learning objective is: "In two weeks, Brian will learn to sit securely on the edge of the bed (or chair), to stand with the assistance of a walker, and to walk twice across the bedroom, using the walker properly with a minimal amount of wasted energy." The objective contains the essential elements: (1) active verbs—sit, stand, walk; (2) a definite time element; (3) a specific distance that is measurable; and (4) standards of performance—securely, using a minimal amount of energy. This objective can be used to measure the patient's progress. Subsequent objectives will increase the amount of activity, decrease the time allocation, and increase the distance to be walked. The objectives should be revised as often as necessary, that is, if the patient completes an objective fully before the end of the two weeks, it should be revised and made more rigorous.

This method of teaching/learning can be exciting and fun for both the teacher and the patient, who can clearly see that goals and objectives are being achieved. Success evokes greater motivation and higher achievement levels.

References

Anderson, C. 1990. *Patient Teaching and Communicating in an Information Age.* Albany, N.Y.: Delmar.

Feagins, C., and D. Daniel. 1991. Management of congestive heart failure in the home setting: a guide to clinical management and patient education. *J Home Health Care Practice* 4(1):31–37.

Fleury-Derenowski, J. 1991. Wellness motivation in cardiac rehabilitation. *Heart & Lung* 20(1):3–8.

Knowles, M. 1978. *The Adult Learner: A Neglected Species*, 2d ed. Houston, Tex.: Gulf.

North American Nursing Diagnosis Association. 1987. *Taxonomy I with Complete Diagnosis*. St. Louis, Mo.: St. Louis University School of Nursing.

U.S. Department of Health and Human Services. 1990. *National Cholesterol Education Program: Report of the Expert Panel on Population Strategies for Blood Cholesterol Reduction. Executive Summary*. Bethesda, Md.: National Institutes of Health Publication Number 90–3047.

Joan A. Panchal

Care Coordination: Case Management

"Case management" is a relatively new component in the organized care of older persons, although the concept is a long-familiar one for families who have had to find and orchestrate their own services required by aging parents or other relatives. However, the term "case management" carries with it a pejorative connotation that may influence the way health care providers actually regard older patients: "case management" encourages us to characterize (and dehumanize) older people as "cases" that need to be "managed." A better term, therefore, may be "service coordination" or "care coordination," which focuses attention on the function of care coordination rather than on the clientele it serves.

The role of a care coordinator is to act as the link between the client and health and social service providers, such as home health care agencies or adult day care centers. Care coordination should be part of the broader notion of "collaborative care." Collaborative care refers to an egalitarian relationship between the patient and the multidisciplinary team (physician, nurse, social worker, etc.) caring for the patient, as well as participation by the family or family substitute. Collaborative care calls for shared knowledge between providers and patients and their families, including full access to charts, fully informed consent regarding services, and some shared power. This last factor is especially critical when it comes to older people, because, for them, feeling autonomous can itself be therapeutic, while docility and passivity of older patients can contribute to iatrogenicity.

The purpose of care coordination is to overcome fragmentation in the service delivery system. Care coordinators can be social workers, nurses, psychologists, or other geriatric specialists. A care coordinator conducts a comprehensive needs assessment, develops an overall care plan, coordinates and monitors the delivery of services, and frequently does reassessments. Social work care coordination adds a clinical or counseling component for dealing with the emotional problems surrounding illness and disability.

Over the past ten years, some 600 for-profit care coordination agencies have developed. These agencies act as surrogates for adult children or other relatives who lack the skills, time, geographic proximity, or emotional capacity to provide the services their older relative needs. One common and troublesome situation adult children face is handling the needs of parents or other relatives living in a distant location. A care coordinator in that location can respond to an older person's needs in ways that would be extremely difficult or impossible for family members living elsewhere to do. Aging Network Services, one of the country's leading care coordination referral services, has ties to 250 private practice geriatric social workers nationwide who find suitable paraprofessionals for the elderly (Aging Network Services, 4400 East West Highway, Suite 907, Bethesda, MD 20814, 301–657–4329).

Private care coordination can be expensive, and it is often not covered by Medicare, Medicaid, or private insurance. Religious charities, hospitals, and other nonprofit organizations also provide care coordination services, usually at a lower cost. Unfortunately, staffers in these organizations tend to have more than twice the number of elderly in their caseloads as do care coordinators in private practice. Since care coordination is generally unregulated, it is important to check credentials and references carefully when looking into such services. At a minimum, care coordinators should have a master's degree in either social work or another human services area, as well as geriatric experience.

Care coordination took place at 20 sites throughout the United States from 1986 to 1989 through the Living At Home Program, supported by 39 foundations. The program explored ways to help people remain at home for as long as possible. Hoping to make a significant improvement in the quality of life for a substantial number of older people, the program provided each elderly person with a broad range of services assembled by a care coordinator skilled both in understanding the unique needs of each elderly individual and in securing the necessary services. What differentiated this program is that the care coordinator developed, orchestrated, assessed, and ensured the satisfactory provision of each individually tailored set of services, including medical, financial, legal, and social, not from one single agency, but from multiple participating agencies.

Although past research has shown that care coordination does not necessarily save money, patients and families with care coordination services report a higher degree of life satisfaction than those who have not had the benefit of such services.

Reference

Butler, R.N., M. Lewis, and T. Sunderland. 1991. *Aging and Mental Health*, 4th ed. New York: Macmillan.

Robert N. Butler

Care Coordination: Social Work Perspective

BACKGROUND

Professional social work had its beginnings in the "friendly visitor" functions of nineteenth century charity organizations. In describing the early social work efforts in helping the sick and the poor, Ida Cannon, a pioneer in health care social work, noted the processes of "steering" and "shoving," the former a milder directing to appropriate assistance, the latter a more aggressive intervention used with unresponsive families or resistant community agencies. The moralistic and paternalistic negatives in these early efforts to allocate resources to the indigent led to a recognition of a need for education and training and, thus, the first School of Philanthropy was founded in 1898.

Two decades later social work was rebuffed in its quest for professional status when Abraham Flexner termed social work a "mediating" rather than an "original" agency. Netting (1992) believes that this placed care coordination in a secondary role, one felt by many social workers to be less than worthy of a true professional mission. Hence, for several decades as social work responded to economic and societal forces, and to developments in the social and behavioral sciences, various emphases occurred within the profession, leading to the primacy of psychological interventions at times, or a primacy of advocacy or systems approaches at other times. Despite these practice fluctuations, however, the imprint of service provision for people in need, on individual, group, and larger population levels, has remained fundamental in the social work image.

Today, the coordinating of care function in social work is well integrated into the professional core of knowledge and skill and is, as well, enriched with a century of intellectual and experiential growth.

WHAT IS COORDINATED CARE?

The social work activities that involve the translation of biopsychosocial assessment data into a client-centered plan of care and the provision of appropriate services to implement that plan are most often labeled "generic social work." Currently, the majority of social workers who work with elderly populations utilize a case management method of service delivery that is synonymous with generic social work or coordinated care, but the semantics of both "case" and "management" are counter to the individualizing and participatory characteristics basic to social work's philosophy of helping. Coordinating care and care coordinator are more auspicious terms for both helper and those in need of help, but this is not to deny the timeliness and efficacy of case management principles.

CASE MANAGEMENT DEFINED

Kane (1983) writes "case management implies a continuity of responsibility for a particular clientele; the concept is most relevant for populations that may predictably experience a sustained period of dependency." The target group for case management services are most often those individuals and families that experience multiple concurrent problems as well as difficulty in negotiating systems. Case management is performed by a variety of professionals with varying degrees of training and with varying success. The positives of the case management concept are several: continuity of care is ensured; there is an economy and expediency in use of professional services and resources; and the model lends itself to evaluation and research. The explicitness of case management programs merges well with sound marketing principles in that unmet needs in specific populations can be identified, programs can be designed to meet these needs, and efficiency of service and ongoing need can be monitored.

White (1986) lists six basic steps in the case management process: (1) case-finding, (2) assessment, (3) care or service planning, (4) coordination, (5) follow-up, and (6) reassessment.

The target population determines the model of case management to be used. If, for example, the problem of elder abuse is identified, a case management program would involve not only the individual patient, but family and caregivers, and relevant community health and social agencies. Interventions would be on a crisis level at first, followed up with individual, family, and group counseling, as well as broader educational and preventive programs. Coordination of agencies and services for initial and continued assessment would be in place, as well as mechanisms for evaluating results and ongoing needs.

On the negative side, Netting (1992) notes that case management has been widely embraced chiefly as a cost-saving mechanism which "if stretched to the limit may be used to cover up the broader issue—that the health and human services delivery system is a non-system." Now that case management is so fully integrated into managed care programs whose primary aim is cost control, it deserves close scrutiny. Case managers who act as brokers, that is, who make clinical and fiscal decisions about services needed, but who do not follow up with providers and who do not identify gaps in resources, are most apt to function without professional values and a client-centered perspective.

In addition, the fact that the broad range of case management functions fits into expectable practice for several professional groups can lead to turf struggles among professionals. Netting (1992) advises that regardless of professional allegiance, all case managers should perform well, protecting people against the unqualified or greedy. Certainly, a number of groups in the elderly population are vulnerable to unscrupulous case management practices.

SOCIAL WORK VALUES AND STRENGTHS IN CARE COORDINATION

It is essential to distinguish the various groups in the ever expanding elderly population (27% of the total population by the year 2000). The majority of Americans 65 and over are productive and self-maintaining; some at this age are corporate presidents, professionals in law, medicine, nursing, and social work; they are caregivers, sometimes even to their own parents, or to their children and grandchildren; they are community leaders and holders of political offices. While many of the elderly thus hold key roles in vital aspects of family and community life, the vicissitudes of the aging process cannot be denied, particularly among the growing frail elderly population with compounded physical and mental health needs.

Social workers in a variety of settings come in contact with the elderly at significant points of need. The well-aged are more apt to be seeking informational, educational, and support services aimed at maintaining physical and mental status quo; in other words, basic primary care programs. Physical and mental breakdowns, both acute and chronic, require more secondary crisis interventions consisting of ongoing individual and family counseling, individual and group support services, and respite care, in addition to a range of skilled nursing and home care services. Social workers in hospitals, under increasing length of stay time pressures, must often initiate or augment such home supports at time of discharge, following medical and mental crises. The first crisis that prompts social work attention is rarely a one-time event in the aged population. More often, it signals the beginning of a chronic condition that fluctuates in severity. Thus, coordinating care efforts with components of continuity, follow-up, and evaluation represent high quality patient care and professional accountability.

Social workers bring to the task of coordinating care to the elderly a unique range of professional strengths. These include:

1. an ecological perspective that best expresses a dual concern with the person

and the person's environment, including family, social, and community relationships;

2. skill in the biopsychosocial assessment that calls for a gathering and assimilation of information on several functional levels. To the social worker's own assessment of the person's internal and external resources, roles, and relationships, is added relevant information and recommendations from all other professionals involved in the person's care. The biopsychosocial assessment is a fluid concept responding continually to new insights in medical and social sciences, forming a vital equation of the physical, emotional, and social significant factors that capture the essence of the person in his/her situation and the problems that require interventions aimed at ensuring acceptable life adaptation.

Additional clinical skills necessary in the helping process demand expertise in a range of treatment methods, such as individual and family counseling and group interventions, as well as the ability to advocate for entitlements and other services. Because social workers, especially with elderly populations, function as intermediary and contact persons in interdisciplinary settings, collaborative skill is crucial in communicating patient/family wishes and needs, and in eliciting and synthesizing interdisciplinary information and opinions, demanding a high level of interpersonal skills, a sense of professional camaraderie, and personal stamina.

Social work espouses the humanistic values of all the helping professions. With its special emphasis on self-determination and choice, however, it finds itself frequently in the midst of ethical conflicts, especially when the community good is threatened. Work with the elderly often produces situations in which the capacity for self determination is diminished, thus requiring continuous professional deliberation and reflection. In the larger political arena that determines social policy, social workers must be vigilant that opportunity for choice is preserved. It is in the utilization of these combined practice strengths and values that "coordinating care for the elderly" maintains a "social work perspective."

References

Austin, C. 1990. Case management: myths and realities. *Families in Society* 71(7):398–405.

Austin, D. 1983. The Flexner myth and history of social work. *Social Service Review* 57:357–77.

Cannon, I. 1913. *Social Work in Hospitals*. Philadelphia: The Russell Sage Foundation.

Kane, R. 1983. Social work as a health profession. In *A Handbook of Health, Health Care, and the Health Professions*, edited by D. Mechanic. New York: The Free Press, 495–522.

Netting, F. 1992. Case management: service or symptom. *Social Work* 37(2):160–64.

White, M. 1986. Case management. In *The Encyclopedia of Aging*, edited by G.L. Maddox. New York: Springer, 92–95.

Susan Blumenfield

Caregivers (Family)

Of the nearly 26 million people 65 years of age and older living in the community, about 23 percent have functional limitations. Ten percent of persons 65 and older (or about 2.5 million) receive help with personal care activities. This need for help is even greater for persons 85 years of age and older. For example, almost half (49%) of people 85+ have difficulties performing personal care activities. Thirty-one percent of persons 85 and older receive help with personal care activities. Yet, at any given time, only about 5 percent of persons 65 and older are in a nursing home. Many of these nursing home stays are for short-term rehabilitation or skilled nursing care following discharge from a hospital.

It is estimated that there are anywhere from 1.5 million to over 7 million households containing at least one caregiver, depending on how caregiving is defined. Families provide the bulk of long-term care for older people. Studies consistently show that 80–90 percent of care older people receive, including medically-related care (e.g., injections, catheters) is provided by family members. This caregiving may last for years. Moreover, several studies have shown that families often continue to provide care following institutionalization of a relative.

Research involving small, purposive samples and representative samples consistently finds that the majority of primary caregivers are women, usually daughters, wives and, to a lesser extent, daughters-in-law. Most care recipients are women. Women live longer than men and in the advanced years people are more likely to suffer from chronic physical and cognitive impairments. Almost all research on family caregiving has focused on either primary caregivers or the primary caregiver–care recipient dyad. In fact, a plurality of studies focus exclusively on daughters caring for mothers. Only a few studies have focused on secondary caregivers. With the exception of adding up the number of people listed as regular or occasional caregivers, little research has attempted to understand caregiving involvement or consequences beyond secondary family caregivers. In fact, some researchers combine all others involved in caregiving, except the primary caregiver, into the category, "secondary caregiver." This implies that anyone other than the primary caregivers is essentially the same in terms of involvement and outcomes. Some research suggests that this is not the case.

Caregiving is often determined on the basis of tasks performed for the care recipient. These tasks are differentiated into activities of daily living (ADLs) and instrumental activities of daily living (IADLs). ADLs include activities such as bathing, dressing, feeding, transfers, continence, and ambulation, while IADLs include activities such as housekeeping, shopping, taking medications, using transportation, using the telephone, cooking, and managing finances. An additional consideration is the type of chronic impairment of the elder (e.g., physical versus cognitive impairment). There may be additional demands or concerns for caregivers that are not captured by the specific tasks. For example, a bedridden elder and a demented elder may both require meal preparation. However, a demented elder may also exhibit disruptive or aggressive behaviors. These would not be captured in a task-based measure of caregiving.

As implied above, there are strengths and weaknesses in using task-based definitions. They allow researchers to compare the experiences of caregivers, such as burden or strain, on the basis of different types of care provided. They also allow researchers to compare levels of involvement of different people (e.g., family versus neighbors and friends). Further, they stress the labor-intensive aspects of caregiving.

There are several shortcomings to this approach, however. Focusing on tasks alone fails to embed caregiving in close personal relationships that include emotions and interpersonal histories. Men and women, for example, tend to focus on different aspects of caregiving. Men are more likely to concentrate on the tasks and their completion. Women, on the other hand, tend to focus on the relational aspects. Thus, for women, seeing that personal and instrumental tasks are taken care of is part of a concern with the overall quality of life for the elder.

Related to this is that a focus on tasks performed for the elder may prevent us from seeing involvement of a larger caregiving system. Males and relatives other than daughters or wives may be less involved in direct care to the care recipient, but they may provide support to the primary caregiver. This may help the primary caregiver sustain their involvement for a longer period of time.

Caregivers take on caregiving responsibilities for a number of reasons: a sense of duty or obligation to care; a sense of affection and commitment to the elder; a desire to reciprocate for care received as a child; a concern about quality of life or autonomy for the elder that may not be possible in an institutional setting; financial inability to hire outside help to provide care; no other relatives may be willing or able to provide care; close proximity to the elder. The existence of a particular caregiver seems to follow certain lines of selection or choice. This has often been referred to as a ''principle of substitution.'' The primary caregiver is usually a spouse; if a spouse is not available, the caregiver is often a daughter or sometimes a daughter-in-law. In the absence of these possible caregivers, another relative assumes the responsibility. In some instances where no relative is available, friends or neighbors may provide assistance.

Caregiving behavior has been conceptualized into four broad categories: emotional support, direct service provisions, linkage with the formal service sector, and financial assistance. Research indicates that women provide much more overall assistance than do men, at least as temporary caregivers. Additionally, the kinds of care provided varies with the gender of the primary caregiver.

Women tend to perform more personal care tasks, while men do more instrumental tasks.

Providing care for an elderly spouse or parent can be burdensome—emotionally, physically, and financially. Moreover, opportunities for the caregiver to socialize or take care of basic needs, such as shopping or errands, can be difficult. All of these burdens appear to lead to different degrees of strain. Caregiver strain (also called burden or stress) has been one of the most commonly studied areas of caregiving. Typically, researchers have looked at correlates of caregiver strain, including assessments of which kinds of caregivers are more strained. More recently, some researchers have begun looking at consequences of caregiver strain (e.g., service use, institutionalization). Some form of emotional strain appears to be the most pervasive outcome of caregiving.

An interesting finding about caregiver strain is that many caregivers do not experience strain or do not experience very high levels of strain. In general, though, greater strain is associated with performing more caregiver tasks, especially personal care tasks, presence of cognitive impairment or dementia, disruptive behaviors (often resulting from dementia), greater physical impairment (leading to a greater need for help with tasks), and role conflicts. Greater support with caregiving and a greater amount of affection for the care recipient have been associated with lower levels of caregiver strain.

There is some evidence that caregiving can have benefits or rewards. Some caregivers are pleased about being able to reciprocate for care they received. Some find that they have developed or renewed a close relationship with a parent.

One area of research that has experienced much activity recently is that of competing demands, in particular, employment. Research suggests that caregivers often make adjustments in work or personal schedules to accommodate caregiving. More than one-third of caregivers in one study reported a change in work status as a result of caregiving. This included taking leaves of absence and changing from full-time to part-time work.

Another common research issue is that of "women in the middle." These are women who are primary caregivers for older relatives and who have additional demands such as employment, care for dependent children, and housework. While there are certainly many women who are in this situation, there is evidence to suggest that this situation may not be as onerous as some have argued. Demographics are such that very few women are in a position to be providing care for an older relative and be caring for dependent children. Moreover, there is some evidence that having multiple roles is beneficial—no one role counts too heavily in assessment of well-being or a sense of success.

Despite the tremendous research activity in the area of caregiving during the past decade, there are still many questions that need to be answered. Several researchers have called for more rigorous designs, attention to measurement issues, and an explicit link between caregiving research and theory.

References

Abel, E.K. 1991. *Who Cares for the Elderly? Public Policy and the Experiences of Adult Daughters.* Philadelphia: Temple University Press.

George, L.K. 1990. Caregiver stress studies—there really is more to learn. *The Gerontologist* 30:580–82.

Montgomery, R.J.V. 1992. Gender differences in patterns of child-parent caregiving relationships. In *Gender, Families, and Elder Care,* edited by J.W. Dwyer and R.T. Coward. Newbury Park, Cal.: Sage, 65–83.

Stone, R., G. Cafferata, and J. Sangl. 1987. Caregivers of the frail elderly: a national profile. *The Gerontologist* 27:616–26.

Stull, D.E., K. Bowman, J. Cosbey, W. McNutt, and M. Drum. 1991. *Institutionalization: A Continuation of Family Care.* Paper presented at the 44th annual meeting of the Gerontological Society of America, November 22–26, San Francisco, CA.

Tennstedt, S.L., J.B. McKinlay, and L.M. Sullivan. 1989. Informal care for frail elders: the role of secondary caregivers. *The Gerontologist* 29:677–83.

Donald E. Stull

Caregivers (Family): Economic Supports

Family members provide extensive amounts of care to elderly persons who become dependent due to chronic physical and mental illnesses. In fact, the family is the primary source of care to dependent elders living in the community. Although caregiving can have positive aspects for the caregiver, it is often stressful as well. Many families report that caregiving is an emotional, physical and, at times, financial burden. Data from a national sample of caregivers reported by Stone, Cafferata, and Sangl (1987) indicate that almost one-third of caregivers do not receive any assistance in their caregiving functions from other informal or formal providers, and that family caregivers are more likely to have lower income and lower self-reported health than the population at large. Multiple factors heighten the need for social policies to address the issue of families' continued abilities to provide care for their dependent family members. These factors include the increasing number of elderly persons with chronic health problems, reduced fertility rates leading to fewer children and fewer siblings to share the caregiving burden for future generations, and decreased availability of females as caregivers due to increased employment.

Over the past two decades, a number of states have developed economic support policies, both tax supports and direct payments to caregivers, in an attempt to assist caregivers to continue to provide care for their dependent family members. The development of these policies has not been driven by states' concerns with the level of caregiver burden per se, but rather with the high costs of long-term care and the hope that such supports could help reduce these costs by preventing inappropriate or premature institutionalization of dependent elderly individuals.

The availability, extensiveness, and financial adequacy of economic supports for family caregivers are limited by beliefs of some policymakers and agency professionals that the state should not pay caregivers to perform a family responsibility, fears that families will abuse these supports through exploiting or taking advantage of their elders, and by concerns that families will ''come out of the woodwork'' to demand financial supports or will discontinue their current caregiving responsibilities if they do not receive payment, thus increasing costs to the state.

A significant number of states have economic support programs. However, these initiatives have received little empirical investigation. Thus, there is little information available as to the outcomes of these policy initiatives, either on reducing caregiver burden or on the effects of the programs on the level of institutional costs.

A number of studies published in the early to mid-1980s suggested that families either had little need for, or little interest in, financial supports. However, other researchers such as Arling and McAuley noted that these early studies asked caregivers their attitudes about hypothetical situations and that different responses might be expected in real caregiving situations. It was also believed that financial assistance programs are often stereotyped as being for the ''poor'' and thus might be seen as stigmatic by caregivers.

There are two broad types of economic support policies for caregivers of the elderly—tax supports and direct payment programs. Tax policies include tax credits, defined as a specified sum of money that an individual is allowed to subtract from taxes owed to the government; tax deductions, defined as a specified sum of money that an individual is allowed to subtract from their gross income before computing the amount of taxes owed; and tax exemptions, defined as a specified portion of an individual's gross income that is free from taxation. Direct payment programs for family caregivers are defined as any program that directly transfers money from the state to an elderly individual or to a household. In some cases, payments (cash or vouchers) are made directly to the family caregiver; in other cases, payments go to the elder client in need who is granted authority for determining from whom services will be purchased.

Tax supports are intended to acknowledge the financial burden that caregiving entails and to offer at least token relief to caregiver households, or to family members who are employed and must hire caregivers for their elders while they are working. Currently, as reported by Isensee and Campbell (1987), twenty-four states offer one or more types of tax supports. There is considerable variation among state policies concerning the amount of tax supports provided by existing legislation, ranging from a $40 credit to a $5,000 maximum deduction. In general, however, tax supports cover only a very small portion of caregiving expenses. There are significant differences among states in tax policy eligibility requirements on a number of variables: age and disability of dependent elder, employment of caregiver, financial support which must be provided by the family caregiver in order to be eligible for a tax benefit, the relationship of the caregiver to the dependent elder, and the requirement that the caregiver and elder must maintain a shared household. There are also differences within particular states that have more than one type of tax support policy.

A 1985 report by the Maryland Office of the Aging found that of the three types of tax supports, tax credits are the most effective, providing the most support to the largest number of taxpayers. However, questions have been raised as to the overall effectiveness or usefulness of tax policy to provide economic supports to family caregivers. A major problem with the use of tax policy to provide economic supports to family caregivers is that there is no way to target expenditures to populations that are most in need of assistance. In fact, if level of functional impairment were to be used as an eligibility criterion, tax policies would be difficult and expensive to administer.

Direct payment programs, as opposed to tax supports, provide greater fiscal resources to families; they also allow for more precise targeting of resources. Direct payment programs tend to be targeted to lower-income elderly at higher risk to a greater degree than are tax benefit programs. Another benefit of direct payment programs is that they can be utilized together with service supports to provide a comprehensive approach to meeting the needs of family caregivers.

Surveys of state level direct payment programs to family caregivers were conducted by Linsk and associates in 1988 and by Biegel and associates in 1989. Linsk and colleagues found that thirty-three states permit some form of financial payments to relatives who provide home care services to the elderly; that is, they either had a payment program in place in at least part of the state, or they did not prohibit payments to caregivers. A follow-up study done in 1990 indicates that the number of states that allow payments to caregivers had remained about the same, although there were some differences in the particular states that allowed payments in the 1985 and 1990 surveys. Using a narrower definition of states actually having a payment program in place, Biegel and colleagues found that twenty states provide some type of direct payments to caregivers.

Most direct payment programs are part of a larger home care or independent living program. As described earlier, tax policies vary considerably from state to state. Direct payment programs differ even more with wide variations in average payments, number of persons served, family income, kinship and residence restrictions, preference for payment of family members (family caregiver as first resort, last resort, or somewhere in the middle), disability requirements, caregiver employment, sources of funding, payment mechanisms, and requirements for training and certification of caregivers. Thus, it becomes difficult to describe a "typical" program. While many states offer direct payment programs to caregivers on a statewide basis, in other states, such payment policies are offered only in certain parts of the state.

Linsk and colleagues believe that direct payment programs are an underutilized policy option that would gain wider support if federal policies, principally those of the Health Care Financing Administration (HCFA), were not aimed at discouraging or restricting such payments. They make a number of recommendations aimed at strengthening and expanding compensated family caregiving. First, they believe that policies need to move away from last resort, residual approaches that compensate caregivers primarily to save the state monies, to a broader recognition of the benefits of compensation for family members as caregivers. Such benefits include the fact that family members are already known by the elder, can provide services flexibly, and can enhance elders' self-esteem and autonomy. In the authors' view, benefits, in the form of cash payments to family caregivers, should be targeted at elders based upon disability levels. Payments to family caregivers should not be seen as a last resort to be used only in the absence of available formal service providers, but rather as a desirable, first resort. Programs should also incorporate services for elders and caregivers as needed, with case management and quality assurance mechanisms built in as well.

SUMMARY

Enhancement of economic supports for family caregivers needs to address the significant inequities and inadequacies of current state programs. The availability and generosity of economic supports for family caregivers often depend on the state in which one lives, or the area within a particular state. Presently, state level economic support programs are often fragmented, with lack of communication between state-level health, social service, and aging agencies. In addition, economic support programs are not well coordinated with available service programs. Indeed, economic support programs suffer from the drawbacks of our fragmented overall system of long-term care in which, as noted by Leutz and colleagues, states lack a single agency with overall responsibility for long-term care. This suggests that to be fully effective, improvements in economic support policies for family caregivers need to be part of a broader reform of the current long-term care system.

References

Arling, G. and W.J. McAuley. 1983. The feasibility of public payments for family caregiving. *The Gerontologist* 23(3):300–6.

Biegel, D., R. Schulz, B. Shore, and R. Morycz. 1989. Economic supports for family caregivers of the elderly: public sector policies. In *Family Involvement in the Treatment of the Frail Elderly*, edited by M.Z. Goldstein. Washington, D.C.: American Psychiatric Press, 157–201.

Isensee, L.C., and N.D. Campbell. 1987. *Dependent Care Tax Provisions in the States: An Opportunity for Reform*. Washington, D.C.: National Women's Law Center.

Leutz, W.N., J.A. Capitman, M. MacAdam, and R. Abrahams. 1992. *Care for Frail Elders: Developing Community Solutions*. Westport, Conn.: Auburn House.

Linsk, N.L., S.M. Keigher, and S.E. Osterbusch. 1988. States' policies regarding paid family caregiving. *The Gerontologist* 28:204–12.

Linsk, N.L., S.M. Keigher, L. Simon-Rusinowitz, and S.E. England. 1992. *Wages for Caring: Compensating Family Care of the Elderly.* New York: Praeger.

Stone, R.I., G.L. Cafferata, and J. Sangl. 1987. Caregivers of the frail elderly: a national profile. *The Gerontologist* 27:616–26.

David E. Biegel

Caregiving (Informal)

At a landmark conference on the family in aging societies held 25 years ago, the reported demise of family solidarity and decrease in the availability of family support were found to be premature. Several pioneers in the area of family caregiving research continued during the 1970s and 1980s to shatter the myth of family abandonment. Today, most researchers, policymakers, and practitioners recognize that the family is the backbone of the service system for the elderly and other disabled persons. In fact, the terms "family caregiving" and "informal caregiver" are quickly becoming a part of our vernacular.

The graying of the population, however, coupled with other demographic trends (e.g., decreasing fertility rates and increased female labor force participation) and increasing fiscal constraints at the federal, state, and local levels, have raised concern among policymakers and service providers about the short—and long-term viability of the family as a major service provider. Some have expressed concern that, given the availability of publicly subsidized services, families will substitute formal for unpaid assistance. The literature to date, however, does not support this fear of "substitution." The key question in the 1990s is not whether the family is abrogating its responsibilities, but what can be done to support and enable families to continue providing care.

MAGNITUDE OF CAREGIVING

The wide variation in the definition of caregiving has important implications for estimating the magnitude of informal care in the United States. Caregivers may be defined by the types of care provided (including physical, emotional, and financial support); the volume, intensity, and duration of care; the relationship of the caregiver to the care recipient; and selected care recipient characteristics including age, the level of disability, and presence of health conditions. Using a very broad definition of caregiving, a recent survey conducted by Harris and Associates found that 30.2 million Americans over age 55 are caring for a sick or disabled spouse, other relative, friend or neighbor, or for their children or grandchildren. Estimates from the 1984 National Long Term Care Survey, which used a more stringent caregiver definition, indicate that at any one time, over 13 million spouses and adult children of disabled elderly persons—7 percent of the U.S. population and one in 11 full-time workers—face significant long-term care decisions. Just under one-third—4.2 million people—provide help with activities of daily living (e.g., eating, toileting, dressing, meal preparation, shopping) to disabled spouses or parents living in the community. Another 3 million relatives, friends, and neighbors are also active caregivers; still others provide informal care to elders in nursing homes. Data from the 1987 National Medical Care Expenditure Survey indicate that over 12 million Americans provide informal, unpaid assistance with activities of daily living to disabled family members or friends across the age spectrum, including physically disabled adults and children as well as the elderly.

While the data on caregiving to persons under age 65 are limited, research has substantiated anecdotal evidence that families and, to a lesser extent, friends and neighbors, provide the bulk of long-term care to disabled elders. A recent comparison of national data on primary informal caregivers to disabled elders in 1982 and 1989 found that family caregiving is still going strong. While there was a slight reduction in the percent of elderly relying solely on informal assistance (from 74% to 67%) over the 7-year period, the vast majority—91 percent—continued to receive assistance from family, friends, and neighbors. Only 9 percent of the disabled elderly relied solely on paid help in 1989.

CAREGIVER STRESS, BURDEN, AND COMPETING DEMANDS

Eight out of 10 caregivers provide unpaid assistance averaging 4 hours a day, 7 days a week. This responsibility falls overwhelmingly on the shoulders of women (23 percent are wives and 29 percent are daughters), many of whom are elderly themselves. While the majority of caregivers are in good physical and financial shape, one out of 3 primary caregivers reports fair to poor health, and 29 percent are poor to near poor.

A voluminous literature has documented that family care is often provided in the face of much emotional, physical, and sometimes financial burden. These caregivers are at risk for symptoms of psychological stress, disruption of social functioning, and even decrements in physical health. Many have suggested that caregiver burden may lead to "burn-out" and ultimately the decision to institutionalize a disabled family member.

A minority, but nevertheless significant, proportion of caregivers juggle multiple responsibilities, including child care and employment. According to data from the 1984 National Long Term Care Survey, approximately 1.7 million women—6.6. percent of all women with children under the age of 15 in the United States—are faced with elder care decisions in addition to their child care responsibilities. Of these potential caregivers, 164,000 are primary caregivers of disabled parents and children. The relatively small number of women with dual responsibilities is not surprising given that almost two-thirds of daughters of disabled parents are either middle-aged or elderly themselves and are more likely to be grandparents than parents of minor children.

National estimates of working caregivers range from 27 to 36 percent, depending on the definitions of caregiving and employment used as well as the source of data. The prevalence of elder care responsibilities among the work force population varies dramatically (from a low of 1.9% to a high of 46%) depending on the definitions of caregiving and work, the population sampled (i.e., a national sample versus employees of a particular firm or series of companies), and the survey response rate.

Among employed primary caregivers, almost 2 out of 3 report that they have had to accommodate their work schedules in some fashion to meet their caregiving responsibilities by working fewer hours, rearranging their schedules, and/ or taking time off without pay. Researchers have found that among nonspousal working caregivers, females, whites, those in fair to poor health, and those who were caring for elders who required substantial supervision or who have a behavior problem were more likely to experience conflict between work and care responsibilities. Another recent study examining the competing demands of paid work and unpaid help found that full-time employment by caregivers reduces the time they allocate to providing unpaid help by 20 hours a week.

CAREGIVER SUPPORTS

A variety of mechanisms have been developed to help reduce caregiver burden and to mitigate the erosion of the informal care system. An array of direct caregiver services have proliferated across the country to help bolster the informal care system. The majority of existing caregiver interventions are educational, information and referral, or social support programs focusing on practical issues (e.g., the aging process, navigating the service system, home care skills). Individual and group psychotherapy and training programs are also offered to enhance the caregiver's ability to manage specific problems and to teach cognitive/behavioral skills within a time-limited framework. Respite care is another strategy viewed by many as a way to help alleviate caregiver burden and perhaps even delay institutionalization by providing temporary relief from care responsibilities. Although programs vary with respect to setting, duration, and level of care, the most frequently requested and utilized service is in-home respite care provided for short periods.

Financial assistance to family caregivers, through cash subsidies or tax incentives, is also seen as a way to "encourage" or sustain family care and to help or delay institutionalization of a disabled person. Research findings indicate that families prefer direct service programs to cash payments or tax incentives. However, the question of whether, and under what circumstances, dollars or services actually provide better support for caregivers remains to be examined.

THE FUTURE OF INFORMAL CARE

There is growing concern that fewer family members will be available to provide informal care in the future. While the aging of the population and technological advances will increase the number of disabled, the size of the future caregiver population should not be extrapolated simply from what is observed today. The next generation of elders, for example, will have more children available to take care of them. Further in the future, however, the more recent decline in fertility rates will reverse this trend. Future generations may also have a different propensity to rely on informal care. Higher incomes of the elderly population may increase their demand for paid care, and some will have private insurance to cover long-term care. Continued increases in female labor force participation may reduce the extent to which women are caregivers. On the other hand, to the extent that they are not offset by delayed childbearing, smaller families of potential caregivers and increased active life expectancy of parents may reduce the conflict between child care and elder care. Although difficult to predict, these changes will affect the demand for long-term care and the mix of informal and formal services.

References

Brody, E. 1985. Parent care as a normative family stress. *The Gerontologist* 25:19–29.

Commonwealth Fund. 1992. *The Nation's Great Overlooked Resource: The Contributions of Americans 55+*. A national survey conducted by Louis Harris and Associates, Inc.

McFall, S., and B.H. Miller. 1992. Caregiver burden and nursing home admission of frail elderly persons. *J Gerontology* 47:S73-S79.

Shone, B., and T.J. Lair. 1992. *Caregivers, Potential Caregivers and Employment: Preliminary Findings from the 1987 National Medical Expenditure Survey*. Paper presented at The Changing Face of Informal Caregiving Conference, Berkeley Springs, W.Va.

Stone, R.I. 1991. Defining family caregivers of the elderly: implications for research and public policy. *The Gerontologist* 31:724–25.

Stone, R.I., and P. Kemper. 1989. Spouses and children of disabled elders: how large a constituency for long-term care reform? *Milbank Quarterly* 67:485–506.

Robyn I. Stone

Caregiving (Informal): Financing Issues

Informal care is broadly defined as care given by families or friends to those in need, without expectation of payment. This definition implies that the costs of informal care are not recovered from the care recipient, but rather paid by the caregiver. The process of locating and evaluating funds to pay for any activity is known as financing. A discussion of informal care financing must consider two main issues:

1. cost finding: identifying the direct and indirect costs of care;
2. financing: identifying the source and cost of funds to meet the care expenses, and analyzing the impact of financing decisions on the caregiver and the care recipient.

The direct costs of informal care are those that can be identified as specific to the care activity. These costs disappear when the delivery of informal care stops. Direct costs vary widely and have a relationship to the acuity of the individual receiving care. These costs may include supplies, medications, health providers' fees, food, clothing, and any other cost that may be directly attributable to the care activity. Included in direct costs is the opportunity cost of informal caregiving. This is value forgone by choosing to give informal care rather than another activity. For caregivers who are or could be employed, the opportunity cost may be estimated by the wages lost due to the time required for care. Opportunity cost estimation should consider not only any decrease in wages, but also promotions lost, and any losses in pension value or other employment benefits due to caregivers' changed labor patterns.

Indirect costs are those not directly associated with caregiving. These costs are analogous to overhead costs in a business. Caregiving to an individual resident in the same household has indirect costs that represent a share of household overhead such as: water, energy, maintenance, and real-estate tax costs. Caregiving to those who maintain their own household involves overhead costs such as caregiver transportation or any portion of the household cost which increases due to caregiving. Indirect costs must be allocated using a formula which represents the portion of total overhead used in the caregiving activity. The simplest method of indirect cost allocation would estimate the percent of the total resource cost used to support caregiving and allocate that portion as the indirect cost.

Current research on informal care recognizes that caregiving imposes both direct and indirect costs. The financing used to pay these costs and the impact of that financing should also be considered.

A household's financial status is measured by net worth, the total value of the financial assets of a household after debt is removed. The decisions that impact household net worth are of two kinds: current consumption decisions that meet immediate needs, or savings decisions intended to meet future needs. The acquisition of assets such as real estate, pensions, insurance, or bequests increase savings and add to the household net worth. Current income used for immediate needs preserves the household savings. If current income is decreased or stops, households meet immediate needs by using savings or incurring debt, thereby decreasing net worth.

Informal care affects both consumption and savings of a household. Because informal care is a partnership between the caregiver and the care recipient, each may contribute to the cost of care using the financial resources available to them.

According to previous research, there are five financing approaches used in informal care:

- caregiver exchange of paid hours of labor for unpaid hours of care
- formalizing informal care
- tax programs
- debt
- bequests

Each financing mechanism has a different impact on household net worth.

CAREGIVER EXCHANGE

Caregiving, whether formal or informal, is labor intensive. Informal caregivers frequently substitute unpaid hours of care for paid employment. Research findings indicate that employed caregivers make this substitution by decreasing hours of paid employment, using leave-of-absence or sick leave, or by early retirement. The effect of exchanging paid hours of labor for unpaid hours of care has both an immediate impact and a long-term impact on household net worth. Any decrease in current income causes the household to either decrease the rate of savings or to draw on savings or debt to meet immediate needs. In either case, the net worth of the household will decrease. Long-term impacts of this financing also decrease net worth and include: a decrease in pension benefits due to lower contributions or zero earning years, a decrease in income expectations due to missed promotions or a lowered base for cost-of-living increases, and decreases in other job-related benefits such as health or disability insurance.

FORMALIZING INFORMAL CARE

Formalizing informal care results when federal or state programs pay informal caregivers for their care. Examples of these programs include the Veterans' Administration which allows monthly benefits paid to housebound veterans to be used to reimburse family caregivers, and state programs that pay family caregivers. These programs will increase household net worth when the informal caregiver did not previously earn a salary. If the caregiving payment substitutes for a previously higher salary, the program will slow the decrease in household net worth.

TAX PROGRAMS

Tax programs that assist the informal caregiver are of three types: tax exemptions, tax credits, and tax deductions. Federal tax exemptions are available to the caregivers of financially dependent individuals residing with the caregiver.

Tax exemptions reduce income subject to tax. They act to increase household net worth by the amount of tax saved. Tax deductions allow caregiving households to deduct a percentage of an amount actually spent in purchasing care, subject to regulations that limit the amount of deduction. Both tax exemptions and tax deductions are a form of reimbursement to households for expenses incurred in providing care. Thus, they buffer the effect of caregiving on household net worth.

The Federal government and some state governments allow tax credits for child and dependent care. Caregiving households may use tax credits to reduce the final total tax bill. Tax credits also increase the net worth of the household by reducing tax liability and are of more benefit to low-income taxpayers than deductions or exemptions. The effect of a tax credit on household net worth is similar to that of deductions. In order to qualify for a tax credit, a household will have incurred caregiving expense. The tax credit replaces some of the dollars used in caregiving and thus slows decrease in net worth.

DEBT

Caregiving households may also use short-or long-term debt to finance caregiving expenses. Estimating the effect of debt on household net worth requires consideration of the risk of debt. If debt is used by a high-income caregiving household, the net worth is reduced by the amount of the debt obligation less the tax deduction for mortgage interest, if applicable. If debt is used by a low-income household, the cost of financial distress and possible bankruptcy must also be considered. Financial distress results when a household has difficulty meeting debt obligations. Costs of financial distress include late payment penalties, increased cost of credit, and decreased financial flexibility. If bankruptcy occurs, the household will bear legal costs and lose assets in order to satisfy creditors. Both financial distress and bankruptcy costs will reduce the net worth of a household by more than the debt obligation alone. These costs should be considered when a caregiving household assumes more debt than income and savings can support.

BEQUESTS

The caregiving household can realize an increase in net worth if a bequest is made to them by the care recipient. Over the last twenty years, the net worth of households has increased. This wealth may be transferred to the next generation in the form of a bequest if it is not needed to pay for institutional care. If living with the caregiver becomes necessary, Federal tax law provides incentives for reduction in care recipients' income in order to qualify for an exemption. Income-producing assets may be transferred to the caregiving household in order to accomplish this.

In summary, those who choose to provide informal care incur both direct and indirect costs. The payment of these costs does decrease the household's net worth. Existing caregiver subsidies slow the depletion of household financial resources, but does not completely preserve them. The prospect of a bequest or a transfer of the care recipient's wealth is the only financing mechanism which might increase the wealth of the caregiver.

Caregivers do not generally identify financial concerns as a major stressor in the caregiving relationship. However, the decrease in net worth due to caregiving activities occurs over the long term. Further research is needed to establish the long-term financial effects of informal caregiving on the caregiver. Failure to understand this important question may result in the impoverishment of former caregivers at a time when there are few resources to assist them.

References

Bass, D. 1990. *Caring Families: Supports and Interventions*. Silver Spring, Md.: National Association for Social Work Press.

David, M., and P. Menchik. 1988. Changes in cohort wealth over a generation. *Demography* 25(3):317–35.

England, S., N. Linsk, L. Simon-Rusinowitz, and S. Keigher. 1990. Paying kin for care: agency barriers to formalizing informal care. *J Aging and Social Policy* 2(2):63–86.

Horowitz, A. 1985. Sons and daughters as caregivers to older parents: differences in role performance and consequences. *The Gerontologist* 25(5):612-17.

Neal, M., N. Chapman, B. Ingersoll-Dayton, A. Emlen, and L. Boise. 1990. Absenteeism and stress among employed caregivers of the elderly, disabled adults, and children. In *Aging and Caregiving: Theory, Research, and Policy*, edited by D. Biegel and A. Blum. Sage Focus editions. Newbury Park, Cal.: Sage, 160–83.

Stone, R.I., and P. Short. 1990. The competing demands of employment and informal caregiving to disabled elders. *Medical Care* 28(6):513–26.

Mary A. Paterson

Caregiving: Obtaining Meaning Through

Research studies of family caregivers have typically viewed the experience of caregiving as stressful or burdensome. While objective and subjective caregiver distress can be documented, the question that has received less attention is, "How do caregivers manage to do so well under difficult circumstances?" Qualitative research findings suggest that caregivers of persons with dementia often say, "I would not have chosen my situation, but given that my family member has dementia, I will choose to make the best out of it."

The construct, finding meaning through caregiving, is adapted from Dr. Viktor Frankl's construct (1963), finding meaning through suffering. Dr. Frankl, a Viennese psychiatrist, was imprisoned in concentration camps during the 1940s.

When observing other victims, he noticed that those who continued to live and do better under these difficult circumstances expressed a sense of hope and ability to find meaning through that experience. Others have also suggested that this construct can be applied to caregiving. "The spouse of a person with dementia lives in a prison, struggles on a battlefield, and languishes in a concentration camp."

THE PROCESS OF FINDING MEANING

Dr. Frankl made four propositions concerning finding meaning, and these can readily be applied to the caregiving process. First, he suggests that persons create meaning by making choices. Caregivers often perceive that they do not have a choice as to whether they will become caregivers. And in reality these choices, particularly for women, have been shaped by our society. In order to freely choose caregiving responsibilities, caregivers must first entertain the possibility of "not" being a caregiver. While entertaining this option, the caregiver may experience a sense of freedom, as well as a "terrifying new series of choices" and "a fear of unwelcome possibility." The challenge to caregivers is to select the caregiving role and the responsibilities out of "true choice" as opposed to fear.

Second, Frankl suggests that values provide a basis for meaning. Values can be expressed through creative means, experiences, and attitudes of life beliefs. Creative values are expressed through jobs, hobbies, or other creative expressions. Caregiving provides opportunities for creative expression as caregivers develop innovative approaches to solving day-to-day challenges or when they use their creative outlets through hobbies or other enjoyable activities. Experiential values focus on relationships and feelings that persons have toward others. Caregivers' experiential values may be expressed as they enjoy relationships with others, focus on who the care-receiver was in the past, while at the same time still enjoying the person for who he/she still is. Attitudinal values include philosophical or spiritual beliefs, as well as orientations that persons develop toward their situation. Caregivers frequently report that their personal attitudes or spiritual philosophy enable them to persevere in their efforts to provide care.

Frankl's third premise suggests that persons have responsibility for right action and conduct. In his work with concentration camp victims, Frankl said that it does not really matter what we expect from life, but what life expects from us: "Life ultimately means taking responsibility to find the right answer to its problems, and to fulfill the tasks which it constantly sets for each individual." Contrary to popular belief, research suggests that family members readily assume caregiving responsibilities for ailing spouses, parents, or other relatives, and work toward finding the best way to provide this care.

Fourth, Frankl suggests that provisional and ultimate meaning exist. Provisional meaning refers to those short-term or transitory experiences that give meaning to life, such as relationships, pleasant activities or experiences. Ultimate meaning is often found as persons embrace their philosophical or spiritual beliefs and explore deeper meanings to life.

FINDING MEANING THROUGH CAREGIVING

Results from a large qualitative study suggested that caregivers acknowledge their present feelings of loss and powerlessness, and might find meaning through caregiving in some of the following ways:

Acknowledging Their Present Loss

Caregivers talked about their feelings of loss "for" their impaired family member and feelings of loss for themselves. Clinical observations suggest that feelings of loss and grief may be experienced in many different ways including: (a) sadness at their family member's illness and/or behaviors; (b) anger or sadness that their own life has changed and is not what they expected; (c) sadness upon the loss of an important relationship; (d) anger or anxiety over having to assume responsibility for things that they and their relative shared in the past; (e) embarrassment at having to provide intimate care such as bathing or toileting; (f) disgust over having to set limits on the behavior and demands of a family member; or (g) feeling overwhelmed by having another adult totally dependent upon them.

Acknowledging Feelings of Powerlessness

Some caregivers talked about feelings of powerlessness concerning their decision to become the caregiver. They talked about feeling a sense of duty, responsibility, and obligation for assuming these responsibilities. Others reported feeling restricted, that they had lost their freedom, that they experienced nothing pleasant about caregiving, that their life was boring, that they felt like they were in limbo, or that they had a sense of hopelessness or endlessness concerning their situation. Sometimes this powerlessness may also be experienced through feelings of: (a) guilt about something caregivers did or did not do in the past, thinking that they did something that may have "caused" the dementia; (b) inadequacy concerning providing good care; (c) "Survivor's Guilt"as expressed by asking, "How can I enjoy life and do things I want, when my family member can no longer enjoy the same things?"; (d) wishing that his/her relative were dead; or (e) resentment toward other family members who "aren't doing enough."

Making Personal Choices

The majority of caregivers talked about having made a choice to develop a positive attitude concerning life and their caregiving situation, and to appreciate the positive aspects of life. Their most common self-talk statements were compiled into "Twelve Steps for Caregivers":

Twelve Steps for Caregivers

1. Although I cannot control the disease process, I need to remember that I can control many aspects of how it affects me and my relative.
2. I need to take care of myself (rest, outside interests, respite) so that I can continue to take care of my relative.
3. I need to simplify my lifestyle so that my time and energy are available for things that are really important to me at this time.
4. I need to cultivate the gift of allowing others to help me, because caring for my relative is too big a job to be done by one person.
5. I need to take one day at a time, rather than worry about what may or may not happen in the future.
6. I need to structure my day because a consistent schedule makes life easier for me and my relative.
7. I need to have a sense of humor because laughter helps to put things in a more positive perspective.
8. I need to remember that my relative is not being "difficult" on purpose; rather, that his/her behavior and emotions are distorted by illness.
9. I need to focus on and enjoy what my relative can still do, rather than constantly lament over what is gone.
10. I need to increasingly depend on other relationships for love and support.
11. I need to frequently remind myself that I am doing the best that I can at this particular moment.
12. I need to draw upon the Higher Power I believe is available to me.

Valuing Positive Aspects

Caregivers reported that they valued family and social relationships, their impaired family member's love for them, the positive relationship they still experienced with their impaired family member, as well as prior memories and accomplishments. Their "Self-Talk" statements, noted earlier, also incorporated these positive aspects of care.

Searching For Provisional Meaning

Caregivers reported that some of the day-to-day experiences with their impaired family member and others provided them with a sense of provisional meaning. Some additional suggestions that caregivers made concerning stress management and methods through which provisional meaning might be found included: (a) sharing feelings with a caring friend or empathetic listener, (b) attending a support group, (c) expressing feelings in a journal, (d) engaging in positive self-talks, (e) learning to relax and maintaining a sense of humor, (f) exercising regularly, (g) participating in adequate leisure activities, (h) maintaining good dietary goals, and (i) avoiding use of nicotine, alcohol, caffeine, and drugs.

Searching For Ultimate Meaning

Caregivers reported being reassured by their philosophical and/or spiritual beliefs. While they suggested that meaningful rituals established prior to caregiving were very helpful in seeing them through this difficult experience, they also acknowledged that the caregiving experience challenged them to develop new methods of finding ultimate meaning and answering life's difficult questions.

Clinical practitioners might assist family caregivers to find meaning by encouraging them to: (1) express feelings of loss and powerlessness; (2) determine what choices can be made, even if it is just a choice of attitude toward their situation; (3) identify positive aspects of their situation; (4) identify ways in which they find provisional meaning through their situation; and (5) call upon their philosophical or spiritual beliefs as a means of finding ultimate meaning through this experience.

Future research efforts should focus more on examining positive aspects of caregiving, developing or using existing instruments that measure the finding meaning construct, and examining this constuct in relationship to other well-known caregiver variables.

References

Brody, E. 1990. *Women in the Middle: Their Parent-Care Years.* New York: Springer Publishing Company.

Farran, C.J., and E. Keane-Hagerty. 1989. Twelve steps for caregivers. *Amer J of Alzheimer's Care & Related Disorders and Research*, November/December:38–41.

Farran, C.J., E. Keane-Hagerty, S. Salloway, S. Kupferer, and C.S. Wilken. 1991. Finding meaning: an alternate paradigm for Alzheimer's disease family caregivers. *The Gerontologist* 31(4):483–89.

Frankl, V.E. 1963. *Man's Search for Meaning.* New York: Washington Square Press.

Levine, N.B., C.E. Gendron, D.P. Dastoor, L.R. Poitras, S.E. Sirota, S.L. Barza, and J.C. Davis. 1984. Existential issues in the management of the demented elderly patient. *Amer J Psychotherapy* 38(2):215–23.

Zarit, S.H., N.K. Orr, and J.M. Zarit. 1985. *The Hidden Victims of Alzheimer's Disease.* New York: New York University Press.

Carol J. Farran

Cholesterol Management

Coronary artery disease (CAD) continues to be the leading cause of death, especially in the western world. Despite significant success in reducing the death rate by 40 percent during the past 30 years, over 1.5 million adults suffer from new heart attacks each year in the United States alone; over 500,000 of them die each year. Along with smoking and high blood pressure, high blood cholesterol (hypercholesterolemia) has been recognized as a major risk factor for CAD. Recent studies have shown that by reducing your cholesterol by 1 percent you can reduce your risk of CAD by up to 2 percent. Added to that, a recent report has suggested that even those who have significant CAD can also expect a reversal of the hardening and narrowing (atherosclerosis) of coronary arteries by lowering their cholesterol levels.

In the United States, a National Cholesterol Education Program (NCEP) was launched in the mid-1980s following the convincing results of numerous cholesterol studies showing the relationship between high levels of cholesterol and CAD. Based on the blood cholesterol results in adults, the NCEP suggested the following three categories:

1. Cholesterol below 200 mg = normal
2. Cholesterol between 200–239 mg = borderline high cholesterol
3. Cholesterol of 240 mg and over = high cholesterol

Before discussing the management of high cholesterol, it is essential to understand the process of cholesterol synthesis and the mechanism of damage caused by high cholesterol; after all, individuals can take the right steps to control cholesterol only if they know the causes of the condition. Cholesterol is a waxy substance that is found in many food items including milk, eggs, cheese, butter, fish, and meat. Some amounts of cholesterol are necessary for the proper functioning of body cells. The synthesis of sex hormones and vitamin D metabolism requires the presence of cholesterol. Most cell membranes require small amounts of cholesterol for healthy functioning. Besides the amount of cholesterol taken from outside in various foods, the liver itself produces a large amount of cholesterol. It is important to remember that all the fat and cholesterol ingested from the diet is first metabolized in the liver. The cholesterol itself is converted into complex particles called lipoproteins. Two most important forms of lipoproteins are: (A) Low density lipoproteins (LDLs), and (B) High density lipoproteins (HDLs).

LDL is also called "bad" cholesterol since it is considered to be a major culprit in causing CAD. High levels of LDL cholesterol (over 130 mg) are associated with a significantly high risk of heart attacks. HDL is often referred to as "good" cholesterol. HDL helps in the transport and excretion of cholesterol from the liver. The normal adult level of HDL is 40–45 mg. Women tend to have higher amounts of HDL than men, at least until the menopausal age. One reason why women become equally at risk of developing heart disease after the age of 50 is the loss of estrogen and decline of HDL levels. With excessive blood concentration, the cholesterol continues to be deposited in the walls of the coronary arteries. Progressive blockage and occlusion of the arteries results in angina (chest pain on exertion) and heart attacks.

Between 35–50 percent of the adult U.S. population is estimated to have cholesterol levels of over 200 mg. In general, blood cholesterol tends to rise with aging. Although the precise cause of higher cholesterol levels remains unclear, altered cholesterol metabolism and the effects of multiple co-existing medical problems are thought to contribute to high cholesterol levels in old age.

Management of high cholesterol requires a clear understanding of the important causes that lead to this problem. Some of the recognized causes of high blood cholesterol are mentioned below.

HIGH DIETARY FAT AND CHOLESTEROL INTAKE

In some countries, such as China and Japan, the dietary fat and cholesterol intake are much lower than that of the United States. While the Japanese consume only 9 percent of the total calories from all types of fat and only 3 percent from animal fat, the typical western diet contains at least 3–4 times the amount of fat and cholesterol when compared to the Japanese diet. While an average adult should not take in more than 300 mg of cholesterol per day, an average American consumes between 500–600 mg of cholesterol. It is also important to understand the difference between saturated and unsaturated fats. Saturated fat is solid at room temperature and is mostly found in foods of animal origin (milk, butter, meat, and poultry). Some vegetable oils including coconut and palm oils also contain saturated fat. While the intake of all types of fat must be limited, it is the saturated fat that is more harmful. Unsaturated fat remains liquid at room temperature and is typically found in oils. Unsaturated fat may be monounsaturated or polyunsaturated. Rich sources of monounsaturated fat are found in corn, sunflower, and fish oils. In general, both monounsaturated and polyunsaturated fats are safer than saturated fats. Most fast foods tend to be rich in saturated fat and cholesterol contents.

COFFEE INTAKE

Caffeine is a stimulant of the nervous system, and helps the tired body and brain work more efficiently. For many years, caffeine has been suspected of being one of the causes of high blood cholesterol. Although the precise relationship of caffeine and cholesterol remains controversial, several studies have suggested a link of high caffeine intake with an increased risk of heart disease. It is advisable to restrict your coffee intake to no more than 3–4 cups per day.

ALCOHOL INTAKE

Although some reports have suggested a beneficial role of moderate alcohol intake (1–2 drinks per day), excessive alcohol intake is certainly harmful. It is not only hard liquor, such as whiskey or rum, that may cause problems; 12 fluid ounces of beer contains the same amount of alcohol as 1.5 ounces of vodka, gin, or whiskey, or 4 fluid ounces of wine or champagne. High alcohol intake is particularly associated with an increased level of triglycerides—a type of blood fat that is increasingly being recognized as an independent risk factor for coronary artery disease.

STRESS

Emotional stress has been recognized as a cause of high cholesterol in recent years. Based on the individual lifestyle, Drs. Rosenman and Friedman classified most people as belonging to two distinct categories, type A and type B personalities. The type A person is always in a rush and is short of time; the type B person has a relaxed personality. It has been reported that the biochemical changes and excessive stress hormone secretion by the glands in a type A person causes high levels of blood cholesterol. For example, it has been noted that accountants tend to have high cholesterol levels during the last four weeks of tax-filing deadline time (April 15).

LACK OF PHYSICAL EXERCISE

Physical exercise has been known to be beneficial for almost all body functions including the heart, muscles, bones, lungs, and brain. The incidence of several diseases such as CAD, obesity, diabetes mellitus, and gallstones is substantially lower in those who exercise regularly; exercise tends to raise the blood levels of HDL cholesterol (good cholesterol) and lower the levels of LDL cholesterol (bad cholesterol).

DIABETES MELLITUS

Diabetes mellitus is an age-prevalent condition. Many diabetics, especially the elderly, do not even know that they have diabetes. Numerous complications of diabetes are well recognized and include CAD, peripheral vascular disease, stroke, kidney failure, nerve damage (neuropathy), and loss of vision (retinopathy). However, the problem of high cholesterol and triglycerides in diabetics is an important one that has only been recognized in recent years. It is essential that all diabetic patients have their blood cholesterol checked at regular intervals. Better control of diabetes is usually sufficient to control high cholesterol in these patients.

MEDICATIONS

Elderly patients tend to have several co-existing age-prevalent illnesses such as heart disease, hypertension, diabetes mellitus, and arthritis. Multiple medical problems usually result in the use of multiple medications. An average older person in a long-term care facility, for example, is known to consume between 5 and 8 medications per day. Common medications such as beta blockers and diuretics may have an adverse effect on the blood cholesterol. These medications may not only raise the total and the LDL cholesterol, but also lower HDL. Patients using these medications must have their cholesterol checked at regular intervals.

LOWERING THE CHOLESTEROL LEVEL: ROLE OF DIET AND DRUGS

If the blood cholesterol is high, it must be reduced to below 200 mg. Besides total cholesterol, blood tests may also be required to check the HDL and LDL levels. In all cases, simple dietary changes (reduction of total calories, fat, and cholesterol) should be tried first. Fortunately, the vast majority of adults with high cholesterol do not require treatment with medication. Dietary changes require a thorough discussion with the physician and/or the dietitian. A complete medical history, family history, drug history, and food habits must be discussed with the physician. Dietary changes should be tried for a minimum of six months. Medication intake to lower the cholesterol may be indicated only if the dietary and lifestyle changes have failed to achieve the desired results.

Several newer agents have been developed to treat the problem of high cholesterol. Common medications that are prescribed for lowering cholesterol include cholestyramine, nicotinic acid, gemfibrozil, clofibrate, lovastatin, and probucol. Unfortunately, none of these medications are completely free from side effects. The use of medications is particularly hazardous in the elderly. Even so-called simpler medications often dispensed over-the-counter, such as nicotinic acid, may have serious side effects. It is strongly advised that all medications for lowering cholesterol be closely monitored and taken only under the direction of a physician.

References

Berg, D., L. Cantwell, G. Heudebert, and J.L. Sebastian, eds. 1993. Cholesterol evaluation and management. *Handbook of Primary Care Medicine*. Philadelphia: Lippincott.

Bilheimer, D.W. 1994. Lipid and lipoprotein metabolism, 1957–62; Disorders of lipid metabolism, 2052–65; Evaluation and therapy of abnormal lipid profiles, 2121–27. In W.N. Kelley, ed. *Textbook of Internal Medicine*, 2d ed., vol. 2. Philadelphia: Lippincott.

McBride, P.E. and G. Underbakke. 1994. Dyslipidemias. In R.B. Taylor, ed. *Family Medicine: Principles and Practice*, 4th ed. New York: Spring, 956–63.

Rosenman, R.H., M. Friedman, and R. Strauss. 1964. A predictive study of coronary heart disease: The Western Collaborative Group Study. *JAMA*, 189:15.

Krishan L. Gupta

Classification Systems of Patients

INTRODUCTION

Patient Classification Systems (PCS) may be broadly defined as "the grouping of patients according to some observable or inferred properties or characteristics" and "quantification of these categories as a measure of the nursing effort required."

The descriptions of patients' nursing care requirements are frequently referred to as critical indicators of care. Patients are assigned to an appropriate care category through assessment of the critical indicators. Two types of PCSs— prototype evaluation (subjective), and factor evaluation (objective)—exist and differ in the design of their classification instruments. Prototype evaluation generally describes the characteristics of the patients typical to each category. Factor evaluation lists a number of critical indicators or descriptions of direct care requirements that are separately rated and then combined to designate the patient category.

OVERVIEW

As early as the 1970s, Patient Classification Systems for home health care patients were described in the nursing literature. Daubert described the Rehabilitation Potential Patient Classification System (RPPCS) as implemented in one home health agency. Daubert's copyrighted method was developed as one component of a quality assurance program to evaluate patient outcomes. Daubert's system, a formal method of measuring patient outcomes, classifies all patients admitted to an agency's illness service program (regardless of the number of diagnoses per patient or the mix of agency services received) into one of five patient groups according to each patient's rehabilitation potential.

Abbreviated descriptions of Daubert's five patient groups are:

Group 1—Patients who will return to pre-illness level of functioning.

Group 2—Patients who are experiencing an acute episode of illness but have the potential for returning to pre-episode level of functioning.

Group 3—Patients with intermediate or advanced chronic diseases who will eventually function without agency services.

Group 4—Patients with advanced stage chronic diseases who will remain at home as long as possible with ongoing agency service.

Group 5—Patients will be maintained at home during the end stage of illness for as long as possible with agency service.

For each patient group, a specific ultimate objective and a separate set of subobjectives apply to all six illness service components: nursing, home health aide, physical therapists, speech therapists, occupational therapists, and medical social work.

During the 1980s, the Visiting Nurse Association of Eastern Montgomery County/Department of Abington Memorial Hospital (VNA) purchased the rights to use Daubert's RPPCS. The VNA has been collecting clinical and financial data on an ongoing basis since the mid-1980s, using the RPPCS and Nursing Diagnosis (ND). Data analysis has been completed in cooperation with staff and graduate students. The outcome of patient care and financial data have been shared through publications.

In the 1980s other PCSs were described in the nursing literature. The Visiting Nurse Association of Omaha developed an ND taxonomy for community health nursing. There are 44 NDs included in this taxonomy that are organized by four broad domains addressed by community health nurses: environment, psychosocial, physiological, and health behaviors. Each ND is described by a list of signs and symptoms. This system also includes general goals and specific, attainable patient behaviors.

The Easley-Storfjell Instruments for Caseload/Workload Analysis were designed to give home health care managers tools to obtain strategic information for planning, monitoring, and evaluating field staff activities simply and effectively. This process encompasses four steps that provide a method of analyzing the home health nurses' caseload and workload, providing valuable information for various levels of agency personnel.

Also during the 1980s, several authors shared findings related to the use of other parameters. Various PCSs used included: (1) using four NDs to represent four broad categories of home care patients; (2) the potential for using ND and/or acuity levels to determine nursing resources; (3) factors that were most predictive of nursing service and total agency service required by cardiac and cancer patients in home care agencies; and (4) the effects of a weighted PCS on the quality of care rendered, as indicated by nursing documentation on the assessment visit.

Additional PCS studies have been undertaken in the 1990s. Saba (1992) conducted a study at Georgetown University School of Nursing for the purpose of developing a method to assess and classify home health Medicare patients in order to predict their needs for nursing and other home care services, including their outcomes of care. A national sample of 646 home health agencies, randomly stratified by staff size, type of ownership, and geographical location were represented. In this study, data on 8,961 newly discharged cases were collected, representing each patient's total episodes of care from admission to, and discharge from, the home health agency. The Preliminary Home Health Care Classification System, based on a nursing model, offers to predict resource requirements for home health Medicare patients. Saba states that it could form the basis for a prospective payment system (PPS). Additionally, the coding scheme can be used for efficient documentation and improved reporting of home health care.

Boston University has begun a study that will refine an existing patient classification system for predicting lengths of home care visits. Another study that could make an important contribution to the Health Care Financing Administration (HCFA) is the ABT-Mathematica efforts to develop a Medicare prospective payment system by generating information on home care utilization by clients with lengthy visits. It is also intended to assist home care agencies to identify and monitor trends in acuity of illness and staffing needs. The Boston researchers will base their study on data to be gathered from more than 3,000 visits made by nurses over a 12-month period from 14 participating Massachusetts home care agencies. The study is being funded by the Agency for Health Care Policy and Research. All payer types will be represented in the study.

SUMMARY

Patient classification systems are useful as management tools for staffing, budgeting, monitoring productivity, costing, program planning, and quality assurance. As of June 1993, there is no single PCS that is accepted by or imposed on home health agencies. Home care administrators and staff must be alert to current and future PCS proposals. Involvement in the development of such a system is imperative and can be accomplished through data collection and analysis at each agency, sharing of findings through publications, and participation in pilot studies. This involvement is important since another issue closely related to a PCS is some still unknown prospective payment system for home care. The HCFA funded a Home Health Agency Prospective Payment Demonstration with ABT Associates, Inc. of Cambridge, Mass. HCFA is slated to receive a final report on the impact of this PPS on the participating agencies by 1997. Mathematica Policy Research of Princeton, N.J. will prepare the final evaluation of the demonstration.

The original 49 agencies in five states who signed on at the beginning of their fiscal year that started on or after October 1, 1990, are testing prospective payment on a per-visit basis. Phase Two is scheduled to begin in January, 1995, and will test PPS on a single payment for an entire episode of treatment, rather than for individual visits. [Henry Goldberg, PhD, ABT Associates, Cambridge, MA, 6/24/94 telephone conversation]

References

Anderson, H.J. 1992. Home care PPS demonstration project edges forward. *Trustee* March:13.

Daubert, E.A. 1979. Patient classification system and outcome criteria. *Nursing Outlook* 6:450–54.

NAHC Report No. 478:4. September 4, 1992. Washington, D.C.: National Association for Home Care.

Saba, V. 1992. *Home Health Care Classification Project.* Executive Summary. Washington, D.C.: Georgetown University.

Storfjell, J., C. Allen, and C. Easley. 1988. Caseload and workload analysis in home health care. In *Home Health Administration*, edited by M. Harris. Owings Mills, Md.: National Health Publications, 322–34.

Visiting Nurse Association of New Haven. 1980. *Patient Classification/Objectives System Methodology Manual.* New Haven, Conn.: VNA of New Haven.

Marilyn D. Harris

Classification Systems of Patients and the Prospective Payment System

The two historic federal legislative acts that have significantly impacted upon the development and expansion of home health services are Medicare and the Prospective Payment System (PPS). The first dealt with access; the second with cost containment.

The passage of Medicare in 1965 achieved to some degree the collapse of financial barriers and the promotion of access to health care for the elderly. Home health services were deemed reimbursable if provided by a Medicare-certified home health agency according to a treatment plan prescribed and reviewed by the physician. However, this could apply only to acute illness, which placed a limitation on the number of eligible beneficiaries. Another limitation was the prevailing cost-based system which favored inpatient care and encouraged prolonged hospitalization in lieu of discharging the patient to a lower level of care.

More recently, the issue of access has been replaced by cost containment. The basis for this was the new concern that the aged are disproportionately high utilizers of health care because of their vulnerability to chronic disease and greater demand for health service. Also, the spiralling increases in national health care expenditures significantly outpaced the growth of the general economy. This provided justification for change in the Medicare reimbursement program. In 1983, Congress legislated PPS for hospital care to replace the existing cost reimbursement system which had produced unacceptable costs and had served as a convenient mechanism to overutilize hospital services.

The implementation of PPS resulted not only in a drop in hospital lengths of stay, but also promoted the transfer of care from inpatient hospital settings to home health agencies. This demand for post-hospital services reaffirmed home health services as a valid and integral component of the care continuum for elderly recovering from acute illness.

From 1965 to the present, the home health industry expanded, as evidenced by the rapid growth in the number of agencies as well as the volume and services provided. According to the U.S. Department of Commerce report *Industrial Outlook—1993*, health spending will continue to rise at a double-digit pace, far faster than the general inflation rate. Reasons cited are: (1) the use of high-priced equipment; (2) increases in the variety and frequency of treatments; (3) costly treatments of major illnesses; (4) increased life span; and (5) the labor-intensive nature of the health care industry and the high earnings for professional, administrative, and technical workers.

ISSUES

Facing the nation is the economic imperative to find alternatives to costly patient hospital care and long-term institutionalization. The issues of affordability and accessibility continue to challenge policymakers, and home health services undoubtedly will continue to emerge as a means to reduce health care costs. Marketplace economics will continue to influence changes in home health care delivery, and efforts will be directed toward providing efficient and cost-effective services. Measuring patients' requirements for home health care, outcomes of services, and determining ways of reimbursing for services are being examined to develop a system that addresses the relevant issues. To achieve a match of patient needs and resources required in an environment where costs are a prime consideration is central to a care management system.

Medical Diagnosis

Although PPS provides reimbursement based on diagnosis-related groups (DRGs) for acute care hospitals, the use of a DRG-like payment system for other forms of care, such as home health care, has received some attention. A literature review suggests that, although the medical diagnosis using the International Classification of Diseases (ICD) serves as the logical basis for the treatment and prognosis of a specific disease, its use as a predictor of the types and intensity of services required or the length of time those services would be needed was judged to be poor. Taylor (1988) reported that medical diagnosis alone is not a reliable predictor of service use, but when combined with age, functional ability, and severity of illness, specificity can be improved. According to Lucke and Lucke (1988), the thoroughness and timeliness of health care for patients with a similar diagnosis vary, which, in turn, explains the variance in resource consumption. Factors thought to contribute to a severity of illness construct are the patient's baseline health status, that is, the degree of independence in physical functioning as related to the debilitating effects of disease, as well as the patient's response to therapy and the effectiveness of coping strategies.

Assessment Instruments

Long-term research has made it clear that patient assessment should focus on impairment and disability rather than on medical diagnosis. The World Health Organization defines impairments as abnormalities of the body structure and system function, and disabilities as the inability to perform activities independently. According to Rubenstein (1983), comprehensive assessment has become the cornerstone of geriatric medicine and implies the quantification of all relevant medical, functional, and psychosocial attributes and deficits to achieve a rational basis for therapy and resource planning.

A plethora of assessment instruments, along with their scales for every aspect of geriatric medicine and long-term care, now exists. The challenge in home health is to arrive at a method to secure relevant information to measure not only the patient's clinical status and progress, but also to evaluate the effectiveness of the home health program, and to establish criteria for admission to or discharge from home care.

Nursing Diagnosis

An approach to the identification of the patient's baseline health status is the Taxonomy of Nursing Diagnoses along with their etiologies and characteristics for nursing practice. The major purpose for such a taxonomy is to standardize nursing nomenclature for patient problems, since they can offer a clinical judgment to provide the basis for therapies for which the profession is accountable. Because nursing is a major component of health care, implementation of nursing diagnoses has been under way in a variety of health settings across the country. The refinement of this taxonomy has been ongoing since 1973. The home health setting, in particular, is viewed as the ideal milieu for actualizing its potential. It offers opportunity to exercise independent judgment regarding patients' health problems, to mobilize family and community resources, and to practice nursing holistically.

CLASSIFICATION

Currently, reimbursement to home health agencies is based on the cost per visit, as predetermined by the Medicare costing method, and accomplished by a utilization review of the patient record and the fulfillment of the 60-day certification and recertification requirements. The increasing use of home health services and the increasing costs of the visit are justifying the need by policymakers to consider PPS to substantiate necessary quality care in the least costly manner. The provision and monitoring of quality services at an affordable cost based on need, and at the appropriate level of care, is the rationale for patient classification. Since 1978, several systems for home health care delivery have been reported in the literature to guide health professionals in assessing patients, diagnosing their problems, planning interventions, and formulating outcome criteria by which progress toward the stated goals can be measured. Major studies conducted in service agencies and academia include:

1. *The Visiting Nurse Association of Omaha, Nebraska* designed a system which consists of a scheme in which patient problems are categorized into four domains: Environmental, Psychosocial, Psychological, and Health Related Behaviors. A rating scale for outcomes for each problem, measuring the concepts of Knowledge, Behavior, and Status provides the framework for action. Four broad areas are specified to describe the nature of the intervention: Health Teaching, Treatments, Case Management, and Surveillance. The system in its entirety simplifies documentation through standard terminology and enables health care professionals and administrators to make informed decisions regarding finances, staffing, and program management.

2. *The Visiting Nurse Association of New Haven, Connecticut* designed a method based on the rehabilitation potential of the patient regardless of diagnosis and mix of services given. Five categories of care, each with an identified set of objectives, are used to group patients. The range from Group I to Group V describes patients recovering from acute illness and returning to normal functioning, to patients who are at the end-stage of disease and in need of maintenance of comfort and dignity.

3. *The Home Health Care Classification Method, Georgetown University School of Nursing*, was designed to predict resource requirements and to measure outcomes. This was accomplished through the analysis of retrospective data on a large national sample of Medicare patients for an entire episode of home care, from admission to discharge. The study produced a 3-cohort model on the length and intensity of episodes of care: Short Term (less than 30 days), Intermediate (30–120 days), and Long Term (120 days plus). Four sets of variables (Nursing, Medical, Functional, and Sociodemographic Assessments) were scored for a value, using a method calculated from the research design. These were used to determine resource requirements in terms of the three cohorts of time and volume of provider visits. In addition, the project provided coding schemes for the Classification of Home Health Nursing Diagnoses and Interventions.

CONCLUSION

Although significant effort has been demonstrated and replicated to produce systems with measurement instruments and scales that relate patient classification to resource requirements or to patient outcomes, research continues. In time, reliable and valid models on which to base an equitable reimbursement program will gain acceptance and guide policymakers in the development of PPS for home care in their overall efforts to contain health care costs.

References

Industrial Outlook—1993. U.S. Department of Commerce. (NTIS No. PB 111276). Springfield, Va.

Kim, M.J. 1989. Nursing diagnosis in home health nursing. In *Home Health Care Nursing*, edited by I.M. Martinson and A. Widmer. Philadelphia: Saunders, 58–65.

Lucke, K., and J. Lucke. 1988. Severity of illness and nursing intensity as predictors of treatment costs. In *Patient Classification and Cost Management*, edited by F.A. Schaffer. New York: National League for Nursing (Pub. No. 20–2155), 181–95.

Rubenstein, L. 1983. The clinical effectiveness of multidimensional geriatric assessment. *J Geriatric Society* 31(12):758–62.

Saba, V.K., and A.E. Zuckerman. 1992. A new home health classification method. *Caring* October:27–34.

Taylor, M.B. 1988. An examination of the relationship between home health service use and primary diagnosis. *Home Health Service Quarterly* 9(4):47–60.

Jennifer Boondas

Cognitively Impaired Elders and Family Care

INTRODUCTION

Today, more and more families are caring for relatives who suffer from a cognitive impairment. Approximately 2 million to 4 million persons in the United States (10% of those aged 65 and older) have some form of cognitive impairment. The proportion increases to 47 percent for the population over age 85. It is estimated that 70 percent to 80 percent of these victims are cared for by their families. In most studies, a higher prevalence has been found for females.

Cognitive change is associated with normal aging. Nevertheless, it is a fallacy that old age creates symptoms of dementia. The term "dementia" is used to describe a group of symptoms. It is not the name of a disease that causes the symptoms. The most common forms of dementia are Alzheimer's disease and Multi-Infarct disease. Other causes include Pick's disease, Parkinson's disease, Creutzfeldt-Jakob disease, and Huntington's Chorea disease. Of these, between 50 percent and 75 percent of dementia cases are caused by Alzheimer's disease.

The overall incidence of Alzheimer's disease ranges from 69 cases per 100,000 to about 127 cases per 100,000. Unadjusted, incidence rates for people age 80 and older range from 1,500 to over 3,000 cases per 100,000. By comparison, these rates are substantially higher than the annual incidence of all cancers combined for the same age group. Differential survival rates by ethnicity have been reported.

MANIFESTATIONS OF ALZHEIMER'S DISEASE

Alzheimer's disease is an irreversible, progressive deterioration of human brain tissue. There are four progressive stages: impairment of recent memory, loss of reason, incomprehension, and the loss of instinctive action. The most common behavioral changes that are exhibited in this type of dementia are: confusion, wandering, suspiciousness, changes in personality traits, agitation, sexually explicit activity, and depression.

The earliest feature is loss of recent memory, for example, the person becomes unable to judge the passing of time. Their confusion is marked by their repeatedly asking the question, "What time is it?" Another characteristic is wandering that occurs at all hours of the day and night. Wandering is most common in the earlier phases of the disease because some degree of functioning is required. Closely related to wandering is searching. An assumption here is that the victim is obsessed with trying to find anything familiar to hold on to as they become more and more confused. Changes in personality produce demanding behavior or even verbal abuse. This behavior signals the family about the person's level of loneliness or fear. Caregivers quickly become aware that if demands are not met (or are redirected), agitation follows. In fact, these individuals often become aggressive and will show heightened levels of suspiciousness. Persons with Alzheimer's disease seem to have a keen sense of their impairment. Often, symptoms of depression are presented.

Some researchers argue that, basically, what dementia patients need is social intervention, not medical intervention. Although physical impairments and cognitive impairments are often related, they are very distinct impairments. Onset of dementia varies by disease. Further, not all cognitive impairments are as severe as Alzheimer's disease nor are all cognitive changes indicators of dementia.

Caregiving for a cognitively impaired individual differs from caregiving for individuals with physical impairments. The manifestations of dementia (e.g., wandering, reversal of day and night, aggressive or embarrassing behavior) are quite different, and appear to be more upsetting to caregivers than are the needs of physically impaired elders. How families respond to the challenge varies according to their own levels of physical and mental health. Reactions are strongly influenced by the caregiver's level of well-being and knowledge of the disease and its symptoms.

FAMILY CAREGIVERS

A critical role in families pertains to care and nurturance. According to Semple (1992), roughly two-thirds of all dementia patients receive their care at home from a family member. The primary caregiver role will generally fall first on the spouse, then an adult child, usually the daughter. Forty percent of family caregivers are daughters or daughters-in-law and over half are wives. Noelker

(1990) found that wives who are primary caregivers are "hidden patients" who need attention and social support. Other researchers see the family as the "hidden victims" of Alzheimer's disease. In general, this is a vulnerable population, subject to varying degrees of emotional effects.

Love, devotion, and loyalty are common reasons given by primary caregivers for taking on the responsibility of care. Yet, studies have shown that a greater amount of strain results when the caregiver-recipient bond is strong. Women get more emotionally attached; they also report the highest levels of emotional exhaustion.

Much of the caregiving literature, including issues of burden and, more recently, conflict, has focused exclusively on caregivers for Alzheimer's elders. Caregivers of dementia patients are at high risk for emotional distress along with reduced levels of well-being. Conflict, burden, and strain are outcomes of home caregiving. What is unclear, though, is how much stress is too much stress, and is the impairment the primary stressor? Some studies assert that the stresses of caregiving are not necessarily associated with the level of elder functioning or involvement, but rather the familial relationship itself. It is the quality of the family's relationship that is significant in determining how the caregiver perceives the consequences of the role and how they cope. Generally, outcomes for family caregivers are declines in emotional well-being, physical health, financial resources, changes in personal goals, and work and leisure schedules. Emotional stress can result from feelings of being overwhelmed from 24-hour caregiving, in addition to a sense of alienation from the rest of the family. Each can lead to depression. Research indicates that the key to successful home care is respite.

These influences also relate to conflict and its effect on caregiving and on caregiver well-being. Family relationships can provoke conflict and lead to caregiver depression. Caregivers' views of their performance as a caregiver—their sense of value and competence—are mirrored through negative self-evaluations. Ultimately, the family's functioning, its physical, emotional, social, and monetary resources are affected. These findings underscore the need for more research into family discourse.

Care of this disease invokes radical changes within the family structure. One of the main reasons is the demand involved in round-the-clock caregiving; however, for families who have an understanding about the disease and know what to expect, the transition is easier. Coupled with ongoing feedback from the health care provider, these families can successfully provide care for many years to persons with Alzheimer's disease. Today, formal behavior therapy techniques can easily be adapted to home care. For instance, the victim can be encouraged to keep a diary. This tool has a dual purpose: it aids the victim's memory and, for the caregiver, it provides a log of the progression of the disease.

Studies suggest that the most satisfying activities for these individuals, at each stage of their dementia, are domestic and social in nature. Activities that help preserve the victim's dignity are reading the newspaper to them (in intervals), having them watch their favorite television program, and having them listen to the radio. Further, prompting them to look regularly at clocks and calendars helps the victim have a grasp on the present.

On the other hand, care requiring hands-on assistance produces high levels of distress for the care provider (e.g., dressing, eating, toileting, and attention to self-care and hygiene). As the disease progresses, increased burden results. Nevertheless, the greatest impact on well-being is the way the caregiver responds; that is, how they cope. Studies indicate that faulty coping styles of family caregivers rank as the primary stressor to the family.

Most literature has focused on the negative effects of caregiving and ignored the positive effects. There is some evidence that positive outcomes result from caregiving for Alzheimer's elders. For example, some caregivers who find they have absolutely no control in certain situations of extreme stressors change focus and search for a richer understanding of the situation. Role-playing with the elder allows the caregiver to spend a few moments exploring the victim's world. This produces positive effects for the elder and the caregiver by lessening levels of distress, enhancing the elder's dignity, and bringing new meaning to the caregiver's role. Role-playing is one aspect of validation therapy used in nursing homes today for the care of Alzheimer's disease residents.

According to some researchers, cognitive impairments are leading predictors of institutionalization. Studies show that families caring for individuals suffering from dementia are a particularly high-risk population for nursing home use. More research is needed that focuses on the social aspects of dementia and its ramifications. Issues of family structure and process also need more attention. Accordingly, information about the meanings of roles, statuses, family interaction, and family histories may help to explain conflict and burden, as well as coping in caring for cognitively impaired family members.

References

Abel, E.K. 1991. *Who Cares for the Elderly? Public Policy and the Experiences of Adult Daughters*. Philadelphia: Temple University Press.

Alzheimer's Disease and Related Disorders Association, Inc. 1990. *Alzheimer's Disease Statistics*. Chicago: Alzheimer's Disease and Related Disorders Association, Inc.

Baldwin, B. 1990. Family caregiving: trends and forecasts. *Geriatric Nursing* July/August:173–74.

Noelker, L. 1990. Family caregivers: a valuable but vulnerable resource. In *The Vulnerable Aged: People, Services, and Policies*, edited by Z. Harel, P. Ehrlich, and R. Hubbard. New York: Springer Publishing Company.

Semple, S.J. 1992. Conflict in Alzheimer's caregiving families: its dimensions and consequences. *The Gerontologist* 32:648–55.

Stevenson, J. 1990. Family stress related to home care of Alzheimer's disease patients and implications for support. *J Neuroscience Nursing* 22:179-88.

Donald E. Stull and Karen L. Rice

Communicating with the Elderly

In 1952, the field of gerontology was considered uninteresting and unchallenging by most young medical students. Fortunately, the knowledge gained about the elderly since then has stimulated interest, caring, and communication with older people. Much of the knowledge we now have about communicating with the elderly was gained through many mistakes and misperceptions. Using appropriate behaviors and language with older persons is extremely important to foster compliance, to gain trust, and to develop a truly open and reciprocal relationship with patients in this older age group.

The reasons for inability to communicate fully with older persons are multiple. A major cause is the person's decreasing ability regarding the senses, especially hearing and vision. There may also be diminished mental acuity and perception. Cognitive impairment may be present as a result of Alzheimer's disease or stroke.

Based on these and other factors, several rules should be borne in mind about behaviors and approaches that are *not* to be used. First, one cannot be patronizing. The immediate use of first names is not advisable, unless this familiarity is suggested by the individual. Older people grew up and were educated in a different, more formal, era. Early in this century, even spouses called one another "Mr. Jones" or "Mrs. Jones," particularly in conversation with others.

Most older persons do not appreciate being treated as though they are old. Eighty-five-year-olds will insist that they are not old, but that the ninety-three-year-old neighbor *is* old. Age, like time, is relative, dependent on such factors as perception, level of self-esteem, state of health, degree of physical and mental ability, agility, and others.

Similarly, older people are not easily impressed with professionals such as doctors, lawyers, dentists, nurses, or others. Their experiences have shown them that most people do not belong on pedestals, and titles or degrees do not inspire awe or subservience.

All patients, regardless of age, should be involved in developing the treatment plan, if they are capable of making these kinds of decisions. They know, better than the physician or nurse, what they can do, like to do, want to do. The goal of treatment is improved health status. Compliance is essential for achieving this and other goals. Without the individual's full and complete cooperation, any well-developed treatment plan is doomed to failure.

Diagnostic testing and procedures should be kept to an absolute minimum. Older persons as a group have the physical problems associated with normal aging—variable alimentary absorption, decreased liver function, and impaired

renal clearance. Performing tests that require high technology may be unnecessary and yield little in the way of useful additional information about the
individual's condition. Those tests that are needed should be explained in detail,
and include the reasons for having them done. Older persons, many of whom
grew up during a time when even television was not commercially available,
may resist the use of technology in their care. The wise provider is aware of
these possible feelings and reactions.

Older people like explanations that really describe what will happen. While
they may not be familiar with medical jargon, they understand when adequately
detailed explanations are given, using stories or anecdotes, and especially if the
descriptions are graphically shown with pictures, drawings, videotapes, or other
kinds of visual aids. Patient teaching, particularly with older persons, requires
great skill and creativity, but the rewards often far outweigh the extra time and
attention given to these important aspects of care.

Older persons may need others to make the final decisions for them. They
may have periods of confusion, or limited attention spans, and may not be able
to take in the situation no matter how carefully it is explained. For these individuals, lengthy explanations and having to choose among several options may
be overwhelming. In these cases, the professional must assist the patient to
decide on the best course of action. Careful reasoning and expressing true concern for the person are particularly important in these decision-making situations, when other family members may need to be included in the process. Avoid
unnecessary details while being precise and concise in providing information or
teaching. Most older people, regardless of mental status, can better take in and
understand short, simple sentences and instructions.

As with patients of all ages, professionals need to listen to what the patient
is saying. The message that older persons are attempting to convey may go
beyond mere words; therefore, it is essential to listen very carefully to everything
that they say in order to pick up clues about how they are feeling, what fears
they may have, or what else needs to be asked or discussed.

STAYING ON TRACK

Because older persons sometimes get off the track, talk about matters other
than why they came for treatment, or simply like to talk, the professional should
keep in mind some strategies for allowing as much interchange as possible
without falling behind in the day's schedule. The provider may need to take
charge of the interaction by anticipating needs and expectations, and discussing
these early in the encounter. These communication strategies include the following.

Request that the patient set priorities. Ask what the major problem is, from
their perspective, then lesser problems. Determine which of these should be
discussed immediately, and which might be deferred to another visit. Review
their list of perceived problems, and decide if the priorities, as set by the patient,

are in the order that the provider believes is appropriate. Priorities are based on severity of the problem, and threat to the patient's health, safety, and functional status. The provider should inform the patient about parameters, with regard to the allotted time, and when the appointment will likely have to end. At the conclusion of the appointment, counteract any disappointment on their part by being encouraging and positive about their progress, cooperation, etc. Let them know that you welcome discussions about their problems, and look forward to their next visit. Try to make each patient feel special. It is important to see the patient on a regular basis to monitor progress. Regular visits, even for asymptomatic geriatric patients, will likely enable them to remain in their present living environment and out of the hospital. Encourage them to call between visits, if a problem comes up that they cannot cope with without assistance. If not given encouragement, older persons frequently hesitate to intrude on a busy provider's time. It is up to the provider to let patients know that they may call at any time. A telephone conversation may allay fears, explain details of the treatment regimen more clearly, and relieve patients' anxieties or confusion.

PATIENT MISCONCEPTIONS

Another cause of miscommunications or incomplete communication is because the patient has, in the past, relied on erroneous or outdated information. Much that is written about health in the popular press does not take into account differences that occur with aging, such as digestion, absorption, effects of drugs, and others. Slight elevations in cholesterol, blood sugar, or blood pressure may not require specific therapy in older people. They often need to be reassured that these and other changes that are occurring as they get older are simply natural aging processes, and not necessarily an indication of decreasing health status or potential problems. What is important for older people to consider is that their senses may be less acute, that it's important for them to arrange their living quarters so that falls can be prevented, that too many drugs can be just as dangerous as not enough of the right drugs and the right dosages of drugs, and that some days are better than others. Older people, in other words, need to become oriented to getting older, get used to new limitations, and adjust to changes as they occur.

One of the overlooked problems that occur with aging is the gradual diminution of short-term memory. Therefore, instructions should be written, be short, be clear. Repetition is frequently necessary in talking with the elderly individual.

However, the provider has the responsibility of sifting through the patient's comments, questions, problems, and symptoms to arrive at real and potential problems that might affect the health and functional status of the person, both short- and long-term. The primary goal of communicating with older persons is to keep them as healthy as possible for as long as possible, by discovering problems early and treating them appropriately to avoid hospitalization or long-term institutionalization. By keeping in mind the special needs of older persons and enhancing communications, this goal can be achieved more easily.

References

Arnold, R., L. Forrow, and L.R. Barker. 1990. Medical ethics and doctor-patient communication. In *The Medical Interview: A Textbook on Medical Interviewing*, edited by M. Lipkin, S.M. Putnam, and A. Lazare. New York: Springer-Verlag.

Bertakis, K.D. 1994. Interpersonal communications with patients. In *Family Medicine: Principles and Practice*, 4th ed. Edited by R.B. Taylor. New York: Springer-Verlag, 24–28.

Schulman, E.D., ed. 1982. The what and how of interviewing: how to get out of the client's way. In *Intervention in Human Services: A Guide to Skills and Knowledge*, 3rd ed. St. Louis: Mosby, 206–243.

Eric G. Anderson

Computers and Home Health Care

Computer technology is revolutionizing the health care industry. Its effects are evident in the majority of today's home health agencies, physicians' offices, hospitals, and homes. Computer technology is used in tomography (CT scan), high speed electrocardiograph machines (ECG), thermometers that take a person's temperature by placing a probe in the ear, and digital blood pressure cuffs that are easy enough for an elderly person to use in the home.

Today's patients come into the hospital sicker and their length of stay is shorter, requiring more home care than that needed ten or even five years ago. The decrease in length of stay and the increasing need for patient follow-up in the home environment is causing home health agencies to become more effective and efficient in administering care. In order to achieve this efficiency, agencies have pursued computerization of financial and clinical data.

HARDWARE

Computers have come a long way since the ENIAC (Electronic Numerical Integrator and Computer) built in 1946 by J. P. Eckert and J. W. Mauchly at the University of Pennsylvania. This computer filled a 20 by 40 foot room and contained approximately 18,000 vacuum tubes. Today's desktop personal computers can process more data in less time than the ENIAC of yesteryear. No wonder personal computers have had a direct effect on the home care industry. The cost and size of the computer has decreased while the power to store and process data has vastly increased. It is estimated that the health care industry will spend more than a billion dollars on computer technology in the next few years.

Computer System

A computer system is a complete electronic information processing center. It can calculate, store, process, and retrieve data. It can take raw data (e.g., numbers) and turn it into valuable information (e.g., a graph). Computer hardware consists of a CPU (central processing unit), computer monitor (a visual display), usually a computer keyboard with a mouse and/or light pen, modem, and printer.

Input Devices. Inputting information into the computer may be achieved via a computer keyboard, touch screen monitor, color monitor, mouse, optical scanner, tape or compact disc read only memory (CD-ROM), and modem (modulation and demodulation—a communications device via telephone lines).

Central Processing Unit (CPU). The CPU is the brains of the computer system. It is where all data are processed into information. The CPU is divided into three components: internal memory (RAM—random access memory—and ROM—read only memory), arithmetic/logic (calculations and step-by-step process), and control (communication between input and output and controls information processing).

Output Devices. Output is the end result of data that has been processed. Common output devices include modems, monitors, pointers, plotters, optical discs, magnetic tape, and floppy disks.

SOFTWARE

Instructions to the computer that tell the computer what to do are called software. These programs include disk operating systems, word processing, databases, spreadsheets, and games. These programs range from launching space ships at Cape Kennedy to producing computerized imaging of malignant tumors.

COMPUTER TECHNOLOGY

By the year 2000, it is estimated that 100 percent of all home health agencies will be computerized. Already, computer literacy is an accepted expectation, and computers are a part of everyday life.

Recipes will be called up on the computer and a printout of the ingredients will be retrieved with information about the nutritional value of the meal, plus contraindications to medications or diet restrictions.

The efficiency of using computer technology is being felt in the home care field. Several issues are forcing automation: increased competition among home health agencies, emergency clinics, diagnostic centers, and group medical practices; increasing numbers of underinsured or uninsured patients; increasing number of frail elderly who would like to stay in their own home; and the enormous amount of paper work required for Medicare and Medicaid.

NURSING MINIMUM DATA SET

Werley and Lang (1988) proposed a minimum data set for nursing to determine what information is needed to provide quality care. They divided the data into the following groups:

• Nursing Care Elements—nursing diagnosis, intervention, outcome, and intensity;

• Client Demographics—identification, date of birth, address, and other universal data;

• Service Elements—service agency number, medical record number, health care provider, episode of care start date and termination date, and expected payer.

In the late 1970s, the Omaha Visiting Nurse Association developed a classification scheme for community health nursing. The classification grouping consisted of four domains: environmental, physiologic, psychosocial, and health-related behaviors. The coding process has proven to be viable and has provided a framework for assuring quality of home care.

The need for a uniform nursing minimum data set is urgent. However, though many classification domains and categories have been defined, more research is needed.

INFORMATION SYSTEMS

An information system is a formalized mechanism for integrating data from various sources to provide information necessary for making decisions. Information systems can process medical procedure data such as ECGs, pulmonary function test results, and laboratory data, while retrieving financial data about insurance and guarantor information. Large amounts of information can be processed into a report that can be instantaneously available by means of a predefined keystroke on the computer keyboard and printed in the main office while copies are being printed in branch offices or other designated locations.

Hospital information systems were originally designed to handle financial information. As hospitals began to recognize the cost saving associated with using information systems, inpatient clinical systems were developed.

Hospitals and home health agencies began using information systems to reduce costs and to save time, thereby increasing the organization's cost effectiveness and efficiency while maintaining quality patient care. Having information systems is also a competitive advantage in today's environment of diminishing resources.

DEVELOPING INFORMATION SYSTEMS

Information needs are determined by the decisions to be made. Management uses information for two major purposes—planning and evaluation. In the planning phase, objectives must be defined and the strategies for meeting the objectives determined. The evaluation phase evaluates the actual outcome by measuring the extent to which objectives are achieved.

Information systems have been successful in providing information that is structured, routine, and predictive for making decisions. Several phases occur in the development of an information system:

1. Needs Assessment—the organization determines precisely what information is needed to ensure optimal operational activities. In one instance, ability to retrieve abnormal laboratory data is necessary. The needs assessment also delineates constraints, such as insufficient funding. Essential to a successful needs assessment is to have those people who will be using the system involved in its development.

2. Structured Analysis—this phase focuses on developing a budget based on the needs assessment. In addition, a schedule for the design and implementation of the project is set up.

3. Hardware—the technical staff decide on the electrical needs and computer hardware required to run the system.

4. Design—the computer staff decide on the number of individual programs to be designed, for example, a separate program for each of the ancillary departments may be needed. Priorities must also be determined. Aspects of the programs to be considered are the purpose, scope, utility, expansion capability, and other similar features.

5. Implementation—this phase requires the development of all coding systems congruent with the information to be processed. Interfaces between or among programs are considered and established as needed.

6. Testing Phase—the system is run experimentally before actual full activation occurs. Errors must be identified and fixed at this phase.

7. Downtime Procedures—at times when the computer is "down" (not operating or being repaired), alternative fill-in procedures must be adopted.

8. Training—training for all personnel who will be using the system must occur simultaneously with implementation and testing, so that when the system is fully activated, people will be able to use it.

9. Activation—the system becomes fully operational. Ongoing monitoring and evaluation of the system are carried out to determine errors, to define areas for expansion, and to decide what additions must be incorporated into the system.

10. Audit and Maintenance—this process is continuous and often determines the ultimate success of the system.

HOME CARE MARKET

Many home health agencies have automated their inventory systems, personnel files, financial data, and are in the process of using laptop computers for entering patient clinical data in the client's home. Information such as the following can be monitored, updated, and stored in the computer.

1. private services—the need for private duty nurses, sitters, live-ins, and housekeepers.
2. Professional intermittent services—visits by professional nurses, therapists, social workers, etc.
3. Medical supplies—hospital beds, wheelchairs, ambulatory aids, etc.
4. High-tech home care—including home infusion, nutritional therapies (TPN), etc.

CONCLUSION

Home health agencies must be competitive while providing quality patient care. With a keystroke and the client's name, a visiting nurse is able to access the care plan, find where to call for a wheelchair, schedule laboratory work for the client, and transfer all information back to the home office via a modem connected to the laptop computer and a telephone. The benefits of automation are reduction in duplication of information, errors, time, and cost, and enhancement of efficiency and quality of care.

References

Fishman, D. 1993. Nursing informatics: the electronic information revolution. *Nursing Issues in the 90s.* Albany, N.Y.: Delmar.

———. 1988. Computers in health care. In *Diversified Health Occupations*, 2d ed. Edited by L. Simmers. Albany, N.Y.: Delmar, 114–24.

———. 1994. Nursing informatics: the electronic information revolution in education and practice. In *Nursing Issues in the 1990s.* Edited by O.L. Strickland and D.J. Fishman. Albany, N.Y.: Delmar, 471–88.

Goodwin, D.R. 1992. Critical pathways in home health care. *J Nurs Admin* 22(2):35–40.

Hettinger, B., and R.P. Brazile. 1992. A database for community health data. *Computers in Nursing* 10(3):109–20.

Martin, K.S., and N.J. Scheer. 1988. The Omaha System: providing a framework for assuring quality of home care. *Home Healthcare Nurse* 6(3):24–28.

Pulliam, L., and E. Boettcher. 1989. A process for introducing computerized information systems into long-term care facilities. *Computers in Nursing* 8(6):251–56.

Werley, H.H., and N.M. Lang. 1988. *Identification of the Nursing Minimum Data Set.* New York: Springer.

Dorothy J. Fishman

D

Dementia and Behavioral Management

Dementia, a condition characterized by impaired cognition and frequently accompanied by behavioral and emotional problems, becomes increasingly common as individuals age. The incidence of dementia in a community-based population of individuals over the age of 85 years has been estimated to be as high as 47 percent. The rapidly growing elderly segment of the population in this country will likely lead to dementia becoming an increasingly common health problem. Demented older adults can remain in their homes with proper care long after the onset of their cognitive decline. However, since dementia predisposes individuals to developing impaired judgment and behavioral disturbances, several issues should be addressed when contemplating caring for a demented individual in the home.

Maintaining a demented individual in the home requires providing for their basic needs. In addition, a comprehensive care approach should be initiated to preserve social and functional skills. Treatment goals should include the management of cognitive impairment and associated behavioral problems. These goals are more easily accomplished when caregivers are cognizant of certain underlying issues related to the care of demented individuals. Although the basic problem in dementia is cognitive loss and therefore appears as a simple neurologic condition, dementia is actually a more generalized neuropsychiatric condition resulting in profound functional loss. Successful care of demented individuals must recognize this generalized functional loss as central. Recognizing dementia as a broad-based loss of function allows a relatively optimistic view toward its management instead of the prevailing narrow view of dementia as a progressive loss of cognition with little or no chance at effective intervention.

A closely related aspect of dementia care is the importance of a multidisciplinary approach. The disease-oriented approach of the traditional medical model is inadequate for elderly health care. The fields of geriatrics and gerontology have long recognized that successful care of the elderly must address functional needs as well as medical problems. In fact, studies have shown improved outcomes for older individuals following illness when their health care delivery is broadly integrated to address psychological and social issues in addition to medical problems. Therefore, health care professionals from a variety of disciplines should participate in the care of the elderly. This is particularly true for demented individuals whose psychological and social needs are often intensive.

An essential component of this care is a primary caregiver (usually a spouse or adult child) who is educated about the dementing condition and has reasonable expectations. Other important components may include a physician skilled in the management of problems of the aged, a home health aide with specialized training, and a case manager (usually an individual with training in social work). Individuals with particularly intensive needs can be admitted to a long-term home health care program (''nursing home without walls''); this permits different services to be delivered under the auspices of a single program. Other care components that can enhance the caregiver's ability to maintain the individual in the home include an adult day care program specialized for individuals with cognitive impairment, and a respite care program that is available to care for the individual for a finite period of time to enable the primary caregiver to take periodic vacations. The abilities of the primary caregiver to have time away and obtain appropriate emotional support through organized support groups dedicated to the caregivers of the elderly demented is critical to the success of the situation.

Caring for a demented individual in the home often requires making specific adjustments to the environment in order to protect the individual from untoward events that may occur as a result of the poor judgment that is often seen in dementia. These include the installation of specific devices to prevent a demented individual from wandering from their home during times when their caregiver is unable to provide close supervision (for example, at night or during bathing). Any devices limiting the demented individual's freedom should include a system to allow escape during emergencies such as fire. It is always a good idea to inform local police and fire agencies of the presence of a cognitively impaired individual.

Unfortunately, there are no clearly effective treatments to reverse or slow the inexorable cognitive decline seen in individuals with the major dementing diseases, including senile dementia of the Alzheimer type (SDAT) and multi-infarct dementia. Although a small percentage of dementias have potentially reversible causes (hypothyroidism, drugs, tertiary syphilis, B12 and folate deficiency), the majority are not amenable to intervention. SDAT is associated with significant decreases in the central nervous system neurotransmitter, acetylcholine, as well as striking reductions in the number of cholinergic neurons. This discovery has prompted a series of trials to administer cholinesterase inhibitors or acetylcholine analogs with promising but inconclusive results. In multi-infarct dementia, impaired cognition stems from areas of nonfunctioning brain tissue resulting from a procession of infarctions due to atherosclerotic disease of cerebral blood vessels. While there is no therapy that will replace lost nervous tissue, there is evidence that low-dose acetylsalicylic acid (aspirin) therapy, as low as 30 mg per day, can effectively lower the incidence of future strokes. In addition, effective control of hypertension can also reduce the incidence of further cerebrovascular accidents.

While there are as yet no clearly effective treatments for the cognitive decline associated with dementia, behavioral and emotional disturbances can be managed effectively. These aspects of dementing illness often prevent the demented individual from remaining in the home. Demented individuals often develop deficient judgment and behavioral disturbances that may resemble primary psychiatric disease. Cognition and judgment problems can be managed by constant supervision. However, dementia-related behavioral disturbances often require specific management techniques to prevent the behaviors from threatening the ability of caregivers to maintain the individual in the home. Techniques for managing behavioral manifestations of dementia incorporate psychotherapy, pharmacotherapy, and various nonpharmacologic modalities.

Contrary to popular thought, psychotherapy may be useful in the management of emotional and behavioral manifestations of dementia. The specific approach must be carefully designed to consider the stage of the individual's dementing condition. The dynamic nature of dementing illness should also be considered when choosing a psychotherapeutic approach. In addition, the approach must include a degree of flexibility to allow for disease progression. Early in the course of dementia, a relatively complex form of psychotherapy requiring considerable involvement and insight from the patient may be used to manage chronic anxiety and depression.

Rage with violent behavior may develop in some moderately demented individuals. This stems from a high level of frustration that results from a significant degree of functional loss that they experience as the dementia progresses. As the dementia progresses and the individual loses the ability to gain insight into the cause of their feelings, a more directive form of psychotherapy with the goal of supporting the patient through their struggle can be applied. A related approach known as reminiscence therapy is often applied in demented individuals because long-term memory may be preserved well into the cognitive decline. Several strategies can be utilized depending on the individual's pre-morbid personality, the stage of their dementing illness, and the involvement of caregivers. The advice of a mental health professional (psychiatrist, psychologist, or other psychotherapist) with training and experience in treating the elderly is invaluable when a psychotherapeutic approach is being contemplated.

Apart from psychotherapy, there are several nonpharmacologic management techniques that can reduce the incidence of dysfunctional behavior. These include socialization, exercise, sensory stimulation, and adequate nutrition. Maintaining social contacts is an important way for demented individuals to preserve their sense of individuality. However, the degree and level of socialization must be appropriate to the individual's cognitive level. Socialization requiring skills beyond the demented individual's capacity may produce feelings of inadequacy. Sensory stimulation includes both passive and active techniques. These are often combined with socialization such as in an adult day care program. Regular exercise is considered beneficial for persons of all ages and the demented elderly are no exception. In this population exercise is particularly beneficial in maintaining normal function in the face of cognitive decline. The demented elderly are at risk for poor nutrition for several reasons including loss of appetite, depression, deglutition problems, and inability to provide for themselves. Therefore, the provision of adequate nutrition for the demented individual is very important and should be a deliberate part of their management.

Behavioral problems often become severe enough to warrant pharmacologic intervention. This treatment should be carried out by a physician who is trained in the use of psychoactive medications and is familiar with their use in this population (psychiatrist or internist/family practitioner with geriatric training). There are several important factors to consider before embarking on a course of pharmacologic therapy to manage dysfunctional behavior in a demented individual. These include age, associated medical conditions, and the nature of the problematic behavior. Major classes of psychoactive medications that are appropriate for the management of dysfunctional behavior in this population include antipsychotics, antiaggression medications, antianxiety medicine (anxiolytics), and antidepressants. Obviously, the nature of the problematic behavior will determine the choice of agent. Within individual classes, individual agent types have various pros and cons and should be chosen on a case-by-case basis, depending on the needs of the individual. In addition, close attention should be paid to the potential for toxic side effects, as well as deleterious interactions with other medications the individual may be taking.

Antipsychotic medications (also known as neuroleptics and "major tranquilizers") are the mainstay of treatment designed to alleviate the behavioral complications associated with dementia. The widespread use of antipsychotics is based more on anecdotal reports and empiric evidence of their effectiveness rather than on an established body of research. The effectiveness of antipsychotics lies mainly in their utilization for situational control where the demented individual develops behavioral disturbances unpredictably. They are effective for a common problem seen in the demented elderly known as nocturnal conceptual disorganization ("sundowning") and are particularly useful for more typical "psychotic" features such as delusions and hallucinations. Antipsychotics do not reverse the cognitive decline of dementia and therefore cannot correct the associated functional loss.

Antipsychotics are grouped into five families based on their chemical structure: phenothiazines, butyrophenones, thioxanthenes, molindones, and loxapines. The main features differentiating antipsychotics are their side effects with a dichotomy between a high-potency, low-sedating, low-anticholinergic and high-extrapyramidal group (such as Haldol and Navane) and a low-potency, high-sedating, high-anticholinergic and low-extrapyramidal group (such as Mellaril and Thorazine). While both groups seem equally effective at treating behavioral disturbances, the high-potency group may be considered more appropriate for the demented elderly because of their relatively low tendency toward sedation and anticholinergic side effects. The typical starting dose for antipsychotic treatment of dementia-associated behavioral disturbances is considerably lower than in younger individuals. For example, the starting dose for Haldol for the treatment of behavioral problems in the demented elderly is typically 0.5 mg once or twice daily.

When behavioral disturbances become exaggerated, leading to aggressive behavior, antipsychotic medication can often be used to alleviate potentially violent outbursts. When antipsychotics are ineffective, other medications have demonstrated effectiveness in controlling aggression. These include carbamazepine (Tegretol), propanolol (Inderal), and lithium. Tegretol, primarily used for seizure disorders, may be limited in its use by a variety of hematologic side effects. Inderal, a beta blocker, is contraindicated in patients with congestive heart failure, sinus bradycardia, and bronchial asthma. A recent report demonstrated the potential effectiveness of estrogen in treating physical aggression in elderly demented men.

Demented individuals often develop a significant degree of anxiety. Antianxiety agents that may be beneficial include ethyl alcohol, barbiturates, meprobamate (a propanediol), benzodiazepines, and buspirone (Buspar). Of these, the benzodiazepines are the most commonly used to treat anxiety and are considered first-line agents. Agents with shorter half-lives ($T^{1/2}$) and lack of active metabolites (Halcion, Ativan, Xanax, and Serax) are more appropriate for this patient population because of the tendency of the longer-acting agents (especially Dalmane) to accumulate, resulting in excess sedation.

Unfortunately, depression may coexist with dementia; differentiating them is often difficult. Uncomplicated depression in an older person may be mistaken for dementia (pseudodementia). However, truly demented individuals may develop dysphoric mood early in the disease course when insight into the future is preserved. When depression complicates dementia, the depressive component is often reponsive to drug therapy. In choosing an antidepressant for the demented elderly, one must be extremely careful about potentially toxic side effects. The tricyclic antidepressants are the most common in use but several are inappropriate for the elderly (amitryptyline, imipramine, and doxepin) because of potentially serious side effects including anticholinergic, sedative, hypotensive, and cardiac problems. Serious anticholinergic side effects include urinary retention, dry mouth, tachycardia, decreased visual accommodation, and impotence. Desipramine and nortriptyline are tricyclic antidepressants with the least anticholinergic side effects and are relatively safe for use in the elderly when begun at reduced doses (25 or 50 mg before sleep).

Other nontricyclic antidepressants that may be more appropriate for the elderly include methylphenidate (Ritalin), which is an amphetamine or "psychostimulant." Two newer agents that are commonly used in the elderly because of low anticholinergic side effects include maprotiline (Ludiomil) and trazodone (Desyrel). When the long 3- to 4-week latency period of most antidepressants presents a problem, amoxapine (Asendin) may be used to treat depression. Another group of antidepressants, the monoamine oxidase inhibitors (MAOIs), particularly phenelzine (Nardil) may be used in place of the tricyclics because of fewer cholinergic side effects.

SUMMARY

The care and treatment of behavioral problems in the demented elderly requires comprehensive assessment, analysis of all existing clues and symptoms regarding the behavioral problems, and meticulous discrimination with respect to pharmacological choices. Intensive watchfulness to detect side effects and other reactions to drug therapy is necessary, since demented individuals may not be aware of specific manifestations of side effects or allergy to drugs. Last but not least, care for the caregiver is a priority in providing care for the demented elderly.

References

Hamel, M., D.P. Gold, D. Andres, M. Reis, D. Dastoor, H. Graver, and H. Bergman. 1990. Predictors and consequences of aggressive behavior by community-based dementia patients. *The Gerontologist* 30(2):206–11.

Kyomen, M.D., K.W. Nobel, and J.Y. Wei. 1991. The use of estrogen to decrease aggressive physical behavior in elderly men with dementia. *J Amer Geriatric Soc* 39:1110–12.

Maleta, G.J. 1988. Management of behavior problems in elderly patients with Alzheimer's disease and other dementias. *Clin Geriatr Med* 4(4):719-47.

Pohlmann, E., and D. Howells. 1990. How to care for dementia patients: case management models in long-term home health care. In *New Directions in Understanding Dementia and Alzheimer's Disease*, edited by T. Zandi and R.J. Ham. New York: Plenum Press.

Wragg, R.E., and D.V. Jeste. 1988. Neuroleptics and alternative treatments: management of behavioral symptoms and psychosis in Alzheimer's disease and related conditions. *Psychiatr Clin North Amer* 11:195–213.

Barry M. Schultz

Dementia and Urinary Incontinence

INTRODUCTION

Alzheimer's disease (AD), multi-infarct dementia, and other brain disorders that impair cognitive function affect an individual's ability to function. Urinary incontinence or loss of urine control is a major functional and behavioral change which may occur with altered mentation secondary to dementia.

Urinary incontinence is defined by the International Continence Society as a condition where involuntary loss of urine is a social or hygienic problem and is objectively demonstrated. It is estimated that 15–30 percent of elderly individuals living in the community experience such difficulties with urine control. The causes of urinary incontinence in the individual with dementia are multiple and interactive; thus, evaluation of all possible contributing factors and the development of an individualized plan of management are important. It is apparent that treatment can improve the problem for most patients and at a minimum lead to better management, negating the belief that incontinence is a hopeless problem.

NORMAL URINATION

Urination (bladder elimination) is a complex function regulated by many factors. At birth, urine control is governed by a basic reflex action that causes bladder filling and emptying at regular intervals without conscious control. With maturation of the brain and spinal cord, voluntary control over urination is achieved through a process of socialization, that is, recognition of the correct time and place to void. In aging, certain changes occur that may alter the normal anatomy and the control mechanisms regulating the bladder. These changes may result in (a) reduced bladder capacity and emptying, (b) increased frequency and urgency in voiding, (c) increased nighttime urination, and (d) reduced control probably related to unpredictable and uncontrollable bladder contractions. Age-related changes make an individual more vulnerable to difficulties with urine control but generally do not cause urinary incontinence.

Normal bladder control is also influenced by functional and environmental factors. For example, (a) an individual must have the physical ability to find and ambulate to the toilet, (b) transfer, (c) undress/dress, and (d) have the ability to overcome environmental obstacles or barriers to reaching a toilet or toilet receptacle. Psychological factors include the need for motivation to be continent. Also, certain medications impact on bladder function.

IMPAIRED COGNITIVE FUNCTION AND URINARY INCONTINENCE

Dementia compounds the problems of reduced control over urination that occur with age. Incontinence generally develops in the middle stages of AD and becomes increasingly prevalent as dementia worsens. The exact relationships between the development of incontinence and the brain changes that occur in AD are unknown, but probably involve both frontal and parietal lobes where the integration of complex behavioral tasks occurs. The resulting impaired ability to attend to the internal cues of the need to void, and confusion as to the place to void, as well as apathy, depression, and reduced physical abilities that occur with AD, all contribute to the prevalence of incontinence. For example, the following clinical behaviors have been identified as possible contributors to the problem: (1) impaired memory, (2) inability to find or recognize a toilet, (3) inability to remember the sequence of steps involved in the toileting process, (4) impaired physical ability to respond to messages from the brain to toilet oneself (apraxia), (5) language difficulties that impair the ability to communicate need, and (6) impaired insight regarding the presence and meaning of incontinence.

EVALUATION

Urinary incontinence is a symptom that requires careful evaluation. Many affected individuals and their families fail to report or discuss the problem, due to shame, embarrassment, or a belief that incontinence is an inevitable part of normal aging. Even when reported to health care professionals, the problem may not be adequately evaluated because of a lack of understanding of the topic. Thus, individuals may be denied effective evaluation and treatment. For individuals with dementia, it is essential that causes other than advancing cognitive impairment be considered when evaluating the problem. Part of the challenge in evaluating incontinent behavior in the demented individual is their inability to give a detailed history and description of the problem. Thus, the description usually must be supplemented by caregiver observations. In this sense, the caregiver must act like a "detective" to isolate the cause of the incontinence.

The evaluation process is a crucial first step in the identification of helpful specific interventions. The initial part of the evaluation process is to identify any potentially reversible causes. The primary care physician or other health care provider should be involved at this stage. Reversible causes of incontinence should be investigated and treated. These might include: (a) delirium (acute confused state); (b) depression; (c) urinary tract infection; (d) atrophic vaginitis from decreased estrogen effects; (e) fecal impaction; (f) illnesses causing problems with mobility; (g) medical conditions including excessive fluid intake, diabetes, congestive heart failure, and lower extremity venous insufficiency; and (h) medications. The initial evaluation may be obtained from a variety of health care professionals including a family physician, urologist, gynecologist, nurse specialist, or community health nurse. If the clinical problems are more complicated, then referral to a specialist or a specialized clinic for urinary incontinence may be needed. It is important that the person chosen be knowledgeable about the topic, able to design a care plan, and available for questioning and follow-up.

In summary, a comprehensive evaluation for urinary incontinence should include a careful description and characterization of the problem. This component of the evaluation process can and should be initiated by the incontinent individual (if they are able) and the caregiver in the home environment. A community health nurse may offer valuable assistance to the family in making observations and clarifying such issues as (a) onset of the problem; (b) duration, frequency, and timing of urination and incontinent episodes; (c) amount of urine lost; and (d) associated circumstances. Also, the nurse may serve as the treatment coordinator. It is important that caregivers keep a voiding record or diary to document specific times the patient is found wet or dry and the results of toileting (urinated, did not urinate).

Observing performance of toileting behaviors and assessment of the home environment provide useful information concerning the person's ability to independently toilet. This information serves as a practical method of assessing the impact of cognitive and physical impairments on toileting skills. It is critical that the task of toileting be conceptualized as a series of behaviors that, when combined, lead to effective toileting behavior. Therefore, toileting is broken down into steps and the identification of specific skills that are preserved or missing can guide caregivers into identifying impaired behaviors for intervention.

MANAGEMENT

Following a careful evaluation of the problem, an individualized plan of care is developed. These treatment approaches may be summarized as (a) general medical, (b) surgical/medication, (c) behavioral, and (d) general.

General Medical

Patients with dementia, like any other patients, may experience the same general medical illnesses that result in increased risk of incontinence. Therefore, treatments for such illnesses as urinary tract infection, gynecological infections and irritations, bowel disorders, or bladder dysfunctions related to medications, to name a few, may be treated by the patient's family physician. If routine evaluations and treatments do not result in an improved function, then referral to a more specialized incontinence program should be considered.

Surgical/Medication

Surgical approaches and medication trials for incontinence may be effective in selected persons if based on identifying the underlying type of incontinence. Individuals in these groups require a detailed evaluation usually by a specialized multidisciplinary clinic before a final decision regarding therapy is made. For individuals with dementia, a careful discussion should take place on the risks, benefits, and expected outcomes of these more complicated forms of therapy.

Behavioral

Behavioral interventions carry little risk and may be the most useful starting point for cognitively impaired individuals. Caregiver involvement is a necessary component in planning and carrying out the intervention. Both habit training and prompted voiding have been shown to be successful in both physically dependent and cognitively impaired persons. Habit training provides caregiver-assisted toileting help at regularly scheduled intervals (usually 1–2 hours) while adjusting toileting times to match actual urination patterns of the individual. Prompted voiding is a toileting approach consisting of (a) regular monitoring of the incontinent person by a caregiver who asks the person to recognize if they are wet or dry, (b) asking the person if they need to urinate and assisting the person to the toilet if the response is yes, and (c) giving positive reinforcement or praise for remaining dry and/or attempting to use the toilet. At night, toileting schedules are individualized.

General

Additional goals and approaches that may be helpful can be summarized as: (a) adequate fluid intake, (b) regular bowel elimination, (c) communication, (d) functional status, (e) environmental barriers, (f) catheters, and (g) protective products and skin care.

Fluid Intake

Adequate fluid intake is necessary to assure a normal signal of a full bladder and the subsequent need to urinate. Limited fluid intake may lead to dehydration, possible bladder irritation, and urinary tract infection. Evaluation of the impact of caffeine-containing liquids, alcohol, and diuretic medications on urination patterns can be helpful.

Bowel Elimination

Severe constipation or fecal impaction can block the bladder outlet and lead to incontinence. Adequate fluid intake, a high fiber diet with adequate fluids, maintenance of activity level, and a routine time for bowel elimination (usually after breakfast) may prevent constipation. If these are not effective, discussing the need for other bowel medications with the health care provider is recommended.

Communication

Caregiver beliefs and expectations can influence continence status. Maintaining a positive belief that the problem can be improved communicates a message of hope. Also, incontinent individuals benefit from praise for positive efforts and results. Criticisms of incontinence should be avoided.

Clear, step-by-step instructions for each step in the sequence of toileting may be necessary. The person may need help with parts of the task ranging from encouragement, verbal guidance, demonstrations, and physical assistance. The person may no longer be able to communicate the need to urinate. Observe for nonverbal signs indicating a need to toilet such as restlessness and pulling at clothing. A kitchen timer may be useful to caregivers implementing a toileting program.

Functional Status

Observation of toileting behaviors will provide an assessment of tasks that require assistance and behaviors that might be improved. Encourage the person to keep active to maintain general health and walking skills. A daily walking program with family members might be all that is needed. Stable footwear (athletic footwear or running shoes) makes walking safer and decreases the risk of falling. Muscle strengthening, range of motion, and gait training assistance by a physical therapist may improve function. Clothing should be simplified for ease in dressing. Velcro closures, elasticized waists, and wrap-around skirts may be helpful. Having the person wear underpants may serve as a reminder to remain dry.

Environment

Chairs of a correct height to permit easy rising can make the task of toileting easier. Grab bars attached to toilets or walls, raised toilet seats, walkers, canes, and other mobility devices are examples of equipment that may facilitate toileting. Bed height should allow feet to rest on the floor when sitting. Well marked bathrooms and other orienting cues, such as leaving the door open, are important for persons who have difficulty finding the bathroom. Eliminate throw rugs to avoid falls. Provide adequate lighting, especially at night, and reduce clutter in the environment to facilitate safe toileting. Depending on the distance to the toilet, speed of walking, and amount of warning time, toilet substitutes such as a bedside commode, bedpan, or urinal may be useful. Privacy should be provided. Wet clothing should be changed so the person does not become accustomed to this condition.

Catheters

Use of indwelling catheters should be avoided in the management of urinary incontinence except for medically indicated reasons. External catheters for men are available but are associated with an increased risk of urinary tract infection. Female external urine collection systems are available but have not been thoroughly evaluated.

Protective Products and Skin Care

Protective covers are available for chairs and beds. A draw sheet (half sheet) can be used with a plastic pad underneath which minimizes full bed linen changes. Absorbent briefs and pant systems are available in both washable and disposable forms. Caution is advised against immediate use of any product without a careful evaluation of the causes of incontinence. The Resource Guide for Incontinent Aids and Services describes products available and is available from Help for Incontinent People. Good skin hygiene with proper cleansing is necessary after incontinence episodes to prevent skin breakdown. Many commercially prepared products are available for cleansing. Moisture barriers are also available and can be helpful in maintaining skin integrity and preventing skin irritation and breakdown.

SUMMARY

Urinary incontinence is a common problem encountered in elderly individuals with dementia. Although there is a strong association between impaired cognitive function and urinary incontinence, many reversible causes besides dementia may be identified and treated. Many advances have been made in understanding the nature of the problem, leading to better evaluation and management. Careful evaluation of the problem by a knowledgeable health care provider is essential for effective management; however, the informed caregiver is also recognized as a vital member of the treatment team.

References

Help for Incontinent People (HIP). P.O. Box 544, Union, S.C. 29379, telephone (803) 579–7900.

Ouslander, J.G., and J.L. Marks. 1990. The management of urinary incontinence in dementia. In *Dementia Care: Patient, Family, and Community*, edited by N.L. Mace. Baltimore: Johns Hopkins University Press, 113–47.

Schnelle, J. 1991. *Managing Urinary Incontinence in the Elderly*. New York: Springer.

Simon Foundation for Continence, Box 835, Willamette, IL. 60091, telephone (800) 23-SIMON.
Urinary Incontinence Guideline Panel. March 1992. *Urinary Incontinence in Adults: Clinical Practice Guideline*. AHCPR Pub. No. 92-0048. Rockville, Md.: Agency for Health Care Policy and Research, Public Health Service, U.S. Department of Health and Human Services.
Weaverdyck, S.E. 1990. Intervention-based neuropsychological assessment. In *Dementia Care: Patient, Family, and Community*, edited by N.L. Mace. Baltimore: Johns Hopkins University Press, 32–73.

Sue E. Nickoley, Mark T. Wagner, and Robert W. Hamill

Depression and Late-Life Bereavement

Every year in the United States there are over 800,000 new widows and widowers, most of whom are elderly. By age 65, over 50 percent of all women and over 10 percent of men have been widowed at least once. Bereavement causes significant alterations in the life of the survivors, leaving them potentially vulnerable to increased substance abuse, worsening of ongoing medical problems, depression, and possibly even increased mortality rates.

Loss on many levels is an accepted concomitant of aging and is known to precipitate or exacerbate depression. The death of a spouse is generally the most traumatic loss faced by an elderly person, often leading to loneliness, demoralization, and sometimes even to frank clinical depression. Depressive symptoms are ubiquitous after bereavement and, in a large number of the elderly bereaved, the symptoms are of sufficient intensity and persistence to warrant the diagnosis of major depression. Therefore, spousal bereavement among the elderly is a risk factor for a potentially major public health problem.

In one of the larger prospective studies, researchers at the San Diego Widowhood Project followed 350 widows and widowers for the first two years after the death of their spouses. The study showed that depressive syndromes are common not only in the first several months of bereavement, but throughout the entire two-year period. Major depressive syndromes are both less frequent and perhaps slightly less severe during the first year of widowhood in late-age widows and widowers than in their younger counterparts. However, the occurrence rate and intensity of depressive syndromes merge with those of younger bereaved spouses over the second year. While there is no single explanation for this phenomenon, the ongoing stress of bereavement with its accompanying life crises may prove overwhelming to some individuals. By the end of the second year, approximately 14% of all late-age widows and widowers can be expected to suffer from a clinically meaningful major depressive syndrome, and many more will experience ongoing depressive symptoms that do not quite fulfill the criteria of major depression.

DEPRESSIVE SYNDROME ASSOCIATED WITH BEREAVEMENT

Common medical practice has long held the idea that depression associated with grief is normative, especially in the months immediately following the loss, and that to treat such depression is to prematurely and arbitrarily interfere with the grieving process, setting the stage for future adjustment problems. However, it should be remembered that while grief is a perfectly normal and expected reaction to the loss of a loved one, major depression is not. Prompt identification and treatment of early syndromes (referred to as "uncomplicated bereavement" in the DSM-III-R) may prevent some of the morbidity (and possibly the mortality) associated with late-life bereavement. Symptoms of depression (poor appetite or overeating, insomnia or hypersomnia, low energy or fatigue, low self-esteem, poor concentration or difficulty making decisions, feelings of hopelessness) lasting longer than two months require prompt, professional intervention.

Indications for formal intervention are often inversely related to the strength of the survivor's support system: a physically and emotionally healthy individual with family, friends, and outside interests is less likely to need intervention than the "high risk" individual who is alone and/or in poor health. Other indications of high risk individuals are those who have a history of depression, have lost someone to suicide or homicide, or have experienced multiple simultaneous losses or accidents in which they were at fault.

TREATMENT

There are varying suggestions for treatment of the depression associated with widowhood that correspond to the varying levels of need. For individuals who are not depressed, but are having difficulty coping, traditional bereavement counseling may suffice. Most advocated psychotherapeutic approaches are relatively brief and time-limited and have been shown to be beneficial. Certain common features can be identified: first, most therapies include an educational component, helping the bereaved to know what to expect, offering perspective on their pain, and "normalizing" their confusing array of feelings and behaviors. Second, therapies encourage the expression of the full range of bereavement emotions and affects. Evocative techniques, such as role playing, writing letters to the deceased, looking at pictures, or even visiting the burial site can be effective. Third, most therapies attempt to help the bereaved come to peace with their altered relationship to the deceased. This usually involves systematic exploration of all aspects of the relationship, both in the past over time and as it has developed since the death. Although the relationship technically is over in one real sense, there are many ways, symbolically or otherwise, that the relationship lives on in a very real way for the bereaved. To disregard this altered relationship is to demean the powerful attachment to the deceased person and the meaning of that bond. Fourth, most therapies attend to the bereaved person's new identity, focusing on an integrated self-concept and a stable world view.

When grief is complicated by a major depressive syndrome, psychotherapeutic techniques such as interpersonal or cognitive-behavioral therapy should be considered to treat the major depression. If depression is mild to moderate, this may be all that is necessary. In more severe depression or when psychotherapy has not been successful, psychopharmacologic intervention should be considered. Medications are particularly indicated when there is a past history of severe depression, suicidal ideation, psychomotor retardation, morbid feelings of worthlessness or guilt, or when psychosocial impairment is substantial. When the depressive syndrome appears early in the bereavement, antidepressant medications may be useful to treat the present syndrome and to prevent later relapse. Such treatment will not prohibit grieving; rather, treatment facilitates adaptive processes, and prevents the distortion and coping interference brought on by depression. However, when treating depressive syndromes associated with bereavement, the clinician should strongly consider an integrative approach, since psychotherapy may be necessary for other aspects of grief.

People like to believe that wisdom and serenity come with age, and that enduring the vicissitudes of life builds strength of character and an increased ability to cope. Unfortunately, this is not always the case. Enduring can be eroding, and resiliency can wear thin. It is important to recognize that what appears to be "normal grief" can mask a potentially harmful, long-term depression which should be evaluated and treated as for any other depression.

References

Clayton, P.J. 1990. Bereavement and depression. *J Clin Psychiatry* 51:34–38.

Gilewski, M.J., N.L. Farberow, and D.E. Gallagher. 1991. Interaction of depression and bereavement on mental health in the elderly. *Psychol Aging* 6:67–75.

Harlow, S.D., E.L. Goldberg, and S.W. Comstock. 1991. A longitudinal study of the prevalence of depressive symptomatology in elderly widowed and married women. *Arch Gen Psychiatry* 48:1065–68.

Osterweis, M., F. Solomon, and M. Green. 1984. *Bereavement: Reactions, Consequences and Care*. Washington, D.C.: National Academy Press.

Pasternack, R.E., C.F. Reynolds III, M. Schlernitzauer, C.C. Hoch, D.J. Buysse, R.R. Hovek, and J.M. Perel. 1991. Acute open-trial nortriptyline therapy of bereavement-related depression in late life. *J Clin Psychiatry* 52(7):307–10.

Zisook, S., and S.R. Shuchter. 1991. Depression through the first year of widowhood. *Amer J Psychiatry* 148:1346–52.

Sidney Zisook and Gretchen Pena

Diabetes Mellitus

Diabetes mellitus is a condition that results when there is an insufficient quantity of insulin to take sugar out of the blood and drive it into the muscles, liver, kidneys, and other body organs to provide energy. Insulin may be totally deficient, as is the case in Type 1 diabetes, formerly referred to as Juvenile Onset diabetes, or present in insufficient quantities, as is the case in Type 2 diabetes, formerly referred to as Adult Onset or Maturity Onset diabetes. Type 2 diabetes is more common in blacks, persons with family histories of diabetes, persons who are overweight (larger fat cells are not as responsive to insulin action), and persons who are older.

BLOOD SUGAR LEVELS

Both forms of diabetes are associated with serious and life-threatening complications if not properly treated. In general, the blood sugar should be maintained in the 120 to 160 mg/dl (milligrams per deciliter—1/10th of a liter or 100 milliliters) range after meals; many physicians will allow blood sugar to rise to as high as 220 mg/dl in older persons with Type 2 disease. Fasting blood sugars should be less than 140 mg/dl. There is a direct correlation between inadequate control of blood sugar and complications including the development of cataracts, electrolyte abnormalities, diseases of the skin, infections, and even large vessel disease including stroke and heart attacks. Every year 500,000 new cases of diabetes mellitus are identified with the highest number being those persons in their 40s, 50s, and 60s.

PREVALENCE, COMPLICATIONS, AND COST

There are approximately 10 million Americans who have been diagnosed with diabetes and probably another 5 million who have the disease and do not even know it. Over 40 percent of all persons with diabetes are over the age of 65.

Diabetes cost American taxpayers $20.4 billion in 1989. Over one-third of this cost was spent on the hospital treatment of complications from diabetes. Diabetes is the leading cause of blindness in America and increases the risk of being in a nursing home by 800 percent for persons under age 45 and by 20 percent for persons over the age of 65. Persons with diabetes have 7 times more cataract extractions, 17 times more renal failure, and 5 times the prevalence of coronary disease and stroke as compared to individuals without diabetes. Clearly, early identification that a problem exists and prompt treatment are essential. For these reasons, it has been recommended that blood sugar measurements be made at periodic intervals throughout one's life.

DIAGNOSIS

Diabetes is defined as a "fasting" blood sugar value of 140 mg/dl or greater on more than one occasion. If a two-hour glucose tolerance test is done, persons who have values at two hours of 200 mg/dl or greater with at least one value during the preceding two-hour interval also of 200 mg/dl or greater meet the criteria for a diagnosis of diabetes.

TREATMENT

While persons with Type 1 diabetes require once or even twice daily injections of insulin given subcutaneously, persons with Type 2 diabetes can be managed under most circumstances with a regimen of diet and exercise. Diet should be individualized to keep the person within 10 percent of average weight for age as established by the Metropolitan Life Tables. Diets should emphasize complex carbohydrates; these nutrients provide a more "even" blood sugar level throughout the day. Fat intake should be limited to no more than 30 percent of the daily calorie consumption; an emphasis should be placed on the ingestion of polyunsaturated fats, 2:1, over saturated fats. Fiber should be increased to 30 grams per day over a period of time, and protein maintained at 0.8 grams/kg of body weight unless otherwise advised by the physician because of some underlying disease state that might result in either an increased or decreased need. Exercise is important and helps keep joints mobile, and muscles firm and active. In addition, exercise has a positive effect on one's psychological well-being. Since exercising muscles takes up sugar with less need for insulin, exercise also helps keep blood sugar in check. Exercise need not be exhaustive, however, or even be vigorous enough to raise the heart rate to have an effect. "Sedentary aerobics" (movement to music while sitting in a chair or even lying in bed) is something most people can do at home. Since Type 2 diabetes is associated with normal or even high levels of insulin, though not enough for a given person, this exercise may help reduce insulin requirements and thus reduce blood sugar levels. Prior to embarking on any exercise program, however, it is imperative that a frank discussion take place with one's physician to define exercise limits as based on other underlying illness(es). Persons who are "bed bound" may benefit from the installation of a "trapeze" above the bed to assist in movement as well as with transfers.

DRUG THERAPY

In certain cases, the combination of diet and exercise will not be sufficient to reduce blood sugar levels to an acceptable range even in the person with Type

2 diabetes. This usually occurs because of the person's inability to stick to an appropriate diet. In this case, the use of oral hypoglycemic agents may be necessary. Newer, second generation agents, glipizide and glyburide, can be taken once or twice a day and, by stimulating the body to make more insulin as well as making the body more sensitive to the insulin that is present, blood sugar values can reach an acceptable range within days. These agents should be taken only under the direction of a physician, and blood sugar should be monitored at home to ensure that adequate control is being achieved. Home blood glucose monitoring can be done using a simple hand-held computer that accepts a drop of blood and instantaneously "reads" the blood sugar value. Whenever these pills are taken, it is important to stay on as regular a diet and exercise program as possible to prevent shifts in blood sugar values that can result in levels that are either too high or too low.

In certain cases, blood sugar values remain too high and insulin injections are required. Dosages must be individualized and may require either a single or twice daily injection. Individuals who have problems preparing the insulin syringes may require assistance. Fortunately, syringes with pre-measured insulin may be kept in the refrigerator for daily use. In certain circumstances, someone may be required to actually give the injection to the affected individual. Family members can easily be taught to do this, or arrangements can be made with a visiting nurse. It is essential that all persons with diabetes be under the care of a physician, that regular podiatric visits be arranged, and that an eye examination be done at least at yearly intervals or sooner if a problem arises. One's daily routine and diet should be as consistent as possible, and any change in one's usual health be brought to the attention of a health care professional.

QUALITY OF LIFE

While diabetes mellitus is a disease that will require daily attention, it need not interfere with one's quality of life. Unfortunately, many persons are functionally impaired as a result of complications of diabetes, many of which could have been prevented through better blood sugar control. Family members should consider being screened for the disease themselves and become knowledgeable regarding aspects of monitoring and treatment. Particular attention should be given to aspects of prevention with an emphasis on good skin care, care of finger- and toenails, blood sugar control, and vaccinations. Blood sugar values should be kept within a predetermined range and monitoring be done on a regular basis at home.

References

Berg, D., L. Cantwell, G. Heudebert, and J.L. Sebastian, eds. 1993. Diabetes mellitus. *Handbook of Primary Care Medicine*. Philadelphia: Lippincott, 515.
Gregerman, R.I. 1991. Diabetes mellitus. In *Principles of Ambulatory Medicine*, 3rd ed.

Edited by L.R. Barker, J.R. Burton, and P.D. Zieve. Baltimore: Williams & Wilkins, 913–51.

Halter, J.B. 1992. Diabetes mellitus in the elderly. In *Textbook of Internal Medicine*, 2d ed. Edited by W.N. Kelley. Philadelphia: Lippincott, 2362.

Rifkin, H., and D. Porte, Jr., eds. 1990. *Diabetes Mellitus: Theory and Practice*, 4th ed. New York: Elsevier.

Steven R. Gambert

Diabetic Foot Disease: Prevention and Care

People with diagnosed or undiagnosed diabetes are at risk for developing foot disease as a result of two common pathologies: peripheral neuropathy and peripheral vascular disease. Early identification of these pathologies is essential to prevent the development of ulcerations that may lead to amputation. Inattention to foot care and inspection by persons with diabetes may also result in foot infections or injury.

Peripheral neuropathy is a disorder of the large or small nerve fibers of the lower extremities. Hyperglycemia appears to contribute to the problem by damaging the nerve fibers. This damage to nerve fibers leads to loss of sensation in the extremity. However, the exact mechanism is not known. Progressive symmetric distal polyneuropathy is the most common form of peripheral neuropathy. This neuropathy results in decreased temperature sensation, paresthesia, or dysesthesia. Paresthesia manifests itself as shooting pains or "pins and needles" sensation. Pain that occurs from stockings or bed clothes is known as dysesthesia. Eventually, there is a loss of sensation in the extremity. Without sensation, the individual with diabetes may be unaware of injury or infection in the foot.

Peripheral vascular disease usually occurs concurrently with hypertension, cigarette smoking, hyperglycemia, or hyperlipidemia. These conditions diminish blood flow within an artery. The diminished blood flow may occur in the femoral, popliteal, or iliac arteries.

SIGNS AND SYMPTOMS

Initially, peripheral neuropathy usually causes burning or shooting pains in the calves, decreased temperature sensation, numbness, or tingling. As the disease progresses, sensation is ultimately absent. Peripheral vascular disease may cause pain in the calves, thighs, or buttocks during physical activity; swelling of the feet or ankles; or cold feet. Symptoms of both diseases may be attributed to lack of potassium, aging, inadequate footwear, or muscle pain.

DIAGNOSIS

The diagnosis of both peripheral neuropathy and peripheral vascular disease is dependent upon a careful history and physical examination. It is vital for the clinician to question the patient about the presence of signs and symptoms of both diseases. Questions must be directed toward the presence of pain, location of pain, timing of pain, and alteration of daily activities. In addition, any known changes in sensation must be documented. It is essential to document the patient's level of glycemic control. A social and work history should be obtained to document possible coexisting causes such as alcoholism, smoking, or exposure to heavy metals. Conditions such as hypothyroidism, vitamin deficiencies, uremia, and chronic obstructive pulmonary disease can cause symptoms of peripheral neuropathy. A medication history is essential to determine the use of such drugs as chloramphenicol, clofibrate, demeclocycline, ethambutol, hydralazine, isoniazid, nitrofurantoin, phenytoin, or tricyclic antidepressants, which have been known to cause symptoms of peripheral neuropathy.

After obtaining a history, the physical examination is done. This examination includes vital signs, gait, general appearance, head and neck, thorax, heart, abdomen, and extremities. Examination of the patient's gait will document any abnormal positions of the feet. Evaluation of the extremities includes both the affected and unaffected extremity. In peripheral neuropathy, the lower extremities may have muscle wasting, absent deep tendon reflexes, foot deformities, abnormal gait, and diminished or absent vibratory sensation. With peripheral vascular disease, the lower extremities may have decreased hair growth, absent or decreased pulses, infections of the feet, shiny appearance of skin, blanching of skin with elevation, or edema.

Prior to initiation of studies to further diagnose peripheral neuropathy, glycemic control should be evaluated. A glycosylated hemoglobin is a simple blood test that provides an average blood sugar level for the past three months. If glycemic control is adequate, nerve conduction studies may be ordered.

If peripheral vascular disease is suspected after a physical examination, segmented Doppler studies are ordered. Blood pressure and characteristics of blood flow to the extremities with ultrasound are documented by means of Doppler studies. The measurements are recorded in percentage of blood pressure in segments of the lower extremity and compared to the upper extremity. A finding of 1.0 or less identifies blockage of blood flow to the extremity. When the results are less than 0.75, the blockage can impair tissue healing or cause claudication.

TREATMENT

Treatment of peripheral neuropathy is essentially palliative. The major objective of treatment is to reduce symptoms and prevent injury. To reduce symptoms, medications may be used. A topical cream (0.075% Capsaicin) may be applied to the affected areas four times daily. It appears that Capsaicin relieves pain by depleting the nerve fibers of substance P which is necessary to transmit pain signals in Type C nerve fibers, which are responsible for mediating pain. Capsaicin is made from jalapeño peppers and can cause local irritation if applied to other body areas. For that reason, care must be taken to keep the cream away from other parts of the body. Another medication, amitriptyline (Elavil), is useful in reducing the symptoms of peripheral neuropathy, by preventing the synaptic uptake of serotonin or norepinephrine. This action seems to inhibit transmission of the pain impulse at the level of the spinal cord, brain stem, or thalamus. Currently, amitriptyline is approved by the Food and Drug Administration to treat depression.

Treatment of peripheral vascular disease is aimed at preventing ulcers, and includes the use of vasodilators and exercise. If the blockage is severe or does not respond to nonsurgical methods, cardiovascular surgery may be necessary. Laser surgical techniques have been successful in restoring blood flow to an extremity.

PATIENT EDUCATION

In addition to medical intervention, patients must be instructed on foot care and inspection. Daily foot care includes cleansing, adequate drying of the skin, application of lotion, and use of powder in areas with excessive perspiration. Any lotion is advisable as long as it contains minimal alcohol. Alcohol dries the skin. After cleansing the skin, the feet should be inspected for any cracks, calluses, color changes, temperature changes, swelling, or signs of infection. Any changes in the feet are promptly reported to the clinician. Nails are trimmed straight across unless other problems are present.

Prevention of foot injury is of great importance. Protective footwear, both socks and shoes, is essential. To prevent injury, shoes must be checked prior to wear for foreign objects. Socks should be loose-fitting and not hampering blood flow. Avoidance of temperature extremes, too hot or too cold, will help to prevent injury. Smoking is discouraged.

PROGNOSIS

By means of adequate glycemic control, injury prevention, daily foot care and inspection, and good health habits, costly injuries to the lower extremities can be prevented. Persons with diabetes must be educated to communicate problems regarding their feet to the clinician as soon as possible. Early identification and treatment strategies can reduce the number of lower extremity problems that could result in amputation.

SUMMARY

Because the signs and symptoms of both peripheral neuropathy and peripheral vascular disease are subtle and often go unrecognized early in their development, clinicians, patients, and patients' families must be aware of these early manifestations of nerve and circulatory problems. Prompt attention to any changes in sensation, appearance, pulses, and reflexes of the lower extremities will help to prevent ulceration, further nerve damage, and potential amputation in those with diabetes.

References

American Diabetes Association. 1991. *Diabetes 1991 Vital Statistics.* Alexandria, Va.
Bays, H.E., and M.A. Pfeifer. 1988. Peripheral diabetic neuropathy. *Med Clin North Am* 72(6):1439–64.
Levin, M.E. 1988. Medical evaluation and treatment. In *The Foot in Diabetes*, edited by G.J. Sammarco. Philadelphia: Lea & Febiger, 41–50.
Sammarco, G.J., and M.W. Scioloi. 1991. Examination of the foot and ankle. In *The Foot in Diabetes*, edited by G.J. Sammarco. Philadelphia: Lea & Febiger, 29–35.

Jane Harley

Discharge Planning

INTRODUCTION

Discharge planning is the process of planning and providing for transition between levels of health care. Usually, discharge planning refers to the transition of a patient from an acute care hospital to other levels of care in the community, such as a nursing home or home care. The discharge planner assesses the continuing care needs of the patient, the resources available to the patient, and develops and implements a plan to provide the services needed in a coordinated and continuous manner. The focus is on ensuring that the patient's needs are met once he or she leaves the hospital or other facility, and that a sudden disruption in the pattern of care does not occur. Effective discharge planning is particularly important for older persons because they are more likely to have complex continuing care needs and lack the social support or financial resources needed for their care.

HISTORICAL BACKGROUND

Discharge planning has been a part of hospital practice since early in this century. Both medical social workers and nurses have been involved in this activity, since it requires knowledge of the patient's health care needs and the system of health and social services available in the community. Despite its recognized importance, discharge planning was not strongly supported in most hospitals, because it was done after the "real work" of the hospital (curing the patient) was completed; it was often an afterthought. The major change came in 1983, with the implementation in hospitals of the Prospective Payment System (PPS) for Medicare patients using the diagnosis related groups (DRGs) methodology. PPS pays a fixed fee for each complete hospital stay, rather than the traditional fee-for-service payment system in which the hospital was paid for each additional day the patient remained in the hospital. Hospitals now have a financial incentive to discharge patients as soon as medically possible; delays in discharge because arrangements have not been completed now cost hospitals money. To lessen the financial incentive to discharge patients too quickly, penalties were put in place for patients who are readmitted to the hospital after a short time because of an inappropriate initial discharge.

As hospital stays became shorter, hospitals began to aggressively move into other health care arenas, partly as a way of ensuring that their patients had access to continuing care services and would not be "backed up" in the hospital unnecessarily. As hospitals became integrated health care systems processing patients at a much faster rate, the role of the discharge planner became more important. In this new context of health care as a business, advocates for the elderly became concerned that the balance between controlling costs and ensuring quality was not being maintained. In 1984, the Joint Commission for the Accreditation of Healthcare Organizations (JCAHO) and the American Hospital Association issued special guidelines on discharge planning. In 1986, the Health Care Financing Administration (HCFA), the federal agency that administers Medicare, amended the Medicare Conditions of Participation to require that hospitals give patients, upon admission, a statement of their rights to appeal discharge decisions and that the hospital have a discharge planning program. This requirement was strengthened in 1987, following action by a broad-based coalition of professionals and consumers. Discharge planning has thus become an important element in the health care system, and is recognized as such by the government, professional and advocacy groups, and patients and their families.

THE PROCESS OF DISCHARGE PLANNING

The discharge planning process usually includes four steps.

Identification of Patients

Not all patients need extensive discharge planning, but it is critical to identify those who will as soon as they enter the hospital, or even before admission. Most hospitals have screening techniques that consider such variables as age, diagnosis, or procedure (e.g., stroke or hip replacement), living arrangements (e.g., living alone or in an unsafe environment), ability to perform activities of daily living (e.g., toileting, bathing) and general functional status, family and social network resources, financial resources, and a history of multiple hospitalizations or difficult transitions from the hospital. Patient screening and discharge planning can begin before admission; for example, an elderly patient living alone in a house with the only bathroom on the second floor and who is admitted for total hip replacement will need continuing care to be able to return home. Marshalling the complex resources needed to make this transition successful does not need to wait until discharge, and a major goal of discharge planning is to identify patients in potential need and begin planning as soon as possible. A variety of personnel, but usually nurses or social workers, make this initial identification, and refer the patient to the discharge planning program.

Assessment

Once a patient has been identified, a multidisciplinary team of professionals assesses the patient's needs for care following discharge from the hospital. The team typically includes the patient's physician and additional physician specialists, nurses, and social workers, with input from other professionals as appropriate, such as psychologists; occupational, physical, and speech therapists, and dietitians. The assessment considers the patient's medical condition, likely course of treatment, psychosocial needs and resources, and financial resources.

Discharge Plan Development

After the multidisciplinary team has assessed the patient's needs for continuing care, the discharge planner develops a plan to match these needs to available resources. Given the fragmented system of health and social services in the United States, finding and coordinating the proper resources is often a difficult and time-consuming process. Discharge planners must have a comprehensive knowledge of the resources available in the community and the health care finance system, with its different requirements and restrictions for each program. The discharge plan identifies the health care and social resources that will be used, and specifies how these resources will be coordinated and paid for. The goal is to develop a plan that meets the patient's needs for continuing care within a realistic framework that reflects the patient's changing condition and caregiving environment.

Discharge Plan Implementation

The implementation of the discharge plan is the most important and complex phase of the process, since many of the coordination activities take place outside of the hospital, and therefore outside of the discharge planner's direct observation and control. Educating the patient, family, or other caregivers as to their responsibilities and avoiding misunderstanding as to expectations is an important component of discharge planning, especially for patients with more complex medical needs returning home rather than remaining in the hospital or going to another institutional setting. A specific individual, either the discharge planner or another professional, is usually assigned responsibility for following the case through its implementation. The physician is the only person legally able to discharge the patient and must be integrally involved in the process for discharge planning to work effectively. The hospital discharge itself is closely coordinated with the arrival of the services anticipated in the plan. Follow-up to make sure that the services planned are in place and that the plan is working as anticipated is the last phase of the implementation process.

DIFFICULTIES ENCOUNTERED IN DISCHARGE PLANNING

In a process as complex as discharge planning, many problems can arise in developing and implementing a successful discharge plan, including:

* inadequate screening, leading to patients in need not being identified in a timely fashion;
* patient needs that cannot be matched to resources in the community;
* patients who do not qualify for reimbursement of the needed services and do not have the resources to pay independently;
* physician and hospital staff resistance to actively participating in discharge planning;
* patient or caregiver "optimism" concerning their ability to care for the patient after discharge that does not match reality (e.g., the frequent comment that patients "will say anything to get out of the hospital"); and,
* rapidly changing patient condition that could not be anticipated, leading to the wrong resources being planned.

All of these problems make the work of the discharge planner challenging. In a fragmented health care and social support system, their job is to hold the pieces together for the patient's sake. For older persons especially, their role is a crucial one that is being recognized as essential for the well-being of those they serve.

References

Birmingham, J. 1992. *Discharge Planning: A Practitioner's Guide to Policies, Procedures, and Protocols*. Los Angeles, Cal.: Academy Medical Systems, Inc.

Hanson, P.C. 1988. *Quality Assurance. A Strategic Guide for Discharge Planning Professionals*. Eagan, Minn.: Healthcare Management Services.

Proctor, E.K., and N. Morrow-Howell. 1990. Complications in discharge planning with Medicare patients. *Health and Social Work* 15(1): 45–54.

Russ, G.H. 1991. *Discharge Management: Policy, Procedure and Tool Design*. Raleigh, N.C.: Continuing Education Resources.

Volland, P.J., ed. 1988. *Discharge Planning: An Interdisciplinary Approach to Continuity of Care*. Owings Mills, Md.: National Health Publishing.

John Feather

E

Emergency Medical Care

The geriatric community has special emergency medical care needs in the home. In 1990, the elderly made an estimated 3.1 million emergency department visits for cardiovascular problems, 1.6 million visits for neurological problems, 1.2 million visits for pulmonary problems, and 1 million visits for fractures and dislocations. Elderly patients differ from younger patients in both the reasons for and presentation of their emergencies. For any typical presentation, functional assessment and polypharmacy evaluations need to be addressed by the home health care provider to ensure comprehensive emergency care.

Several studies have assessed the use of emergency services by elderly patients. A small hospital study found that about 19 percent of all emergency room (ER) visits were made by patients older than 65 years. Elderly patients are more likely to arrive by ambulance, require hospitalization for completion of their care, and incur higher laboratory and procedure costs than younger patients. Another multicenter study compared 418 elderly patients who visited the emergency department with 175 younger controls. As in the previous study, the elderly were more likely to arrive by ambulance, present with conditions that were intermediate to high urgency, and more frequently presented with disease conditions other than the one that necessitated the emergency room visit. These "other" conditions were most likely to be hypertension, coronary artery disease, chronic obstructive pulmonary disease, arthritis, noncoronary vascular disease, and cerebral vascular accidents (stroke). Elderly patients were more likely to present with a medical illness (80%) than younger patients (66%). Injuries were more likely in the younger patients (25%) than in older patients (18%). Of the elderly who presented with an injury, 71 percent were related to falls. In this study, too, the elderly incurred higher costs and were more likely to be admitted to the hospital than the younger controls. When asked why they decided to come to the ER, many elderly patients stated they were "too sick to wait for an office visit." Finally, 21 percent of the elderly seeking emergency care noted a deterioration in their ability to care for themselves as a result of their illness, while only 11 percent of the younger controls noted the same complaint of deterioration. It may be noted that the level of patients' anxiety may play a role in reasons for seeking emergency care.

Polypharmacy is a predisposing factor to adverse events in elderly patients utilizing home health care services. Elderly nursing home patients receive between 6 and 8 medications per day for treatment of multiple disease states. The same could probably be said of the home health care recipients, although this population does differ slightly from that in a nursing home. An estimated 10 percent of elderly patients taking 6 to 10 prescription medications daily have an adverse reaction. These reactions could be drug-disease, drug-drug, or drug-food interactions, or an accumulation of side effects from all causes. Compliance is also a problem with multiple drug use among the elderly. Patients either fail to take their medications properly because they are confused about proper use, lack the proper instructions, or simply lose track of what medications they have taken. Another factor that impacts on compliance among the elderly is economics. Most elderly patients live on a limited income and cannot afford to take a large number of drugs in today's market of escalating drug prices. This may be a serendipitous benefit to many older patients, whose intake of drugs is curtailed because of inability to pay for them.

Disease states often have an atypical presentation in older persons. The presentation of myocardial infarction may include a history of falls and weakness, without the classic crushing chest pain. Pneumonia or urinary tract infection may be present in a patient who has no elevation in white blood cell count and no elevation in body temperature, but is in an acute confusional state. Examples of other diseases that present atypically include pulmonary embolism, congestive heart failure, parkinsonism, transient ischemic attacks (TIAs), hypothyroidism, depression, and malignancy. This change in symptom presentation is not completely understood, but may be due in part to the elderly patient's inability to mount an appropriate physiologic response. *Changes in the elderly patient's mental state, demeanor, or appetite may signify the beginning of an acute medical problem requiring emergency intervention.*

Falls are the leading cause of injury in the elderly. There are several well-defined causes of falls in this age group. The first is generalized muscle weakness which often presents in patients with chronic disease. Gait disturbances may also be manifestations of chronic disease and, when combined with weakness, can greatly increase the risk of falls. Because older persons often have a less compliant cardiovascular system, orthostatic hypotension (a drop in blood pressure on standing) may result in a fall. Several classes of medications have been shown to increase the incidence of falls in the elderly: antihypertensive agents and diuretics can worsen or cause orthostatic hypotension; benzodiazepines, antidepressants, and neuroleptics not only cause orthostasis, but also cause disequilibrium and falls by their central nervous system-mediated mechanism of action.

If the elderly patient does fall, the consequences can often be life-threatening. The most obvious consequence of falls in the elderly is fracture. The most common site of fracture is the hip. Due to the brittle nature of bone in older persons, once these fractures have occurred, they often take extended periods of time to heal. If the fracture does not heal properly, hip replacement is generally required. Hemorrhage is a complication of hip fracture that is life-threatening in the elderly. Pressure sores sometimes develop in the period following fractures because of the limited mobility created by the fracture.

PREVENTION OF ACCIDENTS AND EMERGENCIES

Steps can be taken to prevent accidents and emergencies in older persons. Since emergencies are usually medical problems, the treatment plans for the patient's illnesses should be understood and followed very closely by the provider. The treatment plans should be as simple as possible. If the plan is, or becomes, too complicated, the home health care professional should take steps to simplify it as appropriate. The primary provider should be contacted if the patient shows any sign of unusual weakness, fatigue, change in appetite, or change in mental status. Anticipate situations that could lead to emergencies and have a plan of action that is approved by all providers caring for the individual. Fall prevention strategies should already be in place: improved lighting in dark areas of the home, railings and bars placed where needed, placement of nonskid rugs in the bathtub or shower, etc. Elimination of hazards in the home should have been carried out: removal of clutter, throw rugs, protruding furniture, poor lighting, electric wires across open floor spaces.

What steps can be taken if there is an emergency at home? The appropriate emergency personnel should be called, along with the primary provider. Emergency numbers should be displayed beside the telephone. While waiting for the emergency medical personnel, assess the patient's airway, breathing, and circulation (the ABCs of emergency treatment should be assessed in that order). Standard cardiopulmonary resuscitation (CPR) techniques should be used if needed. The patient's family should be instructed in these techniques beforehand, if they are not familiar with them. First aid techniques can be used when necessary. After the emergency personnel have arrived, provide as much history as possible about the patient's condition and the probable cause of the accident, injury, or emergency event. The patient's medications, along with dosing schedules, should be sent with the patient.

SUMMARY

In conclusion, most emergencies in the elderly are medical in nature and often present atypically. If the emergency is an injury, it is usually a fall. Most emergencies can be prevented if the treatment plan is closely followed and measures taken to prevent accidents or injuries from happening and to safeguard the patient. Any noticeable change in the patient's condition should be reported to the primary provider. If an emergency occurs, call the appropriate emergency personnel and use CPR and first-aid techniques to assist the patient until other help arrives. Remain calm. Be prepared to provide a detailed history to the emergency personnel, which may need to be repeated to the ER staff. Take all of the patient's medications and the dosing schedule to the ER or send it with the ambulance team.

Not all accidents or emergency events can be prevented. Being prepared to manage these at the time they occur is part of the responsibilities of caregivers and providers.

References

Baker, S. 1985. Fall injuries in the elderly. *Clin Geriatr Med* 1:501–12.

Baum, S.A., and L.Z. Rubenstein. 1987. Old people in the emergency room: age-related differences in emergency department use and care. *J Amer Geriatr Soc* 35:398–404.

Eliastam, M. 1989. Elderly patients in the emergency department. *Ann Emerg Med* 18: 1222–29.

Hedges, J.R., B.M. Singal, E.W. Rousseau, A.B. Sanders, E. Bernstein, R.M. McNamara, T.M. Hogan. 1992a. Geriatric patient emergency visits. Part I: Comparison of visits by geriatric and younger patients. *Ann Emerg Med* 21:802–7.

———. 1992. Geriatric patient emergency visits. Part II: Comparison of visits by geriatric and younger patients. *Ann Emerg Med* 21:808–13.

Pinholt, E.M., K. Kroenke, and J.F. Hanley. 1987. Functional assessment of the elderly: a comparison of standard instruments with clinical judgment. *Arch Intern Med* 147:484–88.

Singal, B.M., J.R. Hedges, E.W. Rousseau, A.B. Sanders, E. Bernstein, R.M. McNamara, T.M. Hogan, 1992. Geriatric patient emergency visits. Part II: Comparison of visits by geriatric and younger patients. *Ann Emerg Med* 21:808–13

Dirk S. Lucas and Mark A. Stratton

Ethics in Health Care

INTRODUCTION

Ethics is a systematic and logical process of determining right or best answers to questions regarding moral dilemmas that frequently confront health care professionals when caring for individuals with acute, emergency, or terminal problems. Ethical dilemmas involve choices between equally unsatisfactory alternatives in which there are clearly no best solutions, often involving interrelationships characterized by conflict and tension.

Ethics provides insight for our understanding of philosophical and moral problems and addresses the critical area of the "distinction between what is and what ought to be." Ethics enables us to understand and appreciate the ideal with regard to morals, rules, and principles of individuals and of society, and emphasizes the quality of decisions made and subsequent actions taken.

ETHICAL DECISION MAKING

Four fallacies in ethical reasoning have been described: (1) reductionistic thinking, in which the individuals involved in the dilemma insist that there is only one moral decision in each case, when generally several moral problems coexist; (2) "ethical dominoes," in which the contention is made that bad, but not necessarily related, consequences will result from an action, as when children with severe birth defects are allowed to die, then others say that adult children have the right to kill unwanted elderly parents; (3) "ethical quagmires," that result when all the ethical problems in one situation are considered simultaneously, overwhelming the individuals in the situation to the point where no decisions can be made; and (4) "exception arguments," where individuals may focus only on "miracle cures" or other exceptional outcomes, rather than on the usual and expected outcomes in particular situations. Often, constructing a decision tree will identify the ethical question or problem, and all its ramifications, and lead the thinking process toward a rational, logical, and ethical decision, that is, the best possible decision in that case.

MORAL AND ETHICAL CODES

Morality has been defined as those behaviors that conform to custom. In our fast-paced, culturally diverse world, in which common values, beliefs, customs, and traditions no longer exist, at least for consensus purposes, ethical dilemmas arise frequently.

Most professional disciplines hold certain ethical standards and ideals of practice. An ethical professional has several qualities: (1) maximal competence in the specific discipline, (2) ability to provide a service that has significant social value, (3) ability to practice with a high degree of autonomy, and (4) sound judgment and ability to make reasonable, logical decisions in accordance with the tenets of the particular profession.

Physicians and nurses have their own codes of conduct. These codes often exceed the legal standards for professional practice. While a violation of the code of conduct may not be punishable under the law, the profession may impose sanctions such as reprimands, censure, suspension, or expulsion, depending on the severity of the breach of the code.

PROFESSIONAL AND PERSONAL ETHICS

A difference exists between professional and personal ethics. Professional ethics and conduct based upon ethical principles are subject to public scrutiny, are formalized, represent a tradition, and reflect policies that have developed over time and with experience. Members of professions are held accountable for the ethics of their practice.

Personal ethics are usually not formalized and may not be subject to public scrutiny. However, one's personal ethics and guiding principles play a major role in one's personal and professional life. Some individuals, for example, believe that it is wrong, under all circumstances, to not do all that is possible to save a life. Others believe that prolonging suffering is morally wrong and that saving a life is not the best choice. An alternative view is that it is impossible to make decisions based on "sanctity of life" and "quality of life" because individuals define these concepts differently. Each individual has his or her own collection of beliefs, ideals, morals, and ethics, often held subconsciously and never discussed nor perhaps even recognized.

ETHICAL ISSUES IN CARE OF OLDER PERSONS

Health care of the elderly frequently involves ethical decision making on many levels—societal, family, and individual.

At the societal level, several kinds of ethical problems may arise: (1) adherence to the prevailing standard of care for older people as contrasted with that for younger people, (2) the issue of rationing of scarce or costly health care resources for the elderly, (3) euthanasia, (4) the rights of institutionalized patients, and (5) creating a balance between the need for research and the rights of aged persons to participate or not as research subjects.

Individual and family issues concern decisions regarding (1) when to limit aggressive care, (2) how to handle mental incompetence while preserving the rights and dignity of the individual, (3) preserving autonomy in decisionmaking about health care, and (4) conflict of interests among family members, care providers, and the individual with respect to placement and treatment.

Several strategies can be used in making ethical decisions with regard to care of the elderly: (1) reviewing the values history, in which the patient's own opinions, expressed in the past to family members, physicians, or others are considered, to determine what the patient would wish to have happen; (2) using an ethics committee to discuss the various alternatives, including the patient's family, a member of the patient's religion, and experts involved in the care of the patient; and (3) using legal remedies to resolve such questions as legal

guardianship, power of attorney, and related issues that come under the domain
of the law.

EUTHANASIA

Euthanasia is a controversial topic that is much in the news media today,
partly because of the issue of assisted suicide. The term itself is often not understood, with some people considering euthanasia to be acts by health professionals to maintain comfort but not prolong life (passive), whereas others view
euthanasia as a more active process of actually hastening death. Others question
whether there is any real difference between passive and active euthanasia. In
one survey, however, 23 religious groups refused to condone active euthanasia,
while only three condemned passive euthanasia.

Many contend that euthanasia is the result of inappropriate use of medical
technologies and the failure of the courts and philosophers to reach a consensus
regarding the acceptability of limiting medical care for those in persistent veg-
etative states or with advanced disease or dementia.

Proponents of euthanasia believe that individuals with chronic progressive
incurable disease should have access to easy and painless death by choice, made
either by the patient or by appropriate others.

Opponents of euthanasia generally base their objections on two major reasons:
(1) belief that human intervention with death is immoral on religious and philosophical grounds; and (2) fear that, over time, indiscriminate criteria will be
used to create an atmosphere in which death may become an obligation of all
elderly persons, rather than a choice.

Because of the diversity of cultures, religions, and opinions prevalent in the
United States, it is unlikely that a national consensus regarding euthanasia will
emerge in the near future. Most state laws now support consideration of advance
directives made by individuals regarding the level of aggressive care. Health
care professionals need to be aware not only of euthanasia that may occur without appropriate decision-making processes, but also that advance directives are
not being honored by those caring for the individual.

SUMMARY

Ethics in health care is an essential part of providers' total knowledge and
efficacy in decisionmaking with regard to ethical dilemmas that arise frequently.
Individuals must have internalized values and ethical standards, both personal
and professional, to provide care that is in the best interests and well-being of
patients in all situations, particularly in terminal illnesses.

In reviewing the literature from 1993 regarding euthanasia, one finds that in
nearly every country, active euthanasia is considered to be immoral and illegal.
This conclusion holds true for current thinking and practice in The Netherlands,

often seen as a bastion of extreme liberal thought. Experts distinguish clearly between "killing" and "letting die," the two being separate issues. Most of the writers indicate that this is the critical point of decision, and most consider that, in the "double-effect" situation where, for instance, pain-killers are given to relieve unrelenting pain, and those who give the drug in larger and larger doses know that the other effect might very well be the death of the patient. A further case is made for refusing to administer any treatment that all experts regard as futile for the patient's well-being.

Only in the extreme instance when there is an insoluble conflict between "killing" and "letting die," it may be necessary to perform an action that is, in essence, impermissible. These situations are, fortunately, rare.

References

Jecker, N.S. 1993. Being a burden on others. *J Clin Ethics* 4(1):16–20.

Johnson, D.H. 1993. Helga Wanglie revisited: medical futility and the limits of autonomy. *Cambridge Quarterly of Healthcare Ethics* 2(2):161–70.

Siegler, P.A., E.D. Pellegrino, and P.A. Singer. 1990. Clinical medical ethics. *J Clin Ethics* 1:5–9.

Solomon, M.Z., L. O'Donnell, B. Jennings, V. Guilfoy, S.M. Wolf, K. Nolan, R. Jackson, D. Koch-Weser, and S. Donnelley. 1993. Decisions near the end of life: professional views on life-sustaining treatments. *Amer J Public Health* 83(1):14–23.

van der Wal, G. 1993. Unrequested termination of life: is it permissible? *Bioethics* 7(4): 330–39.

Weisbard, A.J. 1993. A polemic on principles: reflections on the Pittsburgh protocol. *Kennedy Institute of Ethics J* 3(2):217–30.

Ada Romaine-Davis

Ethnicity and Home Care

All ethnic groups provide extensive home care for older relatives, but there are some important differences among these groups. These differences are not in the types of services needed by the older person, but in attitudes toward the use of formal and informal home care and in the interpersonal dynamics between the individual receiving assistance and the caregiver.

The major differences in attitudes toward the use of formal home care stem from (a) the socioeconomic status of the ethnic group, (b) patterns of "family relationships," (c) values within the ethnic group toward home versus institutional care, and (d) the immigration status of the older person and their family.

SOCIOECONOMIC STATUS AND HOME CARE

Although home care services are available from a variety of public agencies, ethnic elderly in more affluent populations may use formal home care to a greater extent than their less affluent counterparts. Unfortunately, despite the increase in income among the older population since the 1970s, ethnic elderly are still likely to be among the population living in poverty. In 1990, the Federal poverty level for older persons (age 65 years or older) was $6,268 for a single person and $7,905 for a couple. According to official Federal government statistics, 16 percent of Americans over the age of 65 were poor or near-poor (125% of the poverty level). The proportions of poor and near-poor were substantially higher among ethnic elderly: 45.1 percent of Black elderly, 33.5 percent of Hispanic elderly.

Care must be exercised when citing income data about Hispanics. Cubans have distinctly higher income levels than Hispanics from Mexico or El Salvador. Among Asians, the situation also varies. Asian Indians have higher incomes than recent arrivals such as Koreans and Vietnamese. Regardless of tribal background, 55 percent of Native Americans living in rural areas are estimated to have incomes below the Federal poverty level. The high levels of poverty among African Americans, Hispanics, some Asians, and most Native Americans have their parallel in low educational levels.

It is important to note that low income is also a problem among younger members of these ethnic groups. The continuation of low income levels among younger cohorts means that unless funding for home care is increased substantially, home care among these ethnic groups will, by necessity, have to be provided by the informal social networks of the older person.

Middle-class ethnic families have more choices about whether to provide home care themselves, utilize formal home care services, or resort to institutional care when these services become too expensive or the task of constant home care too onerous. A study of middle-class Italian men in a suburban Maryland community indicated a more positive attitude toward the use of institutional care for a seriously impaired individual than among a working-class Baltimore population. For less impaired older relatives, middle-class Italian men viewed care for the older person at home as an acceptable alternative.

FAMILY RELATIONSHIPS AND HOME CARE

Family relationships are crucial to home care among the ethnic aged. A primary determinant of the extensiveness of home care provided in ethnic families is the configuration of the family itself. Among Black aged, contact with family members is more extensive than it is among Whites. Some writers argue that the concept of "family" as consisting only of blood relatives is not appropriate for all ethnic populations. Among Hispanics, the concept of family goes beyond blood relationships. Individuals may be linked to the family through a variety of relationships including serving as godparents. This compadrazgo system extends the range of the family system among many Hispanic groups. Among Native Americans living on reservations, the family often comprises a number of families who provide mutual assistance. The extent to which this enlarged family system is currently able to provide all of the home care necessary for a seriously impaired older person is not clear. As Native Americans become a predominantly non-reservation population, the patterns of home care will become more concentrated among fewer individuals.

In order to provide adequate home care, the older person must live in proximity to relatives. Merrill and Dill (1989) found that Italians in Rhode Island have more contact with relatives than other White ethnic groups. Among minorities, Black, Hispanic, and Native American families have larger proportions of relatives living at home or in close proximity.

ATTITUDES TOWARD INFORMAL AND FORMAL HOME CARE

The extensiveness of home care and the relative responsibility of respective family members for it is often based on strong cultural values about the role of the older person and the obligation of the family to provide assistance. In Asian cultures, Confucianism forms a common moral and ethical code of conduct. One of the major thrusts of Confucianism is ascribed behavior patterns for parents and children. These patterns include the respect that children must provide their elders ("filial responsibility") and their responsibility to care for parents. There are signs of erosion of filial responsibility among Vietnamese in the United States. These changes may reflect the availability of forms of care that were not available in Vietnam or shifts in attitudes under the influence of American culture. There are, however, no signs of abandonment of the elderly in any ethnic group.

More striking than a reduction in filial responsibility is the commitment family members make to home care for older relatives. This commitment was evident among women who had migrated to Australia and were providing home care for older parents. As one Croatian woman noted at a focus group session, an acceptable option to home care does not exist in Croatian culture.

A violation of norms of the ethnic culture can also lead to sanctions against the guilty party. In Australia, an Australian-born woman of Greek descent decided to place her mother in a nursing home after her mother had a serious stroke. Shocked by this action, other Greeks came up to her brother in the street and remarked that his sister was "disgusting" because no Greek would ever consider placing their parent in a nursing home. Smarting from these negative comments, the daughter decided to bring her mother home. In this example, the use of institutional care to replace informal care violated the norms of an ethnic group. Even the use of formal home care may be seen by the older ethnic person as a sign of abandonment by the family.

The older person may live alone but still receive home care from a relative. This pattern of home care is likely as the proportion of elderly living alone increases. The older person may live alone because they value their independence. The ethnic older person may live alone in an ethnic neighborhood because they value its cultural hegemony. Chan cites the case of Chinese elderly returning from the suburban home of children to live in the Chinatown area of Montreal because they wanted to live in a Chinese environment.

Among Black families, home ownership is more common among elderly than among younger cohorts. In these cases, if the older person is unable to live alone and no spouse is available, it is likely that a child will be living in the older person's home. Whose home the family resides in may not seem to be important, but if the relationship between the child and the parent deteriorates, home ownership may become an element in emotional conflicts.

IMMIGRATION STATUS

Two aspects of immigration status are important to ethnicity and home care. First is whether the family has legal immigration standing. Second is the generation of immigration of the individual.

Individuals who are illegal aliens may be forced to provide home care because they are able to obtain only low income jobs. These jobs do not provide adequate incomes to pay for any formal services. In addition, illegal aliens may be afraid to have contact with organizations that could provide assistance because they are afraid of inquiries about their immigration status.

Among immigrant populations, as in most groups, there is the expectation that women, particularly daughters, will shoulder the bulk of the home care burdens. The daughter may be required to provide more than assistance with the daily activities of living. The daughter may also be expected to be a social companion for her parent. This added task may result from the parent not being able to speak English. Unless the family lives in an ethnic neighborhood, the parent may become increasingly reliant on her family for both "hands on" home care, and social and recreational outlets.

Generation of immigration represents not only a historical fact but possibly alterations in values. Children of immigrants (second generation individuals) may have less allegiance to ethnic norms about caregiving than their parents. Conflicts with parents may arise about appropriate respect to parents and the appropriateness of employing formal home care providers.

SUMMARY

Home care for the ethnic aged thus involves complex decision making about the needs of the older person, the resources in the family to meet these needs, and the willingness of the older person to accept various forms of assistance.

References

Chan, K. 1983. Coping with aging and managing self-identity: The social world of elderly Chinese women. *Canadian Ethnic Studies* 15(3):36–50.

Die, A., and W. Seelbach. 1988. Problems, sources of assistance, and knowledge about
    services among elderly Vietnamese immigrants. *The Gerontologist* 28:448–52.
Gelfand, D.E., and D. Fandetti. 1980. Suburban and urban White ethnics: Attitudes to-
    wards care of the aged. *The Gerontologist* 20:588–94.
Gratton, B. 1987. Familism among the Black and Mexican-American elderly: Myth or
    reality? *Aging Studies* 1:19–32.
Kramer, J. 1990. *Study of Urban American Indian Aging.* Los Angeles: The Public Health
    Foundation.
McCallum, J., and D. Gelfand. 1990. *Ethnic Women in the Middle.* Report to the Com-
    monwealth Department of Community Services and Health, Canberra, Australia.
Merrill, D., and A. Dill. 1989. *Ethnic Differences in Family Caregiving.* Presented at the
    Annual Meeting, Gerontological Society of America, Minneapolis, November 15–
    19, 1989.

Donald E. Gelfand

Ethnicity as a Policy Issue

INTRODUCTION

The literature regarding ethnicity and home care clearly indicates that issues
regarding ethnicity must be addressed in order to maximize the benefits of home
care contacts for home care workers and their agencies, and for their clients.

HISTORICAL BACKGROUND

While early in the twentieth century it was still generally believed that the
United States was a "melting pot" and that group distinctions would eventually
disappear, it became apparent after 1950 that our society remained one with
diverse groups. In spite of this, research about ethnicity and aging has been slow
to develop; this is reflected in the paucity of literature available regarding ethnicity and home care. The slow development of research on ethnicity and aging
resulted from several factors. Since the 1930s, research on ethnicity tended to
focus primarily on members of minority groups, whereas until the early 1970s,
research on aging focused on Caucasian, native-born Americans. An additional
major factor was that early researchers in aging generally viewed elderly persons
as a homogeneous group in which age leveled all other characteristics, including
ethnicity.

ETHNICITY AND HOME CARE

It is apparent that issues around ethnicity and home care must be understood
and addressed. Some researchers state that culture has a pervasive influence on

an individual's values, goals, interests, roles, habits, and performance. Similarly, Blackburn (1992), writing on multicultural service orientation, emphasizes the need to understand the role played by ethnicity in the provision of home care services. She believes that conflict is implicit in the personal nature of home care and is a widespread problem, occurring particularly in areas of the country in which there are greater ethnic variations.

While Blackburn (1992) suggests that conflicts occur in which either the home care worker or the client may be the victim of discrimination, the literature regarding ethnicity has focused on difficulties experienced by home care workers as a result of institutional and individual prejudice and discrimination. Donovan (1987) states that the home care industry, a significant employer of low income and minority women, is creating many nonprofessional jobs within subemployment systems that keep wages low and give minimal or no benefits. Donovan (1987) believes that these conditions have their roots in U.S. slavery and in the continued segregation of African-American women into work roles as domestic servants in private households. Further, she believes that in the increased development of home care services with the goal of cost reduction, these efforts may be taking their heaviest toll on female minority workers. In developing the practice of contracting with private agencies in order to minimize costs, thereby developing a subemployment system, the government creates a system with low wages and minimal or no benefits.

Cantor and Chichin (1990) looked at the interpersonal relationships of workers and their clients, focusing on the factors that cause stress and strain among home care workers. They identified responses that appeared to be related to ethnicity. There was little evidence of worker demoralization, but the levels that existed were significantly related to functional fluency in English, race-ethnicity, and levels of health and education. It was also determined that although there was little reporting of harassment related to race, color, or language, some experiences of this type did occur. They showed that harassment by clients or families diminished job satisfaction among home care workers. These researchers indicated that questions about harassment of home care workers are sensitive, resulting in probable underreporting.

The literature also addresses systemic and individual problems as they relate to recipients of home care. The research study of Fine (1986) corroborates Donovan's findings, that there are biases against minority low-income women providing home care services, but information suggests biases against recipients of care as well. This study indicates that California's assignment of workers as "independent providers" of home care services under Title XX puts the most needy in the hands of the least trained and supervised, and most exploited, home care workers. Similarly, other researchers who studied privatization of home care services suggest that the trends revealed in their study show potentially negative consequences for clients who are already in marginal positions in society, including those who have low incomes or belong to minority groups.

RECOMMENDATIONS BY RESEARCHERS

Many excellent recommendations have been made to address problems related to ethnicity and home care. These include a national policy for long-term care and changes at the agency and individual levels. Several authors stress the need for home care workers to have adequate training, which will provide advancement and additional educational opportunities among minority home care workers. Blackburn (1992) describes training models.

While improved training is one incentive for home care workers, other incentives in the form of better wages or bonuses, fringe benefits, and involving workers in developing care plans for clients will enhance the status and job satisfaction among minority workers.

Cantor and Chichin (1990) found that much of the supervision of home care workers was conducted via telephone. They recommend that supervision occur face-to-face with supervisors making in-home visits, that support group meetings of home care workers be established, and that a method be developed for workers to quickly communicate problems such as harassment. Several researchers suggested that agencies' governance and staffing represent community and cultural diversity, and that an outreach focus on underserved populations be an integral part of the services.

Obstacles to the use of home care services by potential clients should be explored, particularly among diverse racial and cultural groups in the community. Major obstacles are often language, education, and economic barriers.

CONCLUSION

The research literature regarding ethnicity and home care shows that there are multiple issues to be addressed on many levels. The onus for change must rest with the home care agencies, particularly those related to staff effectiveness, appropriateness, efficiency, and racial and ethnic diversity among administrators and staff. To improve access to and quality of home care, home care administrators need to institute changes, and to evaluate the effects of these changes on each of the various issues and obstacles to be addressed.

References

Bergthold, L.A., C.L. Estes, and A. Villanueva. 1990. Public light and private dark: the privatization of home health services for the elderly in the U.S. *Home Health Care Services Quarterly* 11(3/4):7–33.

Blackburn, J.A. 1992. Achieving a multicultural service orientation: adaptive models in service delivery and race and culture training. *Caring* 11:22–26.

Cantor, M.H., and E.R. Chichin. 1990. *Stress and Strain Among Homecare Workers of the Frail Elderly.* New York: Brookdale Research Institute on Aging, Third Age Center, Fordham University.

Donovan, R. 1987. Home care work: a legacy of slavery in U.S. health care. *Affilia* 2: 33–44.

Fine, D.R. 1986. The home as the workplace: prejudice and inequity in home health care. *Caring* 5:12–19.

Patricia J. Kolb

Ethnicity and Variations in Family Support and Caregiving

The decision for home based care for minority elderly, and variations in types of treatment and involvement of extended family members or community supports, is determined by many culturally related factors besides values. Assimilation, acculturation, generational level, family size and stability, time since immigration, intergenerational conflict, barriers to care, and multiple medical and psychiatric illnesses all contribute to decisions for home care. Care is undoubtedly stressful to many minority families, but special strategies to engage these families are still lacking.

The 1990 U.S. Census estimated that 12.5 percent of the overall U.S. population is over the age of 65. Comprising this 12.5 percent, 0.98 percent African-Americans, 0.46 percent Hispanic Americans, 0.04 percent American Indians, Eskimo, and Aleutians, and 0.17 percent Asian/Pacific Islander-Americans. The lower than expected proportion of elderly minority individuals, compared to the overall population, is partly explained by immigration laws that excluded many minority groups prior to 1943 and excess mortality rates due to lifestyle differences and higher health risks.

Minority elderly have long been known to underutilize formal health care and social services despite need. Although especially low utilization rates of nursing homes and long-term care facilities have been described, it is surprising that even home-bound services and meals are not heavily utilized. Data from the local area agencies on aging and other service utilization data show a general lower rate of use and even declines in participation for many services by ethnic/racial minority elders. One interpretation of these data is to romanticize informal support and reliance on family caregivers as a cultural preference, or a value to keep things within the family. Although this is true to some degree, one cannot discount the influence of low socioeconomic status on the ultimate form that caregiving takes. For example, the low use of formal services by Black or Hispanic elderly is strongly influenced by barriers to care, poor quality of services, inadequate information about available services, absence of bilingual providers, or fears of being treated prejudicially.

Research and demonstration models for service delivery for minority populations, especially low-income minorities, are lacking. Inconsistencies exist between the perceptions of public policymakers and the perceptions of minority elderly about the actual services needed. Since mainstreaming has not been effectively achieved, a debate continues to rage between establishing "culturally sensitive services'' that are largely structured like existing mainstream programs but offer bilingual staff, cultural activities, peer identification, and improved quality (e.g., Hispanic nursing homes or Asian nursing homes), versus establishing fundamentally different services oriented around home-care and community groups.

The main problem in describing ethnic variations and defining family support needs lies in the great diversity among and within ethnic groups along lines of social class, immigrant status, language dominance, degree of assimilation, and openness to assimilation. Cultural adherence and special service needs differ greatly. Overriding clinical issues that these groups present are described, from which several clinical generalizations can be made.

CLINICAL ISSUES

Immigrant Status and Intergenerational Stress

Except for African-American and Native-American elderly, a majority of elderly minority individuals are immigrants. In general, recent immigrant elderly are at highest risk for psychological disturbances due to adjustment difficulties and stress. Mental problems may be especially problematic if there are language barriers, poor education, or lack of resources. In contrast, rates of mental illness may be even lower for "survivors" who have lived in the United States for decades than they are for American-born elderly. This is thought to be related to a survivor effect where only the fittest survive into old age.

The proverbial "generation gap" may be heightened in minority groups with recent immigrant status. Assimilation of American-born generations often leads to differing expectations of family roles, mannerisms, customs, food preferences, values, behaviors, and other attitudes. Some speculate that first- and second-generation relations may actually be more emotionally distant and strained than later generational relations despite a strong feeling of obligation. Thus, care may be provided but under extreme strain and emotional tension. Strain may be even higher for many upwardly mobile minority families who strive to move out of ethnic areas to the suburbs. If elderly remain in the multigenerational household, isolation is often magnified since additional community support networks are lacking.

Similar problems may arise for ethnic groups who have been blocked from assimilation due to prejudicial barriers. Isolation and generational conflict may still be present and might be especially pronounced in upwardly mobile families where there are strong socioeconomic differences between generations.

Timing/Degree and Type of Disability

Ethnic minority elderly often have higher rates of chronic illness at earlier ages than the average. In African-American groups, multi-infarct dementia may be a greater risk due to the high prevalence of hypertension, cardiovascular disease, and diabetes. Black elderly also have higher rates of mobility limitations, activity restriction, and bedfast days when compared to a white group. For Hispanic-American elderly, there are high rates of diabetes, tuberculosis, and obesity, but lower rates of cardiovascular disease. Because of an earlier age of onset for illness, some Hispanic groups consider ''old age'' to start as young as 55 years old, particularly those who have been employed as migrant workers. American-Indian elderly have a life expectancy of 65 years compared to 73.3 years for other groups. They experience disability at a much earlier age than non-Indians (age 45 vs. age 65). This group has higher rates of diabetes, pneumonia, and tuberculosis than other minority groups. Some Asian-American groups have high rates of hypertension, stroke, multi-infarct dementia, and heart disease that may be a result of high salt, high cholesterol diets. In many Indochinese elderly, parasitic diseases and sequelae of toxic exposures may be persisting problems.

Early onset and severity of problems and disabilities can seriously stress primary caregivers who may have competing family demands and economic responsibilities. If frailty appears when the available caregiver is either too young or too old to give care without conflicting demands, caregiver stress will be exaggerated.

Family Size and Extent of Non-Kinship Support

Family size is understandably viewed as an index of support. However, the picture is much more complex since marriage and divorce rates, household size, family structure (e.g., multigenerational households, single parent households), social mobility, occupation, socioeconomic class, and expectations differ among minority groups.

Stable middle and upper income minority groups are more likely to show similar family support patterns to majority groups and approach those rates of formal service usage. Lower income groups or recent immigrants are often more reliant on family and community support networks. Current trends reveal extended social networks from church and friends play a larger role in home care for elderly Black patients than for other ethnic groups. Hispanics tend to utilize multigenerational support more. Mexican-American elderly, in particular, are three times more likely to live in a multigenerational household.

However, an increasing risk for minority elderly is that the range of family supports and resources may not allow optimal care when they need assistance, even if there is a strong preference for home care.

Openness to Collaboration with the Community and Fears of Prejudice

The available data does support the notion that family attitudes is one major reason for the low rates of service utilization by frail minority elderly.

Every ethnic group likes to believe that it has a strong ethic for family affiliation and filial duty for its elderly. Strongly expressed values for close, traditional extended family ties persist in all groups. However, the form of filial obligation often may not remain "traditional." For example, the Japanese norm for responsibility of the eldest son to provide care for the parents is not practiced in the United States. Care in the United States, similar to national trends, is often relegated to the oldest daughter.

In Mexican-American and Chinese-American groups, and many other minority groups, it is more likely that the elderly will receive care from an informal source, usually a spouse or a child, rather than from an outside formal source. Black and white groups tend to use formal services more frequently. Linkages with churches or religious centers are often a major source of support for many groups. Institutionalization is less commonly used by all groups (whites 5%; Blacks 3.5%; others 2%).

The choice of informal care in order to accommodate alternate health belief systems and treatment preferences, such as herbal treatments, massage, spiritual healing, or other approaches, are generally more strongly held by individuals with lower education, lower exposure to health information, or isolation from the dominant culture, such as recent immigrants or the prejudicially excluded.

An additional reason for the preference of informal family care is due to external barriers to care. Frequently, services available to minority populations are viewed by the minority community as inadequate. Fears of stereotyping, misdiagnosis, and mistreatment will prevent caregivers from seeking formal services in many instances. In addition, complex application processes and policies and cost-sharing demands are often intimidating to low-income or low-literate or non-English-speaking minority elderly who comprise a large proportion of minority elderly.

SUMMARY

As this overview shows, there is wide variation among ethnic minority groups regarding utilization of support services, some of which are culturally based, others that are dependent on the health care system in the United States. Differences are evident among minority groups about who will care for elderly family members and how much support will be given within the family and how much will be sought from outside the informal circle. Also evident is that existing behavior patterns are changing.

References

American Society on Aging. 1992. *Serving Elders of Color: Challenges to Providers and the Aging Network.* San Francisco.

Hatch, L.R. 1991. Informal support patterns of older African-American and white women. *Research on Aging* 13(2):144–70.

Heyman, A., G. Fillenbaum, B. Prosnitz, K. Raiford, B. Burchett, and C. Clark. 1991.

Estimated prevalence of dementia among elderly black and white community residents. *Arch Neurology* 48:594–98.
Report of the Task Force on Ethnic Minority Elderly. 1993. Members: K. Sakauye, Chairman, F.M. Baker, R.M. Chacko, R.G. Jimenez, H.W. Nickens, J.W. Thompson, J.M. diFigueiredo, W. Liu, and S. Mason. April.
Sakauye, K. 1992. The elderly Asian patient. *J Geriatr Psych* 25(1):85–104.
Yee, D.L. 1992. Health care access and advocacy for immigrant and other underserved elders. *J of Health Care for the Poor and Underserved* 2(4):448–64.

Rose McCleary and Kenneth M. Sakauye

Expenditure Patterns of the Elderly

INTRODUCTION

A growing part of the U.S. population, as well as of other nations, is elderly. Coupled with an overall improvement in the economic condition of many (not all) of those over 65, the elderly have an increasing effect on the entire U.S. economy. Understanding this impact—for example, on the overall level of savings in America, or the shifts in demand for various goods and services such as food, housing, and medical care—is of major importance.

Researchers at the University of Pennsylvania, in collaboration with scholars at Temple and Fairleigh Dickinson Universities, recently completed a study that explored how the elderly behave as consumers and savers, and which goods and services are particularly important in the marketbaskets of older Americans. Funding in the early stages of this research was provided by the Center for the Study of Aging. The study was primarily supported by a major grant from the A.A.R.P. Andrus Foundation. The other researchers included Dr. Janusz Szyrmer, Associate Director of the Social Science Data Center and Adjunct Assistant Professor of Regional Science, and Dr. Rosenwaike, Social Work, from the University of Pennsylvania; Dr. Joseph Friedman, Economics, Temple University; and Dr. Arthur Dolinsky, Marketing, Fairleigh Dickinson University.

SAVING AND CONSUMPTION

Choices people make between consumption and saving are critical decisions for the household, and in turn have a profound impact on the overall economy. Just now, much attention is being paid to the shortfall of saving that hurts our ability to invest for the future. Investment in turn fuels future economic growth and well-being. This study focuses on the role which age plays in determining the propensity to save and to consume, the split all people make in their income, between putting money in savings and spending.

The research was based on what is called "Life Cycle Hypothesis," which seeks to explain shifts in saving behavior as people grow older. The hypothesis, based on considerable study over the past decades, argues that young people save relatively more, and that the elderly draw down assets, supporting themselves from savings in retirement years. Tests of the Life Cycle Hypothesis, using cross-sectional data, were undertaken in the past, with mixed results. However, findings from the Pennsylvania study utilizing a longitudinal database covering the 1960s through the 1980s, which are more appropriate to such investigations, do not support this hypothesis. The propensity to save was actually found to increase with age; older people spend relatively less and save relatively more than do younger people.

Age, of course, should not be studied separately from other factors. The analysis is enriched by the introduction of the concept of "cohort" as well as analyzing overall rise in income. Those in the generation who share a given environment or experience at a certain stage of their lives, a given cohort, can be expected to exhibit distinct patterns of economic behavior. Thus, those who grew into adulthood in Depression years (which of course is an important group of those now over 65) might well show particular expenditure and saving patterns colored by that traumatic experience. They are different from those who began their work life in the ebullient post-war years some twenty years later. As distinct cohorts are studied, various patterns emerge. For example, data show that Baby Boomers are engaged in a virtual consumption binge well into their middle age, though another recent study, by the researchers at the National Bureau of Economic Research, suggests a return to higher savings by the aging Baby Boomers. In the Pennsylvania study, today's very elderly (those over 85) were found to save, contrary to the ruling hypothesis.

COMMODITIES AND SERVICES

The second phase of the research looked in greater detail at how people spend their money. Various types of expenditures were examined. Particular attention was given the various health-related expenses, as well as food, shelter, transport, and other categories. These were subject to statistical analyses to see how age, long-term trends, cohort, and income level affect shares spent on each class of goods and services.

The most dramatic findings, confirming widely held views and evidence from other studies, are that various health-related expenditure categories (such as medical services, insurance, drugs, and supplies) have increased for all Americans. The share is found to be dramatically higher for households headed by older Americans, and the increase is especially great for the very elderly. The researchers also found that elderly households spend proportionately less on food than do younger ones. A somewhat lesser association with age was found in personal care expenses. Contributions as a proportion of expenditures were higher among older Americans, thus challenging many other findings. Other groups of expenditures were found to be proportionately smaller for households headed by older Americans: transportation, leisure activities, and apparel. Life and personal insurance is not particularly associated with age. Though housing expenses decline with age, the households in which there was a very elderly household head were found to spend more on housing than where the head was counted among the young elderly.

Introducing income as a factor, the results are consistent with most expenditure studies. As other studies show, the Pennsylvania study found that spending for food declines proportionately with higher income, though this difference appears to diminish with age—all elderly spend proportionally less on food. For all ages, housing expenses have come to take a larger bite for lower income households. And the share of health-related expenditures of lower income households exceeded those of other households; it was found to do so for all age groups, and over the timespan covered. Not surprisingly, the budget share of life insurance is greater with income for all age groups. Contributions are related to income, with elderly wealthy giving proportionately the most.

When investigating changes that have taken place over the period from the 1960s into the later 1980s, a number of trends become apparent. During these decades, health-related expenses have proportionately increased for all households. But those effects are felt with particular intensity by elderly households, and more so in the recent past than earlier. Housing as budget share has grown for young households; not so for older households.

Cohort effects have not stood out as sharply for specific categories, though the cohort which has just reached retirement in the mid-1980s did register a steady upward trend in health-related expenses that was greater than that experienced by other cohorts as they aged. This cohort is spending proportionately less in its older years for food and other commodities, too.

The analysis drew on a major data series that until now has not been successfully analyzed on a comparative basis over a longer period. This is the Consumer Expenditure Survey fielded by the Bureau of Labor Statistics. Each of a series of such surveys obtained detailed information from thousands of households all over the country. The initial research has facilitated a broader range of studies now underway by others. Econometric analyses of this rich database were complemented with other statistical analyses. The investigators hope to continue this line of research by looking at regional patterns and differences among urban, suburban, and rural households. Analysis of shifts in the geography of the population, together with aging trends, will have a profound impact on the way our economy works.

Thomas A. Reiner

F

Family Relationships in Later Life

INTRODUCTION

Perhaps the most noteworthy feature of late life families and family relationships is their variety. Whereas early family life focuses upon the couple, late life families may include first-married couples, widowed individuals, adult child-parent units, siblings, or subsequently-married couples. Caregiving for an impaired member is likely to be different in relation to the life stage of a family and the variety of relationships.

Second, late life families are now often characterized by shifting patterns of aid and dependency. Many types of intergenerational and intrafamilial support and care are given as parents and children become members of older generations and grandchildren are middle-aged.

The third important feature of contemporary later life family relationships is the length of time relationships are likely to have endured. Given the increased life expectancy that has occurred within this century, relationships between two family members may endure fifty to seventy years.

Finally, social change as it has been manifested in such features as work, marriage, and family size heavily impacts relationships and caregiving within families. For example, the high divorce rate, increased numbers of working women and fewer children in families have important consequences for who gives care at home as families age.

TYPES OF FAMILY RELATIONSHIPS

Older men are likely to experience different late life family relationships than do older women. Most older men are married, but almost half of older women are widows. In 1986, 80 percent of men between the ages of 65 and 74 were married and cohabiting with their spouses, while 49 percent of women of the same ages were married and 49 percent of older women were widowed. The shorter life expectancy of men and the likelihood of men marrying younger women combine to increase the numbers of women who are widowed. Still, two-thirds of the elderly population are independently living married couples. And, research has long shown that when spouses are able and available, they are usually the designated primary caregivers when home care is needed. Caregiving spouses are divided about equally between wives and husbands because most older men are married and older women often must face their own impairment alone.

Most older couples are in first, long-enduring marriages. Marriages that last tend to be much longer, and thus partners are charting new courses as the length of marriage when one spouse dies is, on the average, 43 years. What is known from research is that these couples are likely to be quite satisfied with their long-term partnerships. Although there are some mixed findings, most studies have shown marital satisfaction is higher for "empty nest" couples than for couples with children living at home. This trend continues through late life. This factor may be important when home caregiving is needed. Close relationships tend to motivate the caregiver to cope with the demands of home care.

Because women are more often widowed than men, they have more opportunity to be socialized for the role. Widows, more than widowers, develop social networks with other women, while men are likely to remarry, given the availability of partners and the acceptability of marrying a younger woman. Widowers also tend to be more isolated because, in the older cohorts, wives tend to make social arrangements. Sometimes, older widowers may even have difficulty in knowing how to initiate social plans with their own adult children; it may be harder to ask for substantive help such as help with activities of daily living (ADL).

A few studies have addressed remarriage in later years and find the marriages characterized by satisfaction, especially when adult children approve. Loneliness and a need for companionship are given as reasons for remarriage. Divorced older persons are more likely to remarry than widows and widowers, and always-single elders are least likely to marry. Whether marriage is new or long-enduring, spouses are the most likely persons to provide needed home care. A hierarchy of care exists whereby adult children are next likely to care for impaired older persons, and siblings are generally third in the hierarchy.

Sibling-shared households have not been carefully investigated, but it is known that sibling relationships tend to be stronger in later life. They are characterized by rather frequent contact and feelings of closeness. Still, the marital or parent-child bonds are the main subject of research and the most prominent family ties.

Older parents are likely to enjoy high levels of interaction with and support from their children. There is an increase in the number of households composed of an older parent and a single adult-child and many older persons who need care live with their adult children's families. Families provide most of the care needed by older members; adult children, together with their families, are responsible for much care despite busy schedules and time conflicts.

PATTERNS OF AID AND DEPENDENCY

Older parents are likely to see their children quite often and to live near them, despite what is commonly thought to the contrary—that industrial and post-industrial societies and transient families have weakened intergenerational relationships. Most older parents (about 80%) live within an hour's driving distance of one of their children, and they are likely to see one of their adult children at least once a week.

Decades of research have shown the devotion and high levels of instrumental and personal care given to older family members across a continuum of need. Families, much more than professionals, regardless of race or socioeconomic status, play the central roles in helping and decisionmaking for their older members. Intergenerational aid, especially financial and instrumental help, commonly flow downward from the parent generation through early old age. A shift often occurs as parents begin to have limiting chronic illnesses that require different types of help, such as transportation and housework assistance. As individuals live longer and families are impacted by divorce and remarriage, there are new combinations of caregiving and care-receiving family members.

SOCIAL CHANGE AND FAMILY RELATIONSHIPS

The facts of divorce, subsequent remarriages, and single-parent families have also augmented the long list of family members. If one does not have good rapport with one's mother, there may be a stepmother or an older half-sister with whom to share. One researcher describes "a matrix of latent relationships" that are resources for family members. Her description refers to the increased numbers and types of relatives that provide potential for a variety of relationships.

Remarriage of widowed persons can be seen as "triadic." In other words, the deceased spouses of both bride and groom are present in the history of the family. Moreover, the families of those departed spouses now may interact with the new spouse's family on occasions of family import such as weddings and graduations. This feature of remarriage among widows and widowers adds to the "matrix" of possible relationships and the complexity of family life for the new spouses. It may also add to the emotional and physical support one might expect to receive in old age.

Another aspect of social change that has consequences for older family relationships occurs in the world of work. First, women are likely to be in the work force, and thus the traditional family caregiver may be absent or only partially available. Sons and other relatives help to fill this void. Second, today's older cohorts of retired persons are the first generations to leave their work and live on for more than a decade, enabling them to devote more time to family ties.

Finally, although there are more and longer-enduring relationships in today's older families, the trend toward fewer children per couple in industrialized societies results in fewer parent-child and older sibling relationships. Persons over 65 typically have at least one sibling living. In the past, most older people had a number of siblings. Though it is still open to speculation, it seems the new relationships derived from remarriages within families offer possibilities for replacement of those ties of the past.

References

Brubaker, T.H. 1985. *Later Life Families.* Newbury Park, Cal.: Sage.

Harris, D. 1990. *Sociology of Aging.* New York: Harper and Row.

Matras, J. 1990. *Dependency, Obligations, and Entitlements.* Englewood Cliffs, N.J.: Prentice-Hall.

Riley, M.W. 1983. The family in an aging society: a matrix of latent relationships. *J Family Issues* 4(3):439–54.

Shanas, E. 1979. The family as a social support system in old age. *The Gerontologist* 19:169–74.

Smerglia, V.L., G.T. Diemling, and C.M. Barresi. 1988. Black/white comparisons in helping and decision-making networks of impaired elderly. *Family Relations* 37: 305–9.

Donald E. Stull and Virginia L. Smerglia

G

Gastrointestinal Problems

Gastrointestinal (GI) problems are common in old age and are responsible for approximately 15–25 percent of all visits to physicians. Normal aging affects the structure and function of the intestinal tract. Loss of teeth, decreased amount of saliva and loss of tastebuds, gastric mucosal atrophy, loss of acid secretion, and motility changes may all contribute to GI problems. Altered dietary habits and the use of multiple medications can influence the functioning of the GI system. In addition, such common non-GI problems as loneliness, depression, and dementia could also have an impact on GI functioning.

Almost all GI problems that begin in young adult life may continue into old age. However, GI diseases also may appear with advancing age. The most common GI problems seen in elderly patients are:

1. hiatus hernia and reflux esophagitis

2. peptic ulcer disease

3. diverticular disease of the colon

4. inflammatory bowel disease

5. GI bleed

6. constipation and fecal incontinence

7. GI malignancy

8. Ischemic colitis

HIATUS HERNIA AND REFLUX ESOPHAGITIS

Hiatus hernia is a common problem in old age. It is estimated that over 50 percent of people, age 70 and over, have hiatus hernia with or without reflux esophagitis. Changes in the sphincter pressure at the junction of the esophagus and the stomach may lead to symptoms of reflux including epigastric discomfort and heartburn. Hiatus hernia and reflux problems are more common in those who drink, smoke, and are obese. Some of the commonly used medications such as calcium channel blockers (used for hypertension and heart disease) and theophylline (used for bronchitis and asthma) may lead to reduced sphincter tone and cause symptoms of reflux. Esophagitis results from acid regurgitation and irritation of the lining of the esophagus. While most elderly patients have reflux esophagitis with hiatus hernia, some patients continue to have reflux symptoms even in the absence of significant hiatus hernia. Unlike the younger adults, in older patients these symptoms may remain poorly defined. In some cases, the patient may continue to lose small amounts of blood from the lining of the esophagus and may gradually become anemic. Gastric contents may be aspirated periodically and this may cause recurrent hoarseness and respiratory infections. Since elderly patients may also have coexisting coronary artery disease, the pain of reflux esophagitis could mimic anginal pain in some individuals. A thorough evaluation by the physician is essential in every case. The management of hiatus hernia and reflux esophagitis is, fortunately, not difficult. Simple steps that are helpful in the management include:

1. weight reduction
2. avoid overeating; eat early in the evening
3. avoid alcohol
4. stop smoking
5. raise the head of the bed by 4–6 inches
6. avoid wearing constrictive garments around the abdomen

There are a number of antacid preparations that may be used, many of them available over the counter. In patients with persistent symptoms, medications that affect the acid secretion (H_2 antagonists) may need to be prescribed by the physician.

PEPTIC ULCER DISEASE

Peptic ulcer disease is common in older patients. Gastric ulcers are far more common than duodenal ulcers in this population; a lower incidence of duodenal ulcers may be due to a decrease in the gastric acid secretion. Since the symptoms may be ill-defined and may, in fact, mimic the symptoms of hiatus hernia and reflux esophagitis, it is essential that all patients with suspected peptic ulcer disease be thoroughly evaluated. Endoscopic examination of the suspected ulcer and a biopsy confirmation of the nature of the ulcer are necessary in most cases. Radiological investigations such as barium meal studies may not be sufficient to exclude a malignancy. Over the last 15 years, with the availability of H_2 receptor antagonists (cimetidine and ranitidine), the management of peptic ulcer disease has been revolutionized. Some patients, with the tendency of recurrence of ulcers, may need to take maintenance doses of these medications for several months. Medical follow-up is vital in all cases to ensure that the ulcer has healed satisfactorily.

DIVERTICULAR DISEASE OF THE COLON

Diverticular disease has been termed a disease of modern civilization; the disease was almost unknown until the twentieth century. With the low fiber content of the western diet, the condition predominantly affects people in the western world. In rural parts of Asia and Africa, where the dietary fiber content remains high, diverticular disease is uncommon. High intracolonic pressure and constipation are thought to cause the small areas of herniation—the diverticuli—in the colon. Diverticuli are more frequently seen in the sigmoid colon. It is estimated that approximately 35 percent of people between the ages of 65–74, and 50 percent of people over 75, are affected by this condition. The presence of diverticuli itself may not cause significant symptoms for many years. Symptoms commonly include change in bowel habits (constipation, diarrhea, or constipation alternating with diarrhea), flatulence, and heartburn. Complications of diverticulitis may be seen in up to 30 percent of cases and include acute diverticulitis, colonic abscess, intestinal obstruction, and perforation. Acute abdominal pain, fever, vomiting, and distention of the abdomen may indicate complications that require urgent medical, and possibly surgical, care.

INFLAMMATORY BOWEL DISEASE

Major inflammatory bowel diseases include ulcerative colitis and Crohn's disease, which usually present in young adult life. However, the symptoms may first appear in old age and could include change of bowel habits, abdominal pain, weight loss, weakness, and anemia. In all cases, if an older person has significant bowel symptoms that persist for more than a few days, the patient requires appropriate medical attention. Special investigations, including barium studies, sigmoidoscopy, and colonoscopy, can aid in diagnosing these conditions with relative certainty. Most patients respond satisfactorily to medical therapy. Failure of medical therapy or the appearance of complications may require surgery. Since ulcerative colitis is associated with a high risk of malignancy, surgical resection of the bowel may be required in selected patients with prolonged history of ulcerative colitis.

GASTROINTESTINAL BLEEDING

Acute GI bleeding is a common condition that is often responsible for urgent hospitalization of the older person. The most common site of bleeding is from a peptic ulcer. A tear at the lower end of the esophagus (Mallory-Weiss syndrome), gastritis, and carcinoma of the stomach are other causes of bleeding. Despite advances in the diagnosis and treatment of GI bleeding, the mortality rate among older persons with acute GI bleeding remains high. There are at least two important factors that affect the outcome for these older patients. First, the hardened vessels do not constrict very well in the elderly, and therefore rebleeding within 24–48 hours of the first bleed is more common in the elderly. Second, despite acute blood loss, often there is a lack of diaphoresis (high pulse rate and low blood pressure) that commonly results in delayed diagnosis. GI bleeding in old age requires urgent medical attention and frequent monitoring.

CONSTIPATION AND FECAL INCONTINENCE

Although difficult to define, constipation may be defined subjectively as a sense of incomplete evacuation of the bowel. Because many elderly people believe that ''auto-intoxication'' may result from the colon, they complain of constipation if they do not have 1–2 bowel movements each day. The fact remains that there is considerable variation in the frequency of bowel movements, and it is not necessary to have 1 or 2 bowel movements per day for perfect health. Poor dietary habits, inadequate fluid and fiber intake, poor motility of the bowel, and drug toxicity are some of the more common causes of constipation in old age. Several significant medical problems including dementia, depression, GI stricture and malignancy, anal fissure, inflamed hemorrhoids, metabolic disturbances (underactive thyroid gland, low serum potassium, and high calcium levels) may also be associated with constipation. In all cases, the management of chronic constipation requires a thorough evaluation by a physician. In most cases, simple steps such as gradual increase of fiber and fluid intake, and a regular physical exercise program may be sufficient to regularize the bowel habits. Fecal impaction is a common cause of fecal incontinence in the elderly, especially those in institutions, and must be treated as a priority before other measures are employed to regularize bowel habits.

GASTROINTESTINAL MALIGNANCY

Although cancers may affect any part of the GI tract, carcinoma of the stomach and colon are the two most common types of cancer. The incidence of carcinoma of the stomach has been, fortunately, declining in the United States in recent years. Patients with pernicious anemia are at particularly higher risk. Symptoms of GI tumors include anorexia, nausea and vomiting, weight loss, abdominal pain, and change in bowel habits. Surgical resection in early stages is the only hope for most patients. Once the cancer has spread to distant organs, there is little that can be done.

ISCHEMIC COLITIS

With progressive narrowing and hardening of the arteries (atherosclerosis), the blood supply of any major organ may be compromised. The blood vessels of the bowel, the mesenteric arteries, may also be affected by atherosclerosis. Gradual reduction of the blood supply to the intestine may cause bowel symptoms, particularly following meals. Abdominal pain and discomfort, malabsorption, and diarrhea are often the presenting symptoms. Unlike the coronary artery bypass for coronary artery disease, there is no satisfactory surgical treatment for ischemic colitis. Medical care is primarily based on treatment of symptoms.

CONCLUSION

GI problems are not uncommon in old age. Since most conditions have non-specific presentation, an elderly person with a change in bowel habits, abdominal pain and discomfort, and weight loss must seek medical attention at an early stage. Appropriate diagnosis can be easily established with thorough history, physical examination, radiological investigations, and endoscopic procedures. Fortunately, most conditions respond well to medical treatment. In all suspected cases, malignancy must be ruled out initially; if malignancy can be detected at an early stage, surgical treatment can be lifesaving for many persons.

References

Berg, D., L. Cantwell, G. Heudebert, and J.L. Sebastian, Jr., eds. 1993. Gastrointestinal medicine. *Handbook of Primary Care Medicine*. Philadelphia: Lippincott.
Kelley, W.N., ed. 1992. *Textbook of Internal Medicine*, 2d ed. Philadelphia: Lippincott.
Taylor, R.B., ed. 1994. *Family Medicine: Principles and Practice*, 4th ed. New York: Springer-Verlag, 685–742.

Krishan L. Gupta

Gender Issues in Health Care

INTRODUCTION

The beginning of the twentieth century brought important changes in the United States regarding health care, including improved and more available medical care, people's greater willingness to seek medical care, the growing number of hospitals that provided care for serious illnesses, the demand by upper-class women for obstetrical care during pregnancy and delivery of their babies under anesthesia in hospitals, and the increased emphasis on improving and maintaining one's general health. These changes rapidly increased the demand for medical care and services, resulting in increased utilization of physicians, hospitals, clinics, and other kinds of health facilities and services. Additional factors in the 1950s and 1960s influencing demand for physician and hospital services were the development of physician-managed contraception, government programs providing prenatal care, the new system of third-party reimbursement through health insurance, and the tremendous growth of the medical-industrial complex.

TRADITIONAL CARE DURING ILLNESS

Before this century, care of illness in both men and women was provided in the home, with women the caregivers. Young girls were taught home remedies and folk medicine to be used in the treatment of various common illnesses and assumed the role of major caregiver as they became wives and mothers. Medical knowledge at that time was not much more advanced than lay care practices, and they both used the same herbs and home remedies to treat illnesses, based on experience and what seemed to work. In wealthier homes, some of the care responsibilities were given to female servants, many of whom were also knowledgeable about folk and home remedies. Men and women with terminal illnesses were also cared for at home, sometimes with the assistance and guidance of a private physician who made regular visits. Care of the poor, and particularly for those with no families, was given, carelessly and haphazardly, in almshouses or other public charity institutions. Transfer to charity institutions and almshouses was resisted by even the poorest and sickest, for this usually meant death.

At the turn of the century, particularly with the improvement in medical education instigated by the Flexner Report in 1910, it suddenly became fashionable for women to have their babies in hospitals, where they could be carefully watched and be delivered with less pain by means of new anesthetic methods developed in Germany, using scopolamine and morphine. Women's supposed delicate and sensitive physical and emotional needs, particularly among the wealthy class, were catered to by physicians who saw this population as a means of promoting themselves and their professional services, and increasing their revenue. It was socially and culturally acceptable for women to be sick, and to seek health care for a variety of "women's ailments." Men, on the other hand, were seen as strong, brave, and not needing health care. Traditionally, men did not seek health care until the later stages of disease or disability, when improvement was not expected.

HEALTH CARE UTILIZATION TODAY

A relatively large discrepancy exists between genders in all populations regarding the greater proportion of women who seek and receive health care. Many theories have been put forward to explain the causes of this discrepancy between the sexes and health care. Among these theories are that women report more illnesses than do men because it is culturally more acceptable for women to admit to being ill and needing help or care; that the social role of women is more compatible with the adoption of the sick role; that women are actually more in need of care than are men, perhaps because of the demands on their time and energies from children, husbands, and other family members; and that women's responsibilities as the bearer of children with all its attendant complexities and problems, both physical and psychological, account for their seeking health care more frequently than men. It is likely that all of these possible explanations play a part in the causes of gender differences in health care.

EXPENDITURES FOR HEALTH CARE: MEN AND WOMEN

The most recent information shows that overall expenditures for health care of women below the age of 65 are 22 percent higher than for men in the same age group; for women above 65 years of age, the difference is 15 percent, which is congruent with the fact that those in older age groups, both men and women, require more health care than younger age groups. Even greater differences are seen when types of health care are examined: hospital expenditures for women below 65 are three times that of men's hospital costs, indicating that more women receive care in hospitals than do men. Hospital costs for women and men over 65 are about the same, which again supports the fact that both sexes in the older age group have more need for hospitalizations than younger age groups. However, costs for women receiving nursing home care are twice that for men in the older age group, indicating that women, in general, live longer and therefore require more nursing home care. Women in both younger and older age groups spend twice as much for drugs as do men. Indications are that, as the number of older persons increases over the next several decades, the cost of health care for this population will increase tremendously.

For many years, white women sought health care in all settings more than did women of different races and cultures. However, recent studies show that these data are changing dramatically. Until recently, women had more problems accessing health care than did men, primarily because of health care costs and the lack of personally owned wealth and property by women. Language and cultural factors continue to be barriers to care for both men and women, but these factors weigh less heavily now than 20 years ago.

AGE AS A BARRIER TO HEALTH CARE

Aging persons require more health care than younger persons, because of the number and complexity of diseases and conditions related to the aging process. More time is required for history taking and physical examination of older persons because of the elderly's slowed thought processes and movements. Also, disease processes are not as apparent in the elderly. It is not uncommon for symptoms of disease in older persons to be absent, atypical, or ignored by practitioners; in older people, subtle deterioration of functional capacity or cognitive abilities may be the only indication of serious pathology. An extensive evaluation may require several visits, and diagnostic tests may prove physically and psychologically taxing, and so must be spread over a longer time. Older persons are more likely to require treatment for terminal illness than younger patients, which adds to time and cost expenditures.

WOMEN AS CAREGIVERS

The traditional role for women in most societies is that of caregiver to all other family members. Today, providers find that older women are not only in need of care themselves, but are also expected to care for their spouses or aged parents or parents-in-law. Caregiving produces added stress and burden to older women, and may increase the incidence and severity of their own illnesses. The provider needs to keep these aspects of care of older persons in mind, and to suggest alternatives to ease the burdens of caregiving that an older female patient may be carrying. Interventions through a social worker or home care agency may provide relief for the overburdened caregiver.

GENDER BIAS

Vestiges of bias against women by society and persons in professional roles exist even today. Physicians may not attend carefully to women's complaints or may dismiss them as unimportant. Sometimes, if the women's husband is present, the physician will address his remarks only to the man and ignore the female patient, giving the impression that the woman is unable to understand complex instructions and concepts. This type of bias may be even more apparent when the patient is of color or from a culture other than white America.

Gender bias is not as widespread as it was even 20 years ago, however, and does not pose as large a barrier as it once did. Data from the late 1980s and early 1990s indicate that women of color and from different cultures are receiving care on a par with white women from the same socioeconomic level.

THE SELF-CARE MOVEMENT

Beginning in the 1960s and 1970s, the so-called self-care movement appeared, during which women, in particular, assumed more responsibility for their own health and health care, relying less on physician care and more on care provided by midwives, acupuncturists, and other alternative care providers. Once again, folk and home remedies, and the use of herbs and plant compounds, became popular, particularly among younger people, both men and women. Women became less passive and more assertive, less willing to accept the guidance of professionals, especially physicians. Births outside of hospitals became more common, and birthing centers and nurse-midwifery practices developed in both urban and rural areas.

People of all ages became more involved in improving their own health by means of self-help, and placed more emphasis on healthful diet and exercise programs as a way to prevent illness and to improve their physical and mental health. Moderation or cessation of smoking, and alcohol and drug consumption was stressed.

These practices helped to ease the upward spiral of health care costs to some extent and to improve the health of many younger people. The continuation of these good health practices, and the increased understanding of the role of prevention in maintaining health, may show improved health among younger people in the decades ahead, as this generation of young people age.

However, costs for health care of older people during this same period continued to escalate, largely because many of these people were developing illnesses caused by years of smoking, and the effects of alcoholism and poor diet.

THE WOMEN'S HEALTH INITIATIVE

One of the most recent positive advances for the health care of older women especially, is embodied in the National Institute of Health's (NIH) Women's Health Initiative, which established the Office of Women's Health during the tenure of its former director, Bernadine Healy, M.D., in the late 1980s and early 1990s. This initiative is limited to menopausal and postmenopausal women, and addresses the health care needs of older women in the areas of cardiovascular disease, stroke, and osteoporosis. Most clinical research and clinical trials of new drugs that had been done at NIH since its establishment in the 1930s focused only on men's health problems and involved only males as research subjects. Now, in the wake of women's health activism, a greater emphasis exists regarding women's health problems, and women's participation in clinical trials and as research subjects. This initiative provides funding to 15 vanguard centers around the country to participate in cooperative research studies on older women's health problems. Separate NIH programs exist to study the health problems of younger women, such as breast and colon cancer, sexually transmitted diseases (STDs), and AIDS.

In the most recent federal government report of the health status of minorities, there is also evidence that minorities are receiving preventive screening and other kinds of health care services at the same rate, proportionately, as whites. Health care for minorities from the lower socioeconomic level occurs primarily in public clinics, health departments, or hospitals, particularly for the uninsured, but access to adequate health care seems to be approaching a more equitable state. Health care reform may result in even better care for the nation's underserved and minority populations, both men and women.

References

Finkler, K. 1994. *Women in Pain*. Philadelphia: University of Pennsylvania Press.
Hodgson, T.A., and A.N. Kopstein. 1984. Health care expenditures for major diseases

in 1980. National Center for Health Statistics. *Health Care Financing Review* 5:1.

Marieskind, H.I. 1980. *Women in the Health System: Patients, Providers, and Programs.* St. Louis: Mosby.

Network for Continuing Medical Education. 1992. *The NIH Women's Health Initiative: Status Report One.* Videocassette tape produced by Roche Laboratories, a division of Hoffman-La Roche, Inc., Secaucus, N.J. Washington, D.C.: U.S. Government Printing Office.

Ada Romaine-Davis

Gerontological Nurse Practitioners

The increasing number of elderly in the United States, predicted to comprise 13 percent of the population by the year 2000, requires additional health care providers in all settings to care for people as they age. Along with family physicians, nurse practitioners and physician assistants are important providers of care to the aging population.

Nurse practitioners (NPs) are registered nurses, prepared at the master's level in nursing, who assume advanced practice roles in caring for people of all ages, depending on the specialty area of the individual nurse practitioner. A nurse may choose any one of a number of specialties such as adult, family, pediatric, obstetric/gynecologic, and gerontological nurse practitioner (GNP).

The education of GNPs focuses on the field of gerontology and the special needs of aging persons. In 1993 there were about 1,600 certified GNPs and a total of 45,000 NPs altogether in the United States. The need and demand for GNPs rise every year, as the proportion of the elderly population increases. The preparation of gerontological nurse practitioners includes acquiring in-depth knowledge of health problems affecting older adults. GNPs strive to maximize functional abilities, promote health, prevent further progression of disease and disability, and help the older individual to remain independent as long as possible. Most states require that advanced practice nurses—NPs, nurse-midwives, nurse anesthetists, and clinical specialists—take national certification examinations in a specialty area. Certification examinations for these highly educated and specialized nurses are offered by the American Nurses Credentialing Center (ANCC), which is a separately incorporated center through which the American Nurses' Association (ANA) provides the credentialing service, and other similar national accrediting and certifying organizations. The goals of ANCC include promoting and enhancing public health by certifying nurses and accrediting organizations using ANA standards of nursing practice, nursing services, and continuing education. ANA standards of nursing practice have been developed for all specialty and general areas of nursing, for example, public health nursing, critical care nursing, primary health care nurse practitioner. A master's degree in nursing *and* completion of a graduate level program that prepares gerontological nurse practitioners are required for certification in this specialty. Didactic content of programs includes a review and application of theories and concepts from the physical, behavioral, social, medical, and nursing sciences, and supervised clinical and preceptorship experiences with physicians or nurse practitioners that include health assessment, health promotion, and advanced assessment and management of health problems of the older adult population. The student is expected to become adept at performing a comprehensive history and physical examination, making accurate diagnoses, and developing an appropriate plan of care, which includes the ability to perform laboratory tests such as urine analysis and microscopy, in order to confirm diagnoses and to treat appropriately. Students gain skills in clinical judgment, decisionmaking, consultation, collaboration, research, and the change process.

NPs can provide, according to the Congressional Office of Technology Assessment (OTA), between 50 and 90 percent of the health care normally performed by physicians. Working together as a team, the NP can increase physician output and productivity by 20 to 50 percent. Often referred to as a physician substitute, recent research indicates that there is an impact that the NP provides that far exceeds the medical care substitute role. This finding is likely related directly to the nursing background that NPs bring to the care of patients.

Although many legislative and organizational barriers exist, not the least of which are state medical practice acts and prescriptive regulations, NPs and other providers are providing care to people of all ages in a variety of settings. For example, at the Geisinger Clinic in Pennsylvania, which is a private, multi-specialty group practice, more than 100 NPs and PAs (physician assistants) complement the work of more than 500 physicians. Similarly, the Community Health Plan in Albany, New York, a model HMO (Health Maintenance Organization), reports that over 150 NPs, PAs, and CNMs (certified nurse-midwives) deliver care to their patients. A 1992 report prepared by the Bureau of Health Professions, Health Resources and Services Administration included information that revealed that 88 percent of rural community and migrant health centers either already employ or are seeking advanced practice nurses and PAs.

A managed care delivery system in Minneapolis-St. Paul, Evercare, uses gerontological nurse practitioners and physicians to provide health care services to about 700 nursing home patients. Under a collaborative agreement with a physician, the GNPs may prescribe drugs and order tests, send patients to the hospital when necessary, and make recertification visits required by State and Federal regulation. The GNP also makes urgent medical visits and decides whether the physician should see the patient. Because of the focus on preventive care within the nursing home, Evercare reports that its members use about half as many inpatient hospital days as the national nursing home population. NPs are used widely in home care and often make up the largest proportion of providers to this specific population.

National health care reform is at the top of the domestic policy agenda. To meet the demands and stresses that health care reform will place on the existing delivery system, it is essential to improve the utilization of nonphysician health care providers such as GNPs. In many different settings, health care organizations are utilizing nonphysician providers in new ways to address the concerns about cost, access, and quality of care, particularly of the aging population.

References

American Nurses' Association. 1987. *Standards of Practice for the Primary Health Care Nurse Practitioner*. Kansas City, Mo.: ANA.

American Nurses Credentialing Center Certification Catalog. 1993. Washington, D.C.: ANCC.

Hereford, R.W., L. Rutter, and A.S. Levine. 1993. *Enhancing the Utilization of Nonphysician Health Care Providers*. Washington, D.C.: Office of the Inspector General, Department of Health and Human Services.

Melillo, K.D. 1993. Utilizing nurse practitioners to provide health care for elderly patients in Massachusetts nursing homes. *J Amer Academy Nurse Practitioners* 5(7): 19–26.

Swenson, M.M. 1992. Primary health care of elderly women. *J Amer Academy Nurse Practitioners* 4(4):143–47.

Ada Romaine-Davis

Gynecologic Problems

Gynecologic problems and concerns are not uncommon in women of any age, but may not receive as much attention in an older woman as they may in a woman of reproductive age. Some of the potentially serious gynecologic problems common to the elderly are minimally symptomatic, particularly in early stages. Other problems, while not life-threatening, may be annoying enough to interfere significantly with daily activities and well-being. Many situations can be detected by attention to symptoms and routine care of the perineum (the skin around the vagina and anus), whether by the client, a family member, home health care worker, or other health professional.

PREVENTIVE CARE

Women may hesitate to mention gynecologic complaints or concerns for several reasons. Many older women were raised in an environment where talk about gynecologic problems was considered impolite or improper and may cause embarrassment. Some women may be confused when symptoms cannot be correlated by visual inspection, particularly if bowel or bladder problems also exist. If the home care attendant is uneasy dealing with gynecologic issues, it will be even more difficult for the client to discuss her concerns. The most useful approach is to include questions about gynecologic well-being along with other health history items.

A review of the client's health history should include patterns of sexual function, bladder function, and any symptoms of vaginal or vulvar irritation or bleeding. An annual pelvic examination should include visual examination of the vulva (the skin folds surrounding the vagina) and vagina, and bimanual examination. In 1992, the only recommended gynecologic cancer screening test is the Pap smear, but there is controversy about the frequency of screening. If there have been three consecutive negative (normal) smears and the woman is not at risk for sexually transmitted disease, the interval between Pap smears can be increased from a year to every three to five years. Women who have had a complete hysterectomy for benign disease may not need Pap smears, but many clinicians continue to screen with Pap smears every three to five years.

Hygiene should consist of gentle cleansing of the perineal skin including the vulva. Soap or detergent may dry the vulvar tissue excessively. Plain water, baby oil, or mild non-astringent solutions are usually better choices. If the skin folds are moist, cornstarch or other unscented powder will absorb excess perspiration. For skin or vulvar itching, oatmeal (Aveeno™) or oilated baths may be soothing. Baby care products such as "wipes" containing aloe or lanolin are useful for cleansing between baths.

Estrogen replacement therapy (ERT) has many potential benefits as well as several possible risks. Women with adequate estrogen effect of the vagina and vulva are less likely to have sexual dysfunction or atrophic vaginitis. ERT may result in vaginal bleeding, necessitating biopsy. ERT must be given with a progestational agent (another hormone) in any woman who has a uterus; ERT without a progestin will increase the chance of uterine cancer.

PHYSIOLOGIC CHANGES

In the postmenopausal period, estrogen production normally declines. If estrogen levels are low, the epithelium (skin and mucous membranes) of the vagina and vulva changes from its premenopausal state. There is a decrease in blood supply, and the epithelium becomes thinner due to a decrease in number of cell layers; in addition, the cells forming the epithelium are not as mature. Well past menopause, the vulva become much smaller and the labia minora (the inner portion of the vulva, consisting of the skin folds closest to the vaginal opening) may be virtually absent. The vagina may become shorter and narrower. The decrease in moisture of the vagina may lead to discomfort during sexual activity. There are wide variations in the amount of change present in individual women. These changes will be less marked in women who have higher estrogen levels, either naturally or as a result of ERT, and in women who are regularly sexually active.

VAGINITIS AND VULVITIS

Vaginitis refers to any irritation or inflammation of the vagina. Vulvitis, or inflammation of the labia minora and/or majora (the vulva), is also common. On the basis of symptoms, it can be difficult to distinguish vaginitis from vulvitis, and the two are discussed together.

Atrophic vulvo-vaginitis may occur when the thin epithelium is irritated by minor mechanical trauma or contact with bodily fluids, soaps, medications, or other substances. The initial event may be trivial and may never be identified. Itching is usually the major symptom, although ''pressure'' or more severe discomfort is quite possible. On inspection the vulva may be reddened with some swelling. Some vaginal discharge may be present. The vagina, cervix, and vulva may be so fragile that an examination causes bleeding. Treatment should initially be directed toward removing any irritating agent. Urine, which may be acidic, is a common irritant. If the woman is using incontinence pads, breakdown of urine may lead to ammonia and alkaline by-products that are also caustic. Soap is also a common irritant. If removing the irritant doesn't resolve the vaginitis, then estrogen will usually improve symptoms, frequently dramatically. An estrogen cream in small dosage (e.g., 1–2 gms of conjugated estrogen cream two to three times a week) is often the easiest to use although systemic estrogens (ERT) can be given instead. Short-term local estrogen use is rarely associated with side effects, but long-term use can result in any of the problems associated with systemic use as the absorption by mucous membranes of the vagina is considerable.

Yeast (monilia) infections will also result in itching of the vulva and vagina, with swelling, white discharge, and occasional excoriations from scratching. It is more common in women with diabetes or antibiotic use, and is treated with vaginal creams or suppositories of an anti-fungal drug. Less than 10 percent of infections are resistant to commonly used drugs, but recurrent yeast infections may be a sign of immunosuppression.

Trauma to the vulva and vagina may occur from medical examinations or hygiene if the tissues are very fragile. Falls may also result in trauma, particularly straddle falls. Straddle falls may occur on a toilet or bathtub rim if the woman is unsteady. Sexual abuse is another cause of trauma which is certainly underreported.

Women with vulvar dystrophy may have itching and discomfort of the vulva, or may be relatively symptomatic. The itching is often initially misdiagnosed as an infection, but if the vulva are inspected, irregular thickening and change in coloration (either darker or lighter) may be seen. Diagnosis is made by biopsy. Biopsy is necessary as vulvar cancer may have an identical appearance. If a vulvar dystrophy is confirmed by biopsy, local treatment will result in improvement in most women. Steroid creams or testosterone creams are the two medications most likely to be effective.

VAGINAL BLEEDING

Vaginal bleeding is a symptom which alarms both patient and caretaker. While bleeding should never be ignored, there are many causes of vaginal bleeding that are not serious.

The first step is to determine the source of the bleeding, which is not always obvious. Bleeding from the urinary tract or bleeding from the bowels may be confused with vaginal bleeding. The relationship of the bleeding to urination or bowel movement is helpful but not always clear. Sometimes, a small tampon or piece of gauze placed in the vagina will help determine the source of the bleeding.

Bleeding from the urinary tract can include bleeding from urinary tract infection, stones, or tumor. Another cause of bleeding in older women is urethral prolapse, where a small portion of the terminal urethra is extruded. The prolapse appears as a small cyanotic (dark blue) cluster of tissue at the opening of the urethra. The dark coloration is often alarming, but the situation is entirely benign. No treatment may be necessary, or local estrogen cream may be helpful, with minor surgery reserved for only a few cases.

Bleeding from the bowel may be due to hemorrhoids or anal fissuring, colitis, diverticulitis, or bowel tumor.

Vaginal bleeding may be due to atrophic vulvo-vaginitis or trauma. The atrophic cervix may be so delicate as to bleed on touch. Cervical polyps may result in irregular bleeding. These are benign and easily removed; removal is usually advised because of the anxiety that is created by the bleeding. Vulvar cancer may occur at any age, although in younger women it is associated with cigarette smoking. Any lesion of the vulva which does not resolve promptly should be evaluated, as vulvar cancer can have a variety of appearances. Primary vaginal cancer is rare, but the peak incidence is in elderly women. Cervical cancer has a peak incidence in younger women (30–60 years old), but may also occur at any age. The epidemiology of squamous cell cervical cancer, the most common type, is well described. Squamous cell cancer is associated with multiple sexual partners, early age at first intercourse, other risk factors for sexually transmitted diseases, and immunosuppression. A risk factor history may not be easily obtained from elderly clients. Some cervical cancers, particularly adenocarcinomas, arise spontaneously and are not associated with the risk factors described for squamous cell cervical cancer. Since any cancer may have abnormal blood vessels, a biopsy of a suspected cancer should take place only where there are facilities to deal with unexpected bleeding.

Vaginal bleeding may indicate bleeding from the uterus. This may occur from benign changes in the endometrium (the lining of the uterus) which may occur with variations in estrogen level. Endometrial polyps and leiomyomata (fibroids) are also benign causes of bleeding from the uterus. Endometrial (or uterine) cancer becomes progressively more common into the eighth decade of life. Any of these situations may result in irregular bleeding of various amounts, and neither the pattern nor amount of bleeding is helpful in determining the cause. Diagnosis is made by physical examination to determine the size and consistency of the uterus, and by biopsy of the endometrium, the lining of the uterus. Biopsy is done by passing an instrument with a diameter of several millimeters through the cervix. This is frequently an easy and quick procedure, which can be done in a bed if necessary. However, in some women, the cervix may be too tight to admit the instrument or there may be technical problems in the pelvic examination which make biopsy difficult. In that situation, a dilatation and curettage ("D & C") procedure would have to be done, using local or general anesthesia.

Ovarian cancer, which is the third most common type of female reproductive tract cancer after uterine and cervical cancer, and Fallopian tube cancer, which is very rare, may sometimes cause vaginal bleeding as an initial sign. These cancers may be strongly suspected based on physical examination, ultrasound testing, or other radiologic tests, but definitive diagnosis is made by operative biopsy.

PROLAPSE

The uterus and vagina are held in their normal anatomic relationships by a set of ligaments and supporting tissues. These tissues may become weakened and stretched, resulting in uterine prolapse (uterus protruding into the vagina or through the vaginal opening), cystocele (prolapse or dropping of the bladder), rectocele (prolapse of the rectum through the vaginal wall), or any combination of these. There may be symptoms of pelvic pressure, but severe pain is not common. If there is bladder prolapse, it may be difficult to empty the bladder completely, leading to frequent urination and bladder infection; conversely, there may be some degree of incontinence. Rectocele may make defecation more difficult. Usually the prolapse is noticed as a bulge of tissue coming out of the vagina; at the outset, it may be noticed only if the woman is standing. She may be able to push the prolapse back into the vagina, and some women report that they push the prolapse in whenever they need to urinate (or defecate). When prolapse has happened, the exposed epithelium of the cervix and vagina are subject to drying and trauma, and bleeding may occur. Factors associated with prolapse include age, heredity, nutrition, childbearing, and increased intra-abdominal pressure such as caused by obesity and chronic lung disease. Diagnosis is made by physical examination.

Mild degrees of prolapse may be treated conservatively. Stool softeners may reduce the amount of straining. Weight loss may reduce intra-abdominal pressure. Muscle-strengthening exercises may improve the tone of the pelvic floor. While the existing prolapse may not improve dramatically, these measures may also prevent a small degree of prolapse from progressing and requiring major interventions.

Pessaries can be used to replace and retain the prolapse in its proper position. Pessaries are usually made of rubber or synthetic rubber material and may have a metal core; they are available in a variety of shapes and sizes. A properly selected pessary will hold the prolapsed organs in place, while the pessary is held in place by the muscles around the vagina and pelvic floor. Since pessaries are a foreign body, they may damage the vagina through direct pressure or through infection. After placement of a pessary, it is necessary to check the vagina for excessive irritation. The pessary itself should be removed and cleaned at least once a month and preferably much more frequently; pessaries are often used with an estrogen cream which can be replaced at the time of cleaning.

Pessaries may not be useful if the pelvic muscles are too weak to hold the device in place, or if they lead to discomfort despite adjustment of size and type, or if vaginal sexual activity is desired. Surgical treatment of prolapse will be the preferred treatment in many circumstances. Most primary operations are done through a vaginal approach and can be done with a regional anesthetic. Generally, these operations are well tolerated, even in debilitated patients, because of the anesthetic options and the lack of bowel disturbance. The improvement in well-being may be substantial. Home care may be simplified postoperatively, as both pessaries and prolapse have been eliminated.

SUMMARY

Many gynecologic problems affect older (as well as younger) women. Many of the problems are a result of aging and the change in hormonal levels and other physiological changes that occur with aging. However, early recognition of problems can lead to early diagnosis and treatment, with complete resolution of the problem, and increased comfort and well-being.

References

Galask, R.P., and B. Larsen. 1981. Identifying and treating genital tract infections in postmenopausal women. *Geriatrics* 36:69–79.

Herbst, A.L., D.R. Mishell, M.A. Stenchever, and W. Droegemueller. 1992. *Comprehensive Gynecology*, 2d ed. St. Louis: Mosby Year Book, Inc.

Notelovitz, M. 1978a. Gynecologic problems of menopausal women, Part 1: Changes in genital tissue. *Geriatrics* 33:24–30.

——— 1978b. Gynecologic problems of menopausal women, Part 2: Treating estrogen deficiency. *Geriatrics* 33:35–42.

——— 1978c. Gynecologic problems of menopausal women, Part 3: Changes in extragenital tissues and sexuality. *Geriatrics* 33:51–58.

Peckham, B.M., and S.S. Shapiro. 1983. *Signs and Symptoms in Gynecology*. Philadelphia: Lippincott.

Lynn Borgatta

H

Health Services Utilization Among the Elderly

There are a number of reasons for studying health service utilization. From an economic perspective, the study of health service use offers a way to understand and control the rising costs of health care. Health expenditure from 1980 to 1988 increased at a rate of 14.8 percent compared to 4.6 percent for the consumer price index during that same time period. From a social equity perspective, the study of health service use provides information about the distribution of health care services. Elderly individuals comprise the largest single group of consumers of health care services in the United States. Although elderly Americans represent only one-eighth of the population, they account for over one-third of all health care expenditures. Moreover, the changing demographic structure of society suggests that this trend will continue well into the twenty-first century. The third reason for studying health service use is to evaluate outcomes, particularly the relationship between use and overall health of the population. Although the United States has the largest per capita spending on health, its health outcomes tend to be poor due to an estimated 38 million persons who are excluded from the health care system. Partly as a result, the United States ranks 19th in life expectancy rates for men.

TYPES OF HEALTH SERVICE USE

Of the estimated $661 billion spent on health care in 1990, 89 percent was for personal health care with the remainder spent on administration, research, and construction of medical facilities. The primary expenditures for personal care are of two types: hospital care (43%) and physician services (23%). Nursing homes account for an additional 9%, and in-home health services account for less than 5%.

Hospital Use

In 1984, excluding newborn infants, adults aged 65 and over accounted for 30 percent of all hospital discharges. Not surprisingly, hospital use increases markedly with advancing age. Examining discharge rates per 1,000 population in 1984, rates were 208 for those aged 55–64 years, 320 for those 65–74 years, 498 for those 75–84 years, and 591 for those 85 years and over. Older adults accounted for longer hospital stays as well. Average length of stay increased from 7.5 days for those aged 55–64 to 9.8 days for those aged 85 and over.

Although it is frequently assumed that older adults are a relatively homogeneous group, there is remarkable heterogeneity of health and health behavior among the elderly that parallels the nonelderly population. Recognition of this diversity among older adults has led to the realization that it is not age per se that is responsible for high use, but rather medical need. High users of hospital care represent only 1.7 percent of the total population but account for almost 55 percent of those requiring hospital treatment. Regardless of age, high volume users have poor health, severe functional limitations, and the presence of multiple medical conditions. In addition to the severely ill, heavy users tend to be people in the end stage of life. An analysis of Medicare expenditures revealed that a substantial proportion went to recipients in their last year of life.

Physician Visits

The pattern for physician visits is similar to that of hospital use: a relatively small proportion of the elderly consistently use more physician services. According to one estimate, high users of ambulatory medical services represent only 4.5 percent of the population but account for 32 percent of all those making ambulatory visits. Although there tends to be a monotonic increase in the rate of use of physician services with age, this relationship continued across all age groups. The result is an inverse J-curve in which physician use increases with age until approximately age 80, then begins to decline. A number of explanations have been put forth to explain this phenomenon, including the substitution of formal and informal services, an increasingly stabilized regimen, or increasing pessimism on the part of the patient, the physician, or both.

Nursing Homes

In 1986 slightly over 4 percent of Americans aged 65 and over resided in nursing homes. The life time probability of institutionalization for any given individual age 65 or over, however, is substantially higher, increasing to 10 percent for persons 75 years and over, and 22 percent for persons age 85 and over. Over 70 percent of nursing home residents are women. Since women tend to live longer than men, they are more likely to be widowed and without a caregiver. As with acute hospital care and use of physician services, medical need is an important predictor of nursing home entry. In contrast to these other services, however, nursing homes generally provide custodial rather than rehabilitative care. The majority of elderly enter a nursing home directly from an acute care hospital with only about one-third ever discharged back into the community. It is also noteworthy that, while medical need is a strong predictor of nursing home use, for every person in a nursing home, there are at least two persons who have comparable impairments living in the community.

In-Home Health Services

In 1988 only about one-fourth of public expenditures for long-term care went for home care; the large majority went for nursing home care. Given the strong desire of the elderly to live at home, however, there is strong interest in expanding funding for home care. Since Medicare is by far the largest third-party payer for home health care, most of the information comes from use under this program. In 1986 the Medicare use rate of home health care among all older persons was approximately 5 percent. This rate must be interpreted in the light of other evidence that suggests that unlicensed and uncertified home health care providers may outnumber Medicare-certified agencies and be providing care through out-of-pocket or private insurance payment. As with other health services, use of home health care increases sharply with age. For both men and women, use rates for those 85 years and over are twelve times the rates of those aged 65 to 74. It is also noteworthy that diagnosis alone is a poor predictor of Medicare home health use.

MEASURING AND PREDICTING HEALTH SERVICE USE

Models of Health Service Use

Two conceptual approaches are most frequently used to explain the relationship between predictor variables and health service use: Andersen's behavioral model and Rosenstock's health belief model. The behavioral model identifies predisposing, enabling, and need factors as being the primary determinants of service use. Predisposing factors are presumed to create a "propensity" toward use by family members and are captured by such variables as age, sex, marital status, race, family composition, and health beliefs. Enabling factors reflect the fact that even though families may be predisposed to use services, certain conditions must be met to enable families to attain them. Enabling conditions primarily include family resources and community resources. Assuming a predisposition to use services and the ability to do so, the family must also see a need for a particular service. Need, viewed in the behavioral model as the most immediate or proximal cause of service use, is assessed by the extent of illness perceived by the family. Empirical support for the behavioral model in explaining the health behavior of the elderly has been largely disappointing. In general, need variables have tended to perform best, but the total amount of variance in service use explained by the model has tended to be modest (generally from 9% to 25%). The model has been even less effective in explaining the health behavior of the elderly (the largest users of health care) than the general population in the United States. Moreover, the effects of predisposing and enabling factors on service use have frequently been found to be extremely small, if not substantively unimportant.

The health belief model has been less widely used in studies of service use. This approach suggests that an individual's readiness to perform a health-related action is a function of several factors: (1) a person's beliefs about their susceptibility to a particular illness and the severity of its consequences; (2) the costs and benefits of acting, including physical, financial, psychological, and social costs; and (3) access to "cues" that trigger appropriate health behavior. Cues can be either internal (e.g., perceptions of changes in bodily states) or external (e.g., communications from the mass media). Although there has been no single study to test the health belief model in its entirety, several studies of the various components of the model have confirmed the general utility of taking into account subjective or attitudinal factors by service users.

Issues in Measurement

In evaluating predictive models, it is important to note that different services (e.g., hospital use vs. physician use) have different predictors. Even within a particular type of service, however, the way that health service use is measured will have consequences for the predictive model. Health service utilization has been variously represented as contact (yes/no), volume (number of contacts in a specified period), contact per illness episode, and recency of contact.

Another measurement issue concerns the distinction between objective and subjective measures of health status. Objective measures focus on the presence or absence of disease states; subjective measures generally focus on the older person's self-report of how healthy they are. As a result, objective measures tend to represent "need," whereas subjective measures tend to be more representative of "demand" for health services. One consequence is that objective measures may be better predictors of nondiscretionary health services (e.g., hospitalization), while subjective measures may tend to be better predictors of discretionary services (e.g., annual physical exam).

Finally, the way in which use measures are collected will likely influence empirical relationships between predictors and use. For example, with self-report data, older adults in poor health have been found to overreport physician visits, and those with greater levels of utilization tend to have more error in estimates of use.

Measurement issues such as these highlight the difficulties inherent in predicting health service use. Undoubtedly, these measurement issues are also responsible for much of the variability in estimates of service use and the relatively poor predictive ability of contemporary models.

References

Glandon, G., M. Counte, and D. Tancredi. 1992. An analysis of physician utilization by elderly persons; systematic differences between self-report and archival information. *J Gerontology: Social Sciences* 47:245–52.

Hanley, R., and J. Weiner. 1991. Use of paid home care by the chronically disabled elderly. *Research on Aging* 13:310–22.

Harrington, C. 1992. Health-care financing. *Encyclopedia of Sociology*. New York: Macmillan.

Hughes, S.L. 1992. Home care: where we are and where we need to go. In *In-Home Care for Older People*, edited by M.G. Ory and A. Duncker. Newbury Park, Cal.: Sage, 53–74.

Kahana, E., and S. Brittis. 1992. Nursing homes. *Encyclopedia of Sociology*. New York: Macmillan.

Walinsky, F. 1990. *Health and Health Behavior Among Elderly Americans*. New York: Springer.

Karl Kosloski

Hearing Impairment

THE PROBLEM

Hearing impairment is a common problem in older people. It may range from failure to understand words in conversation and to appreciate sounds such as a telephone ringing or a knock at the door, to total deafness. The National Institute on Aging reported that 30 percent of adults age 65 to 74, and 50 percent of those 75 to 79, suffer some degree of hearing loss. In the United States alone, it is estimated that more than 10 million older people are hearing impaired.

Hearing loss often means living in a world of silence, particularly for those who are moderately or severely impaired. Its toll can be devastating because hearing loss contributes to loneliness, isolation, and frustration. Those who deny that a hearing problem exists, or do not seek treatment or assistance in coping with this loss, are vulnerable to depression. Withdrawal from social interaction and unwillingness to participate in social activities intensify their loneliness and isolation.

THE HEARING MECHANISM

The delicate and intricate process of human hearing is dependent on a series of mechanical and electrical events that enable sound waves in the air to be channeled through the external ear before striking the ear drum. The drum vibrates and transmits the vibration to three bony structures in the middle ear. The vibrations are amplified so that the sound passes on to the snail-shaped cochlea of the inner ear, which contains microscopic hairs that convert sound waves into electrical impulses. These impulses are then carried by nerve receptors within the spiral of the cochlea. These nerve receptors come together to form the acoustic nerve, which leads to the brain. The brain, in turn, receives and interprets the sounds.

TYPES OF HEARING IMPAIRMENT

Complete or partial inability to hear is most commonly the result of an ear disease, injury, or degeneration of the hearing mechanism because of aging. There are three common types of impairment.

1. When sound conduction is impeded before it reaches the cochlea in the inner ear, the hearing impairment is considered to be a conductive problem. The leading causes of conductive impairment are buildup of wax (cerumen) in the external ear; a perforated ear drum as a result of injury, sudden pressure, or infection; and middle ear infections (otitis media). Less common is the condition of otosclerosis in which the bony structure of the middle ear loses its mobility.

2. When the delicate workings of the inner ear are damaged, the hearing impairment is a sensorineural problem. As people age, hearing ability declines. This decline is so gradual and progressive that by ages 60 to 70, 25 percent of older people notice hearing impairment. This problem, referred to as presbycusis, is becoming a growing concern. It is associated with the degeneration of the hair cells and nerve fibers in the inner ear. Sounds become less clear, and tones, especially high frequency, become less audible. It is known that continued exposure to loud noises, diminished blood supply to the inner ear due to arterial disease, and continued use of drugs such as salicylates, certain antibiotics, and diuretics can damage the inner ear.

3. A third type of hearing impairment which relates to central auditory dysfunction is caused by damage to the auditory nerve centers in the brain, due to such events as tumors, head injury, and stroke. In this type, sound cannot be totally received or interpreted by the brain even though the ear is without a conductive or sensorineural problem.

DIAGNOSIS AND TREATMENT

Hearing problems that may be successfully diagnosed and treated by the family doctor are ear infections or removal of impacted wax. Complicated cases,

however, require the expertise of an ear specialist (otologist) who will be responsible for a comprehensive medical history and ear examination. Referral to
an audiologist, a health professional educated in the science of hearing, may be
needed in order to identify and measure the hearing problem. Audiological testing includes a battery of tests to determine the extent and pattern of the hearing
deficit by testing how well sounds are heard at different frequencies, how well
the ear drum and middle ear conduct sounds, and how well the individual is
able to discriminate human speech and sound. The results from the family doctor, ear specialist, and audiologist will determine the nature of the hearing problem and the best treatment for that specific problem. Most often, the hearing
loss of the elderly is irreparable, but there are known strategies that can be
undertaken to reduce the effects, primarily the use of a hearing aid.

THE HEARING AID

The hearing aid is a miniaturized battery-operated electronic device designed
to fit inside the ear. It consists of a tiny microphone to pick up sounds, an
amplifier to increase sound volume, and a tiny speaker to transmit sound through
the ear. By providing the extra power to amplify sound, the cochlea in the inner
ear is stimulated. To benefit from such a device, there must be some hearing
capability. That is why professional advice is necessary to determine whether a
hearing aid is indicated for one or for both ears and, if so, to determine what
design, model, and brand match the needs of the individual. Hearing aid users
must recognize that the electronic device cannot make up for lost hearing, but
rather enhances communication by making sound loud enough for it to be heard.
When purchased, it should be understood that after a 30-day trial period, it can
be returned for reimbursement if the device is not satisfactory. Life adjustments
will be necessary to accommodate the sensitivities of the individual, and counseling must be provided in the proper use and maintenance of the aid. Success
depends on the individual's attitude and motivation as well as the quality of the
product and service. Periodic professional follow-up is recommended to assure
compatibility of the individual to the hearing aid itself.

The usefulness of the aid is enhanced with speech reading and auditory training. The former enables the hearing impaired to receive visual cues from lip
movements, facial expressions, and body language; the latter enables the hearing
impaired to manage specific communication problems. The focus of this type
of training is essentially to help the individual to understand and to maximize
capabilities and accept limitations.

LIVING WITH IMPAIRED HEARING

Assisting the individual to make the best use of limited communications abilities and promoting a positive attitude help the individual to cope, and improve
confidence and self-image. People with hearing problems should be encouraged

to be open about their hearing deficit and not feel self-conscious when it is necessary to ask another person to repeat a word or a phrase. Reading lips and understanding body language are important in supplementing hearing. Shouting should be avoided as it distorts sound, which could be very irritating. Conducting a conversation as if the impaired person were not there adds to feelings of isolation and frustration. Also, speaking directly into a person's ear doesn't help, either, because the listener cannot make use of visual cues. In the course of a conversation, always look directly at the person. If the listener fails to understand what is being said, rephrasing in short, simple sentences is suggested. Speaking at a distance of three to six feet and in good lighting facilitates communication. Competing environmental sounds in the home (TV, stereo, radio, etc.) should be minimized for more effective communication.

Modern technology has produced assistive devices for sound amplification associated with the use of telephone, TV, and radio. This technology allows other family members to continue to listen at the normal volume level. Television telecaptioning is also available for those with good vision but whose hearing is not sufficient to benefit from amplified sound.

Many elderly are on various drug treatment regimes for specific conditions such as infections and hypertension. One must always bear in mind that the problem of drug-induced hearing loss is real. Drugs as common as aspirin, antibiotics (streptomycin, neomycin), and diuretics (furosemide) are referred to as ototoxic because they can damage the delicate inner portion of the inner ear, which is responsible for both hearing and balance. While under medication, one should be aware of possible toxic side effects and report sudden changes or worsening of the hearing impairment, ringing in the ears (tinnitus), or problems in balance, all symptomatic of inner ear dysfunction. Such symptoms should be reported to the physician for a reassessment of the therapeutic plan before further damage is done.

There are a number of organizations concerned with the problems of the hearing impaired. The National Information Center on Deafness at Gallaudet University, Washington, D.C., in particular, provides updated information on deafness and hearing loss. All available resources should be tapped by the hearing impaired and their family members to learn as much as possible about the condition and ways of adjusting to it. Joining a self-help group for the hard of hearing facilitates the sharing of experiences, including difficulties and challenges, and developing solutions for common problems.

OUTLOOK

Scientists continue to explore ways to help the profoundly deaf adult who is unable to benefit from the more traditional approaches. The cochlear implant shows some promise. Unlike the hearing aid, which amplifies sound, this device uses tiny electrodes to apply electrical stimulation directly to the auditory nerve fibers. Implantation of the device requires surgery either inside or outside the cochlea. At the same time, a miniature receiver is implanted under the skin, either behind the ear or in the lower part of the chest. Although the usefulness of the implant is not reliably predicted, it is generally thought that the implant enables the user to hear the rhythms of speech and the intonation of the voice. At present, its use is limited; however, research continues to produce advances in electronics, audio engineering, and the science of hearing.

References

Abrams, W.P., and R. Berkow, eds. 1990. *The Merck Manual of Geriatrics.* Rahway, N.J.: Merck & Co., Inc., 1083.

The American Medical Association. 1989. *Encyclopedia of Medicine.* New York: Random House.

The National Information Center on Deafness. 1991. *Aging and Hearing Loss.* Washington, D.C.: Gallaudet College.

The National Institute of Aging. 1991. *Age Page: Hearing and Older People.* Bethesda, Md.: Public Health Service.

The National Institute on Deafness and Other Communication Disorders. 1982. *Hearing Loss: Hope Through Research.* Bethesda, Md.: Public Health Service.

Jennifer Boondas

Hispanic Informal Support Systems

INTRODUCTION

The physically and mentally impaired elderly are a subgroup in our society whose special needs are not being adequately or appropriately met. In spite of the extensive interest in alternatives to institutional care, there are relatively few community alternatives to institutionalization. Not only is there a lack of appropriate services in the community, but also an underutilization of the existing services by the elderly and their families.

The present system of long-term care for the elderly in the United States provides large amounts of public funds for institutional care, but minimal funding for community-oriented supportive services. As a consequence, older people are forced into institutions prematurely or, in some cases, unnecessarily.

The accessibility of a family support system appears as the primary factor in reducing the probability of institutionalization for the chronically ill person. Families for the most part will go to extraordinary lengths before institutionalization is considered. In addition, a substantial amount of care is provided by friends and neighbors, augmented by community supported long-term care services. This accounts for the large number of persons who need long-term care services and yet are able to remain in the community.

Most older people are tied into a network of social support in which the children, primarily, and friends and neighbors secondarily, provide important supportive services. Children occupy the key role in the informal support systems of the elderly, while other relatives serve as a reservoir of kin from which replacements and substitutions for missing or lost relatives can be obtained.

Family, friends, neighbors, civic organizations, and religious groups constitute an important source of social support for the elderly, particularly to the Hispanic elderly. It is to these informal supports that the elderly first turn for help. There is no doubt that the circumstances surrounding the lives of the elderly Hispanic demand the use of significant persons with whom to interact and on whom to depend.

INFORMAL SUPPORT SYSTEMS AND THE HISPANIC ELDERLY

The prevalence of family and informal support systems is strong within the Hispanic society and serves as an important role for the elderly. Socioeconomic barriers encountered by the Hispanic elderly may make them more dependent on their families than their white counterparts. Despite the changes that the Hispanic family has undergone in the United States, it continues to retain many aspects of its ethnic identity and cultural values. One such value, known as familism, places a great emphasis on family unity, supports family integrity, and gives shape and direction to the behavior of its members. In being family centered, members feel an obligation to relatives and duty to help in time of crisis.

In the Hispanic community, the family is a source of strength for individuals of all ages. The Hispanic cultural heritage is one that underlines family responsibility for care of those in need. This tradition means that the family is a significant primary provider of social services. In accordance with cultural norms and values, and as a practical necessity in Hispanic families, the extended family concept is still of great importance. For instance, many Puerto Rican elderly share a household with a child or relative. The fact that Puerto Rican aged are more likely to live in households with other relatives is a function not only of the value system of this community, but also a matter of economic necessity. The shared household is one way poorer families meet their housing needs and, in addition, the grandparents often take care of the children in the increasing number of single parent families, or in families where both parents work.

The importance of the informal system in the Hispanic community has been a focus of research in recent years. The belief that informal support systems within the Hispanic community serve as a resource in meeting personal needs continues to be supported in the literature. Contrary to various opinions about its demise, there is evidence to suggest that Hispanics utilize the system in a most significant manner.

Delgado and Delgado (1982) emphasized that in the Hispanic communities the informal support system serves to minimize the use of formal resources. The extended family and religious institutions are important parts of this support system.

The Hispanic culture places a high value on the concept that life is a network of interpersonal relationships. Family consists not only of the nuclear family but extends to distant relatives and includes close friends.

Informal support systems in the Hispanic community play an important role in assisting individuals in crisis and have a potential impact on the utilization of services. This natural support system has four important components: the extended family, including friends and neighbors, folk healers, religious institutions, and social clubs that function totally or partially to help individuals in distress. Weeks and Cuellar also pointed out the importance of the informal support system among Hispanics. They stated that Hispanics show a great reluctance to turn to professionals for help. If a family member is not available, they turn to friends and neighbors or other community support.

The existence of an informal support system composed of family members, and friends and neighbors among the Puerto Rican elderly was amply documented by research conducted on widows. This study also demonstrated the importance of the informal support system for the well-being of elderly women. The activities carried out by means of the widows' informal support system can be summarized in four major categories, listed in order of importance and frequency: emotional support, practical support, economic support, and liaison with agencies. Principally, the daughters and then sons, sisters, and other family members were involved in these activities. Friends and neighbors provided mainly emotional support, which included visits, telephone calls, and advice.

Similarly, the research on the group support program for Hispanic caregivers indicated the existence of an informal support system among the elderly Hispanics in New York City. This system was mainly composed of relatives, friends, and neighbors. Daughters, in-laws, sisters, grandchildren, spouses, friends, and neighbors of the Hispanic elderly took primary responsibility in the caregiving role. Caregiving activities involved a variety of services ranging from emotional support, instrumental activities of daily living, and financial assistance to linkage services. Emotional support emerged as the most frequent activity performed by the caregivers, followed by instrumental activities such as shopping, meal preparation, light housecleaning, laundry, and personal hygiene. Providing emotional support and personal care were the most frequent problems mentioned by the caregivers in their caregiving role. However, more caregivers reported lack of conflict in their caregiving situation than those who reported having any conflict. Project findings sustained the notion that families do not diminish or give up their responsibilities when formal services exist. One of the most significant aspects of this project was its documentation of the strong communitarian primary group tradition among Hispanics, especially as it relates to the care of the elderly.

IMPLICATIONS AND RECOMMENDATIONS

When one looks at the situation of ill and impaired older people in the community, and what they need in order to remain in their familiar surroundings, it is clear that they need an array of supports and services—financial help, clothing, shelter, personal assistance, emotional support, and activities that at least occupy their days and, more ideally, make lives worth living. If one looks at this list, it is obvious that families, friends, and neighbors (the informal support system) are best able to do certain things, while the responsibility for other tasks is best assigned to the formal organizations. For example, most older people rely on Social Security or Supplemental Security Income for their basic income, but families often provide extra money. Both contribute to the older person's standard of living and at the same time serve to articulate family devotion and responsibility.

In general, there is a division of labor between family and organization. A corollary to this is that the ill and impaired elderly do better if both family and formal organizations are available to them. Families, particularly children, are extensively involved in the care of their elderly relatives and are carrying a major burden of support. It is important, however, not to view the family support system as one best left alone by the formal system. Clearly, the caregiving population needs the collaboration of the formal system. Especially in the case of Hispanics, where a strong familial system still exists, and in times of fiscal constraints or crisis, there is the danger of viewing the family support as a "cost effective" approach in the care of the elderly.

While the concept of the informal support caregiving network is not new, there is little general knowledge of the specific roles, stresses, needs, and problems that caregivers face. There is a need for educating and training of health and social professionals as well as enhancing and supporting this informal support structure. Caregivers usually seek information, advocacy, peer support, and help in their caregiving role.

Finally, inherent strengths exist in the Hispanic informal support system. For this reason, human service providers should not undermine a system of service delivery that has always existed. At the same time, however, human service providers should not use the existence of this natural support system as a pretext not to provide services. The natural support system should be supported and should be a focus of further research. There is still much to learn about how the Hispanic culture has managed to support its elderly and frail members amid all the constraints that they encounter.

References

Cruz-Lopez, M., and R. Pearson. 1985. The support needs and resources of Puerto Rican elders. *The Gerontologist* 25:483–87.

Delgado, M., and D. Delgado. 1982. Natural support systems: a source of strength in Hispanic communities. *Social Work* 27(1):83–90.

Rogler, L., and R. Cooney. 1984. *Puerto Rican Families in New York City: Intergenerational Processes* (Monograph No. 11). New York: Hispanic Research Center, Fordham University.

Sanchez, C.D. 1992. Mental health issues: the elderly Hispanic. *J Geriatric Psychiatry* 25(1):25–30.

——— 1989. Informal support system of widows over 60 in Puerto Rico. In *Mid-Life and Older Women in Latin America and the Caribbean*. Washington, D.C.: Pan American Health Organization: 265–77.

——— 1987. Self-help: model for strengthening the informal support system of the Hispanic elderly. *J Gerontological Social Work* 9(4):117–31.

Weeks, J., and J. Cuellar. 1981. The role of family members in the helping networks of older people. *The Gerontologist* 21(4):388–94.

Carmen Delia Sánchez

Hispanic Informal Support Systems: A Research Study

INTRODUCTION

The population of those 65 years and over in Puerto Rico has increased from 2 percent in 1898 to 9.7 percent in 1990. According to the 1990 population census, there were 340,884 persons 65 years and over in Puerto Rico. The progressive increase of the Puerto Rican aging population in the last decades has created the need to study this group from different perspectives, particularly the nature of its support system.

Considerable attention has been paid to the importance of the social support system in the lives of elderly persons. The social support system comprises a range of basic entitlements and services provided by both public and private large-scale organizations characterized as having a formal component, and the more personal idiosyncratic assistance received from the family and significant others such as friends and neighbors, known as the informal support system.

This research study focused on the extent to which a group of Puerto Rican elderly have an informal network of friends and neighbors, and the nature of their interaction.

CONCEPTUAL FRAMEWORK

The primary component of the informal support system of the Puerto Rican elderly (relatives, friends and neighbors) provides a variety of services that are ongoing, generally nontechnical in nature, such as providing emotional support, and which involve a long-term commitment. This reliance on the informal support system in no way denies the acceptance by the elderly and their family, friends, and neighbors of the role of the government and other formal organizations in the provision of a range of services and entitlements. Rather, the empirical data appear to support the theory of shared functions between formal organizations and primary groups as delineated by Litwak, which is the theoretical formulation underlying this study.

The nature of the functions that each primary group is able to carry out will be determined by the particular characteristics that distinguish each group. The family system, for example, distinguishes itself by the permanency of the relationship between its members. Therefore, the tasks that this group will be in the best position to deliver will be those implying a long-term commitment. On the other hand, neighbors and friends are characterized by geographical proximity and face-to-face contact between individuals. They will be better able to be involved in those tasks that require such proximity and do not require a long-term commitment.

The relationship between the elderly, friends, and neighbors has been recognized as a resource of emotional support and intimacy, which is needed for the psychological well-being of the aged person. Friendship and neighboring are prevalent forms of social intercourse through which people exchange services, assistance, information, advice, and intimacy in a form not always available within family settings. Intimacy, characterized by close and communicative exchange, is an important dimension of interpersonal relationships among the elderly.

For those elderly persons who live alone or lack available relatives, friends and neighbors constitute a crucial support system. The research conducted by Powers and Bultena demonstrated the validity of the principle of family member substitution by showing that widows had a greater degree of intimacy with friends and neighbors than did elderly married women.

The particular situation that surrounds the lives of the elderly population in Puerto Rico demands the inclusion of significant others to expand their interaction, both at instrumental and affective levels. The Puerto Rican culture places a high value on the concept that life is a network of interpersonal relationships. Family consists of blood relatives and a wide-ranging constellation of "adopted relatives" who fulfill either informal or formal functions within the extended family. These members consist of close friends and neighbors who have engaged in important family matters and events.

The ritual kinship process known as "compadrazgo" formally includes friends and key neighbors as well as distant relatives in the family. This ritual is widely used among the different Hispanic groups.

In the study by Sanchez (1989) on the support system of elderly Puerto Rican widows, neighbors and friends were designated by the widows as the persons who helped them most with health and personal problems in the absence of children or other close relatives.

RESEARCH FINDINGS

The purpose of this exploratory-descriptive study was to examine the role of friends and neighbors in the lives of a group of elderly Puerto Ricans; to find out to what extent elderly persons, living in high-rise housing, have a network of friends and neighbors; delineate the characteristics of such networks; and determine the nature of the interactions among the groups. Through a random sample process, a total of six housing projects were selected from the twenty-five projects providing housing for the elderly, developed by the Department of Housing in metropolitan San Juan. The total sample consisted of eighty-four (84) randomly selected persons aged 62 years and older. Structured formal interviews were conducted with the participants, to collect information on measurable factors such as income, living arrangements, family composition, health problems, and the assistance provided by friends and neighbors. Factors related to perceptions on the support received from friends and neighbors, as well as the level of satisfaction with this support, were derived from the interviews. For the purpose of the study, a friend was defined for respondents as a person with whom the elderly person shared intimacies and feelings, interacted one or more times monthly, had no consanguineal or legal ties, and need not live in the same building. A neighbor was defined as a friend who lived in the same building.

The ages of the participants ranged from sixty-two (62) to ninety-two (92) years, healthy enough to live in independent housing. The majority of the respondents were females (75%), reflecting the unbalanced sex ratio that generally characterizes the aged population. Over half of the respondents (59%) had nine years or less of formal education, which is higher than the average for the total aged population in Puerto Rico. Seven percent of the group studied had no formal education.

The income of elderly persons in Puerto Rico is extremely low in relation to the income of the general population. In the group under study, 62 percent had a monthly income of $400 or less, which represents an annual income of $4,800. People 65 years and over in Puerto Rico depend on the income they receive from Social Security, the Nutritional Assistance Program, or their retirement pensions. Over half of the respondents in the study (52%) received income from both Social Security or a pension plan. Fourteen percent received income exclusively from Public Assistance.

Marital and health status were examined. Data on marital status revealed that only seven percent of the respondents were married, while forty-eight percent were widowed. Ninety-three percent lived alone. Forty-five percent of the participants indicated that they had health problems, mainly musculo-skeletal problems such as arthritis, rheumatism, or movement problems.

Over three-quarters of the respondents had an extended immediate family composed mainly of children, grandchildren, nieces, nephews, and cousins. However, nineteen percent had no children. These findings indicate that the

Puerto Rican elderly continue to be part of an extended family, even though it is evident that families are getting smaller.

Availability of the family was also examined. Fifty percent of the elderly had their relatives living within a half-hour's travel from home. It is notable that in one-third of the cases who reported having family, most of their immediate relatives lived outside of Puerto Rico. Nevertheless, respondents stated that they maintain communication with their relatives through visits (2%), telephone (6%), visits and telephone (83%), and telephone and letters (7%). These interactions are on a daily basis in 37%, and once or twice weekly in 42% of the cases. Ninety percent of the respondents reported receiving some type of assistance from their relatives, basically at emotional and instrumental levels. Only 4 percent of the participants received no assistance from relatives.

All except one of the respondents indicated that they had a relationship with friends and neighbors in addition to their family. The majority (55%) reported having seven or more friends of the same age, whom they knew through living in the same housing complex or a previous neighborhood, previous work experience, or church attendance. Similar findings were reported by Sanchez (1989) in the study on the support system of elderly widows. Almost all of the respondents indicated having some form of communication with neighbors. As with family members, the most frequent form of interaction with friends were visits and telephone calls (83%). Face-to-face contact and visits were the most frequent forms of interaction with neighbors.

The findings of this study demonstrate that friends and neighbors are a very important support system for the Puerto Rican elderly, basically in the provision of emotional support. Visits, companionship to social and religious activities, telephone calls, and support in time of illness and emergency situations were the most common activities carried out by friends and neighbors. All of the participants in the study reported satisfaction with the assistance provided by friends and neighbors, and indicated that this assistance was important in maintaining and enhancing their lifestyle.

CONCLUSIONS AND RECOMMENDATIONS

Data from this study indicate clearly the existence of an informal support system among the Hispanic elderly in San Juan. For the Puerto Rican elderly, relatives, especially children, are the main component of their informal support system. Friends and neighbors are also an important element of this support system. Activities such as companionship, advice giving, transportation services, and sharing of social and religious activities, were among the supportive functions performed by friends and neighbors. Little or no financial assistance was offered by this system. Most of the participants expressed satisfaction with the support received by their friends and neighbors. Even for those elderly with relatives that provided assistance, there were important social and support activities that they considered only friends and neighbors could fulfill.

Additional studies should be done to analyze in greater depth the levels of intimacy and reciprocity between elderly friends and neighbors. The examination of the Puerto Rican elderly support system is also helpful in determining needs and services in this population.

References

Cantor, M. 1979. Neighbors and friends: an overlooked resource in the informal support system. *Research on Aging* 1(4):434–63.

Litwak, E., and J. Szelenyi. 1969. Primary group structures and their functions: kin, neighbors and friends. *Amer Sociological Rev* 24(3) :465–81.

Parris, S.M., and M. Bernstein. 1984. Social support and well-being among residents of planned housing. *The Gerontologist* 24(2):144–48.

Peters, G.R., and M.A. Kaiser. 1985. The role of friends and neighbors in providing social support. In *Social Support Networks and the Care of the Elderly*, edited by W.J. Sauer and R.T. Coward. New York: Springer.

Powers, E., and G. Bultena. 1976. Sex differences in intimate friendships of old age. *J Marriage & Family* 25(4):739–47.

Sanchez, C.D. 1987. Self-help: model for strengthening the informal support system of the Hispanic elderly. *J Gerontological Social Work* 9(4):117-28.

——— (1989). Informal support systems of widows over 60 in Puerto Rico. In *Mid-Life and Older Women in Latin America and the Caribbean*. Washington, D.C.: Pan American Health Organization, 265–77.

Carmen Delia Sánchez

Home Care Policy

Home care policy in the United States is a patchwork of public programs that has been described as decentralized, categorical, and limited. Federal initiatives have, for the most part, relied on decentralized authority and state discretion, leading to the development of at least 50 systems of home care nationwide.

In 1993 the nation will spend an estimated $108 billion on long-term care. Only 31 percent of these expenditures, however, will go to home and community-based care—despite the fact that four out of five disabled and almost three out of five severely disabled Americans live at home or in some community setting. This low proportion of spending on home care is attributed, in large part, to the fact that most noninstitutional care is provided informally by family and friends, and to the institutional bias of the Medicaid program, which is the largest public payor of long-term care expenditures.

Federal and state government expenditures represented almost three-quarters of the $33 billion to be spent on home care in 1993. While the newest generation of long-term care insurance policies tend to include some level of coverage for home care as well as nursing home care, private insurers covered less than five percent of home care expenditures in 1993.

FEDERAL PROGRAMS FOR HOME CARE

Medicare

The Medicare home health benefit is part of an entitlement program, requiring coverage of in-home services for all persons who satisfy the eligibility requirements. This program pays for skilled nursing care; physical, occupational, or speech therapy; home health aide services; medical social work services; and durable medical equipment and supplies for Medicare beneficiaries who are certified by a physician as in need of skilled nursing services on an "intermittent" (as opposed to continuous) basis, and who are "homebound." Medicare covers only personal, custodial care when skilled nursing services are also required. It is, therefore, seen as a post-acute, rather than a long-term care, benefit. Home health care is the fastest-growing Medicare benefit, increasing by 583 percent since 1980 and by 26 percent since 1990.

Medicaid

Medicaid, the federal/state match health insurance program for the poor, finances home care services through three different options in state Medicaid plans: (1) home health care services; (2) personal care services; and (3) home and community-based waiver services. States are required to cover home health services for certain groups of Medicaid enrollees; personal care and waiver services are optional, allowing, but not requiring, states to provide coverage for these services.

Medicaid home health services are usually the same set of services as those provided under the Medicare home health benefit, although states may have different rules concerning the amount, duration, and scope of coverage. Personal care services are semi-skilled or non-skilled services, prescribed by a physician, supervised by a registered nurse, and provided to Medicaid beneficiaries who need assistance with basic activities of daily living (e.g., bathing, dressing, housekeeping). As of January 1990, 30 states provided personal care services as an optional benefit under their state Medicaid plans. Spending for personal care services, however, is highly skewed across the states; New York alone accounts for over 80 percent of all personal care spending.

To promote more extensive investment in home care, section 2176 of the Omnibus Budget Reconciliation Act of 1981 authorized a waiver of Medicaid requirements allowing states to provide a broad array of nonmedical, community-based services including case management, day care, personal care services, transportation, homemaker services, and respite care. The waiver authority permits states to liberalize some income standards to broaden coverage, but limits potential cost increases by allowing states to restrict eligibility to specific geo-graphic areas and population groups. States must demonstrate that spending for home and community-based care will be offset by reduced expenditures for nursing home care of at least an equal amount. Persons receiving services under the waivers must meet the same level of care criteria that are used by states to certify Medicaid coverage for nursing home care.

In 1989, 36 states operated one or more waiver programs for aged and phys-ically disabled Medicaid enrollees. Spending for all home and community-based waiver programs grew rapidly in the 1980s, reaching $943 million in 1989. Two-thirds of Medicaid spending for home and community-based waiver serv-ices are for children and adults with mental retardation and other developmental disabilities, with the remaining one-third covering services primarily to the dis-abled elderly.

A 1990 Medicaid provision allows states to provide home and community-based services as a state option, rather than through waivers. Although the cost-effectiveness requirements are not applicable, the circumstances under which these services can be provided as a regular state option are quite proscriptive. Another limitation is that total federal and state expenditures for these optional services are capped in each fiscal year, exposing states to considerable financial risk.

Other Federal Programs

Two federal social service programs also authorize a broad range of home and community-based services—the Social Services Block Grant (SSBG) under Title XX of the Social Security Act, and Title III of the Older Americans Act (OAA). These programs do not carry as stringent restrictions on eligibility and on the scope of services to be provided as do Medicare and Medicaid. But they do have the ability to provide significant funding for in-home and community-based care. The Department of Veteran Affairs also operates a range of programs for disabled veterans living at home or in alternative residential care facilities.

States have broad authority to spend their SSBG allocations on a wide array of social services, of which home care for the elderly and disabled is only one. In 1986 at least 38 states used some portion of their SSBG funds to support home and community-based services for the frail elderly, with over 50 percent of this spending attributed to California's In-Home Supportive Services Pro-gram.

Through the OAA, the Administration on Aging allocates federal grants to states for the development of comprehensive and coordinated community-based systems of services for the elderly. Although all persons over age 60 are eligible for benefits without means-testing, the program focuses special attention on eld-erly persons with the greatest economic and social needs. In 1987 OAA amend-ments for the first time targeted funds to provide in-home services for frail older persons, expending $4.6 million in FY 1989. Just over one-half of all program funds in FY 1989, however, were used for nutrition services (i.e., congregate meal and home-delivered meal programs), with another third funding supportive services including information and referral, transportation, home repairs and maintenance, as well as home health aide and homemaker services. OAA programs make an important contribution to the publicly-financed home care system by supporting the infrastructure through which resources can be coordinated. State Agencies on Aging and local Area Agencies on Aging (AAAs) serve a major information and referral function, with many AAAs formalizing their roles as providers of case management services.

STATE FINANCING OF HOME CARE

States also use their own general revenue funds to support home care programs, with most of the dollars going toward state matching requirements under Medicaid and the OAA. Many states, however, provide additional funding for home care by supplementing SSBG and/or OAA programs; targeting State Supplemental Payments to federal Supplemental Security Income (SSI) benefits to elderly and disabled persons requiring some level of home care or living in supervised residential settings; and developing ''stand-alone'' programs that provide home and community-based care to disabled persons.

STATE VARIATION IN HOME CARE PROGRAMS

Given this patchwork of public financing for home care, it is not surprising that there is quite a bit of variation in home care programs across the states. Oregon, for example, has developed the most consolidated and centralized structure for administering home care, offering a continuum of care from home-delivered services to assisted living residential facilities. New York uses Medicaid's personal care services option to target an intensive service package to financially eligible disabled persons. In contrast, the Massachusetts program uses state-only revenues and SSBG funds to serve a broader range of clients at much lower levels of intensity. Illinois has pooled resources to create a statewide entitlement to home care for individuals of all ages and income levels who meet functional/medical criteria for nursing home admission. Wisconsin uses a combination of Medicaid, SSBG, OAA, and state-only funds to provide a wide range of home and community-based services, as well as cash grants, to poor and near-poor disabled of all ages. Programs are administered at the county level and consumers have much discretion in the services that will be used. Finally, California and Michigan use individual providers (including family members) who are hired and directed by the clients themselves.

HOME CARE POLICY REFORM

There has been much debate concerning the appropriate mix of informal and formal home care, and the respective roles of the public and private sectors and the family in assuring access to services for all persons in need of home care. Policy options range from incremental changes in Medicaid to a national social insurance program for home and community-based care. The Clinton administration's plan for health care reform is expected to include provisions for the expansion of home and community-based services for people of all ages. As the debate rages at the federal level, state and local governments, as well as the private sector, will continue to experiment with alternative ways to finance and deliver home care.

References

Advisory Council on Social Security. 1991. *The Financing and Delivery of Long-Term Care Services: A Review of Current Problems and Potential Reform Solutions.* Washington, D.C.

Benjamin, A.E. 1992. An overview of in-home health and supportive services for older persons. In *In-Home Care for Older Persons*, edited by M.G. Ory and A.P. Dunker. Newbury Park, Cal.: Sage Publications, 9.

Office of the Assistant Secretary for Planning and Evaluation, U.S. Department of Health and Human Services. 1992. *Public Financing of Long-Term Care: Federal and State Roles.* Paper presented at the Four Nations Social Policy Conference, Pennsylvania State University, September 15–17, 1992.

The Pepper Commission. 1990. *A Call for Action.* Final Report, S. Prt. 101–114, Washington, D.C.: U.S. Government Printing Office.

Prospective Payment Assessment Commission. 1992. *Medicare and the American Health Care System.* Report to the Congress. Washington, D.C.

Stone, R.I., M. Bernardin, L.A. White, and B. Owen. 1992. *State Variation in the Regulation of Long-term Care Insurance.* Washington, D.C.: American Association of Retired Persons.

Robyn I. Stone

Home Care Use: Predictors

Because of the continued health care crisis in the United States and the view that institutionalization is neither appropriate for nor preferred by many elderly with disabling conditions, home care is the most rapidly growing segment of the health care industry. This rise in importance has not been without growing pains, however. It is often unclear who the most appropriate clients of home care may be, nor is it clear whether home care programs typically offer service arrays that meet most of the elderly's major needs.

BACKGROUND

The history of formal home care programs dates from the mid-nineteenth century. The first hospital-based home care program was established by the

Boston University School of Medicine in 1855. For many years, growth in the home care industry was rather slow, but a resurgence of these programs occurred in the 1970s and again in more recent years.

The mid-1970s interest in home care programs came about because of rapidly rising costs of institutionalized forms of long-term care, and because of concerns that institutionalization was often inappropriate as a way of dealing with the social and medical needs of many aged people. At the time, it was hoped that home care programs would substitute for nursing homes or other forms of institutional care, thus increasing the ability to meet the needs of the aged while saving money.

Despite a lack of convincing evidence that home care is indeed a cost-effective substitute for nursing home care, the resurgence of home care programs continues. Recent growth stems in part from a desire to control hospital inpatient costs in the context of prospective payment systems for inpatient care. Prospective payment systems are used by the Medicare program, many State Medicaid programs, and some private payers. These systems contain strong incentives to reduce the length of inpatient stays. As a result, hospital discharge occurs sooner, and a market for post-acute rehabilitative care outside inpatient units has developed. That market includes home care services or services in other settings such as hospital swing beds, adult day care facilities, and nursing homes.

The earlier hope that home care would substitute for more costly institutional care and the more recent focus on shortened hospital stays have direct impact on predictors of home care use, because they influence the types of patients who want and can benefit from that care.

DEFINITIONAL ISSUES

Growth in the home care industry has been characterized by the variety of programs that offer different types of medical and social services. This wide array of service types and the differing eligibility criteria have been cited as evidence that no clear definition of home care services exists. This diversity, it is argued, often leaves the elderly and their families unaware of the range of services available or their potential eligibility for service use.

In addressing definitional issues, the first priority is a formal definition of home care for the elderly and examining briefly eligibility criteria for that care. The formal definition is a modified version of adult day care proposed by the federal government:

[Home care] is a program of services provided under health leadership [at home] for [the chronically impaired] who do not require 24-hour institutional care but who are incapable of full-time independent living due to physical or mental impairment. (*Federal Register* 41(6):1604, January 9, 1976)

There are three phrases of immediate interest in this definition that bear relationship to predictors of home care use. The first relates to care provided under health leadership. The second refers to the absence of need for institutional care. The third notes the importance of both physical and mental impairment. All of these components are discussed.

Services Provided Under Health Leadership

Federal and State governments are major payers for home care services. These governments have set eligibility criteria for home care services that typically focus predominantly on medical services or medical social work services. The federal government began offering reimbursement for home care services in 1965, when Medicare legislation was passed. To be eligible for that care, patients had to be homebound, meaning that trips away from home were generally restricted to medical care visits. Services included skilled nursing care, speech therapy, and physical or occupational therapy. Services had to be ordered by a physician and were intended to address relatively short-term needs. State Medicaid programs and other State programs often offered similar services and also typically required that care be prescribed by a physician.

The influence of health care reform measures designed to reduce the cost and length of inpatient stays has also led to the medicalization of home care. As Steel (1991) notes, "virtually any service provided in the hospital can be provided in the home if the patient has an adequate support system (both formal and informal), if physical constraints do not contravene its provision, and if the physician is willing to authorize and oversee the care plan in association with a home care coordinator." Examples of these services include blood tests, ECG, flu shots, intravenous antibiotics, respiratory therapy, dialysis, phototherapy, parenteral therapies, chemotherapy, other therapies that require the use of infusion pumps, ventilator therapy, pain management, post-burn treatment, and decubitus treatment.

Medical services are provided in most home care programs, but the limited mobility and frailty of the home care population has also resulted in the demand for nonmedical services. Hereford (1989) describes the Supportive Services Program for Older Persons, a series of grants funded by the Robert Wood Johnson Foundation (RWJF), in which venture capital was provided to 11 local agencies. Eligibility for the grant money required the agencies to assess the demand for services by the elderly population. Telephone surveys and focus groups with older people showed that the most-desired services were not medical in nature. Rather, they related to house-care and included minor repairs and maintenance, plumbing and electrical work, and yard maintenance. Other services desired included help with shopping and transportation. These services correspond roughly to the need for help with instrumental activities of daily living (IADLs).

The surveys of demand for care identified unmet needs of many home care programs that focused primarily on medical and social work services. It is interesting to note that five of the 11 grantee organizations were visiting nurse agencies and two were local departments of health.

Absence of Need for Institutional Care

In the early 1970s, home health care was proposed as a means of avoiding institutionalization. Steel (1991) cites evidence from the Channeling project that some nursing home care may have been avoided by the use of home care social services, but Garner and Mercer (1982) note that home health care is a cost-effective substitute for nursing home care only when disability is not too severe. This comment is consistent with findings from earlier demonstration projects showing limited impact of home health care on nursing home costs and thus increased total long-term care costs when home care was used.

If home health care is not a cost-effective substitute for institutional care, who should use it? Various studies of home care describe participants as having at least some functional limitations in activities of daily living (ADLs or IADLs). In the RWJF grant projects, most clients lived alone, about two-thirds had significant ADL limitation, and 80 percent had difficulty performing heavy chores around the house. Beland (1987) notes that the appropriate candidates for home care are those with relatively few functional limitations, but whose limitations are nevertheless severe enough to lead to neglect in their living environment. These candidates tend to be women, those who need some medical care, help with shopping, meal preparation, and heavy housework, those who could benefit from substantially improved social networks, assistance with transportation, occupational therapy or physiotherapy, and social work services. Hannan and O'Donnell (1984) show that home care patients are very similar in levels of functioning and need for care to adult day care patients. They also noted limitations in ADL and IADL activities, as well as frequent lapses in mental alertness. Thus, all of these factors may be good predictors of home care use.

Physical and Mental Impairment

Early home care programs followed Medicare's lead in stressing the need for services provided by a physician. Though eligibility criteria vary widely by funding source, many Medicaid or other State-based programs required some limitation in ADL capability. Jackson et al. (1992) criticize early programs for an over-reliance on physical limitations. These programs excluded elderly who had the capacity to function well physically, but who often failed to remember to perform those activities or needed cues to complete an activity. They argue that both physical and mental health needs should be considered as criteria for appropriateness of home care.

Jackson et al. (1992) estimate the number of elderly in the United States with various levels of ADL and cognitive limitations, using data from the 1984 National Long Term Care survey. They show that the proportion of people with limitations is very sensitive to the criteria used to measure ADL and cognitive limitation. As a result, anywhere from 1.6 percent to 14.0 percent of the elderly population could be considered as potential home care users.

PREDICTORS OF HOME CARE—A FOCUSED REVIEW

In the literature regarding predictors of home care use, about 20 papers can be found; these are listed in the Medline database maintained by the National Library of Medicine. Of the 20 papers, 13 provided the results of statistical tests of hypotheses concerning home care use. The most significant risk factors for home care are ADL and IADL status, perceived physical status, actual physical status, lack of social supports, age, living arrangements, income, marital status, cognitive functioning, infrequent contact with children, level of depression, and prescription drug use. The number of predictors for home care use is larger than the number of factors expected to predict institutionalization.

Factors in common with those that emerged in the study regarding predictors of institutionalization include age, income, marital status, ADL and IADL limitations, social group involvement, and living arrangements. Gender was not identified as a factor in predicting either home care use or institutionalization.

Studies such as these provide a fairly good indication of the predictors of home care use.

CONCLUSION

Though it may not be a cost-effective substitute for nursing home care, home care has the potential to meet significant medical, social, and environmental needs of a substantial number of elderly persons. The rapid growth of the home care industry underscores this supposition. Earlier studies showed the limited impact of home care on nursing home costs. It will be of interest to note the impact of home care on alternatives such as swing-bed care in hospitals and adult day-care programs. Like home care, swing-beds were originally proposed as short-term sites for treating post-acute needs of the elderly in tight nursing home markets. The early swing-bed demonstrations were confined to rural areas, but the Health Care Financing Administration is considering expansion to urban areas as well. Like home care, the literature on swing-bed use suggests that it is not a complete substitute for nursing home care; it may indeed be a competitor to home care programs across the country. Further research needs to be done to determine which form of care is more appropriate, or whether competition among alternative programs will reduce the cost of treatment and enhance access to care for the nation's elderly.

References

Beland, F. 1987. Identifying profiles of service requirements in a non-institutionalized elderly population. *J Chronic Diseases* 40:51–64.
Federal Register 41(6):1604, January 9, 1976.
Garner, J.D., and S.U. Mercer. 1982. Meeting the needs of the elderly: home health care or institutionalization? *Health and Social Work* 7:183–91.
Hannan, E.L., and J.F. O'Donnell. 1984. Adult day care services in New York State: a comparison with other long-term care providers. *Inquiry* 21:75–83.

Hereford, R.W. 1989. Developing nontraditional home-based services for the elderly. *Quality Review Bulletin* 15:92–97.

Jackson, M.E., B. Burwell, R.F. Clark, and M. Harahan. 1992. Eligibility for publicly financed home care. *Amer J Public Health* 82:853–56.

Steel, K. 1991. Home care for the elderly: the new institution. *Arch Internal Med* 151: 439–42.

Ronald J. Ozminkowski and Laurence G. Branch

Home Health Care: National Trends

LONG-TERM CARE AS PERSONAL HOME CARE

"Financial Gerontology" is the field of applied and basic research that explicitly examines the connections among the financial and social dynamics of rapidly aging societies. Personal care at home is recognized as an important alternative to the "nursing home solution." In many circumstances, it can be both less expensive than nursing home care and a more human response to the needs of older individuals.

Despite public imagery that portrays an aging population as synonymous with a dependent and bedridden society, in fact, 95 percent of older people do not live in nursing homes, and 75 percent of older people do not require personal assistance on an everyday basis. Nonetheless, long-term care is a critical medical, social, and financial issue for a society with rapidly expanding numbers and proportion of old and "older-old" citizens.

Long-term care is usually discussed in the context of institutional care and nursing homes. It is increasingly recognized, however, that many, if not most, older men and women continue to live in their own homes even when they have some level of disability. The capacity to continue to live at home, even with illness or disability, is made possible by new medical procedures, sophisticated pharmaceuticals, creative prosthetics, and innovative community-based nutrition and social support services.

Each of these, separately and in combination, contribute to the increased capacity of older individuals to continue to live with their families, in homes and neighborhoods. From a humanitarian as well as financial perspective, such inventions and social programs offer older women and men the resources to stay out of nursing homes, when in an earlier time institutionalization might have been the only possible response to a condition of even limited disability.

Research over the past 20 years has identified a range of situations in which the assistance of another person in the household environment can be the appropriate response to a condition of limited disability. Applied gerontological research has produced a standard way to measure such limitations, known as the Activities of Daily Living (ADL) scale. This tool asks if the older person can perform each of five everyday activities without help, or if he or she needs the assistance of another person to regularly perform the activity: bathing, dressing, moving from bed to chair, going to the toilet, and eating.

The distinction between home care to assist in the successful performance of these daily activities and the alternative "nursing home solution" is straightforward: without the assistance of "that other person" in the home to help with these everyday tasks, the older person would likely be institutionalized. In other words, when the problem is linked to an older person's difficulty in performing an activity, such as eating or taking a bath, then the logical solution is to provide assistance with eating or bathing.

THE DEMAND FOR AND THE SUPPLY OF PERSONAL
HOME CARE

Given the desirability and appropriateness of personal home care as an alternative to nursing home care for a substantial number of men and women, the demographic magnitude of population aging transforms home care from an individual issue to a societal issue. This points to two fundamental questions: First, how much ADL-related home care is our aging society likely to demand over the next several years? Second, where is the supply of this care likely to come from?

Research clearly demonstrates that there is a positive correlation between age and functional limitation. For each of the five ADLs, the pattern is the same: the older the age, the higher the rate of personal care assistance needed to accomplish the tasks. However, the strength of the correlation varies. Eating has the weakest relationship with aging, and bathing the strongest. For purposes of the following discussion, an older person is defined as being "in need" if he or she needs assistance with any one or more of the five standard ADLs.

Information describing the ADL rates for different age groups is derived from the 1984 Supplement on Aging to the Health Interview Survey, a nationally representative sample of 11,500 respondents age 65 and older. For now, it is assumed that these 1984 rates accurately describe the older population over the next 10 to 20 years. This assumption is then modified in anticipation of a time when personal and societal health practices will extend old age longevity.

Combining the ADL rates with census projections of the size of the older population in future years produces estimates of the overall societal demand for personal care over the years 1980 to 2010. The 2 million men and women age 65+ with one or more ADL limitations in 1980 are projected to increase to 3.6 million persons by 2010, an increase of 80 percent. A significant pattern within this overall trend, however, is that the demand for personal care in the older-old (85+) age group is projected to increase by 173 percent.

Who are the providers of personal care? Systematic research as well as anecdotal accounts confirm that most personal care is provided by the daughters and daughters-in-law of the older care recipients. To estimate the aggregate societal-level supply of potential caregivers, researchers use the number of middle-aged women (age 55–64) as a surrogate for daughters/daughters-in-law caregivers. During the same period that the overall demand for personal care is projected to rise by 173 percent among the older old, 1980 to 2010, the number of middle-aged women will increase by only 58 percent.

THE CAREGIVER RATIO

These trends identify the projected demand and supply components of the caregiver relationship: the number of older persons with one or more ADL dependencies, and the supply of middle-aged women as potential caregivers. Combining the two components produces a Caregiver Ratio (CGR) which summarizes the demand-supply relationship into a single index number: the number of caregivers for each individual care-recipient. During the period between 1980 and 2010, there are about 5–6 caregivers projected for each care recipient.

ALTERNATIVE VIEWS OF THE FUTURE

How realistic is it to use the 1984 ADL rates to project the future demand for personal care? Not very. Despite improvements in life expectancy, *recent research indicates that dependency within the older population is increasing, not decreasing.* As new medical procedures extend the lives of older men and women, some are kept alive in a less healthy, more dependent state. The reduction in tuberculosis, for example, increases the number of people who will survive into old age, and who are thus at risk of cancer and cardiovascular disease. Similarly, reduction of deaths from cancer and heart disease again increases the number of elderly, and thereby increases the overall number of persons who are at risk of getting Alzheimer's disease and other conditions that result in disability.

Variations in Demand

More dependency in the future means that there will be a greater need for home care. Examination of these alternative futures is based on two additional sets of Caregiver Ratios that "simulate" increased ADL rates: 1) ADL rates 25 percent higher than the 1984 rates, and 2) 50 percent higher than the 1984 rates. Using the 25 percent higher ADL rates, the total number of older persons with one or more ADL limitations increases by 125 percent, from 2 million in 1980 to 4.5 million in 2010. Using the 50 percent higher rates, the need for personal care increases by 170 percent overall, and by more than 300 percent among the older-old population.

Variations in Supply

Not all the middle-aged women enumerated in the census are the daughters or daughters-in-law of dependent older persons. Among middle-aged women who do have living parents, many may be unable or unwilling to provide home care. Many middle-aged "empty-nest" women have returned to the paid labor force; others live too far from their parents' home; still others may simply prefer not to be caregivers. For these reasons, Caregiver Ratios using a 50 percent reduction in the number of middle-aged women caregivers are included in the "alternative futures" analysis.

The most extreme version of the Caregiver Ratio produced by these alternative future demand and supply projections shows that if the need for personal home care services should rise by 50 percent, and if only 50 percent of the daughters should be available to provide care, the magnitude of society's need for caregivers will be substantial.

CONCLUSION

The demand for personal care is driven by the combined force of two inescapable and intertwined dynamics: age-correlated patterns of need and the demographic growth of older age groups. Therefore, the assessment of future patterns of demand and supply suggests that social policy in both the private and public sectors should be directed toward increasing the supply of caregivers. Public policies should endorse home care benefits alongside the community-based nutrition and social services now available. Medicare should emphasize well-compensated home care as a matter of long-term health care policy. Private insurance should include generous home care provisions and benefits. The real bottom line is that we cannot hope to attract and retain motivated and caring people to take care of our parents and grandparents, and then pay them minimum wage or less. Whether we use current rates of need or modest estimates of increases in the rates of the need for home care, projections of demand and supply of caregivers show that the future needs will be great.

References

Brody, E.M. 1981. Women in the middle and family help to older people. *The Gerontologist* 21:471–80.

Cutler, N.E. 1991. Personal care, home care, and long-term care insurance. *J Amer Society of CLU & ChFC* November:31–34.

———— (1992). The emerging dynamics of financial gerontology: individual aging and population aging in the new century. In *Age, Money and Life Satisfaction: Aspects of Financial Gerontology*, edited by N.E. Cutler, D.W. Gregg, and M.P. Lawton. New York: Springer.

Haan, M.N., D.P. Rice, W.A. Satariano, and J.V. Selby. 1991. Living longer and doing worse? Present and future trends in the health of the elderly. *J Aging & Health* 3:133–37.

Katz, S.T., T.D. Downs, H.R. Cash, and R.C. Grotz. 1970. Progress in the development of the index of ADL. *The Gerontologist* 10:20–30.

Neal E. Cutler

Home Health Care: Public Policy Issues

INTRODUCTION

As the elderly portion of the population in the United States continues to expand, issues relating to the financing and regulation of home health care become increasingly important. Both the federal and state governments have responded to this growing need with initiatives that have encouraged the development of home health care programs. The purpose of this chapter is to provide a brief overview of financing and regulatory issues currently impacting home health care in the United States. Coverage for home health care (HHC) services has been provided by Medicare, a federal program designed, since its inception in 1965, to ensure access to high quality health care to individuals over age 65. Medicaid, a combined federal-state program designed to ensure health care access for the poor, also began to provide for HHC coverage in 1965, although it was optional for states until 1971. Occasionally, Medicaid-provided HHC can be important for older persons because of coverage differences with Medicare. Subsequently, new federal programs were initiated to fund HHC because of increasing need.

HOME HEALTH CARE REIMBURSEMENT

Favorable legislation in the 1980s stimulated tremendous growth in the HHC industry. However, despite the increased supply of home health agencies (HHAs), coverage for HHC through governmental programs and other third-party payers remains inadequate. Public reform initiatives are limited and narrow, usually emphasizing eligibility criteria and cost-effectiveness rather than appropriateness and comprehensiveness. One consequence of this inadequacy is that approximately 75 percent of all disabled elderly rely on unpaid, informal caregivers (family and friends) for home care. Another indirect result is that HHC coverage remains unaffordable to those elderly most in need. Finally, those who do qualify for home care through public funding must sort through the many different programs that underwrite home care services. These programs include Medicare, Medicaid, the Older Americans Act, the Social Services Block Grant, and the Department of Veterans Affairs.

Medicare is the largest third-party payer (private or public) for post-acute HHC services. During the 1980s, Medicare HHC expenditures nearly quadrupled due to the demands of an aging population. Under Title XVIII of the Social Security Act, Medicare Part A reimbursement for HHC requires the beneficiary to meet several criteria (in addition to basic Medicare criteria) including that the beneficiary must be homebound, must be under the care of a physician who certifies the home health plan and reviews the plan every two months, the care needed must include part-time skilled nursing care, physical therapy, or speech therapy, and the HHA providing the services must be a certified, participating Medicare agency.

Once the above criteria are fulfilled, Medicare will reimburse for several services including part-time or intermittent skilled nursing care and home health aide services; physical, speech, and occupational therapy; medical social services provided under the supervision of a physician; medical services provided by a resident in an approved teaching program; and medical supplies and equipment. Medicare will cover a combination of skilled nursing and home health aide services for up to 7 days per week, up to 28 hours per week, and up to 21 days per illness episode. Upon documentation verifying the "need for and reasonableness of" additional care, the beneficiary may receive up to 35 hours per week of combined skilled nursing and home health aide services. Home health aides are provided through Medicare Part A at no cost to the recipient. Durable medical equipment is covered under Medicare Part B with a 20 percent copayment by the recipient.

Medicaid is the primary public payer of long-term care (LTC) services for the elderly (primarily because Medicare pays only for the first 100 days of post-hospital care). The key to Medicaid coverage is that in order for a middle-class person to become eligible for long-term care services, an individual must "spend down" their savings so that they meet low-income criteria. Medicaid HHC benefits, legislated by each state, encompass a broader spectrum of services than Medicare (e.g., they include personal services). Medicaid's HHC expenditures have also skyrocketed in the last decade from being less than half of Medicare's costs to matching them by the end of the 1980s. Under Title XIX of the Social Security Act, Medicaid coverage for HHC services requires beneficiaries to qualify in one of several categories that reflect the need for income assistance.

Home health services covered by Medicaid differ by state. The basic framework incorporates a series of services including nursing, home health aides, medical supplies, appropriate medical equipment, and physician home visits. Other available services, depending on eligibility, may include physical therapy, occupational therapy, speech therapy, audiology, private duty RN/LPN services in-home beyond just intermittent visits if the additional services are physician-recommended, prescribed drugs, dentures, prosthetic devices, orthopedic shoes, and eyeglasses. Certain states will also reimburse for nonprofessional personal care services prescribed by a physician and performed under RN supervision in the home, and home- and community-based services (under waiver agreement) that specifies that the services are needed to prevent the individual from being institutionalized.

   Title III of the Older Americans Act of 1965 was designed to provide a variety
of home- and community-based services to the elderly. All those 60 years or
older are eligible for benefits regardless of income, with emphasis on services
for low-income, minority, and isolated elderly. Under Title III the federal government issues funds to states for the provision of senior centers, supportive
services, and home-delivered meals. Following the introduction of Medicare's
Prospective Payment System (PPS) for hospitals in an attempt to reduce health
care costs associated with hospitalization, agencies dealing with the aged experienced a large increase in referrals for in-home services such as case management, home nursing services, and housekeeping and personal care services.
As a result of PPS, $858 million was allocated for this program under Title III
in 1989. Supportive services include outreach, housekeeping, home health aides,
personal care, chores, visiting and telephone reassurance, residential repair, and
health services. Allocation of funds to each service type is decided by individual
states. Services provided under Title III are free of charge although donations
are accepted.

   The Social Services Block Grant (SSBG) from Title XX of the Social Security
Act was designed to provide funds for social services and nonmedical home
care and has been the primary source of federal funding for these services since
1975. States receive federal grants to spend on state-identified needs. Some
states coordinate the administration of Title III of the Older Americans Act with
SSBG funds to maximize targeting of services under both programs. SSBG, like
Title III, also targets its services to low-income populations. States provide variable services through SSBG. Often, these include home-based services (e.g.,
homemaker, chore aide, home management, etc.) and home-delivered meals.
Vendors are paid by fee-for-service, contract, and vouchers. Beneficiary copayment is determined by state program criteria.

   The Department of Veterans Affairs provides hospital-based (Veterans Administration Medical Center) HHC to eligible veterans who require medical care
following hospitalization. Home care is available to qualifying veterans living
within a thirty-mile radius of one of the 49 Veterans Administration (VA) Medical Centers with a home care unit. The services covered include physician
services, skilled nursing care, rehabilitation therapy, social services, nutritional
services, prescription drugs, and medical equipment and supplies. When available at a hospital-based home care unit, home health aides and physical, occupational, speech, and respiratory therapy are also covered. Primary health care
is available for homebound veterans who require long-term therapy to maintain
status and retard decline, for terminally ill veterans, and for those who (with
their families) need short-term HHC training to remain at home. Copayment for
services is based on eligibility category, secondary insurance status, and ability
to pay.

   Private insurance for HHC differs by plan and company, but is generally
limited and often expensive (with age-dependent rates). Home care benefits under private insurance usually follow the Medicare program and are therefore

limited to the immediate post-hospital period. Private insurance for long-term HHC will most likely continue to reflect the general state of long-term care insurance in this country, which is restrained by high rates and limited coverage.

CLASSIFICATION OF HOME HEALTH AGENCIES

A home health agency is a public or private agency specializing in the provision of skilled nursing services at home. Historically, HHAs originated from nonprofit visiting nurse associations started in the late 1800s. There are five primary types of HHAs representing 95 percent of all Medicare-certified HHAs (approved for Medicare funding): public/governmental, visiting nurses associations, hospital-based (public and private), private nonprofit (voluntary), and proprietary (for profit). The population and services provided for by these different types of HHAs differ, depending on the agencies' incentives and resources.

Medicare-certified HHAs experienced unprecedented growth in the 1980s as a result of favorable legislation. Congress legalized certification of proprietary HHAs in 1980. The Omnibus Reconciliation Act of 1980 eliminated the requirement of a minimal three-day hospitalization under Medicare Part A and a $60 deductible under Medicare Part B before qualifying for HHC benefits. In response to the general aging of the population and to the introduction of the prospective payment of hospitals, the number of Medicare-certified HHAs exploded from 2,967 in 1980 to 8,105 in 1989. In 1989 for-profit HHAs made up about 34 percent of the total certified HHAs serving over 25 percent of the Medicare beneficiaries. The number of private hospital-based HHAs has also risen since the mid-1980s due to the increased demand for post-acute services resulting from the implementation of the Medicare Prospective Payment System for hospitals. Hospital-based HHAs constituted less than 13 percent of all HHAs in 1980, but grew to constitute 31 percent of all HHAs in 1989. In conjunction with the expansion of proprietary and hospital-based HHAs in the 1980s came the decline of public HHAs (which represented the largest sector of the market prior to the 1980s) due to state government budget cuts.

Public HHAs provide needed community services and serve a much larger proportion of indigent and Medicaid clients than private agencies. Although Medicare is the primary payer to all HHAs, public agencies rely more heavily on Medicaid for reimbursement than nonpublic agencies and therefore tend to provide more long-term care; public HHAs cost less for visit charges and reimbursement than other HHAs partly because they provide fewer specialized services such as physical, occupational, and speech therapy. The clientele of public agencies have longer durations of enrollment, receive lower intensities of services, and have more total visits compared to private agencies. These characteristics reflect the fact that public HHAs tend to service indigent and chronically ill elderly.

Alternatively, proprietary HHAs exist to maximize revenues. Proprietary agencies have greater flexibility in choosing the types of clients they serve and the types of services they provide. They receive a greater proportion of their payment from Medicare than public agencies. Their clients are usually well-insured. The clients have short durations of enrollment, receive the highest intensities of services, and often remain at home after HHC. These characteristics reflect the fact that proprietary HHAs service more middle-class and less ill elderly.

HOME HEALTH AGENCY REGULATION

Several mechanisms were devised in an attempt to assure high quality in HHAs. In some cases, an agency must be certified by public funding sources in order to receive reimbursement. For example, HHAs must be certified by Medicare or Medicaid reimbursement in order to receive funding. Other attempts to assure quality occur through the efforts of nonprofit advocacy groups that attempt to exercise influence through public opinion and industry-wide acceptance. The National Home Caring Council accredits homemaker and home health aide services. The National League for Nursing and the American Public Health Association accredit skilled-care agencies. The Joint Commission on Accreditation of Hospitals accredits hospital-sponsored HHAs.

THE HOME CARE TEAM

Home health care typically requires a team of health care professionals. These teams should include the patient, the family, the physician, a social worker/case manager, and a nursing coordinator. Depending on individual needs, the team may also include registered nurses (RNs) or licensed practical nurses (LPNs), home health aides, a homemaker, companions, therapists (physical, occupational, respiratory), speech pathologists, clinical psychologists, and a nutritionist. The physician and nurse should devise the home health treatment plan, and check it periodically to ensure that the patient is receiving appropriate care, based on ongoing patient care outcome evaluation data. The team should make critical decisions about patient care as a group.

References

Benjamin, A.E. 1992. An overview of in-home health and supportive services for older persons. In *Home Care for Older People: Health and Supportive Services*, edited by M.G. Ory and A.P. Duncker. Newbury Park, Cal.: Sage, 9–53, 193–99.

Fanale, J.E. 1988. Home health care: what's available and what Medicare pays for. *Geriatrics* 43:15–21.

Institute on Law and Rights of Older Adults. 1991. *Entitlement and Advocacy Training: Medicaid in New York State*. New York: Brookdale Center on Aging, Hunter College.

Wieland, D., B.A. Ferrall, and L.Z. Rubenstein. 1991. Geriatric home health care: conceptual and demographic considerations. *Clin Geriatr Med* 7:645–63.

Williams, B.C., S.A. Mackay, and J.C. Torner. 1991. Home health care: comparison of
patients and services among three types of agencies. *Med Care*, 29:583–87.

Barry M. Schultz and Theresa T.H. Nguyen

Home Health Care: Supportive Services

INTRODUCTION

The development of a national health care policy that will meet the variable needs of the American population, young and old, is an exceedingly important challenge for this nation. The nature and character of the policy, particularly the long-term care aspects, will be heavily influenced by factors related to an aging population, such as the rapid increase in people who live to be 85 years and older.

Though frailty and physical decline are not inevitable aspects of aging, many older Americans do depend on others for some assistance with basic tasks of daily living. There are two basic options available to people who need long-term care assistance: care provided in institutionalized settings, such as nursing homes; or community-based care, where services are provided in the person's own home or in the home of another. Community-based care offers individuals an opportunity to remain independent for as long as possible and is the preferred option among older people, their families, and policymakers alike. Much of the assistance provided in the community is provided by family and friends. But formal services are needed to complement the care provided by the informal network. While nursing home care is an integral part of the long term care continuum, in-home care and supportive services is a particularly important aspect that needs special attention.

DEFINING THE CONCEPT

In the 1980s a dramatic growth was noted in the home health care industry, largely the result of policy attention to the "nursing home problem" (e.g., rising costs, inappropriate placement, inadequate care, and ineffectual regulation) and changes in federal policy (i.e., introduction of the prospective payment system, less restrictive eligibility requirements for federal reimbursement, and waivers to stimulate the assisted living industry). But the home care system is in crisis and often characterized by inaccessibility, poor care, unskilled personnel, high out-of-pocket costs, and inadequate linkages to other related services. Recognizing the need for an intensified research effort to guide programmatic and policy decisions for strengthening the U.S. health care system, the U.S. Bipartisan Commission on Comprehensive Health Care (The Pepper Commission,

1990) issued recommendations for long-term care reform, highlighting the need for additional research on the implementation of home and community-based care. The Clinton administration's early discussions of health care reform have similarly emphasized the need to expand such service.

The concept of "in-home health and supportive services" is defined to include a broad array of professional and paraprofessional post-acute and long-term care services provided in nonmedical residential settings. Services include treatments for acute and chronic illness, rehabilitation, and management of disabilities of older persons. A range of medical, social, and personal services can be delivered depending on the level of needs and impairment of the person living in the community. At one end of the continuum are medical and technical services provided by physicians, nurses, and therapists; at the other end are less technical services provided by home health aides, housekeepers, and volunteers. Of course, since family and friends provide much of the assistance needed by older persons, the informal support network is a critical component of home-based care.

DETERMINING THE IMPACT OF HOME CARE

Largely in response to a steady growth in health care expenditures and dramatic increases in nursing home use, early research on home care, such as demonstration programs and evaluation efforts, have placed undue emphasis on home care as a substitute for expensive institutional care for people who are frail and elderly. Much of the research in this area has fallen into the "cost-effectiveness" trap and has kept researchers from devoting sufficient attention to the complexity of this area of research. However, there has been a gradual shift in focus to include broader issues related to need, use, effectiveness, costs, as well as how to better organize, coordinate, and integrate services provided under different models of home care (high-tech, hospice, skilled home health care, and low-tech custodial, respite, etc.). Coordinating services to accommodate multiple and changing needs are of special concern.

Access and Coordination

The complex mix of existing funding sources and the divergent eligibility criteria for different types of home care services have been major obstacles for responding to the home care needs of older Americans. As conceptualized by Susan Hughes (1992), a leading expert on home health care, this distinctive financing system has led to the evolution of four distinct models of home care in the United States: high-tech home care, hospice, skilled home health care, and low-tech/custodial care.

Review of the models points to the overlap between acute care and long-term care, as well as the dynamic nature of long-term care. For example, high-tech home care represents the acute care nature of home care and refers to the transfer of technology-intensive care (e.g., chemotherapy) to the home. This is a fast-growing segment of the home care market and services may be used by the young and the old, particularly in light of legislative changes in Medicare that encourage earlier discharges from hospitals.

Hospice care refers to palliative rather than curative care for those who are not expected to live beyond six months. Young and old who are terminally ill (and their families) may benefit from a range of services, such as nursing care, social services, physician services, and counseling. Older people are most likely to use skilled home health care services if physicians have prescribed the need for skilled nursing care and/or physical, speech, or occupational therapy. The need for this subacute care increases with age and is found to be predominantly used by women. Custodial/low-tech care is generally provided to those who are chronically ill and physically and/or mentally impaired. Anywhere from 600,000 to one million older people are estimated to reside in low-tech care homes known as domiciliary care, personal care, adult foster care, board and care, and assisted living facilities. There is still much to learn about providers and clients of this form of care, but services usually include paraprofessional homemaker and chore/housekeeping services.

The services provided and outcomes expected in each model are not mutually exclusive. The care required by a client may be a reflection of the stage in the progression of a chronic or acute illness. The chronically ill person may experience acute illnesses that require high-tech services (i.e., respirator/ventilation therapy) for some period of time but, once stabilized, will require custodial care only. Or, a client may receive high-tech services in the early stages of a disease (e.g., cancer) but will require only palliative care in the later stages. While improvement is generally the most desired outcome, maintenance of some level of functioning may be the best to be expected for clients who use certain types of care, such as high-tech or low-tech care. In the same way, decreased hospital use may be the most reasonable outcome for clients needing skilled home care or hospice. The needs of the home care clients are variable and change, depending on a number of factors: stage and type of illness, age, availability of informal assistance. For this reason, flexibility and appropriate targeting are important requirements for maximizing the potential of the home care market.

FUTURE RESEARCH NEEDS

Just as the home health care market is complex, so too is research which examines the quality of services provided in the home. First, the heterogeneity of the population requires that needs be identified within different subgroups in the population to determine whether services are available and/or accessible to those who need them. Second, a more concerted effort must be made to describe the nature of the home care services delivered and the variations they have on the populations who use them. It is necessary to consider what it is about a service that yields a positive or negative outcome within a specific group. Third, research is needed on how different home settings vary with respect to populations and resources. Setting and population characteristics will have an effect on how care is delivered and what outcomes can be expected. Finally, it is extremely important for research to address the adequacy of service, the degree that the solution for a problem matches the magnitude of the problem. More information is needed on how well the quantity and scope of benefits fit the level of need for special populations (e.g., minorities, rural elders) in need of service.

Though research is limited, a foundational base has been established on which to develop future research on the structure, process, and outcomes of home care. In addition, important insights can be obtained through experiences aimed at meeting the long-term care needs of special populations, such as persons with AIDS or Alzheimer's disease. Our ability to learn from research and practical experiences is an important key to our success in developing a home health care policy that is reliable, accessible, and adequate.

References

Benjamin, A.E. 1992. An overview of in-home health and supportive services for older people. In *In-Home Health Care for Older People*, edited by M.G. Ory and A.P. Duncker. Newbury Park, Cal.: Sage.

Estes, C.L., and J.H. Swan. 1993. *The Long-Term Care Crisis: Elders Trapped in the No-Care Zone*. Newbury Park, Cal.: Sage.

Hughes, S.L. 1992. Home care: where we are and where we need to go. In *In-Home Health Care for Older People*, edited by M.G. Ory and A.P. Duncker. Newbury Park, Cal.: Sage.

Ory, M.G., and K. Bond. 1989. Introduction: health care for an aging society. In *Aging and Health Care*, edited by M.G. Ory and K. Bond. London: Routledge.

Ory, M.G., and A. Duncker. 1992. Introduction: the home care challenge. In *In-Home Health Care for Older People*, edited by M.G. Ory and A.P. Duncker. Newbury Park, Cal.: Sage.

Pepper Commisson (U.S. Bipartisan Commission on Comprehensive Health Care). 1990. *A Call for Action*. Washington, D.C.: Government Printing Office.

Marcia G. Ory and Donna M. Cox

Hope in the Elderly: Clinical Assessment

It has been suggested that the overall function of hope is to enable persons to deal with situations where needs and goals are not met, and to make life under stress bearable. Research on hope in the elderly has focused on community-based "healthy" samples, the recently widowed, those awaiting institutionalization, and in persons post-stroke. Additional studies have examined hope in

chronic illnesses, such as cancer, multiple sclerosis, amyotrophic lateral sclerosis, and cardiac problems. More recently, researchers have begun to examine
the role that hope plays in psychoneuroimmune responses.

Poets, philosophers, psychologists, sociologists, theologians, and clinicians
suggest that hope is an essential characteristic of the human condition. Hope
can function as a way of feeling, a way of thinking, a way of behaving, and a
way of relating to one's world. Hope has the ability to be fluid in its expectations, and in the event that the desired object or outcome does not occur, hope
can still continue to function.

While numerous instruments that measure hope have been developed or used
by nurse researchers, often these instruments cannot readily be adapted to the
clinical setting. As a way of helping clinicians to conduct a qualitative assessment of hope, the acronyms HOPE and GACT have been identified.

H = HEALTH

Whether it be physical or mental health, current research suggests that there
is a relationship between hope and health. A clinical assessment of hope would
examine how hope and health are related in older adults; how hope, or its
absence, is being expressed; the person's level of hope; and whether the person's
illness is challenging existing hope structures.

O = OTHERS

Hope has been inextricably associated with personal relationships, and Erikson suggests that hope is based upon trust in others. A clinical assessment of
hope examines whether the older adult demonstrates a general trust in others
and how others might be helpful in bolstering a reality-based hope. This assessment would also note whether the older adult and others in his/her family
are relating to a larger community or whether they are isolated and alone.

P = PURPOSE

Hope is often linked to one's purpose in life or one's religious/spiritual orientation. A clinical assessment of hope would examine the person's source of
hope—whether it be a Higher Power, relationships with others, inner strength,
or some combination thereof. If persons clearly identify a more religious/spiri-
tual basis for their hope, a more detailed spiritual assessment can be included.

E = ENGAGING PROCESS

The process of hoping is an engaging one that includes setting G = GOALS,
taking A = ACTION, maintaining a sense of C = CONTROL, and placing the

process of hoping into some T = TIME frame. This process of hoping generally includes the setting of nonspecific, reality-based, and flexible G = GOALS. A clinical assessment of hope determines what outcome the older adult hopes for, and whether there is congruency between the older adult's and significant other's hope-related goals, thoughts, emotions and behavior.

To hope also implies A = ACTION. Hopeful persons generally are active in terms of planning, creating, imagining, and engaging in hopeful attitudes or behavior. A clinical assessment of hope determines how actively the older adult participates in this process, and whether there are any conditions or situations such as depression, that interfere with this active process. The process of hoping also denotes a functional sense of C = CONTROL in the face of uncontrollable events. Sometimes it has been found that if older persons try to exert too much control over situations that cannot be controlled, that they may become discouraged or hopeless. It has been suggested that feelings of "Things are under control," as opposed to "I am in control," are much more functional over time.

Hope is also based upon a T = TIME perspective—including the past, present and the future. Past positive experiences help persons to deal with present difficult experiences and can reassure persons that they can cope with future difficult experiences. A clinical assessment of hope would determine whether the individual's hope is oriented in one's past, present, or future, and if the older adult can apply these earlier experiences to this present situation.

A multidimensional clinical assessment of hope can provide the basis for implementing interventions that assist persons to maintain existing, or to regain their potential, hope.

References

Christman, N. 1990. Uncertainty and adjustment during radiotherapy. *Nursing Research* 39(1):17–20.

Erikson, E.H. 1963. Eight ages of man. In *Childhood and Society*, 2d ed. New York: Norton, 247–74.

Farran, C.J., K. Herth, and J.M. Popovich. 1994. *Hope and Hopelessness: Relevant Clinical Constructs*. Newbury Park, Cal.: Sage.

Farran, C., and J. Popovich. 1990. Hope: a relevant concept for geriatric psychiatry. *Arch Psychiatr Nursing* 4(2):124–30.

Farran, C., C.S. Wilken, and J.M. Popovich. 1992. Clinical assessment of hope. *Issues in Mental Health Nursing* 13:129–38.

Herth, K. 1990. Relationship of hope, coping styles, concurrent losses, and setting to grief resolution in the elderly widow(er). *Research in Nurs & Health* 13:109–17.

O'Leary, A. 1990. Stress, emotion and human immune function. *Psychological Bulletin* 108(3):363–81.

Carol J. Farran

Hospice Care

INTRODUCTION

Hospice is a philosophy of caring for the terminally ill and their families. Contemporary hospice care in the United States is a comprehensive approach to providing palliative medical, social, emotional, and spiritual support to individuals whose life expectancies are medically diagnosed to be limited to days, weeks, or months. Although the majority of hospice patients are elderly, hospice care is not limited by a person's age and is available for terminally ill persons of any age.

HISTORICAL BACKGROUND

Hospice care has existed throughout history, with reference to hospices, also called hospitals, hotels, and hostels, dating back to ancient times. With the rise of Christianity, hospices grew as places of rest and care for the sick, impoverished, and homeless. The American hospice movement has been influenced by the work of Dame Cicely Saunders, M.D., a British physician who founded St. Christopher's inpatient hospice in London in 1967. The writings of Elizabeth Kubler-Ross, M.D., who advocated home care as a choice for the care of terminally ill, have also contributed to the growth of hospice in the United States. The first American hospice, The Connecticut Hospice, began providing hospice home care in 1974. Since then, hospice services have expanded to be available in every state.

OVERVIEW

A hospice team works with patients and their families or caregivers to keep a person as comfortable as possible during the final stage of life. The goal of hospice care is to help patients maintain their dignity and comfort during the dying process. Hospice care is based on patient advocacy and ensures that the patient's choices are maintained. Hospice team members work to help people remain in their own homes whenever possible, throughout the terminal stage of illness up to the last day of life. In cases where a patient is no longer able to stay at home, a patient and the caregivers may choose to have hospice care delivered in an inpatient setting, such as a hospice unit, hospital, or nursing home or other facility.

The services that a hospice patient receives are individualized, depending on the person's own physical, emotional, and spiritual needs. Since comfort is a primary goal, medications are frequently administered to decrease a patient's pain. There is a wide range of medications available for hospice physicians and nurses to work with when trying to alleviate a patient's discomfort. Although there are some types of pain, such as bone or nerve pain, that are more difficult to eradicate, the hospice concept encourages trying different medications and therapies until a patient's comfort level is increased. Nonpharmacologic measures for symptom control are also applied and taught to patients and caregivers. These types of interventions may include frequent position changes, modifying feeding techniques, and the periodic use of oxygen.

Hospice care also recognizes that a person's pain may be heightened by emotional or spiritual concerns. In addition to medical personnel such as physicians and nurses, a hospice team is composed of social workers, chaplains, and pastoral counselors who are trained to provide emotional and spiritual assistance to hospice patients and their caregivers. These team members are available for home visits to counsel patients and their caregivers about issues and stresses that develop throughout the dying process. Hospices also offer bereavement groups and services for families and caregivers to assist them with their grief.

There are many daily activities required in caring for a terminally ill person, such as bathing, dressing, and feeding. Hospices offer home health aides and community volunteers who assist caregivers in providing personal care needs for the patient. Volunteers also support caregivers in other ways, such as performing errands or staying with the patient for a brief period to give the caregiver a respite break.

Patients may also benefit from certain therapies, such as physical and occupational therapy, and speech-language therapy for problems in this area. If patients choose to seek these services, the treatment plans are designed to help maintain them at the highest possible level of functioning. For example, patients may be taught how to use a walker and portable oxygen so that they can get out of bed for meals with the family. Dietitian services and nutritional counseling are available to assist patients and caregivers to better understand the changes in nutritional needs and food choices that a terminally ill patient often undergoes.

Hospice services are reimbursed by means of a number of sources. One of the largest payers is the Federal government. Legislation enacted in 1982 created the Medicare hospice program (Public Law 97–248, Section 122). A patient may choose payment of hospice services through the Medicare hospice benefit if certain provisions are met. Requirements include a physician's certification that a patient is terminally ill with a prognosis of six months or less. The hospice care must also be delivered through a Medicare-certified hospice. Covered services under this government benefit include all of the personnel described above, plus items such as medications that are used for care of the terminal illness and medical equipment such as oxygen, hospital beds, walkers, and wheelchairs. Based on the growth of the Medicare hospice benefit, many private medical insurance plans have now included forms of hospice coverage within their policies. A Medicaid hospice benefit is available in 35 states for those patients under 65.

As of this writing, there are 1,288 Medicare-certified hospices, which serve 156,583 patients. There are a number of noncertified hospices that also provide care. This group of hospices is not subject to the same Medicare regulations, nor are these always required to be state licensed. Traditionally, noncertified hospices have relied more heavily on volunteers to provide services than have Medicare-certified hospices. The volunteer-based hospices coordinate with other health care agencies to supplement services provided through other resources.

CONCLUSION

Hospice care in the 1990s has changed dramatically since the first hospices began in the 1970s. Most services are now home based. The hospice philosophy, however, remains intact. By choosing hospice, the terminally ill elect to maintain a standard of comfort and dignity for their final days of life. With the support of a hospice team, the terminally ill are assisted in experiencing their lives to the fullest for as long as they are able.

References

Kaye, P. 1991. *Symptom Control in Hospice and Palliative Care.* Essex, Conn.: Hospice Education Institute.
Kubler-Ross, E. 1969. *On Death and Dying.* New York: Macmillan.
Quill, T.E. 1993. *Death and Dignity: Making Choices and Taking Charge.* New York: Norton.
Siebold, C. 1992. *The Hospice Movement: Easing Death's Pains.* New York: Twayne.
Stoddard, S. 1991. *The Hospice Movement: A Better Way of Caring for the Dying.* New York: Vintage.

Pamela C. Buncher

L

Living at Home/Block Nurse Program

A Living at Home/Block Nurse Program (LAH/BNP) is a community program that draws upon the professional and volunteer services of local residents to provide information, social and support services, nursing, and other professional services to their elderly neighbors who might otherwise be admitted to nursing homes. It is initiated and developed by community residents.

The LAH/BNP is the merger of two Minnesota models that coordinate and provide services for the elderly in neighborhoods. The Living at Home model has operated successfully in two communities, and the Block Nurse Program in five. A 1991 evaluation of the Block Nurse Program documents that 38 percent of the clients would be in nursing homes without the model, at a cost of $2,000 a month in a nursing home, compared to $300 and $500 a month at home. The Living at Home Project and Block Nurse Program complement each other and have been merged so that the best aspects of both can be utilized. By 1992 the combined model spread to 14 communities throughout Minnesota and is expected to expand further in 1993. Two other sites in different states are being developed.

In the Living at Home/Block Nurse Program, there are two categories of services: (1) informal services that are provided by volunteers, and (2) formal services that are paid for.

Volunteer services are planned, coordinated, and delivered through the community board. They might include caregiver support, respite for a caregiver, socialization for someone who is isolated, information about available services, and a myriad of other services such as balancing checkbooks, cleaning a yard, having birthday parties, and many other activities. The community becomes sensitized to the needs of the elderly and creates a volunteer system that helps keep the elderly at home.

Closely related to volunteer services are activities that provide information, prevention (perhaps in classes arranged through the county extension agent or through community education), or early intervention by the nurse so that a crisis does not occur. In one community, 85 percent of referrals to the nurse are by word of mouth because neighbors recognize a need.

For the frail elderly, a registered nurse who, ideally, lives in the community, works with the community board of directors to develop a care program for residents in need of services. Home health aides, homemakers, and volunteers who also, ideally, live in the community provide services to elderly residents and families under the supervision of the Block Nurse. These team members are called the Block Nurse, Block Companion, and Block Volunteer.

Block Nurses assess the need for care, incorporate information and orders from the client's physician, and information and wishes of the client and the family, into a care plan that is acceptable to all concerned. Other professionals are often used: social workers; occupational, physical, and speech therapists; dietitians, and others.

Block Companions—home health aide/homemakers—are oriented to the family, as appropriate, and assist in care implementation. Care is monitored by a Block Nurse, and revision of the care plan occurs periodically. The Block Nurse provides coordination of the formal and informal caregivers so that the goal of safe, effective care that promotes health and independence is achieved.

Block Volunteers are used as needed, and perform a wide variety of services.

Two different categories of staff are necessary for the LAH/BNP model.

1. *Administration in the community.* This category includes all the administration that is necessary in the community, and can be divided into five different functions:

- *nursing administration*: operationalizes and maintains the integrity of the LAH/BNP nurse practice model of case management and service delivery, in collaboration with a contract nursing service agency (RN required; BSN/PHN preferred).

- *other client services administration*: organizes and administers comprehensive support services to meet the needs of seniors in the community (individual client level).

- *volunteer administration*: organizes, implements, monitors, and evaluates all volunteer activities associated with LAH/BNP.

- *community organization/outreach administration*: facilitates development and implementation of LAH/BNP among community groups and citizens (organizational level, not individual client).

• *program management administration*: administers and provides leadership to the LAH/ BNP under the direction of the community board of directors.

These functions may be combined according to community needs and the skills/qualifications of available personnel. For example, program administration might be combined with nursing. Volunteer and outreach functions might be appropriate for an individual who has the necessary experience and skills. In a smaller community, one person working full-time might perform all functions. Ongoing communication and collaboration of all functions by individuals in the designated positions and with the contracting nursing service agency is critical to success of the program.

2. *Service delivery in the community.* The second category of staff are nurses (Block Nurses) and home health aides/homemakers (Block Companions) who provide care in homes. Ideally, they are from the community and are hired through an agreement by the board with the local county public health nursing service or the visiting nurse association, called an agency or vendor. The board recruits the staff, interviews them, and makes hiring recommendations to the vendor. The vendor supports the philosophy of the LAH/BNP.

A high degree of flexibility is necessary from the vendor so that the program designed by the community can become operational. For example, the board may want to combine home health services (paid by Medicare) with homemaker services (paid by Title XX) so that one person does both. This saves mileage and travel time and is less confusing to the elderly when only one person delivers all services.

Because the nurses and home health aides/homemakers are hired by a nursing agency, all entitlement programs are billed on behalf of eligible clients. This includes insurance, Medicare, Medicaid, HMOs, VNA, and others. Services for which there is no reimbursement are billed to the client on a sliding fee scale which considers the ability of the client to pay. Grants from foundations and state and federal governments support the difference between what the client is able to pay and the remainder of the cost. Current LAH/BNPs generate some of the money to pay for nonreimbursed care.

The LAH/BNP arranges any service necessary to maintain the elderly in their own homes and communities. The LAH/BNP delivers formal care such as skilled nursing, and provides health education, prevention programs, and early intervention that link most effectively with the community's volunteer services. A community-based volunteer system augments these services and arranges for volunteers to provide services to those persons who need social support and assistance prior to needing more organized, formal care.

A community-based volunteer network can begin with a few committed, interested people. They know of or learn about others who are willing to commit time and energy to attend meetings, assemble facts and figures, converse with people, and do the detail work necessary to launch a new venture. This pooling of knowledge, experience, insight, and sensitivity from community-minded people who are concerned about the status of the elderly in their area provides a rich resource to the organization and implementation of an LAH/BNP. Those in the community know how to get things done, know who the leaders are, who the movers and shakers are. They know who needs to be included in the planning process in order for things to work. It may be a community resident who always seems to be leading causes, it may be the local banker, county commissioner, or clergy.

Networks are not circumscribed. Their tentacles are unknown. They intersect, link, are interconnected, sometimes form a chain, are often twisted and irregular, and cannot be controlled. However, a network is a structure, albeit an ill-defined system. Networks are intrinsic to and alive in communities. The community network can be used to organize and coordinate volunteer services and other activities to provide the long-term care services needed by elderly residents. The challenge for agency and government people is to ask the right questions, stimulate constructive discussions, and facilitate the process so that the program "belongs" to the local community.

Once in place (and this takes time), the program collaborates with organizations delivering long-term care. This is where agency people intervene to remove system barriers so that the linkages among community groups can operate smoothly. Community residents become exhilarated about their involvement and the potential for assisting in the creation and implementation of a noninstitutional long-term care system, each one unique to the individual community.

ROLE OF THE LAH/BNP, INC.

The Living at Home/Block Nurse Program, Inc. is an organization that fulfills two objectives: (1) it provides consultation to communities who wish to plan for implementing the model, and (2) on behalf of all LAH/BNPs, it is working toward the acquisition of permanent funding to support the nonreimbursable services required by clients and communities to maintain elderly persons in their own homes.

A Replication Manual that outlines specific steps for setting up an LAH/BNP in a community and which contains additional helpful information is available from: The Living at Home/Block Nurse Program, Inc., 475 Cleveland Avenue North, Suite 322, St. Paul, MN 55104, (612) 649–0315.

Reference

Jamieson, M.K. 1992. *Forming a Community-Based Volunteer Network*. St. Paul, Minn.: Minnesota Department of Human Services.

Marjorie K. Jamieson

M

Medicare, Medicaid, and Other Federal Programs

In the more than 25 years of their existence, Medicare, Medicaid, and the Older Americans Act have demonstrated success in enabling older adults to receive medical and nursing care, and other supportive services, that they might otherwise not have been able to afford. These federal programs were legislated and enacted in 1965, during the presidency of Lyndon B. Johnson.

MEDICARE

The Medicare program is a federal health insurance program for people 65 or older and for certain disabled people. It is administered by the Health Care Financing Administration of the U.S. Department of Health and Human Services (formerly the Department of Health, Education, and Welfare). Applications for Medicare are accepted by Social Security Administration offices across the country, which also provide general information about Medicare.

Medicare has two parts: Hospital Insurance (Part A) helps pay for inpatient hospital care, inpatient care in a skilled nursing facility (SNF), home health care, and hospice care. Medical Insurance (Part B) helps pay for services rendered by physicians, and by nurse practitioners in many instances, hospital outpatient services, durable medical equipment, and a number of other medical services and supplies that are not covered by the hospital insurance part of Medicare.

Part A of Medicare has deductibles and coinsurance, but most people do not have to pay premiums for Part A. Part B has premiums, deductibles, and co-insurance amounts that one must pay for, either out-of-pocket, or through coverage by another health insurance plan. The premium, deductibles, and coinsurance amounts are set each year according to formulas established by law. New payment amounts begin each January 1. Individuals are notified about specific amounts when increases occur.

People age 65 and over can get premium-free (no monthly payments) Medicare Part A benefits, based on their own or their spouses' employment. If people meet the age requirement, they can also get Medicare benefits if (1) they receive benefits under the Social Security or Railroad Retirement system, (2) are eligible to receive benefits under Social Security or the Railroad Retirement system but have not filed for them, or (3) the individual applying for Medicare, or spouse, had certain government employment.

People under age 65 can get Medicare Part A benefits if they have been a disabled beneficiary under Social Security or the Railroad Retirement Board for more than 24 months. Certain government employees and certain members of their families can also receive Medicare benefits when they are disabled for more than 29 months. These individuals should apply through the Social Security Administration as soon as they become disabled.

Another group of people who are eligible for Medicare Part A benefits are those who require continuing dialysis for permanent kidney failure or if they have a kidney transplant.

Individuals should inquire of the Social Security Administration whether they have worked long enough under Social Security, Railroad Retirement, as a government employee, or under a combination of these systems, to be eligible to get Medicare Part A benefits. In general, if either an individual or a spouse has worked for a minimum of 10 years, under any of the above situations, they are eligible for Medicare Part A benefits.

Anyone who is eligible for Medicare Part A benefits based on length of work experience under the situations listed above are also then eligible for Medicare Part B. By enrolling in the program, and paying the monthly Part B premiums, individuals may receive Part B benefits.

If individuals over 65 do not have enough work credits to be eligible for Medicare Part A, they may apply for both Part A and Part B benefits, or just Part B, by paying monthly premiums. People who are disabled may also pay monthly premiums to receive Part A and Part B, if they have lost their Part A benefits solely because they are working.

Those people over 65 who are already receiving Social Security or Railroad Retirement benefit payments will automatically receive a Medicare card by mail. The enrollment period for applying for Medicare occurs each year from January 1 through March 31. If individuals do not apply for Part B during this enrollment period, they must either pay a late enrollment fee, or wait for the next enrollment period. These requirements regarding late-enrollment and late-fee regulations also apply to Part A.

INSURANCE INTERMEDIARIES AND CARRIERS

The federal government contracts with insurance organizations called intermediaries and carriers to process claims and make benefit payments. Intermediaries handle claims on behalf of the individual by hospitals, skilled nursing facilities, home health agencies, hospices, and other providers of services. Individuals generally do not deal directly with intermediaries.

Carriers handle claims for services by physicians and other providers designated under Medicare's Part B program. All states and U.S. territories have specific Medicare carrier offices that can answer questions about Part B insurance. A listing of these offices is available through the Social Security Administration.

PEER REVIEW ORGANIZATIONS

Peer Review Organizations (PROs) are groups of physicians and other health care providers who are paid by the federal government to review the care given to Medicare patients. Each state has a PRO that decides, for Medicare payment purposes, whether care is reasonable and necessary, is provided in the appropriate setting, and meets the standards of quality accepted by health care professions. PROs have the authority to deny payments if care is deemed not necessary or is not delivered in the most appropriate setting. PROs respond to requests for review of notices of noncoverage issued by hospitals to beneficiaries; and to beneficiary, physician, and hospital requests for reconsideration of PRO decisions. PROs also investigate individual patient complaints about quality of care provided by inpatient hospitals, hospital outpatient departments, hospital emergency departments, skilled nursing facilities, home health agencies, ambulatory surgical centers, and certain health maintenance organizations (HMOs). Medicare PRO offices are available in each state.

MEDICAID

Medicaid, Title XIX of the Social Security Act, is the major means for financing health care services for low-income people. Enacted in 1965, Medicaid enables states to furnish medical assistance and rehabilitation to the aged, blind, disabled, and families with dependent children whose income and resources are insufficient to meet the costs of needed health care.

Medicaid is a state-administered program, operated under federal regulations, which has been implemented in all states (except Arizona) and in the Territories. Program costs are shared by the federal government and the states, with the federal share dependent on per capita incomes. Sharing ranges from 50 percent in states with a high per capita income, to 78 percent in Mississippi where the per capita income is the lowest in the nation. Within the limits of federal legislation and regulations, states have broad discretion in terms of eligibility criteria, benefit packages, and reimbursement rates.

Coverage must be provided by all states to all recipients of the Aid to Families with Dependent Children (AFDC) program and, with some exceptions, to beneficiaries of Supplemental Security Income (SSI) and the federalized blind, disabled, and aged welfare program. Eligibility criteria relating to income are determined by each state and may extend coverage to the "medically needy." These are persons or families who meet SSI or AFDC eligibility criteria but whose incomes are no more than 133 and 1/3 percent above welfare levels in the state. At their option, states may cover other categories as well, such as families headed by an unemployed male, children who are financially eligible but not in a federal welfare category, spouses who are "essential" to the well-being of an SSI recipient, and persons eligible for, but who voluntarily decline, AFDC or SSI cash payments.

States are required to provide Medicaid benefits that cover hospital and skilled nursing facility care, home health, physician, laboratory, X-ray, family planning services, early and periodic screening, diagnosis and treatment of children under 21, and rural clinic services. Optional services include outpatient prescription drugs, dental services, eyeglasses, intermediate care facilities, prosthetic devices, and care for patients over 65 in tuberculosis and mental institutions.

Since 1970, under Social Security Amendments, states are required to provide home health coverage to any Medicaid beneficiary who is covered for SNF care under Medicaid. This extends coverage for home care to all adults over 21 years of age. States may elect to cover skilled nursing facility and home care to people under 21.

Under Medicaid, home health care is not defined precisely, although regulations require states to include a minimum range of home health services such as nursing care, home health aide services, and equipment. Medicaid does not require "skilled" nursing care, and patients need not be homebound. Services provided to eligible recipients include:

- intermittent or part-time nursing services furnished by a home health agency
- intermittent or part-time nursing services of a professional registered nurse or a licensed practical nurse under the direction of the patient's primary care provider, when no home health agency is available to provide nursing services
- home health aide services provided by a home health agency
- physical therapy, occupational therapy, speech therapy, and audiology services provided by a home health agency or by a facility licensed by the state to provide rehabilitation services.

Regulations specify that these services can by provided only upon the written recommendation of a physician, and the plan of care must be reviewed every 60 days. In most states, there is no limit to the number of home visits.

OLDER AMERICANS ACT OF 1965, TITLES II, III AND IV

In 1965, the Older Americans Act (OAA) established the Administration on Aging (AOA) in the Department of Health, Education, and Welfare. Several of the programs authorized by this Act are administered or assisted by the AOA and relate to home health services for persons 60 years or older.

Title II of the OAA, Grants for State and Community Programs on Aging, is for the purpose of strengthening or developing at the state and local levels a comprehensive and coordinated program to help elderly Americans maintain an independent lifestyle. Many of these projects contain home health service components, such as visiting nurse and other home health services for the homebound elderly, homemaker services, health education, immunization and screening programs, home repairs, and home-delivered meals. Some Title III projects train geriatric aides to monitor the health status of homebound elderly and provide support to improve the well-being of older persons through nutrition and socialization programs. Meals and support services are provided in congregate settings as well as in the home.

A requirement under Title III is that area agencies on aging (AAA) must spend at least 50 percent of their social service allotment on three priority services: (1) access, including transportation, outreach, and information and referral services, (2) legal and other counseling services, and (3) in-home services.

Under Title IV of the OAA, funds are provided for research and demonstration projects directed to models for alternatives for living and service delivery arrangements for older Americans who, without such services, would otherwise be institutionalized.

References

Kansas Employer Coalition on Health, Task Force on Long-Term Solutions. 1991. A framework for reform of the U.S. health care financing and provision system. *JAMA* 265(19):2529–31.

The Medicare 1993 Handbook. U.S. Department of Health and Human Services, Health Care Financing Administration, 6325 Security Boulevard, Baltimore, MD. 21207.

Spiegel, A.D. 1993. *Home Health Care.* Owings Mills, Md.: National Health Publishing.

Susan Appling and Ada Romaine-Davis

Medication History Intake

INTRODUCTION

Among the many responsibilities of the home health care nurse, obtaining and maintaining an accurate medication history is one of considerable importance. The majority of home health care patients are usually medically managed, which often means polypharmacy, especially with elderly patients. Obtaining a complete and accurate medication history is necessary before one can assess the patient's medication regimen. Taking a medication history is more than simply confirming the prescription medications the provider ordered. Most patients use nonprescription medications on an "as needed" basis, and the use of nonprescription medications by patients over 65 years may account for 40 percent of their medication regimen. In addition, patients often "share" medications, or take herbal or home remedies. Clearly, the provider and case manager need to know everything the patient is taking before proceeding with other treatments. The following is an accounting of items, by category, that should comprise the medication history.

DEMOGRAPHICS/BASIC INFORMATION

Obvious information that should be on the medication history form are the patient's name, age, sex, height, and weight. The latter factors are necessary to calculate the patient's creatinine clearance, a laboratory value, which guides the dosage of those medications that are excreted through the kidneys. Also important are the patient's diagnosis(es), to assess possible drug-disease interactions.

ALLERGY HISTORY

A detailed history of any drug allergies is important to know at the outset, because it influences all prescribed and nonprescribed medications in the future. Necessary information regarding drug allergies includes the name of the drug if known, how the allergy manifested itself, and when it happened with respect to time of dose and time of allergic reaction. Knowing what was done to counteract the allergic reaction may prove helpful, if known. Specific questioning will almost always yield specific answers, if the patient knows or can remember the events.

SOCIAL AND PHYSICAL HISTORY/OTHER

Information needed under this category includes the patient's amount of intake of such substances as coffee, tea, chocolate, soft drinks, herbal teas, beer, wine, liquor, and illicit drugs. A tobacco history is essential.

Coffee, tea, chocolate, and caffeinated soft drinks often contain significant amounts of caffeine. Amounts of 250 mg of caffeine is considered a pharmacologically active substance, and can affect how the body reacts to other medications. Caffeine can also cause nervousness, insomnia, restlessness, irritability, tremor, headache, and is known to react with such drugs as theophylline, estrogen, and oral contraceptives.

Alcohol is a central nervous system depressant, whose effects are additive with antihistamines, barbiturates, benzodiazepines, and antipsychotics. Also, concomitant alcohol use with warfarin (Coumadin) or aspirin greatly increases the risk of bleeding. Alcohol taken during nitrate administration increases the risk of hypotension; with oral hypoglycemics, the hypoglycemia may be increased. There may be significant interaction between alcohol and drugs such as antabuse (Disulfiram), chlorpropamide (Diabinese), and metronidazole (Flagyl).

Smoking or tobacco use can have adverse effects when combined with other drugs. For example, patients who smoke and are taking theophylline will require a higher dose of the drug because of increased metabolism secondary to smoking. If the patient is taking an estrogen product or oral contraceptives, smoking greatly increases the risk of cardiovascular problems, such as stroke.

Health professionals are often surprised to learn how many patients take herbal supplements or herbal tea. Herbal products may contain pharmacologically active substances such as coumadin- or digoxin-like elements. These products may cause excessive diureses (high urine output or sweating), gastroenteritis, abnormal electrolyte imbalances, and anticholinergic effects. The history taker must again ask specific questions related to symptoms to ascertain whether the patient who is taking herbal preparations is experiencing side effects from these substances.

Home remedies include such substances as catnip, syrups, turpentine, poultices made of mustard or seeds or other substances, and bizarre topical products—remedies that are rubbed into the skin.

In addition, the history taker must inquire about whether the patient is taking any kind of supplemental feedings, such as those that are fluid food supplements that can be bought in cans. Any of these enteral feedings may be continuous or intermittent, and may interfere with drug absorption. If the patient has a nasogastric (NG) tube in place that allows for liquid feedings directly into the stomach, it is important to recognize that not all medications can be administered via the NG tube.

If the patient has a colostomy or ileostomy in place, it is essential that they receive "immediate" release pharmaceutical dosage forms, to facilitate drug absorption. The more bowel that is removed, the less potential a drug has to be absorbed. These patients should not be given sustained release forms of any drug.

People who have difficulty swallowing solid, oral forms of drugs may be given the same drugs but in a different form of the drug—solutions, suspensions, suppositories, or transdermal forms.

Knowledge about the patient's financial resources is necessary to fully assess the medication regimen and its effectiveness. The history taker needs to ask such questions as whether the patient can afford to pay for medications, whether they have ever omitted having a prescription filled by the druggist because of lack of funds, or whether they routinely take less of the drug than is prescribed to make the amount "last longer." Obtaining the name of the patient's pharmacist is often useful, should there be a need to discuss issues related to the patient's drug regimen.

PRESCRIPTION MEDICATIONS

When one begins the medication history, the patient is asked to bring all medications that they are presently taking. In looking over the collection of medications, one often identifies multiple prescriptions for the same drug under more than one name. The drug may be prescribed by both its generic and trade name, for example. If the history is done in the home setting, the patient shows where the current medications are stored. Most patients store medications in the bathroom or kitchen, which are not optimal storage locations because of heat and humidity; these increase drug degradation.

The first question to be asked is to name the medications taken every day, and what they are used for. In recording these medications, it is sometimes useful to compare them to the physician's form, the referral to home health care, where medications to be taken at home are listed. This comparison does not always provide accurate information regarding the discharge medications, which may have been changed since the patient's discharge from the hospital or nursing home.

Next, it is important to learn when the medications are taken, and what the patient does if a dose is missed. Occasionally, it is evident that the patient takes medications differently from what is prescribed, either by dose or by time. These differences should be carefully noted, for later discussion with the patient.

For each prescription medication, the history taker notes the drug name, dose, frequency, route of administration, start and stop days, reason for discontinuation, and the name of the prescribing physician/provider. Any difficulties the patient has in reading the labels, removing the cap from the bottle, or in taking the proper dose, should be carefully assessed. If there appears to be a problem with compliance, this too should be noted.

NONPRESCRIPTION MEDICATIONS

After information regarding prescription medications has been obtained as fully as possible, information about "other" medications is needed. Often, the patient will answer "no" to this question, because many people believe that over-the-counter (OTC) drugs, or home remedies, are not medications. Most patients do not understand the implications of combining prescription and nonprescription drugs. The nonprescription drugs can cause adverse effects, drug interactions, and other problems similar to those found with prescription drugs. To illustrate this point, 20 percent of drug-related admissions to hospitals are because of nonprescription drug use.

It is not sufficient merely to ask the patient "do you take any other medications?" The history taker must methodically mention each OTC drug category and ascertain symptoms specific to the drug category. The use of simple terms is necessary, such as "What do you take when you have heartburn or indigestion?" rather than "Do you take antacids?" The list of OTC drug categories includes those used for diarrhea, constipation, hemorrhoids, nausea or vomiting, cough or cold, aches or pains, insomnia, or eye, ear, or skin problems. The list also includes vitamins, minerals, and iron products.

FINAL ASSESSMENT

Once the complete medication history is known, a complete assessment of the medication regimen can be made by evaluating the therapeutic appropriateness of each drug, any duplication of drug therapy among those that the patient is taking, barriers to or difficulties with compliance, potential drug interactions, appropriateness of drug dosage, or problems with allergies.

An essential part of the assessment is to discuss the entire therapeutic regimen with the patient and to provide education where needed so that the patient has full understanding of the drugs being taken, why they are being prescribed, the consequences of missing or skipping doses, and the expected outcomes of drug therapy. The latter is important so that the patient has a grasp of how the drugs affect health status, and that much depends on their cooperation and self-care. Drug therapy is greatly enhanced when the patient understands the relationships among the major areas of medication therapy.

Mary Lynn McPherson

Minority Issues: A Social Work Perspective

DEFINITION OF THE MINORITY

Traditionally, the term "minority" describes a group of people with an insignificant representation in terms of its number. Today, this term symbolizes differences, powerlessness, conflict, and resistance. The definition of a minority goes beyond individual differences in terms of race, gender, age, and other acquired characteristics; it further includes an oppressed social status which is correlated with an individual's history and experience, lifestyles, lack of power and resources, and cultural differences.

Issues related to minorities are usually associated with their differences that are treated as problems that require immediate attention, rather than identified as resources that provide insight and linkage for social integration. This "problem-oriented" assumption has intensified the feelings of resistance—minority groups refusing external intervention, and the majority's lack of motivation to accept differences.

A formal definition of the minority elderly is not included here because when differences, power, and conflict enter the picture of defining minorities, every elderly individual can be perceived, at some point, as a minority. Despite the fact that minorities may include any group of individuals with unique characteristics (acquired or achieved) that are associated with powerlessness and oppression, people of color seem to suffer the most. Thus, when the elderly individual is also a person of color, the minority status of this individual is often perceived as disadvantaged. Nevertheless, the Census Reports separate data for African-Americans, American Indians, Asians and Pacific Islanders, and Hispanic Americans—the traditionally defined minority groups. Therefore, while the following discussion addresses minority issues in general, attention is given to these specific ethnic groups.

REPRESENTATION

"Aged over 65" has been commonly used in public policies and social service programs to define older adults. According to the 1980 and 1990 Census, the 65+ population has increased by 22 percent in ten years. In 1980 the 65+ population was 25,549,000—89.8% Whites; 8.2% Blacks; 0.8% Asian Americans and Pacific Islanders; 0.3% American Indians, Eskimos and Aleuts; 0.9% other races. Among them, 2.8% were people of Hispanic origin. Ten years later, in 1990, the 65+ population is 31,224,000—89.1% Whites; 8% Blacks; 1.5% Asian Americans and Pacific Islanders; 0.4% American Indians, Eskimos and Aleuts; and 1% other races. Among these elderly individuals, 3.7% are of Hispanic origin.

These statistics reflect the fact that the minority elderly population has been increasing. Although the distribution of the elderly population among different ethnic groups is proportionally stable, there is a 31 percent increase in the non-white populations as opposed to a 21 percent increase in the white population. However, the growth rate of the African-American elderly (19% increase) is slower than that of the White elderly (21% increase). Nevertheless, the growth rate of the elderly population is very high among Asian Americans (129% increase) and American Indians (63% increase). Also, there is a large increase (141%) of the Hispanic elderly population.

"MINORITY" ISSUES

In the last two decades, research on the minority elderly has focused on analyzing problems and issues related to specific ethnic groups. With a focus on barriers to home care for the elderly, these issues can be grouped into three interrelated areas: individual, relationship, and political and institutional issues.

Individual Issues

Over a decade ago Manuel (1982) studied the social psychology issues affecting the minority aged. These issues, which have been significantly impacting older minority individuals, include differential life expectancy, economic and health issues, retirement, and death. Gelfand (1982) identified stress, emotional needs, income, living conditions, and health status as important considerations. Even recently, the focus of aging studies has not varied much. These issues have been discussed with additional information on images of aging, perception of personal needs, homelessness, safety, and issues related to culture, gender, and race.

Relationship Issues

Closely tied with the individual issues, relationship issues affect the elderly's long-term emotional needs, life satisfaction, friendship, and health. Informal caregiving is one of the most important family values, along with close family relationships and a family-oriented kinship system. Expecting the family to be the center of caregiving, many minority elderly people have been disappointed because this traditional belief may not be supported by their family members. Some elderly people do not even have a family and others have a family facing traumatic cultural changes. Many elderly people who have been caught between the old and new values experience relationship problems with their families. Feelings of isolation become a consequence.

The majority of these individual and relationship issues are common to most elderly individuals, regardless of their ethnic differences. One major reason is that these factors are closely related to the perception and reality of an elderly person's health status. Many people assume that being old is a developmental process for all individuals. When a person is getting older, health care and caregiving will become priority needs. However, when physical and family factors are compounded by environmental and political influences, minority elderly people are more vulnerable than their majority counterpart.

Political and Institutional Issues

A first issue is related to the changing expectation of family involvement. Family caregiving for the aged members has been considered one of the most important milestones among most minority families. Because of racism, discrimination, unequal treatment, and lack of adequate opportunities, many families are unable to provide or continue their caregiving function. Poverty, illness, unemployment and lack of resources are a few of the external factors that also interfere with this expectation. Power differential is a unique aspect explaining the minority elderly's experience.

A second issue is the gap between needs and services. Jacobson (1982) found that many data that measure service utilization and quantity of benefits are "most often incomplete, inaccurate, or misleading when it comes to measuring participation of minorities." As opposed to the overrepresentation of problems by teen minorities in the juvenile justice system or by minority parents in child protection services, minority elderly people have been underrepresented in the social service system. Gelfand (1982) offers the following explanations: (1) lack of knowledge of available services, (2) unwillingness to utilize services, (3) unwillingness to travel to services, (4) lack of available transportation, (5) low expectation of services (compared to what they would have received from the family), and (6) preference to maintain ethnic culture. Cheung (1988) adds two other factors: (1) cultural mismatch between the professional and the client, and (2) lack of familiarity with the social service system.

A third issue is related to the cultural adjustment process. Beyond the expectation that a minority family will take care of its elderly members, society has also imposed a value on minorities that assimilation into the mainstream culture will promote social integration. Cheung (1988) argues that social services should focus on social adjustment rather than cultural assimilation because the culture of the minority elderly should be respected. Changes are recommended only when they will help empower the elderly to improve their situations. Cheung (1988) also identifies an additional minority elderly group—immigrants and refugees who not only try to maintain their family tradition but also adjust to a new culture.

FOCUSING ON STRENGTHS, NOT PROBLEMS

The change of a social and political environment will cause difficulties for any individual. Minority elderly individuals face most of the same issues as other elderly individuals do, plus other socioeconomical barriers against minorities. From the analysis of problems and issues, we should realize that most of these issues are caused by our insensitivity because we focus too much on rationalizing why our services have not been successfully delivered. Some of us blame the elderly individual for having language and cultural barriers but fail to recognize that we have not been willing to listen to their concerns. We realize that it is important to have multicultural staff to clarify misunderstanding of new immigrants, but at the same time fail to address political and social pressure on these individuals who come forward in an unfamiliar environment.

Through many years of research and studies on these "problems," we should have collected facts on the psychosocial and economic factors affecting the minority elderly people. Based on these facts, we should have invested our interest on the strengths of these minority elderly people. Looking at problems from the social perspective provides an opportunity to examine strengths from the elderly's perspective. If the issues are health care, life satisfaction, and discrimination, we should focus on the strengths of minority elderly individuals, including their informal family network, adaptability, and collective power.

SOLUTION-FOCUSED RECOMMENDATIONS

Problems related to the minority elderly have been addressed and studied over and over again. If the main purpose of addressing these problems is to raise individual awareness, it has not been successful, since we are still investing our efforts in studies of problems rather than utilizing the strengths that families and individuals have in problem solving. The minority elderly draws society's attention because of the increased visibility of problems associated with these individuals. From a social work perspective, our intervention should focus on how to make use of society's attention and the minority elderly's strengths to resolve issues and problems.

Many people thought that the melting pot idea would help to streamline differences and thus eliminate problems. However, social integration is not a one-directional process and differences do not equate with wrong-doing or dysfunctional individuals. In order to achieve social integration, participation of everybody in the society is required. Forget about what problems are related to the minority elderly; ignore the definition of minority; and start thinking about a solution-focused question: "What would life be without minority issues?" Home care would be an option for everybody if society will learn from the strengths of the diverse ethnic groups. For example, how might society instill in today's young people the idea that respect for the elderly is a socially desirable and laudable trait?

Before we can effectively serve the minority elderly populations and empower them to best utilize their strengths and resources, three questions should be challenged. First, how may limited resources be distributed equitably, efficiently, and effectively among the growing elderly population? Second, how may we objectively determine the criteria of needs and the degrees of vulnerability among different ethnic populations and at the same time reduce competitiveness for services among these groups? Finally, how may we promote the awareness of the elderly's strengths and utilize them to design a comprehensive service network for all elderly people?

The last question brings out the minority issue among all elderly people—a lack of public and personal awareness of the strengths of a culturally diverse society.

References

Ade-Ridder, L., and C.B. Hennon. 1989. *Lifestyles of the Elderly: Diversity in Relationships, Health, and Caregiving.* New York: Human Sciences Press.

Cheung, K.M. 1988. The elderly Chinese living in the United States: assimilation or adjustment? *Social Work* 34(5):457–61.

Gelfand, D.E. 1982. *Aging: The Ethnic Factor.* Boston: Little, Brown & Co.

Jacobson, S.G. 1982. Equity in the use of public benefits by minority elderly. In *Minority Aging: Sociological and Social Psychological Issues,* edited by R.C. Manuel. Westport, Conn.: Greenwood Press.

Manuel, R.C., ed. 1982. *Minority Aging: Sociological and Social Psychological Issues.* Westport, Conn.: Greenwood Press.

Markides, K.S., and C.H. Mindel. 1987. *Aging and Ethnicity.* Newbury Park, Cal.: Sage Publications.

Kam-fang Monit Cheung

N

Nursing Home Placement

At any given time, around 1.5 million persons 65 years of age and older are in about 19,000 nursing homes in the United States. Twenty percent of persons 85+ are in nursing homes. The cost of this care is over $40 billion per year and rising, with about half of this cost paid for by public expenditures (e.g., Medicaid and Medicare). While only about 5 percent of people 65+ are in a nursing home at any given time, a proportion that has not changed for 20 years, the odds of entering a nursing home are estimated to be about 1 in 4. Not all people in nursing homes are there for long-term care. Many residents are admitted for short-term, skilled nursing care and rehabilitation following discharge from a hospital. Only a minority of older persons prefer nursing home care; most would prefer to be cared for in their own homes if they are unable to care for themselves.

Residents of nursing homes are more likely to be older, white women, unmarried or never-married. These women do not appear to have a caregiver available at the time that they have a relatively high need for care. Incontinence and mental impairment are other factors that distinguish older nursing home residents from their community-residing counterparts. Moreover, there appear to be variations among ethnic groups. Nonwhite, ethnic elderly are much less likely to reside in nursing homes, especially at older ages (85+). For example, of those 85 and older, 23 percent of white people versus 14 percent of black elderly are in nursing homes. The extent to which nonwhite families have larger and more involved informal support systems is, however, still a point of debate.

There are multiple pathways from living in the community to nursing home care and multiple causes of nursing home placement. George and Maddox (1989) note three factors important in the decision to institutionalize. First, the timing of placement is often primarily in the hands of family caregivers. When they reach a point where they can no longer provide care, caregivers often decide to institutionalize. Second, physicians appear to play a role by advising families to institutionalize older relatives, particularly following hospitalization. Finally, nursing home placement is often the result of a precipitating event, in addition to caregiving and the stress caregivers experience. In many instances, the decision to institutionalize is best for both the caregiver and the elder.

Despite the large body of research demonstrating that caregiving is stressful, little research has focused on the effects of caregiver stress as a predictor of nursing home placement. The small amount of research that exists suggests that caregiving burden is an important factor in the decision to institutionalize. Yet for every older person in a nursing home, there are at least two older people with equal impairments receiving care in the community. Clearly, more research needs to be conducted in this area.

Limited information exists about family involvement following institutionalization. In contrast to the image conjured up by the ''myth of abandonment,'' evidence exists that families continue to maintain contact with their relatives, even provide care, following institutionalization. We have, however, very little knowledge about the quality of interaction between residents and their family members. What information is available indicates mixed findings regarding changes in family relationships following institutionalization of older relatives. Quality and, to a lesser extent, quantity, of family interaction is an important aspect of the well-being of community-residing elderly. Some researchers argue that there is no reason to expect this situation to be any less important for elderly residing in nursing homes.

A related matter is the family's role in institutional care and the nursing home experience. Most families do not have previous experience with nursing homes. Consequently, family members seldom know what to do during visits in nursing homes. They may have to improvise in their interaction with staff and in the extent of involvement in the care of their relatives. Some research suggests that when nursing home staff encourage and assist families in their involvement with relatives, adjustment is enhanced for family members and residents.

Following nursing home placement, families experience a variety of reactions, including guilt, helplessness, failure, anger, depression, and relief. Findings indicate few changes in psychological outcomes for family members following nursing home placement of elders. However, the nature or type of distress may be different following institutionalization. For example, financial concerns are likely to increase and there is new stress associated with interaction with staff. The method used to measure stress may be important in assessing changes in psychological impact. Some researchers noted that post-placement caregivers reported no greater stress than for caregivers still providing care. The former, however, did report greater use of psychotropic drugs following institutionalization of the elder.

Interaction of family and nursing home staff has received little attention from researchers. What information is available suggests that families may have unrealistic expectations (at least from the staff's perspective) about the care that should be provided. Moreover, there is a concern that family involvement in nursing home care may interfere with the staff's ability to provide care. The family's perceptions of the quality of care provided by staff is associated with satisfaction with placement. If family members are concerned about the care provided or have complaints about staff, they will be less satisfied with placement and feel more angry or guilty about nursing home placement of their relative.

In summary, there is sufficient accumulated research data to show the differences between nursing home residents and their community-residing counterparts. The data are less informative about why some older persons are institutionalized while many more who are equally impaired remain in the community. Moreover, it is unclear why there are such great ethnic differences in use of nursing homes. Research findings suggest that families continue to care for relatives at home as long as possible and that they continue to provide some care following institutionalization. The decision-making process regarding institutionalization is complex. Families often place their relatives when all other options are exhausted. In many instances, institutionalization is best for both caregivers and care recipients.

References

Barresi, C.M., and D.E. Stull. 1993. Ethnicity and long-term care: an overview. In *Ethnic Elderly and Long-Term Care*, edited by C.M. Barresi and D.E. Stull. New York: Springer.

Colerick, E.J., and L.K. George. 1986. Predictors of institutionalization among caregivers of patients with Alzheimer's disease. *J Amer Geriatrics Society* 34:493–98.

George, L.K., and G.L. Maddox. 1989. Social and behavioral aspects of institutional care. In *Aging and Health Care: Social Science and Policy Perspectives*, edited by M.G. Ory and K. Bond. London: Routledge, 116–41.

Pratt, C., V. Schmall, S. Wright, and J. Hare. 1987. The forgotten client: family caregivers to institutionalized dementia patients. In *Aging, Health and Family: Long-Term Care*, edited by T. Brubaker. Newbury Park, Cal.: Sage, 197–215.

Stull, D.E., J. Cosbey, K. Bowman, W. McNutt, and M. Drum. 1991. *Institutionalization: A Continuation of Family Care*. Paper presented at the 44th annual meeting of the Gerontological Society of America, San Francisco, November 22–26.

Townsend, A.L. 1990. Nursing home care and family caregivers' stress. In *Stress and Coping in Later Life*, edited by M.A.P. Stephens, J.H. Crowther, S.H. Hobfoll, and D.L. Tennenbaum, 267–85.

Donald E. Stull

O

Osteoporosis

Primary osteoporosis affects 15 to 20 million persons in the United States. It is an age-related disorder characterized by a generalized decrease in bone mass and an increased risk of developing fractures because of the loss of bone tissue. About 1.2 million fractures occur annually as a result of the condition, mainly in those 45 years of age and older. It is likely that 32 percent of women and 17 percent of men who live to be 90 will experience a hip fracture. In this group of people who have hip fracture, there is a 12 percent to 20 percent mortality within the first 3 to 4 months postfracture. In those who survive the hip fracture, the physical, psychological, and socioeconomic toll is formidable. The estimated annual cost of osteoporosis in the United States was 7 to 10 billion dollars in 1986.

The two major causes of osteoporosis are estrogen deficiency and aging. Known risk factors include Caucasian race, a sedentary life-style, long-term cigarette smoking, prolonged bed rest, no childbearing, and diabetes mellitus.

Peak bone mass is reached at about age 35. Factors that influence peak bone mass include general health, sex, race, nutritional status, heredity, and level of physical activity. Bone mass is about 30 percent greater in men than in women and 10 percent greater in blacks than in whites. The normal dynamic process of bone remodeling occurs to balance bone formation and bone resorption. Over the life span, women lose an average of 35 percent of cortical bone and 50 percent of trabecular bone. Type I or postmenopausal osteoporosis occurs in the first 3 to 7 years following natural or surgical menopause, causing women to lose bone mass at the rate of 2 to 5 percent a year. During the first 15 to 20 years postmenopause, vertebral fractures and Colles' fractures of the forearm are most common. The vertical fractures are of the "crush" type and are generally deforming and painful. It is the loss of bone mass and vertebral fractures that cause the "dowager's hump" in the upper back of so many older women. Loss of teeth during this period is also common.

Type II or senile osteoporosis occurs in women over 70 and in men, causing fractures of the hip, upper arm, lower leg, pelvis, and lower arm. Neither Vitamin D nor calcium supplements have been shown to prevent bone loss or to increase bone mass in osteoporotic patients.

PREVENTION

Care of elderly persons should include prevention and management of already established osteoporosis. A regular pattern of physical exercise, particularly walking, will help to prevent many conditions, including osteoporosis, and also add to the person's feeling of well-being. The exercise should be geared to the person's age and physical stamina. Estrogen replacement therapy begun in the first 5 to 6 years following menopause is highly effective in preventing osteoporosis in women. However, this type of therapy should be given only to those women who are most at risk of developing osteoporosis, as estrogen also has side effects such as causing uterine bleeding, endometrial hyperplasia, and perhaps endometrial cancer. The risk of endometrial cancer can be reduced by adding progestin. Estrogen apparently decreases bone resorption, thus reducing the incidence of fractures.

Calcium, together with estrogen therapy, seems to be more effective in maintaining bone mass than when calcium is given alone. As indicated, it has not been shown definitively that increasing calcium affects bone mass. Nevertheless, encouraging patients to maintain or increase their intake of dietary calcium in the form of milk and other dairy products is recommended. The daily calcium intake should be between 1,000 and 1,500 mg of calcium. An 8-ounce glass of milk contains about 275 to 300 mg of calcium. For those with weight problems, skim milk contains as much calcium as whole or low-fat milk.

TREATMENT

There is no known treatment of osteoporosis other than those measures discussed above. Prevention is the best method. In those in whom osteoporosis already exists, education of the patient is essential regarding environmental hazards to prevent falls, and the importance of reporting localized pain in the back or limbs that might indicate fractures so that they can be treated appropriately. Patients should be encouraged to stop smoking, to establish a suitable exercise pattern, and to take in additional dairy products to increase the amount of calcium available for bone formation.

SUMMARY

Osteoporosis occurs with aging in those individuals with risk factors, although heredity may be the key factor as to its occurrence. Appropriate preventive and treatment modalities can be instituted in older people, especially in postmenopausal women, who are at greatest risk of developing osteoporosis. Education can help to raise patients' awareness of what they can do to prevent the condition, or to slow its progress and thus prevent fractures.

References

Barker, L.R., J.R. Burton, and P.H. Zieve. 1991. Osteoporosis. *Principles of Ambulatory Medicine*, 3rd ed. Baltimore: Williams & Wilkins, 994–96.

Lyles, K.W. 1992. Osteoporosis in the elderly. In *Textbook of Internal Medicine*, 2d ed. Edited by W.N. Kelley. Philadelphia: Lippincott, 2371–77.

Report of the U.S. Preventive Services Task Force. 1989. Screening for postmenopausal osteoporosis. *Guide to Clinical Preventive Services: An Assessment of the Effectiveness of 169 Interventions*. Baltimore: Williams & Wilkins, 239–43.

Ada Romaine-Davis

P

Pain Control: Drug Regimens in Cancer

When designing a pain protocol for older persons, one should consider

(1) their increased sensitivity to pain medication, both in terms of the analgesia and the drug's side effects (a good rule of thumb is to "start low and go slow");

(2) use of a fixed schedule with rescue dosing, which can be monitored frequently based on the drugs prescribed. A PRN (as needed) schedule should not be used. The goal of therapy is to break the pain cycle; this will reduce the total drug requirement and, in turn, lessen any side effects;

(3) informing the patient or family about the degree of pain relief to be expected and any side effects that may occur.

A most important aspect of caring for patients with pain is having a consistent, reproducible, reliable tool that allows the provider to make a complete evaluation of the patient and also permits monitoring the response to pain therapy. The Brief Pain Inventory or its Short Form, as developed by Cleeland (1990) and his group, is recommended. It combines both the use of a visual analog scale (VAS) and a specific descriptive pain vocabulary. This tool, although not specifically for use in caring for the elderly, has been used throughout the world in cancer pain management. In addition, a daily pain diary method has been used in a variety of settings to ascertain the degree, frequency, and duration of pain episodes, and to monitor therapy.

TREATMENT OPTIONS

Nonpharmacologic

The elderly are susceptible to the use of massage therapy, relaxation techniques, and psychological intervention. These treatments are not often considered as aspects of a pain management plan. However, these modalities are far less "toxic" as to risk/benefit than is pharmacologic therapy. The provider and the family need to discuss all possible methodologies that can be used to deal with the patient's pain. Usually, a combination of non-pharmacologic and pharmacologic treatments are best, and are usually synergistic.

Pharmacologic

The use of agents for the treatment of cancer pain in the elderly, for want of a better strategy, has been approached using the World Health Organization's pain ladder, described below.

Step I: Nonsteroidal anti-inflammatory drugs (NSAIDs). This class of agents is important in cancer pain management. They are not only the first line agents but also are the building block for the addition of other agents. As prostaglandin inhibitors, they are very effective in relieving bone pain due to metastasis. Two agents which have enjoyed the greatest amount of popularity are aspirin and acetaminophen (technically not NSAIDs). Diminished renal function, so common in the elderly, causes a build-up of salicylate, the active ingredient of aspirin, which can lead to intoxication. Salicylate intoxication in the elderly can be quite difficult to detect unless one has a high index of suspicion. Another potential problem of using aspirin in the elderly is that of gastritis or possibly gastrointestinal bleeding. Although there is no convincing evidence that aspirin causes more serious gastrointestinal problems than any of the NSAIDs, subjectively many elders will complain of aspirin intolerance. The advantage to a trial of aspirin compared to NSAIDs is the lower cost. Acetaminophen does not possess the anti-inflammatory properties that aspirin has. Since inflammation plays a major role in many of the pain syndromes, it may not be effective in treating elderly cancer patients.

In addition to aspirin and several of its salicylate derivatives, there are approximately thirteen other NSAIDs composed of five different chemical classes available in the United States. All have various half-lives, duration of analgesic action times, and times to peak of pain relief. Unfortunately, there is no definitive evidence to support that any of these agents is superior in analgesic action to aspirin or any of the other NSAIDs. Similarly, there is no evidence to suggest that any one NSAID is safer than another, as to its gastrointestinal toxicity, that is, bleeding, or renal toxicity. None of the NSAIDs have less renal side effects than any other with regard to the various hypersensitivity reactions, including interstitial (within the tissues) nephritis. Indomethacin, because of its relative potency as a prostaglandin inhibitor, probably is the most detrimental, relative to renal hemodynamics. There is no "magic" when prescribing NSAIDs or when switching from one to another. Logic would suggest that if one class of NSAIDs does not work in two weeks, one should choose one from another class. The use of ibuprofen 400 mg three times a day or salsalate 500 mg three times a day would be an acceptable starting regimen.

When one embarks on chronic NSAID therapy, monitoring for toxicity, especially in the elderly, is important. Most physicians recommend, as baseline data, the following laboratory tests: hemoglobin/hematocrit, BUN and/or serum creatine, and a stool guaiac sample. Subjective complaints of gastrointestinal upset should be carefully evaluated.

Step II: The Weak Opioids. These drugs are classified as morphine agonist, morphine antagonist, and mixed morphine agonist-antagonist, a classification based on their ability to displace morphine from its receptor sites. The mixing of these agents can lead to major complications, for example, sudden withdrawal symptoms. Since these agents do not offer any analgesic benefit to the elderly, this discussion will be limited to agents that act as morphine agonists. When non-narcotic analgesics have been ineffective, the WHO ladder suggests adding a "weak" narcotic given by the oral route. Codeine or oxycodone are good agents to begin the regimen. In fact, there are many "combination"formulations available. It is important to appreciate that these combinations can have limited flexibility because of toxicity related to the NSAIDs. In patients for whom NSAIDs are contraindicated, both codeine and its related compounds can be used as single agents. The narcotic-like agent, propoxyphene, is a poor choice in the elderly because of a toxic metabolite, norproxophene, that can accumulate in patients with poor renal function.

Step III. The Strong Opioids. When pain is not relieved with standard doses of the weak opioids, the use of stronger opioids is recommended. Agents such as meperidine and pentazocine should not be used as oral analgesics due to their relatively poor oral bioavailability. Recalling the problem of reduced renal function in the elderly, a metabolite of meperidine, normeperidine, can accumulate, leading to seizures. Pentazocine, because of its unacceptable incidence of central nervous system side effects, should be avoided. Methadone, although relatively inexpensive, is difficult to use in the elderly. The extremely long half-life of methadone leads to prolonged somnolence and not pain relief. Morphine, because of the many new formulations, new dosing recommendations, and newer sustained release preparations, is the opioid of choice for the elderly patient with cancer pain. Unfortunately, new data suggest that the metabolites of morphine are the active form of the drug. As predicted, they can also accumulate in the elderly who have poor renal function, leading to a prolonged half-life and toxicity. The reader is referred to standard texts that will outline regimens explaining how to convert to strong opioids from weak ones, the role of sustained release products, and the important concept of rescue dosing.

ISSUES ASSOCIATED WITH OPIOIDS

The elderly are very susceptible to the one effect of the opioids that does not lessen as the drug is continued—constipation. This condition, if and when it occurs, should be treated concomitantly with opioid therapy. Somnolence usually clears within a few days of starting the opioids, but will return every time a dosing increase occurs. The patient and the family must be told what to expect in this regard. It is important to remember that many individuals with untreated cancer pain will have been sleep-deprived. Itching is an unusual problem, but when it occurs, it is best treated by stopping the opioids.

NOVEL DELIVERY TECHNIQUES

Beside those routes of delivery that do not involve direct application to the neuraxis, several other routes are available, especially for administering opioids. These newer routes of delivering opioids are especially attractive when trying to avoid impractical situations. For example, in hospice care, frequent intramuscular or intravenous bolus injections would be difficult in the best of circumstances. By using sublingual or buccal liquid morphine sulfate in the patient with bowel obstruction or an inability to swallow, a satisfactory level of pain control can be achieved. A newer route, that of transdermal fentanyl, is available but is not without problems in the elderly. Other routes and delivery systems include subcutaneous and patient-controlled analgesia. These newer approaches to pain management, which will be used in the elderly, must be tested in a rigorous manner in this population in order for proper application and dosages to be prescribed for the best results.

SPECIAL PAIN SYNDROMES

Headache

In addition to the usual causes of headache, that is, tension or migraine, the cancer patient may experience this symptom as a result of intracerebral metastasis. Dexamethasone 12–16 mg per day in divided doses is the drug of choice. The use of radiation therapy depends on the lifespan of the patient. In situations where it is a matter of a few days or weeks, steroids are quite satisfactory.

Neuropathic Pain

The patient with this type of pain will complain of allodynia, pain caused by a minor stimulus, e.g., shirt touching the skin; dyschesia, a rather unpleasant sensation such as burning or electrical in nature; or causalgia dyschesia, associated with sympathetic nervous dysfunction. These symptoms are also seen in Herpes Zoster (shingles), phantom limb, or in nerve damage such as brachial plexus infiltration by tumor. Opioids alone will generally not control these painful problems. The drugs used for this type of pain are called adjuvant analgesics. They include the tricyclic antidepressants, anticonvulsants, steroids, and the oral local anesthetics. These agents can be given in small doses, for example, nortryptyline 10–50 mg per day, carbamazepine 100–300 mg per day in addition to an opioid. Careful titration is required in the elderly.

Delirium

The sudden onset of confusion, behavioral changes, particularly agitation, hallucinations, paranoia, and/or acting-out nightmares can prompt a patient's caregiver to call for help more quickly than any other complaint. The health care worker must be familiar with the patient's background in order to assist in this situation. In particular, one must know if there is a background of dementia. All patients in this age group should have a Folstein's minimental status examination performed on admission to home care, as a baseline study. Delirium and dementia can usually be distinguished by their temporal course (dementia— slow onset), association with hallucinations and psychosis (delirium), and fluctuating nature (delirium). However, these two can occur together, requiring complex management. The principles of care are: (1) exclude precipitating causes such as infection, drugs, electrolyte abnormalities, renal or hepatic failure, and unresolved anxiety related to death fears. The extent of the evaluation again is determined by the stage of the patient's disease; (2) stay with the patient. Use reassurance, light the room to avoid shadows or darkness. If the patient wants to walk, be at their side and avoid using restraints. If medication is required, use diazepam 5–10 mg by mouth or by rectum, or haloperidol 0.5–2 mg by mouth or by intramuscular injection. The dose and frequency of dosing depends on previous medications and response. When associated with terminal agitation, midazolam can be used as a continuous subcutaneous infusion at a dose of 15–25 mg per day.

SUMMARY

Home care of elderly cancer patients is a rapidly expanding field. The knowledge needed to be successful is also undergoing changes, particularly in the area of pharmacology of pain drugs, the role of the interdisciplinary team, and bereavement care and counseling. As in other areas of heath care, frequent self-evaluation is required in order to deliver state of the art excellence.

References

Cleeland, C.S. 1990. Assessment of pain in cancer. In *Advances in Pain Research and Therapy*, edited by K.M. Foley, J.J. Bonica, and V. Ventafndda. New York: Raven Press, 47–55.

Ferrell, B. 1991. Pain management in elderly people. *J Association Gerontology Soc* 39: 64–73.

Ferrell, B.R., B.A. Ferrell, M. Rhiner, and M. Grant. 1991. Family factors influencing cancer pain management. *Post Grad Med* 67:s64–s69.

Holdsworth, M., and W.B. Forman. 1993. Geriatric pain management. In *Drug Therapy in the Elderly*, edited by E. Bressler. St. Louis: Mosby.

Kaye, P. 1989. *Symptom Control in Hospice and Palliative Care.* Essex, Conn.: Hospice Educational Institute.

Twycross, R.G., and S.A. Lack. 1990. *Therapeutics in Terminal Care.* New York: Churchill Livingstone.

Walter B. Forman and Richard J. Roche

Parish Nurse

The crisis in health care delivery in the United States is inspiring new thinking about people, their beliefs, and their institutions. In response to the fragmentation in the current health care system, one of the community-based movements which has emerged is that of parish nursing. Nurses are seeing needs within their congregations and communities, and responding creatively to meet these needs.

Over the past 100 years, a gap between the church and medicine developed. Health care agencies were addressing the care of the body while religious institutions emphasized the spirit. More recently, this pattern is changing; churches are now being seen as important partners in dealing with the health care needs in this country.

Parish nursing grew out of the work by Reverend Granger Westberg (1990), a Lutheran chaplain and former professor at the University of Chicago, who began the Wholistic Health Centers in the early 1970s. He recognized the role that faith and beliefs play in a person's health. He further believed that churches needed to regain their role of healing, along with preaching and teaching. In 1984, Westberg approached the Lutheran General Health Care System (LGHCS) to request support and assistance in the implementation of a program where nurses would be hired in cooperation with the hospital to work in congregations. Initially, the Department of Pastoral Care assumed administrative accountability and invited six congregations to participate. Of the first six Parish Nurse Programs, two were established in Roman Catholic churches and four in Lutheran and Methodist churches.

Not only has the program grown at Lutheran General, but across the country as well. Today, there are approximately 1,000–1,500 parish nurses serving in churches of various denominations, locations, and sizes. Also evident is the increasing number of parish nurses who are volunteering their time. Many of these nurses hold full-time or part-time positions in nursing, but see parish nursing as a way to utilize their skills within the congregation. Many nurses are serving in churches of denominations other than the one in which the nurse is a member. For instance, some Catholic nurses serve in Protestant churches.

The parish nurse is congregationally-based and the nursing role has a strong pastoral dimension. Early on, it was decided that parish nurses would not be involved in providing direct patient care; thus, the role is distinct from the home care nurse, the school nurse, or the doctor's office nurse. Judith Ryan (1990) defines parish nursing in the following way: "Parish Nursing is coming to be understood as a noninvasive, nurturing role, focused more on creating the physiologic, psychologic, spiritual, and sociocultural environment in which the client can gain or maintain health or healing, than on the diagnosis and treatment of human response to disease."

The parish nurse role has five components: (1) health educator, (2) personal health counselor, (3) referral source to the congregation and community, (4) coordinator of support groups and volunteers, and (5) interpreter of the close relationship between faith and health. As health educator, the parish nurse fosters a greater understanding of the relationship of health to a person's attitudes, habits, life-style, and faith. Parishioners utilize the parish nurse as a personal health counselor for a variety of concerns, such as questions about a diagnosis, treatment, medications, health care access issues, and relational issues. Often, parishioners will have their blood pressure checked by the parish nurse and, in the course of the conversation, share very personal concerns.

The parish nurse serves as a referral source to church and community resources and often advocates on behalf of the parishioner. Because the current complex health care system overwhelms many individuals, the parish nurse can help the person or family navigate through the system to receive the care and assistance that are needed. For example, parish nurses accompany families as they visit nursing homes, to select one in which they will place a loved one.

The parish nurse recruits and trains volunteers to reach out to families who have recently sustained a loss, who are providing care for a hospitalized family member, or to isolated shut-ins. For example, an elderly shut-in parishioner needed someone to do her grocery shopping. The parish nurse knew of a teenager whose grandmother had recently died. By pairing these individuals, a relationship and support have developed which is beneficial to both. Volunteers bring food, flowers, and communion as they visit the homebound elderly.

The nurse may also organize support groups as the need arises. The most frequent support groups organized have been for "caregivers." Other support groups address parenting issues, smoking, weight control, and chronic illness. Through all of these activities, the parish nurse helps parishioners to understand the relationship between faith and health.

In 1990, LGHCS received a grant from the W.K. Kellogg Foundation to document and evaluate our six-year experience in parish nursing. As part of this initiative, in August, 1992, *Looking Back: The Parish Nurse Experience* was published. It describes the structure, resources, goals, activities, and accomplishments of 40 parish nursing programs affiliated with Lutheran General HealthSystem in Illinois. A partner in this project was United Medical Center in Moline, Illinois. Together, these programs include churches in urban, rural, and suburban settings. Congregations vary in size from 50 worshipers per week to those with over 3,000 per week. In these 40 congregations, there are 32 parish nurses, with some nurses serving more than one congregation.

In 1990, a total of 12,857 contacts were made by parish nurses with parishioners and community members at the 40 sites. For nine months of 1991 (January through September), a total of 7,865 contacts were documented. Contacts occurred for a variety of reasons; some were initiated by the parishioner while others were initiated by the nurse, often on the request of the pastoral staff. Five main reasons for contact with the parish nurse in 1990 were relational/parenting concerns, hospitalization, hypertension, living arrangements of aging, and death/ dying/grief/loss. Relational/parenting concerns generally addressed concerns with the parenting of children, dealing with teens, aging parents, and relationships with a spouse or other family member. Hospitalization included contacting an individual before, during, and after hospitalization. A growing number of people have been contacting parish nurses with questions regarding their blood pressure, medications, and diet. As the elderly and their families face decisions regarding the safety and living arrangements for an elderly person, they turn to the parish nurse for advice and counsel. Frequently, questions are directed toward the many options available, and the pros and cons of choosing one option over another.

People of all ages face times of grief and loss, and parish nurses assist in providing education, support, and direction during these difficult times. The loss of a spouse in the later years is one of the more common events; other losses include children, family members, severe injuries from automobile or farm accidents, loss of jobs, loss of farms or homes, and the problems encountered when friends or family members have HIV/AIDS.

An underlying concern described by parish nurses is the loneliness and isolation experienced by elderly persons. These feelings are enhanced by changes in family structure and the mobility of today's families. A major challenge for the parish nurse is to mobilize resources within the congregation to minister to shut-ins and to keep them connected to the life of the congregation.

Parish nurses see individuals in a variety of locations, including the church, hospital, home, nursing homes, and other sites. About one-third of the contacts are by telephone. The greatest percentage of contacts are with individuals in the 66–80 age group. In 1990, 56 percent were in this age group. In 1991, these contacts dropped to 46 percent, although there was an increase in the number of contacts with individuals over 80. The number of contacts with individuals over 80 rose from 1 percent in 1990 to 13 percent in 1991. When the over-65 and over-80 age groups are combined, the total number of contacts account for 57 percent of all contacts in 1990, and 59 percent in 1991.

The parish nurse utilizes a variety of strategies to promote health awareness within the congregation. Besides individual consultation, they coordinate and sometimes present educational programs, write columns for newsletters and bulletins, and develop posters and health displays on a regular basis. Programs are offered for all age groups from ''Your Body—God's Gift'' for young children, to a walking class for seniors. Addressing life-style issues such as smoking, exercise, alcohol and drug use, and sexual behavior have been a major focus for the parish nurse.

Often, parish nurses emphasize monthly educational offerings on topics related to the National Health Observances published by the National Public Health Department. For example, since February is identified as American Heart Month, one parish nurse created a health display entitled, ''Heart Care: Your Heart Beats for Your Health.''

Through educational programs and individual health counseling and referral services, parish nurses are addressing many of the objectives listed in the *Healthy People 2000 Objectives*, published by the U.S. Department of Health and Human Services. Parish nurses and congregations have the opportunity to support this initiative in order to improve the health of the American people.

Parish nurses address environmental factors in church buildings that particularly affect the older adult, for example, hearing devices, large-print bulletins, blankets for warmth, safety bars in bathrooms, and lighting in hallways. They promote serving more nutritious foods both at home and at various church functions.

Along with these many activities, parish nurses function as members of the pastoral team and are involved in the spiritual life of the church. They have demonstrated involvement in a variety of ways, such as attending and planning liturgies and funerals, participating in healing services, and working with volunteers. Parish nurses also incorporate into their home visits activities such as biblical reflections, music, prayer, and communion.

In summary, the parish nurse program is more than the presence of a registered nurse in a church. The parish nurse program is a ministry of the church which encourages physical, emotional, spiritual, and social well-being in the context of one's relationship to God, family, and neighbors. The parish nurse facilitates and mobilizes resources within the congregation to reach out more effectively to their fellow parishioners and community members, particularly to the elderly.

References

Djupe, A.M., and R.C. Lloyd. 1992. *Looking Back: The Parish Nurse Experience*. Park Ridge, Il.: National Parish Nurse Resource Center.

Djupe, A.M., H. Olson, J.A. Ryan, and J.C. Lantz. 1991. *Reaching Out: Parish Nursing Services*. Park Ridge, Il.: National Parish Nurse Resource Center.

Marty, M.E. 1990. Health, medicine, and the faith traditions. *Healthy People 2000: A Role for America's Religious Community*. Chicago: Park Ridge Center.

Ryan, J.A. 1990. Liability for parish nursing practice. Paper presented at the Fourth Annual Granger Westberg Symposium, Northbrook, Illinois, September 26-28.

Solari-Twadell, P.A., A.M. Djupe, and M.A. McDermott, eds. 1990. *Parish Nursing: The Developing Practice*. Park Ridge, Il.: National Parish Nurse Resource Center.
Westberg, G.E., and J.W. McNamara. 1990. *The Parish Nurse*. Minneapolis: Augsburg Publishing Company.

Anne Marie Djupe

Parkinson's Disease

Parkinson's disease (PD) is a neurodegenerative disorder occurring mainly in the later years. PD comprises a syndrome (a combination of usually three specific symptoms) that involves rigidity, tremor, and bradykinesis (slow movements). Other manifestations occur as the disease progresses: postural changes, gait disturbance, eye disturbance, and autonomic disorders such as postural hypotension, loss of muscle tone in the large bowel, and esophageal spasm.

Parkinson's disease is defined as a dopamine-deficiency state within the brain resulting from disease, injury, or dysfunction of the dopaminergic neuronal system. Dopamine is a neurotransmitter in the neuronal system and is usually in balance with other biochemically dependent systems in the brain. One of these other neurotransmitters is acetylcholine, a neurotransmitter in the striatum. The decreasing amount of dopamine results in an imbalance between these (and other) neurotransmitters. The ultimate effect is seen at the level of the final common pathway of the motor system, the anterior horn cell, where there are two basic defects: (1) increased inhibition of the gamma motor neuron, and (2) increased alpha motor neuron activity, resulting in the characteristic signs and symptoms of parkinsonism.

The largest number of cases of parkinsonism fall into the category known as paralysis agitans (Parkinson's disease). The disease usually begins between the ages of 50 and 65, and can occur in both sexes and in all races. No evidence exists that points to a hereditary factor, but a familial incidence is supported by many authorities.

The pathologic findings are neuronal loss and depigmentation in the substantia nigra, particularly the zona compacta. Similarly, loss of cells and pigment occurs in the locus ceruleus and in the dorsal vagal nucleus of the brain stem—the section of the brain toward the back and underneath, which connects with the spinal cord. The pathologic hallmark of Parkinson's disease is the Lewy body, an eosinophilic intraneuronal inclusion body seen on a prepared slide with the aid of a microscope.

The cause of the pathologic changes and of the manifestation of Parkinson's disease has not been uncovered. Some authorities believe that environmental pollutants may play a role. However, opponents of this theory state that the disease existed long before environmental toxins and pollutants were widespread. Parkinson's disease was recognized before the onset of the industrial revolution.

SIGNS AND SYMPTOMS

A Severity Rating Scale was developed in the late 1960s by Hoehn and Yahr:

1. Unilateral motor symptoms, usually with minimal functional impairment.
2. Bilateral or midline motor symptoms, without impairment of balance.
3. First sign of impaired righting reflexes (e.g., trouble with maintaining steadiness during turns); some restriction of everyday activities, but the patient is still physically capable of living independently.
4. Fully developed, severely disabling disease; the patient is still able to walk and stand without assistance but is markedly incapacitated in other activities.
5. Patient is confined to a bed or wheelchair unless assisted.

Because the onset of PD occurs gradually, the early signs are often so subtle that it is difficult even for affected individuals to know precisely when they first became aware of any problem. Because the disease tends to begin in the middle years, there is a tendency to attribute the general early signs simply to the aging process: slowness, gradual loss of agility, slight tremor, and depression. Another person, often a colleague or a neighbor, may be the first to notice that the person has a loss of mobility in the facial expression (facial masking), with infrequent blinking, fixed postural positions, hesitation on rising from a seated position, and growing inability to sit down easily. There is a tendency for the person to remain in one attitude or position for longer than usual periods of time. It is not until the person experiences more uncontrolled tremor activity (a "pill-rolling"movement of the thumbs and index fingers) or inability to move arms or legs that the realization occurs that something is really wrong. Tremors are of particular concern because of their visibility and because they could carry the insinuation of emotional instability. Rigidity of muscles is almost universally present in people with parkinsonism. The rigidity occurs in only a few muscle groups at first, but spreads to larger areas of the body later in the course of the disease.

In long-established Parkinson's disease, typical body posture is easily recognized: when the person stands, the head is bowed, the upper part of the body is bent forward, the shoulders droop, and the arms are flexed at the elbows with the hands held toward the front of the body and often showing the typical "pill-rolling" tremor. The knees may be flexed, so that the person seems to take on the position of football players on the defensive. These changes in position of the body parts tend to change the center of gravity, making it difficult for the person to stand erect without falling backward. The gait tends to become festinating, characterized by small steps which, when combined with the forward-leaning of the trunk, results in progressively propulsive forward uncontrollable movement, so that the person has to run into a chair or a wall in order to stop the forward movement and prevent a fall. The most frustrating aspect of the disorder that the individual must contend with is the inability to rapidly and easily carry out even the most routine activities. Sometimes movement becomes so slow as to be at a standstill. However, there are times when those with far advanced parkinsonism who have become almost totally immobile, suddenly get up and move normally. This is known as paradoxic akinetic reaction, which leads unknowing caregivers to remark, "He can do it if he really wants to— he's just being stubborn," which is not the case at all; the individual has virtually no control over his movements.

DIAGNOSIS

The presence of Parkinson's disease is evident in the history and physical examination, obviating the need for further tests to corroborate the diagnosis. From the initial diagnosis, the provider simply follows the progress of the patient and prescribes appropriate medication(s). The follow-up examinations include blood pressure readings in lying and standing positions, to detect any evidence of orthostatic hypotension (fall in blood pressure on standing); an assessment of response to stress; assessment of functional ability; and other tests as deemed necessary. Each of these assessments will demonstrate how well the patient is responding to medication(s), and the degree of change in physical and mental capacity.

TREATMENT

Therapy is aimed at restoring the dopaminergic systems in the brain through the administration of Levodopa, which is transmitted to the brain through the blood circulatory system. In the brain, Levodopa is converted to dopamine. A similar drug is Carbidopa (trade name—Sinemet). Levodopa can cause side effects, which the caregiver needs to be aware of so that the primary care provider can be informed. The most common side effects are nausea, vomiting, and abdominal distress. Along with Levodopa, anticholinergic drugs may be given such as ethopropazine (Parsidol). Antihistamines (such as Benadryl) may also be ordered, some of which have mild anticholinergic properties. Additional or substitutive drugs may be prescribed, depending on the patient's response and degree of symptoms. Patients with parkinsonism must be followed carefully and assiduously evaluated on a regular basis.

CARE OF THE PATIENT WITH PARKINSON'S DISEASE

Much of the care required by these patients relates to assisting them with activities of daily living, guarding against accidents or unintentional injury, and maintaining adequate hydration and good nutrition. Some patients have memory lapses or periods of confusion, especially if they are in strange environments. In these situations, they may wander off and become lost. Caregivers must always be on the alert.

PROGNOSIS

Although the introduction of Levodopa has resulted in considerable improvement of the physical condition of patients with parkinsonism, Parkinson's disease still significantly reduces the life span in those who have developed the generalized form of the disease in their fifties or sixties. Because the neuronal loss cannot be alleviated, the patient's condition continues to decline despite appropriate treatment. The effect of medication decreases over time, and the patient's condition deteriorates. Ultimately, the patient generally becomes bedridden and dies as a result of infection such as pneumonia.

References

Berg, D., L. Cantwell, G. Heudebert, and J.L. Sebastian, eds. 1993. Parkinson's disease. *Handbook of Primary Care Medicine*. Philadelphia: Lippincott, 703–9.

Brownlee, H.J. 1994. Parkinsonism. In *Family Medicine: Principles and Practice*, 4th ed. Edited by R.B. Taylor. New York: Springer-Verlag, 502–9.

Gilroy, J. 1990. Movement disorders: Parkinson's disease. *Basic Neurology*. New York: Pergamon Press, 105–12.

Hoehn, M.M., and M.D. Yahr. 1967. Parkinsonism: onset, progression, and mortality. *Neurology* 17:427–42.

La Rue, A. 1992. *Aging and Neuropsychological Assessment*. New York: Plenum Press, 199–219.

Yahr, M.D. 1989. Parkinsonism. In *Merritt's Textbook of Neurology*, 8th ed. Edited by L.P. Rowland. Philadelphia: Lea & Febiger, 658–71.

Ada Romaine-Davis

Pet Therapy

INTRODUCTION

Animal-assisted therapy involves the use of companion animals to help people with special needs. Companion animals can offer an opportunity for exchange of affection, stimulation, socialization, diversion, distraction, physical activity (playing with the animal and grooming), emotional fulfillment (bonding with the animal and volunteer), unconditional love, and opportunity to nurture and to feel needed. Animal visits can provide reality therapy, add structure to the day, assuage loneliness, and compensate for sensory loss. They can increase confidence, self-esteem, and verbalization. Animals can teach people trust and those feelings can be transferred to human relationships. Specific studies show a decrease in physiological parameters (heart rate, blood pressure, repeat cardiac incidents, need for post-operative analgesics), while others show an increase in self-care measures (improving adherence to medication regime and regularity of meals). Animal-assisted therapy can be a motivating force toward wellness.

OVERVIEW

VNA-Community Services, Inc. (VNA-CS), located in the Philadelphia area, is a voluntary, community-based agency that provides in-home support services as one of its multiple services. VNA-CS initiated its animal-assisted therapy program in February 1990 after two years of development. The in-home program includes two parts: a research and a nonresearch component.

The purposes of the research portion are to: (1) determine psycho-physiological changes in homebound persons who receive pet visits on a periodic basis, and (2) improve the quality of life of those patients who choose to participate in the Animal-Assisted Therapy program.

Objectives are: (1) to determine changes in vital signs, (2) to assess changes in personal adjustment, (3) to describe interactions between pets and older persons, and (4) to improve the quality of life of homebound persons.

Specific questions to be answered include:

1. Over a period of eight weeks, do changes occur to the blood pressure, pulse, and respirations of a homebound older person when a pet is present?
2. If there is a change in the vital signs, is this change sustained through the next week?
3. Is there a different physiological response to the pet if the participant is on antihypertensive medication?
4. Is there a change in the general well-being rating?
5. What kind of describable interactions occur between the older person and the pet?
6. Does a negative response to the pet influence the general well-being rating or physiological response?

The research project is coordinated by a master's-prepared medical social worker (MSW). The MSW, registered nurses, and volunteers who own certified therapy dogs are involved in the project. In addition to collecting positive subjective and descriptive data, the results of the monitoring of physiological and psychosocial parameters have been positive. A graduate student intern helped design a computer program for data input. A faculty member from an area educational facility is assisting with statistical analysis. Many of our patients request and receive continued visits in the post-research period.

In response to community interest, new programs were developed:

- non-research homebound visits
- individualized rehabilitation treatment plans for VNA-CS patients with occupational, physical, speech therapists and registered nurses
- teen and adult inpatient psychiatric groups
- geriatric outpatient mental health program
- educational programs covering many health-related topics
- community coalition/pet aid service.

The non-research component of the home care program involves visits by volunteers with certified therapy dogs, after an initial evaluation by the coordinator. Physiological and psychosocial parameters are not measured. The patient's subjective response to the scheduled animal visits are the determining factor.

VNA-CS PROGRAM CHARACTERISTICS

The VNA program is recognized as a unique animal-assisted therapy service, distinct from animal visitation or demonstration activities. Staff review the human-animal bond and the interactions it evokes as therapeutic. Specific unique characteristics of the program are:

- Homebound elderly focus (95% of the nation's elderly live in the community; 30% live alone).
- Large volunteer population.
- Various breeds of dogs—all certified for health, obedience, temperament, and sociability.
- Data collection.
- Increased time between client and animal.
- Strong community support.
- Professional facilitation of individual/group goals.

Regarding professional facilitation, the program had a registered nurse with a bachelor of science in nursing degree as coordinator for the first two years. Now that role has been assumed by the master's prepared medical social worker who has had extensive experience in the health care delivery system, including geriatrics, group facilitation, and home care.

COMMUNITY RESPONSE

The media's interest in the program has been exciting. The three major network television channels in the Philadelphia area taped interviews or made home visits. A telephone interview was done on National Public Radio. Several newspapers have printed articles and photographs. An article written by two program staff was published. We have received numerous inquiries from local community members in response to the media coverage. Other groups across the state and country have contacted the program requesting information about the concept of animal-assisted therapy, and how to begin a program. Thus, this program has served as a networking force to further promote animal-assisted therapy.

FUNDING

To date, funding has been provided by the VNA-CS board of directors, a local grant, and contributions. The entire program costs cover coordination and consultation fees. The program is offered free of charge to homebound elderly and relies heavily on volunteers. The long-range goal is to obtain grant funding and contributions in sufficient amounts to continue the program at no charge to patients. In the future, it may be possible to obtain third-party reimbursement for this health-related service.

BENEFITS OF THE PROGRAM

The objective and subjective evaluations of the program have been positive. After preliminary analysis of 80 percent of the study group, heart rate and blood pressure have decreased during pet visits, and positive changes have been documented in the subscales on general health, anxiety levels, and feeling of well-being. Some of the subjective comments of patients were: "I look forward to having a visitor and a pet," "The visits with the dog helped to brighten my day," "The visit was uplifting when I was having chronic pain," and others of a similar nature. Patients in a hospital's inpatient psychiatric unit said: "This makes me want to get better so I can go home and be with my dog," "I forgot how good a dog can make you feel." From a retirement center activities director: "They [the persons who participated] talked about your visits for days," and "One woman who had been ill and exhibiting a very flat affect seemed almost transformed by the visits."

The program volunteers have reported great satisfaction with their involvement in the program and have increased their time commitments. The human/animal team represents committed, enthusiastic volunteerism and, by involving secondary organizations and networking, the program has provided a design for two-way community outreach.

SUMMARY

Animal-assisted therapy acts as a bridge across gaps. It brings renewed joy to older persons' lives, motivation, stimulation, and promotes interactions with others who might not otherwise have had these experiences. The program will continue to meet the needs of our patients. Future plans include:

- expanded interdisciplinary cooperation in relation to animal therapy benefits (i.e., use of pet therapy with physical therapy, mental health counseling, and other arrangements by physician prescription).

- expansion of other services such as pet adoption.

- publication of research results to promote the concept of pet therapy and to highlight the success of this program.

- expand the research study to include additional variables such as diet, house care, and other self-care parameters.

- publication of a biannual newsletter.

- expand services to: pediatrics, adult rehabilitation, mental health, intergenerational community programs, and humane/environmental education.

References

Akrow, P., ed. 1987. *The Loving Bond: Companion Animals in the Helping Professions.* Saratoga, Cal.: R & E Publishers, Inc.

Baun, M., N. Bergstrom, N.V. Langston, and L. Norma. 1984. Physiological effects of human/companion animal bonding. *Nursing Research* 33:126–29.

Erickson, R. 1985. Companion animals and the elderly. *Geriatric Nursing* 6(2):92–96.

Friedman, E., A.H. Katcher, J.J. Lynch, and S.A. Thomas. 1980. Animal companions and one-year survival of patients after discharge from a coronary care unit. *Public Health Reports* 95:307–12.

Harris, M., and M. Gellin. 1990. Pet therapy for the homebound elderly. *Caring* 9(9): 48–51.

Rosenkoetter, M., and D. Bowes. 1991. Brutus is making rounds. *Geriatric Nursing* 12(6):277–78.

Marilyn M. Harris and Mindy S. Gellin

Physical Therapy and Physical Agents in the Home

Health care delivery settings are diverse and include the traditional hospital, outpatient clinics, mobile units, and the home. The purpose of this entry is to describe the appropriate use of physical agents commonly used by physical therapists in the care of homebound patients. Use of physical agents, such as heat, cold, compression, and electrical stimulation are common adjuncts used in physical therapy treatment. Many of these agents lend themselves to either independent or supervised use in the home. Physical agents are typically used in the home as adjuncts to exercise, manual therapy, and wound care.

There are three general ways in which physical agents may be utilized in the home. Often patients who are receiving physical therapy in a hospital or clinic are instructed in a home program to be performed in addition to the clinical program. Such a home program may include the use of physical agents, and patients should have received instruction for appropriate and safe use in an unsupervised setting.

A patient may not require ongoing physical therapy treatment but may need periodic monitoring to assess treatment effectiveness and to make necessary adjustments in treatment parameters. For example, an individual using transcutaneous electrical nerve stimulation (TENS) for pain management is likely to receive several follow-up visits to determine optimal current parameters and/or electrode placement. The patient requires continued instruction to achieve full independence.

In situations where the home has become the primary care setting, physical agents are used in the same manner as in the clinic setting. However, not all agents lend themselves to home use because of practical constraints, such as size and safety.

Physical agents commonly used in the home are heat, cold, compression devices, and electrical stimulators. Each of these modalities will be briefly described and common indications, contraindications, and precautions for their use will be discussed.

HEAT

Therapeutic heat is divided into two categories: superficial and deep. In the home setting, common superficial heating agents include commercial hot packs, moist and dry electrical heating pads, and paraffin baths. Portable ultrasound units (deep heating) are available for use in the home by a physical therapist.

Heat has long been used as a means for pain relief, relaxation, and sedative effects. Heat has been classified as a counterirritant and affects the pain-spasm-pain cycle by providing sensory feedback that may inhibit pain perception. Heat may also directly affect the contractile properties of muscle, producing a decrease in motor activity which in turn interrupts the pain-spasm-pain cycle by acting on the muscle spasm.

Increased blood flow and an increase in metabolic rate in response to heat stimuli are well documented and may be helpful in promoting healing and in the removal of chemical irritants found with prolonged edema. Use of heat may also result in edema formation, and caution should be used in patients with acute inflammatory conditions.

Heat increases tissue extensibility by acting on the viscous components of the connective tissues. In conditions such as rheumatoid arthritis, in which joint stiffness is common, heat may be beneficial prior to the performance of range of motion exercises. Heat may be useful in promoting residual elongation of connective tissue when used in conjunction with stretch for the resolution of joint contractures.

Contraindications and precautions for heat application are decreased circulation, decreased sensation, acute inflammation, malignancy, infection, and site of recent hemorrhage. There are additional contraindications and precautions for deep heating agents, such as ultrasound. Ultrasound is contraindicated over the low back and abdomen during pregnancy and directly over cardiac pacemakers and should be used cautiously over growing bone.

Commercial hot packs are available for home use but may not be practical for all patients. These hot packs require preliminary heating for at least 15 minutes, have no means of temperature control, and are heavy. Layers of toweling between the hot pack and skin need to be adjusted based on individual response to heat. Skin checks should be made after the first ten minutes of application or more often based on subjective information from the patient.

Moist and dry electrical heating pads are easy to use and require only minimal preliminary heating. Temperature settings can be adjusted but are not precise. Unlike commercial hot packs that lose heat after 20 minutes of application, electrical heating pads are maintained at a constant temperature. This may be desirable in some instances, but provides a potential for burns.

Home paraffin units consist of a mixture of melted paraffin wax and mineral oil in a small heated basin. They are excellent for arthritic conditions involving hands and feet. Paraffin has a lower specific heat than water, so higher temperatures are tolerated. A paraffin "glove" is formed by repeatedly dipping the hand into the paraffin which serves to retain heat and moisture, but there is no means of temperature control once applied. Use of paraffin baths is limited to small, distal joints and is not practical for larger, more proximal joints such as the hip.

Ultrasound is a deep heating agent that works by transmitting high frequency sound waves through soft tissues, and produces both thermal and mechanical effects. It can therefore affect muscles and deeper joints more directly. Home units are available for use by health care professionals trained in the use of ultrasound. These units are not purchased by patients, but rather the treatment is administered by a physical therapist during the home visit as determined by the therapeutic goals.

COLD

Cold has an inhibitory effect on acute inflammation as evidenced by reduced edema, lower leukocyte counts, reduced analgesic intake, increased pain threshold, and decreased muscle spasm and soreness. Use of cold during the acute phase of injury decreases the metabolic rate and capillary permeability, thus limiting edema formation. Vasoconstriction as a result of cold application also assists in controlling edema and bleeding after trauma.

Connective tissue extensibility is decreased with cold application. Despite this, cold is sometimes used on arthritic joints prior to exercise because of its analgesic effect. Like heat, cold is a counterirritant and may interrupt the pain-spasm-pain cycle.

Caution is to be used when treating patients with hypertension, open wounds, regenerating peripheral nerves, or certain rheumatic diseases. Contraindications include cold urticaria, cryoglobinuria, compromised circulation, vasospastic disorders such as Raynaud's phenomenon, and hypersensitivity to cold.

Home application is a matter of patient preference. Tolerance to cold should always be checked prior to application, and an interface should always be used to ensure uniform distribution. The interface can be either wet or dry depending on patient tolerance. Commercial packs are reusable and can be conveniently stored; however, they do not maintain their temperature for prolonged periods. Home-made ice packs are less expensive and maintain cold temperatures longer; however, they are less convenient.

Ice massage is an alternative method of cold application but is effective only for smaller areas. It is also a means of assessing patient response to cold prior to application of a cold pack.

COMPRESSION

Compression is used in the management of edema and to assist in circulation. Two types of application are common in the home care setting and include elastic bandage wrapping and pneumatic compression devices. Proper application is essential to ensure that circulation is not further compromised. Elastic bandage wrapping is commonly used in shaping residual limbs post-amputation and patients may require initial instruction and continued monitoring until stump size has stabilized. Pneumatic compression devices typically consist of an inflatable cuff that intermittently applies compression to the limb segment. They have prescribed settings based on the extremity being treated and patient tolerance. Often a gradual increase in the pressure settings is necessary before achieving optimal pressure. Elastic bandage wrapping following pneumatic compression treatment may assist in maintaining the reduction in edema.

ELECTRICAL STIMULATION

Transcutaneous electrical nerve stimulation (TENS) and high-voltage pulsed current (HVPC) units are small and portable, and both lend themselves to home use. TENS provides relief of many painful conditions, including reflex sympathetic dystrophy and those associated with rheumatic diseases. Electrode placement and use of different stimulation parameters need to be assessed and adjusted to enhance effectiveness. Care of the electrodes and the unit should be included in instruction to the patient.

HVPC can also be used to promote wound healing by decreasing edema, stimulating beneficial cellular changes, increasing blood flow, and inhibiting bacteria in dermal wounds. Accelerated healing and wound closure with improved tensile strength have been demonstrated after treatment of ulcers with electrical stimulation. Stimulation parameters are determined by the stage and type of wound. Whether treatment is monitored in the clinic or at home, a physical therapist is involved throughout the course of treatment to assess changes in wound appearance and drainage, and to make appropriate adjustments in the parameters.

Some medical conditions may make the use of electrical stimulation an inappropriate choice. These include the presence of demand cardiac pacemakers, pregnancy, cancer, and epilepsy. The use of electrode gel and tape may lead to irritation or breakdown in patients with hypersensitive or fragile skin.

SPECIAL CONSIDERATIONS FOR THE ELDERLY

Age-related changes that impact physiological responses include decreases in thermoregulation, circulation, and sensation, changes in mentation, and altered mobility. Elderly patients may exhibit difficulty in dissipating heat because of the changes in thermoregulation and circulation, thus necessitating use of lower temperatures or application of heat over limited surface areas. Decreased sensation may alter perception of heat, cold, and painful stimuli. Changes in mentation associated with aging may impact judgment and memory, affecting safety and compliance. Decreased mobility may not affect treatment directly but may interfere with patient positioning. These changes are not contraindications to treatment with physical agents, but rather may influence method of application, the overall duration of treatment, the need for more frequent monitoring, and the nature of instruction to patients and caregivers.

References

Gentzkow, G.D., and K.H. Miller. 1991. Electrical stimulation for dermal wounds. *Clinics in Podiatric Medicine and Surgery* 8(4):827–41.

Gersh, M.R., ed. 1992. *Electrotherapy in Rehabilitation*. Philadelphia: F.A. Davis.

Jackson, O., ed. 1989. *Clinics in Physical Therapy: Physical Therapy of the Geriatric Patient*, 2d ed. New York: Churchill Livingstone.

Kloth, L.C., and J.A. Feedar. 1988. Acceleration of healing with high voltage, monophasic, pulsed current. *Physical Therapy* 68(4):503–8.

Lehmann, J.L., ed. 1990. *Therapeutic Heat and Cold*, 4th ed. Baltimore: Williams & Wilkins.

Michlovitz, S.L., ed. 1990. *Thermal Agents in Rehabilitation*, 2d ed. Philadelphia: F.A. Davis.

Kristin Von Nieda and Philip W. McClure

Polymyalgia Rheumatica

Polymyalgia rheumatica is a systemic rheumatic disease of unknown etiology which affects the elderly. It is characterized by aching and stiffness, usually gradual in onset, affecting the shoulders, arms, hips, thighs, and the neck or torso. There is also evidence of an underlying systemic inflammatory process manifested by malaise (generally not feeling well), fatigue, weight loss, fever, anemia, and elevated erythrocyte (red blood cell) sedimentation rate. Diagnosis requires that patients be older than 50 years of age and that the symptoms persist for longer than four weeks. The presence of another specific disease, such as rheumatoid arthritis, systemic lupus erythematosus, chronic infection, polymyositis, or malignancy excludes the diagnosis of polymyalgia rheumatica.

The severity and duration of the syndrome vary widely. Usually, polymyalgia rheumatica is a benign disease which responds well to treatment with low-dose prednisone. In untreated patients, however, there is a gradual worsening of symptoms over several months with progressive fatigue, aching, and stiffness followed by gradual recovery after one or two years. A certain proportion of patients with the syndrome become incapacitated by the pain and stiffness to the point of being bedridden. The immobility may in turn result in significant muscle weakness and atrophy (shrinkage) as well as joint problems such as "frozen shoulder," which is frequently seen in severe cases.

The symmetry of the pain of polymyalgia rheumatica is classical, even though in an occasional patient the symptoms may start in an asymmetric fashion. The proximal location of the pain is also characteristic for the syndrome. The pain may be severe enough to wake the patient from sleep. The stiffness classically occurs in the morning and lasts for about 30 to 60 minutes. The pain and stiffness frequently seem out of proportion to the objective (physical examination) findings. The physical examination may show limitation of active (performed by the patient) movements due to the pain. Passive range of motion (performed by the examiner) may be normal if the patient is relaxed during the examination. In the occasional patient with severe disease who develops "frozen shoulder," even the passive range of motion is limited. There is usually no objective weakness of muscles detected. The absence of proximal muscle weakness helps to distinguish polymyalgia rheumatica from polymyositis, while lack of muscle tenderness on palpation speaks against a possibility of fibromyalgia.

There is usually only minimal, if any, evidence of inflammation of the small peripheral joints, manifested by swelling, increased temperature, and tenderness of the periarticular areas. The absence of synovitis (inflammation of the joint lining) helps in differentiating polymyalgia rheumatica from rheumatoid arthritis, which typically presents with morning stiffness and synovitis of the small joints of the hands and feet. The synovitis of polymyalgia rheumatica, which is present in about 20 percent of patients, is classically evanescent and does not result in deforming or destructive arthritis.

The diagnosis of polymyalgia rheumatica remains a clinical one, as there are no specific tests available to establish the diagnosis with certainty. Diagnosing polymyalgia rheumatica is important not only because there is an effective treatment available, but also because diagnosing polymyalgia rheumatica has broader implications vis-a-vis its association with temporal arteritis. About 15 percent of patients with polymyalgia rheumatica are found to have evidence of arteritis (inflammation of the arteries) on temporal artery biopsy. Performing routine temporal artery biopsy in patients with polymyalgia rheumatica is controversial. However, biopsy is indicated if patients also report headaches, scalp tenderness, claudication (pain in jaw and tongue when chewing), or other symptoms characteristic of temporal arteritis. These patients are at risk of developing visual complications of temporal arteritis, including irreversible blindness, and thus require high-dose steroid therapy.

Otherwise, the treatment for polymyalgia rheumatica is prednisone in low doses, usually 7.5 to 15 mg per day. Clinical response to this regimen is usually rapid and dramatic. Patients who were incapacitated by their illness frequently recover completely within 24 to 48 hours. This favorable and rapid response to small doses of steroids distinguishes patients with polymyalgia rheumatica from those who suffer from other rheumatic diseases like rheumatoid arthritis or polymyositis. The prednisone is usually reduced by 0.5 to 1 mg per month after clinical remission has been maintained for several weeks on a current dose. The majority of patients are free of disease within two years and clinical relapses are rare.

References

Bleecker, M.L., and C.J. Meyd. 1993. Polymyalgia rheumatica. In *Principles of Ambulatory Medicine*, 3rd ed. Edited by L.R. Barker, J.R. Burton, and P.D. Zieve. Baltimore: Williams & Wilkins, 1091–92.

Kelley, W.N., ed. 1992. *Textbook of Internal Medicine*, 2d ed. Philadelphia: Lippincott, 1002–3.

Norris, T.E. 1994. Polymyalgia rheumatica. In *Family Medicine: Principles and Practice*, 4th ed. Edited by R.B. Raylor. New York: Springer-Verlag, 907.

Anna M. Plichta

Prescriptions and the Frail Elderly in the Home

The elderly are a rapidly growing segment of the U.S. population. Currently, 12 percent of the population is over the age of 65. By the year 2000, 13.1 percent of the population will be over 65. This group is also responsible for a large percentage of the annual medication expenditures. The elderly consume an estimated 31 percent of prescription drugs and 40 percent of nonprescription medications used in the country each year. Unfortunately, not all these medications are used appropriately. Of all drug-related deaths in 1986, 51 percent occurred in individuals over the age of 60. Polypharmacy, pharmacokinetic changes, pharmacodynamic changes, and compliance require consideration by health care professionals to ensure safe medication use and thus to improve the quality of life for older persons.

Research substantiates the figures mentioned above. In one study, an estimated

80 percent of the elderly took at least one prescription medication daily. In another study, elderly individuals living independently took an average of four medications per day, while those in nursing homes took between six and eight medications per day. The number of medications that an elderly person takes predisposes them to adverse reactions and drug-drug interactions. Adverse reactions or drug-drug interactions occur in 4 percent of patients taking five medications or less, 10 percent of those taking six to ten medications, 28 percent taking 10 to 15 medications, and 54 percent taking more than 16 medications. Because of diminished physiological reserve in the elderly, these reactions carry high morbidity and mortality rates.

PHARMACOKINETICS

Absorption, distribution, metabolism, and elimination are pharmacokinetic parameters that can be affected by age, and can result in food-drug interactions. The amount of acid produced in the stomachs of older persons is often less than in younger persons. This diminished amount of stomach acidity can result in incomplete dissolution of tablets and capsules, and poor absorption of medications. First-pass metabolism of medications may also be decreased in the elderly, leading to increased absorption of those medications that undergo extensive first-pass metabolism, such as nitrates and estrogens. Diseases often seen in the elderly, such as diabetes mellitus and congestive heart failure, can also affect absorption times and rates.

In general, older persons have an increase in body fat and a decrease in lean body mass, which can affect the distribution of some drugs. Those drugs that are water-soluble and distribute mainly to lean tissues have decreased volumes of distribution in older patients. Because of this reduction in volume, drugs such as digoxin (Lanoxin®) and lithium will require smaller doses to achieve the same blood concentrations. Conversely, the volume of distribution of fat-soluble compounds is increased. This can delay the excretion of some medications such as benzodiazepines. This increased volume of distribution could lead to drug accumulation in the body, causing adverse events. Plasma protein concentrations do not decline with age as was once thought. However, due to catabolic states such as infection and poor nutrition, a portion of the elderly do have decreased plasma proteins. This reduction in plasma proteins can enhance the activity of highly protein-bound medications such as warfarin (Coumadin®), phenytoin (Dilantin®), and valproic acid (Depakote®).

The metabolic reactions that are responsible for drug metabolism can be classified as either phase I or phase II reactions. Phase I reactions are decreased in older persons. The half-life (the time it takes for 50% of the drug to be excreted from the body) of medications metabolized by these pathways are increased, leading to increased drug concentrations and adverse effects. Examples include diazepam (Valium®) and chlordiazepoxide (Librium®). Phase II reactions do not diminish with age. Inactivation of medications metabolized by these routes are not affected and would require no dosage adjustment. An example of a drug that undergoes only phase II metabolism is lorazepam (Ativan®). Cardiac and pulmonary disease states can also alter drug metabolism by reducing the amount of blood flow through the liver.

Kidney function can decline with age. An estimated 35 percent of the elderly have no change in renal function if diseases such as hypertension and diabetes are not present. The remaining portion of the elderly who do have a decline in renal function with age may require a decrease in dose or an extension of the interval between doses, if the medications they are taking are eliminated via the kidneys. Vancomycin, aminoglycosides, digoxin, and salicylates are examples of medications that may require decreased doses for older persons.

PHARMACODYNAMICS

Drug pharmacodynamics, which is defined as the observed clinical effect of drugs, may be altered in the elderly. The beta-adrenergic receptors in the elderly seem to be less sensitive to both agonist and antagonist activity. The cholinergic receptors, however, appear to be more sensitive to antagonist activity. Drugs with anticholinergic side effects, which include dry mouth, dry eyes, drowsiness, constipation, and urinary retention, may be extremely troublesome to the elderly patient. Examples of drugs with anticholinergic side effects include antihistamines, antidepressants, and clonidine, an antihypertensive. The dopaminergic receptors also appear to be more sensitive in older people, as shown by an increase in parkinson-like side effects seen with the use of phenothiazines.

COMPLIANCE

Compliance should also be a concern when considering drug therapy for older people. Elders are often confused about the proper way to take a medication. The print on the bottle is often too small to be read. Older persons may be less likely to ask questions about specific directions regarding when and how to take medications because of wanting not to seem "confused." The more complex the regimen, the less likely the patient will be to comply. This problem is multiplied in the elderly, who often take a larger number of medications. Drugs may be taken twice rather than once, or missed altogether for a day. Devices such as clock faces of paper, set for the time when a medication is to be taken, or individual pills or capsules placed in a row by order of time of dose, can be most helpful in these situations. It is best to eliminate any drugs that are not absolutely essential. Choosing drugs that need be taken only once or twice a day are preferred, to improve compliance.

Informing the patient about what medications are being prescribed, their purpose, and the correct way to take the drug is probably the most important part of the provider's responsibilities. Repetition is useful, and having the patient repeat back the information is confirming to both patient and provider. If the patient has decreased visual acuity, printing instructions in large letters will assist them to assimilate the information. Vocal information is the kind of communication least understood and soonest forgotten; use as many of the patient's senses as possible—vision, hearing, touch, and vocal repetition.

Many, if not all, of these problems may not exist with many older persons, but when present, they must be addressed so that the quality of patients' lives is not diminished.

A SYSTEMATIC APPROACH TO DRUG THERAPY DECISIONS

The health care provider should approach decisions regarding appropriate drug therapy in a systematic fashion. An accurate drug history is necessary, with emphasis on what drugs the patient is now taking and how they are being taken. If possible, information should be elicited about previous medications, particularly any that had associated problems. The history should include prescription and nonprescription drugs, home remedies, and alcohol use.

An accurate diagnosis of the person's health problem(s) is essential so that accurate and appropriate drug therapy can be instituted. If the patient who is already taking medications voices new complaints or has new symptoms, current drug therapy should be ruled out as a cause for the new complaints and symptoms before prescribing other medications.

With certain conditions, such as the new Type II diabetes (formerly Adult Onset Diabetes), diet and exercise may be prescribed as the initial therapy, thus delaying the use of drug therapy. Diet therapy is also effective in hypertension and increased cholesterol. When the decision to begin drug therapy is made, the right drug for that patient should be started. The possible drug choices should be screened for drug-disease, drug-drug, and drug-food interactions. The appropriate dose for a younger person may be inappropriate for an older person. The rule of thumb in initiating drug therapy for the elderly is to "start low and go slow." Because the human mind is not infallible, the provider should never hesitate to consult an appropriate drug reference.

Once medications are prescribed, based on reasonable goals for treatment, the provider must monitor the patient carefully. Failure to achieve a goal is an indication to re-evaluate the treatment plan. Choices that can be made include using alternative drugs, increasing or decreasing the dosage, or discontinuing drug therapy altogether. If the patient responds well to drug therapy and treatment in general, periodic re-evaluation of the patient is still required to monitor changes that might indicate further adjustments in drug therapy. It is important to inform the patient as carefully as before regarding changes, and that previous drugs should not be taken in favor of the new one(s).

When properly used and evaluated, drug therapies can improve the quality of life and, in some instances, prolong life in the elderly. As pointed out, however, there are numerous pitfalls in prescribing medications for older persons. Polypharmacy increases the chances of therapeutic misadventures and drug-drug interactions. Changes in pharmacokinetic and pharmacodynamic properties of medications in the elderly predispose this population to adverse reactions and overmedication. Using a systematic approach to prescribing drug therapy, the provider can enhance benefits to the patient and prevent inappropriate drug use.

References

Everitt, D.E., and J. Avorn. 1986. Drug prescribing for the elderly. *Arch Intern Med* 146: 2393–96.

Goldberg, P.B., and J. Roberts. 1983. Pharmacologic basis for developing rational drug regimens for elderly patients. *Med Clin North Amer* 67:315–31.

Greenblatt, D.J., D.R. Abernathy, and R.I. Shader. 1986. Pharmacokinetic aspects of drug therapy in the elderly. *Ther Drug Monitoring* 8:249–55.

Montamat, S.C., B.J. Cusack, and R.E. Vestal. 1989. Management of drug therapy in the elderly. *N Engl J Med* 321:303–9.

Pucino, F., C.L. Beck, R.L. Seifert, G.L. Strommen, P.A. Sheldon, and I.L. Silberqleit. 1985. Pharmacogeriatrics. *Pharmacotherapy* 5:314–26.

Vestal, R.E. 1978. Drug use in the elderly: a review of problems and special considerations. *Drugs* 16:358–82.

Dirk S. Lucas and Mark A. Stratton

Preventive Care and Health Maintenance

The fastest growing segment of the U.S. population is that of persons aged 65 and older. While this segment currently comprises 12 percent of the U.S. population, it consumes 30 percent of all national health funds and 50 percent of the Federal health budget. Although the elderly are generally more prone to develop severe disabling conditions, elderly individuals who require skilled assistance and nursing home placement are clearly in the minority. Only 3 percent of men and 6 percent of women over age 65 reside in nursing homes. Most people over 65 live at home, frequently with the help of a family member.

Although the normal aging process cannot be prevented, many persons have prematurely "accelerated" their otherwise genetically predetermined age. Environmental factors, diet, and life-styles are just a few variables that determine how well we will age. In many cases, an accelerated aging process has resulted in functional incapacity and disease. While many diseases cannot be prevented, they should be identified and treatment initiated as early as possible. Unfortunately, this is often a difficult task during later life, given the common nonspecific manner in which diseases may become manifest. This entry will discuss three aspects of preventive health care, all important if we are to remain as functional as possible. This is important for everyone and we must not forget those elderly people who are homebound. They may also benefit from proper preventive health care.

PRIMARY PREVENTION

Primary prevention is aimed at reducing the risk of disease before its onset. In many instances, life-style changes and medical interventions have been shown to decrease the age-specific risk of fatal diseases such as heart attack, stroke, and lung cancer. Caregivers and health care workers must assess and attempt to modify behaviors such as smoking, alcohol use, diet, and exercise habits, since it is never too late to prevent disease.

Exercise, with an emphasis on aerobic conditioning and cardiovascular fitness, has been studied in particular. There has also been an emphasis on the decline in physical functioning and one's ability to carry out self-care activities as we age. It is not clear how much of this decline is unavoidable, but a sedentary life-style has been associated with muscle wasting, thinning of the bones, and poor balance, among other factors.

Elderly people should be ecouraged to remain active. It is well documented that even small increases in physical activity can greatly improve one's functional ability and continued independence. Recent studies also suggest that feelings of well-being and self-image improve with regular exercise. Someone who has become very sedentary can begin walking short distances; simple stretching exercises may appeal to others as a beginning. Those who have remained active throughout their lives may begin some mild aerobic activity. Prior to initiating any change in physical activity, however, a physician should be contacted as to limits and advice regarding what is the best form of exercise, given individual capabilities. Even persons who are confined to their homes or who are bedbound, have been shown to benefit from an exercise program, no matter how modest. A "trapeze" above the bed can help maintain upper body strength, flexibility, and mobility. Sedentary aerobics, even below that level which raises heart rate, can have psychological benefits as well as improve muscle mass, bone strength, and prevent contractures.

Nutritional status is also of concern in primary prevention. Although the prevalence of frank malnutrition in the United States is unclear, there are definitely segments of our population who are at risk of developing calorie, vitamin, and mineral deficiencies. Insufficient calcium intake is almost a universal problem. Older people with severe chronic illnesses, particularly those institutionalized or homebound, should be evaluated with respect to their current nutritional status and their ability to obtain and consume an adequate diet. Obesity may also be a problem. The overweight individual should be encouraged, with the aid of a dietary consultant, to achieve healthy weight reduction. In addition, the risk of having an elevated cholesterol must be assessed. Anyone subsisting on less than 1,500 calories is at high risk and at a minimum should take a daily vitamin.

Another issue for primary intervention is the prevention of falls or other accidents. Traumatic injuries are the fifth leading cause of death in persons over 65 with the majority occurring in or near one's own home. Older people are much more likely to suffer death or prolonged disability because of accidents. Falls, in particular, are of great concern because they often result in fractures and subsequent complications. Immobility of older persons, caused by falls, can result in greater loss of bone density and muscle wasting. Elderly, frail people are more susceptible to these events for a variety of reasons, including decreased vision, hearing, and strength. They may have poor balance and coordination leading to gait abnormalities. Poor judgment, as a result of cognitive decline, may also be contributory. Assessment for falls should include an evaluation of vision, hearing, and cognitive function in addition to musculo-skeletal strength and coordination. Efforts should be made to maintain a safe environment including no loose rugs, good lighting, and the elimination of obstacles wherever possible. Assistive devices should be employed when appropriate, for example, handrails, etc.

Elderly persons are at increased risk of developing serious illnesses from medications, including over-the-counter (OTC) preparations. Medication side effects and drug interactions may result in the need for hospitalization and can be life-threatening. Periodic medication reviews must be done and all prescriptions should be evaluated with regard to kind, dosage, and need.

Finally, no discussion of primary prevention is complete without mention of immunizations. Influenza vaccination should be received on a yearly basis, particularly for those with chronic disabling conditions. Although the rate of complete protection is variable, the vaccine is highly effective in reducing the degree of illness, need for hospitalization, and death. Pneumonia is a leading cause of death in the elderly and pneumococcal pneumonia is the leading cause of lower respiratory infections. The pneumococcal vaccine is capable of treating over 85 percent of pneumococcal infections and is recommended for all persons over age 50 and anyone younger with chronic illness, as a one-time dose. Some studies now recommend a booster every 7 to 10 years. Based on serologic studies, at least 40 percent of people over 65 lack adequate levels of tetanus and diphtheria antitoxin. Since 50 percent of reported cases of tetanus occur in people over age 60, it is recommended that these vaccinations be done as a primary series in all elderly people who have no history of having had them, followed by a booster injection every 10 years.

SECONDARY PREVENTION

The goal of secondary prevention is to identify and treat persons with early, minimally symptomatic diseases in order to improve the outcome and maintain function. Hypertension and hypercholesterolemia are leading risk factors for the development of atherosclerotic heart disease and stroke. Even in the absence of a problem, elderly persons should regularly have blood pressure screening every 1 to 2 years and cholesterol screening every 5 years. Recently, it has been shown that systolic hypertension is an independent risk factor for stroke. Hypertension can be easily treated with life-style changes, medications, or a combination of both. Hypercholesterolemia may require modification of diet, a change in exercise habits, and perhaps medication.

Any neurologic impairment and/or functional decline must be recognized. Signs of a significant decline in mental functioning are not a normal part of aging. Elderly persons with evidence of cognitive decline must be thoroughly evaluated for potentially reversible diseases including metabolic abnormalities and depression that are known to be capable of influencing one's mental status. If a patient is diagnosed with a progressive and irreversible dementing illness, caregivers must maintain a secure and familiar environment for that individual.

Elderly persons are at high risk of developing cancer. Although many studies have documented the benefits of early detection and treatment of some cancers, the aged have been underrepresented in most studies. Despite this, several organizations have established specific recommendations for breast cancer screening in the elderly. Approximately 50 percent of all breast cancers occur in women over the age of 65; these women respond to therapy in much the same way as younger women. A yearly clinical breast examination and mammography are recommended. Cervical cancer in women also responds well to therapy if detected early. Although its incidence is relatively low in women over age 65, 41 percent of deaths attributed to cervical carcinoma occur in this age group. Many of these women report never having had a Pap smear. Current recommendations are to have routine Pap smears done annually until age 65. If there have been two negative smears in the preceding years, then a Pap smear is suggested every five years until age 74. Regardless of the Pap test, women should have an annual pelvic examination as the risk of developing a cancer of the uterus increases with age.

Colorectal cancers peak at around age 80 with 60 percent of these cancers occurring in persons over 65 years of age. Survival rates for treated cases appear to be the same at five years for those aged 56 or 75. Currently, there are two methods of early detection available. Fecal occult blood testing is recommended every year and sigmoidoscopy every 2 to 3 years for those over 65. A variety of other cancers may be screened for at the yearly exam including skin cancers, oral cancers, and prostate cancers. Annual digital rectal examination is the single best way to detect prostate cancer early.

TERTIARY PREVENTION

Finally, strong efforts should be made to prevent the progression of conditions already affecting the individual. This is referred to as tertiary prevention. Vision and hearing examinations should be done every two years unless there is a reason to do it more frequently, for example, diabetes mellitus, glaucoma, etc. Older people should visit a dentist routinely to assess teeth and gums, and treat problems that exist. Foot care is also important, particularly for those with vascular disease or diabetes. Osteoporosis should be identified; alterations made to one's diet or the use of calcium pills as a supplement can help maintain calcium balance and at least prevent further bone loss. Many progressive processes may be slowed through identification, treatment, and rehabilitation.

CONCLUSION

Preventive health care during later life is frequently difficult to ensure. Many people cannot afford to visit the doctor. Arrangements for transportation, particularly for the homebound, may be complicated and costly. Sometimes older people are afraid to report symptoms or are unaware of them, assuming that they are part of normal aging, until a state of advanced illness develops. Caregivers must recognize and assist the elderly to overcome these difficulties. This entry has outlined some of the more conservative recommendations made by various health organizations. As noted, these recommendations do extend to the group of elderly people who are homebound. Above all, health maintenance and preventive care must become a priority for all.

References

Report of the U.S. Preventive Services Task Force. 1989. *Guide to Clinical Preventive Services: An Assessment of the Effectiveness of 169 Interventions.* Baltimore: Williams & Wilkins.

U.S. Department of Health and Human Services, Public Health Service. 1992. *Personal Health Guide.* Put Prevention into Practice Program, ODPHP National Health Information Center, P.O. Box 1133, Washington, D.C. 20013-1133.

Katherine Katsoyannis and Steven R. Gambert

Psychological and Psychiatric Disorders and the Elderly

The most common psychiatric disorders among elders in the community are depression and dementia. Some overlap between these two conditions can occur, and other psychiatric problems can be associated with both depression and dementia.

DEPRESSION

Depression is a syndrome characterized by depressed mood and markedly diminished interest or pleasure in activities.

Incidence

In community samples of elders above age 65, the incidence of major depression is between 2 percent and 4 percent. If those with more general depressive symptomatology are included, the rate is 10 percent to 15 percent. However, risk of depression in physically ill elders increases threefold, and 50 percent to 70 percent of elders receiving home care have emotional problems or mental disorders including depression, anxiety, disorientation, confusion, agitation, restlessness, abuse of alcohol, hostility, cognitive impairment, fearfulness, lonesomeness, and paranoia. There is a high risk of suicide among elderly white males: 42.5 per 100,000 between ages 75 to 79, and 50.2 for men above age 85, versus a rate of 21.2 for females. Losses associated with aging and social isolation are considered contributing factors to the high male suicide rate, but it may also be a generational (cohort) effect rather than a phenomenon associated with aging.

Assessment

Depressed elders may present with the classic symptoms of depression that include depressed moods; markedly diminished interests or pleasure in activities; changes in appetite, sleep, psychomotor activity, and energy; feelings of worthlessness or guilt; diminished ability to concentrate; and recurrent thoughts of death or suicidal ideations or attempts. They may also exhibit atypical or "masked" depression if they deny feeling depressed and instead voice somatic complaints such as constipation, dry mouth, gastrointestinal disturbances, headaches, and muscle pains. Other characteristics relevant to assessing depressed moods in elders include: irritability, apathy, increased criticism of significant others, expressing feeling of emptiness, crying, flat monotonous voice, lack of eye contact, flat affect, unkempt appearance, reports feeling sad if asked, and dark physical environment. Suicidal ideations may not be overtly expressed but clues are likely to be present. These include verbal clues such as "You would be better off without me," behavioral clues such as giving away prized possessions, scheduling appointment with a physician for no apparent physical cause or very shortly after the last visit, and situational clues such as death of a spouse.

A number of standardized depression scales with specific cut-off points to indicate clinical depression are available. Examples are the Center for Epidemiological Studies Depression Scale (CES-D), the Beck Depression Inventory (BDI), Geriatric Depression Scale (GDS), the Hamilton Depression Rating Scale (HAM-D), and the Zung Self Rating Depression Scale (SDS). None of these replace the value of a good clinical interview, but they can provide additional information and be useful in following an individual's affective state over time.

Psychosocial and Physical Health Factors

The assessment of underlying causes of depression in elders must include psychosocial and physical health factors. Psychosocial factors include major personal losses (thus differentiating depression from grief reaction); changes in living arrangement and financial resources; changes in family, friends, and support systems; and changes in problem solving abilities. All of these factors can contribute to loneliness and depression. In addition, the fatigue and stress levels of family members need to be assessed and evaluated for possible indications of elder abuse. The correlation between depression in elders and physical illness or disability is particularly striking. Physical factors to be assessed include chronic pain, a general evaluation of all body systems, level of inactivity related to pain and physical illness, and the presence of comorbid physical illnesses. Also, a record of all medications, including over-the-counter drugs, must be made, since over one-third of major depressions found in a community sample were associated with medication use. Antibiotics, analgesics, and sedatives, cardiovascular medications and other prescribed or recreational drugs can also cause depression.

Intervention

Somatic and psychosocial treatment modalities, either separate or combined, are effective in treating depression in elders, but interventions must be tailored to specific patient situations as identified in the assessment process. Particular attention to the presence of physical illness is warranted; treating physical problems appropriately can often resolve the underlying depression. Conversely, treating primary depressive illness can enhance recovery from concurrent medical conditions.

Somatic treatment includes the use of antidepressant medication and electroconvulsive therapy (ECT). Antidepressants such as nortriptyline, desipramine, doxepin, fluoxetine, and trazodone can be given in lower doses than in younger patients while still achieving therapeutic effects. Tertiary-amine tricyclic antidepressants (e.g., imipramine, amitriptyline) are less well tolerated by elders because of anticholinergic side effects and orthostatic hypotension. Family members need to be involved in supervising or administering medication regimes at home. They need to be taught how to recognize medication side effects or sudden changes in behavior (e.g., falls, constipation, disorientation) or suicidal ideations that may require hospitalization. ECT has also been used very successfully as both an outpatient and inpatient treatment modality.

Psychosocial interventions effective with depressed elders include supportive therapy, interpersonal therapy, cognitive-behavioral strategies, and reminiscence or life review. These can be implemented as individual or group modalities. The social context of the elders' living arrangements can positively or negatively affect mood. Therefore, it is important to address the family's coping skills and resources. Opportunities for venting frustrations over difficult behaviors in the elder need to be provided, and when personal and financial resources become strained, the continuation of in-home care needs to be discussed. Government support programs may need to be activated. If elder abuse is suspected, the State Department of Human Services must be notified. The overall goal is to strengthen the family's and the elder's adaptive coping responses.

DEMENTIA

Dementia is a syndrome of persistent cognitive impairment. The most common cause is Alzheimer's disease, followed by multi-infarct dementia, and then mixed cases of both conditions. In addition, delirium or acute confusional states have features of cognitive impairment.

Incidence

Approximately 60 percent of cases with progressive dementia are diagnosed as probable Alzheimer's disease (Primary Degenerative or Senile Dementia of the Alzheimer Type—SDAT). The onset of this condition is age-related. Based on community samples, a prevalence rate has been reported of 10.3 percent between ages 65 and 74; this rises to 18.7 percent for ages 75 to 84; above age 85, the rate is 47.2 percent. Approximately two-thirds of demented elders live in the community. Multi-infarct dementias (MID) comprise less than 15 percent of all cases, and mixed diagnoses of Alzheimer's disease and multi-infarct dementia another 15 percent. The incidence of delirium or acute confusion also increases with age but rates of occurrence are not well documented. In elderly hospital patients, the incidence is at least 30 percent and probably higher. Since more than 20 other terms have been used to describe delirium (including acute confusional state, acute brain syndrome, acute organic psychosis, reversible toxic psychosis, toxic confusional state), it may be one of the most common forms of psychopathology in later life.

Assessment

Criteria for the evaluation of dementia include: impaired short- and long-term memory; impaired abstract thinking; impaired judgment; aphasia, apraxia, agnosia, or constructional difficulty; disturbance of work, social relationships, or activities; and reasonable presumption of an organic etiologic factor. In "mild" dementia, work and social activities are impaired; in "moderate" dementia, independent living is hazardous; and in "severe" dementia, continual supervision is required. Reisberg's Global Deterioration Scale provides a more comprehensive description of seven stages and phases, each with characteristic cognitive and functional manifestations. Frequently used standardized scales to assess cognitive and functional levels of demented elders are Folstein's Mini Mental State Examination, Pfeifer's Brief Mental Status Questionnaire, Reisberg's Brief Cognitive Rating Scale, and Fillenbaum and Smyer's Instrumental Activities of Daily Living Scale. In trying to distinguish between SDAT and MID, time is the critical factor. While the onset of SDAT is insidious, has a slow, linear progression and is irreversible, the onset of MID is abrupt, progress is unpredictable, staccato, and there is a stepwise decline.

It is often difficult to distinguish dementia from depression since elders with cognitive impairment frequently suffer from depression and depressed elders have memory deficits. The term pseudodementia has been used when elders appear demented and depressed, and exhibit marked dependency behavior. In most of these cases depression is the underlying cause. Pseudo-demented elders often have a history of psychiatric illness. Crucial signs for a diagnosis of delirium are a reduction in the ability to focus, maintain, and shift attention. Time of onset is abrupt as in MID, but progression is reversible. Underlying physical causes must be determined (e.g., infection, metabolic disorders, toxins/drugs); in addition, acute confusional states can be caused by major changes in the elders' environment or sensory deprivation.

Interventions

To date, there is no known cause and no cure for SDAT. Given the progressive decline of independent functioning in persons with SDAT, education and support to family caregivers is essential so that they can provide necessary care. In addition, all families, even those whose older members appear healthy, must be alert to sudden changes in behavior that could indicate physical problems or medication toxicity associated with MID or delirium.

Somatic treatment involves the use of memory enhancing drugs such as piracetam, dihydroergotamine mesylate, physostigmine, or tetrahydroaminoacridine, although these remain experimental with only small positive, temporary effects being reported for some SDAT patients. Treatment of behavior problems in SDAT (e.g., anxiety, excitement, emotional lability, uncooperativeness) with antipsychotic medications such as thioridazine or loxapine is no more effective than placebo. However, concomitant depression in early stages of SDAT can be treated effectively with antidepressants at doses and blood levels comparable to those used in the treatment of elders with primary depression. Antidepressants with low or no anticholinergic effects (e.g., nortriptyline, desipramine, trazodone) should be used. Somatic treatments of MID and delirium are guided by underlying causes. Adequacy of treatment for hypertension and diabetes mellitus must be evaluated in MID patients. In delirium, any infection must be treated or drugs with known toxicity must be discontinued. Either decreasing or increasing environmental stimulation may help. Delirium can also be treated with haloperidol on an as-needed basis.

Psychosocial interventions form the majority of care in SDAT and MID cases. Caregivers, predominantly spouses and adult daughters, must be advised that they have to take charge of family finances and monitor their own health and stress levels. They must also be taught how to prevent and manage behavioral disturbances in the elder. There are published guidelines that provide help in dealing with common problems to provide a safe, caring environment for the elder, and to support the caregivers.

References

Agency for Health Care Policy and Research. 1993. *Depression in Primary Care: Vol. 2: Treatment of Major Depression. Clinical Practice Guideline, Number 5*. Rockville, Md.: U.S. Department of Health and Human Services, Public Health Service Agency for Health Care Policy and Research. AHCPR Pub. No. 93-0551.

Ebersole, P., and P. Hess. 1990. *Toward Healthy Aging*. St. Louis: Mosby Yearbook.

Harper, M.S. 1991. *Management and Care of the Elderly*. Newbury Park, Cal.: Sage.

Sadavoy, J., L.W. Lazarus, and L.F. Jarvik. 1991. *Comprehensive Review of Geriatric Psychiatry*. Washington, D.C.: American Psychiatric Press, Inc.

Stuart, W.G., and S.J. Sundeen. 1991. *Principles and Practice of Psychiatric Nursing*. St. Louis: Mosby Yearbook.

Wright, L.K. 1993. *Alzheimer's Disease and Marriage*. Newbury Park, Cal.: Sage.

Lore K. Wright and Gail W. Stuart

R

Retirement Attitudes and Adaptation

DEFINITION AND MEASUREMENT

A wide variety of measures have been used to assess attitudes toward retirement, including willingness to retire, expectations for retirement, and whether retirement is viewed in positive or negative terms. In some studies respondents are asked to evaluate retirement as a general phenomenon, as it might be experienced by most people, while other studies examine individuals' expectations or evaluations of their own lives in retirement. These disparate measures reflect the multidimensional nature of retirement, but lack of measurement consensus limits the ability to make comparisons among the studies, especially when researchers report contradictory results.

Attitudes toward life in retirement, along with other measures of reported psychological well-being, such as life satisfaction and personal happiness, are frequently used to assess an individual's adaptation to retirement. An important distinction to make between retirement attitudes and retirement adaptation is that attitudes represent evaluations individuals make about retirement at a given point in time, while adaptation implies a process. Although retirement attitudes often change over time, they alone cannot be used to represent processes of adaptation or adjustment to retirement.

The very concept of retirement has no clear, agreed-upon definition. Retirement has been measured variously as the number of hours worked during a specified period of time, receipt of retirement benefits such as private pensions or Social Security, or the individual's self-identification of retirement status. Conceptual problems associated with defining and measuring retirement are greater for women and members of racial-ethnic minority groups, who are more likely to have sporadic work histories and less likely to work in jobs covered by a pension plan.

EXPLAINING RETIREMENT ATTITUDES AND ADAPTATION

Factors that are important in understanding retirement attitudes and adaptation derive largely from the circumstances under which retirement is likely to be experienced. Health and income, which predict a favorable orientation toward retirement and satisfactory retirement adjustment, also predict satisfaction with life in general. Studies of retirement have also documented the importance of occupation and industry, family and friends.

Health

Workers with poor health are more likely to expect to retire, to anticipate retirement in less favorable terms, and to report more problems following their retirement. In contrast to the popular belief that men suffer physically and emotionally when they retire, research shows that workers of both genders are likely to retire when in poor health, but that retirement itself does not cause poor health.

Income

Most studies report a positive effect of income, with higher-income groups expressing more favorable attitudes and responses to retirement. In addition, individuals who expect an adequate retirement income often choose to retire early.

Occupation and Industry

Studies of retirement published during the 1950s and 1960s stressed the importance of the worker role for men, especially those occupying high-status occupations. Due to a strong commitment to their work, these men were thought to resist retirement and to be at greater risk for problems in retirement. Subsequent empirical research has challenged this assumption by showing that occupational status does not necessarily predict work commitment, and that commitment to work is largely unrelated to retirement attitudes and responses. Further, though researchers agree that occupational status is an important factor to consider when examining retirement attitudes and adaptation, studies to date have provided inconsistent and contradictory results. As an additional challenge to this assumption, studies have failed to document gender differences in commitment to work.

Clearer effects of occupation, as well as industry, are revealed when wages and benefits are considered. Higher-status occupations, and occupations located in core industries (such as manufacturing, transportation, finance, and professional services), command higher wages and are more likely to provide retirement benefits. As noted, higher income is associated with more positive retirement attitudes and adaptation; pension coverage also shows this pattern of effects. Since women and members of racial-ethnic minority groups are less likely to occupy high-status occupations or to work in core industries, consideration of these factors can help to explain why women and minorities tend to hold less favorable attitudes toward retirement.

Family

Retirement orientations and responses derive not only from individuals' occupational and personal characteristics, but also from their family circumstances and relationships as well. In this context, family includes not only the "traditional family" of a married couple with children, but also extended family members, homosexual couples, and heterosexual cohabitants. Consideration of the family context for retirement represents a relatively new direction in the literature, which can help to explain why most researchers in this area have focused rather narrowly on the marital dyad. Subsequent researchers can provide a fuller understanding of the retirement experience by including other family members as well.

Among married couples, decisions to retire typically are negotiated between the spouses and joint retirement is becoming increasingly common. However, women's retirement decisions are more sensitive than men's to their spouse's work status, with women more likely to retire if their husbands are retired. Women's retirement is also more likely when an ill or disabled family member requires assistance. Research suggests that the retirement satisfaction of women who retire in response to family need is lower than that of women who retire "on-time," or when they had planned to retire.

Available evidence also suggests that expectations held by married couples for their lives in retirement often are not realized. Couples in which the husband is still working anticipate more changes in their activities following retirement than are actually reported by couples who have retired. In addition, married women who are still working expect that retirement will bring a more egalitarian division of household labor, but married women who have retired report that they continue to perform most of the household work. Performing housework can have positive effects on post-retirement adaptation for both women and men, though for different reasons. Women who do not feel that they have been pressured into a traditional housewife role apparently obtain intrinsic satisfaction from performing housework, while men may obtain a sense of accomplishment from housework if they are ill and unable to perform other types of activities or if their spouse is ill.

Social Participation

Formal and informal social participation have also been reported as predictors of retirement attitudes and adaptation, but they have not emerged strongly or consistently in the retirement literature. Some researchers have argued that the usual research focus on frequency and quantity of interaction is misdirected, and that continuity in social participation is a critical element to consider: individuals who are able to maintain friendships and social networks established prior to retirement express greater retirement satisfaction.

Life Course Context

Viewing retirement holistically thus requires consideration not only of current family ties and social relationships, but also individuals' experiences over their life course. Research suggests that retirement adaptation is affected by the timing as well as the accumulation of life events such as divorce, illness, or death of a family member or friend, and change of residence. In addition, longitudinal studies reveal that attitudes held by individuals prior to their retirement are among the strongest predictors of post-retirement attitudes and adaptation, reinforcing the importance of a life-course perspective.

The Larger Social Context

More broadly, retirement orientations and experiences are influenced by events that occur at the societal level, including changes in government policy. For example, changes enacted in the Social Security system during the 1970s increased the value of Social Security benefits, which in turn contributed to the trend toward early retirement observed among many men and some women. This trend may be less pronounced in the future, however, because economic restructuring of U.S. society has produced more marginal jobs with low pay and few or no benefits. In addition, changes in the labor market structure have produced increasing discontinuity in many workers' labor force histories. A likely scenario for the future is that more older persons will continue working for economic reasons, or will re-enter the labor force following their retirement. Those who will have the greatest difficulty obtaining adequate post-retirement employment are also those who have had greatest difficulty obtaining adequate preretirement employment, specifically members of racial-ethnic minority groups, and women.

TRENDS IN RETIREMENT ATTITUDES AND ADAPTATION

It is important to understand why some individuals and groups express more or less favorable retirement attitudes and adaptation compared to others. However, it is also important to place these variations in a relative context: overall, most individuals hold favorable attitudes toward retirement, look forward to the experience, and are satisfied with retired life. These patterns contrast with studies of the 1940s and early 1950s, when researchers reported strong opposition to retirement. With the development of Social Security and private pension programs, retirement has become a normative, expected event. However, if changes in the economic structure continue to produce marginal jobs and dislocated work histories, the historical trend toward more favorable retirement attitudes and adaptation is unlikely to continue.

References

Calasanti, T.M. 1988. Participation in a dual economy and adjustment to retirement. *International J of Aging and Human Dev* 26(1):13–27.

Hardy, M.A. 1991. Employment after retirement: who gets back in? *Research on Aging* 13(3):267–88.

Matthews, A.M., and K.H. Brown. 1988. Retirement as a critical life event: the differential experiences of women and men. *Research on Aging* 9(4):548–71.

Szinovacz, M. 1992. Is housework good for retirees? *Family Relations* 41(2):230–38.

Szinovacz, M., D.J. Ekerdt, and B.H. Vinick, eds. 1992. *Families and Retirement.* Newbury Park, Cal.: Sage.

Zsembik, B.A., and A. Singer. 1990. The problem of defining retirement among minorities: the Mexican Americans. *The Gerontologist* 30(6):749–57.

Laurie Russell Hatch

Rural Anglo-Americans

INTRODUCTION

When considering the characteristics of Anglo-American elderly individuals living in rural areas, it is necessary to address certain issues: (1) the definition of the term Anglo-American, (2) the use of the term rural, and (3) the status of research on rural elderly, particularly Anglo-American elderly. Data from several ethnographic, qualitative aging studies show how this type of research, together with survey data, helps to provide an in-depth understanding of the behavior and attitudes of rural elderly.

TERMINOLOGY

Anglo-American

The term Anglo-American (Anglo) is used in two ways in social science literature: (1) as a specific reference to people of British ancestry (English, Scottish, and Welsh), or (2) as a broader term which, in addition to people of British ancestry, includes those who identify as "Americans." Anglo in its broader sense is used as the definition here.

Although studies of rural elderly do not always identify the ethnicity of the respondents, many of these studies have been conducted in states of the Midwest and South that were primarily settled by Anglo-Americans or by those who now identify as Americans. The studies of rural elderly that do not identify ethnicity and are not specifically about Blacks, Asians, American Indians, Hispanics, or Eastern European/Mediterranean elderly can be assumed to be about those who are predominantly Anglo-American in ancestry.

Rural

While the rural/urban distinction can theoretically be viewed as a continuum, the most common designation of rural is ecological, based primarily on community size, but also including density and location. The Census Bureau historically has considered as rural an area of less than 2,500 in population. Later, the distinction of farm/nonfarm was added and more recently a designation of "nonmetropolitan," which refers to an area with population of up to 50,000 but not included within a SMSA (Standard Metropolitan Statistical Area).

In addition to the above definitions for the term rural, other distinctions exist: geographical variations such as those between regions of the country, for example, the South, the far West, and the Midwest, and gender distinctions—more elderly women live in rural areas than men.

Another aspect of rural aging is reverse migration, that is, urban migration to rural areas, which began in the 1970s, continued until 1984, and resumed in 1988. Migration to rural areas introduces the additional factor of people who are more comfortable with mobility, and who may or may not have been born and reared in a rural environment. Their needs and reactions to aging promise to be different from those who have aged in place in the rural community.

What was once an easily understood distinction between urban and rural has been complicated by the continuing process of population movement that has developed in the twentieth century.

STATUS OF RESEARCH ON RURAL ELDERLY

Included here is an analysis of the trend that research has taken since the 1960s and a discussion of some of the limitations of aging studies. Several excellent reviews of aging research include those by Krout (1986); Coward and Lee (1985); and Youmans (1967).

When Youmans (1967) published his pioneering work on rural elderly people, he lamented the lack of research on rural elderly. In 1986, although recognizing the tremendous growth in studies of the elderly, Krout could still point to the paucity of research on rural elderly, particularly the lack of data on the effects of reverse migration, as well as the lack of studies where one can make valid comparisons between rural and urban aged.

Rowles (1983) voiced another concern when he noted that policymakers seem to have ignored the role of "natural" support systems and the ability of rural elderly to solve their problems without the benefit of social service intervention. He expressed particular concern about the paradox between the studies of socioeconomic status that suggest that rural elderly are generally disadvantaged, with greater poverty, inferior housing, inadequate transportation, poor health, and few social services, and the studies that indicate that life satisfaction of the rural elderly is high and morale good.

Much of the research on rural elderly focuses on the statistical analysis of the conditions under which rural elderly live, detailing their needs. Less attention has been paid to the behavior of rural people or their own perspectives on aging. As late as 1989, Van Willigen cautioned that we continue to lack the kinds of studies that tell us about the behavior of the elderly. He is critical of the focus of social gerontology on an ameliorative perspective which then poses as justification for particular social service programs (such as those, for example, based on "activity theory"). He claims that a lack of concern for the cultural and historical context and the depersonalization of the mass survey studies have decontextualized individuals and reduced them to a set of variables.

CHARACTERISTICS OF RURAL ANGLO-AMERICAN ELDERLY

Krout (1986) summarizes quite well the traits that most researchers agree characterize the values associated with rural populations. Others argue that the identifying cultural features were characteristic only when the elderly were young and no longer constitute a set of identifiable variables.

Although there is no complete agreement on the characteristics that are associated with the rural elderly and the question of values has not been adequately researched, several writers argue that important differences in values still exist between rural and urban populations. According to these researchers, rural people are practical, efficient, friendly, honest, and have a strong religious commitment. They believe in hard work, are social conservatives, and have a mistrust of government.

Rowles (1983) cites studies that suggest that there are certain aspects of rural residence that compensate for poor conditions. These include higher levels of social participation, reduced fear of crime, and a cultural setting which allows more gradual processes of retirement and transition to the elderly status for both men and women. Rowles describes the slower pace of life, more gradual processes of change within the physical environment, and the smaller scale of rural life.

Further, Rowles argues that the rural milieu nurtures a sociospatial support system that can sustain older people. He categorizes these supports into explicit and implicit groups. The indigenous informal support networks include family members, neighbors, confidants, and fellow members of the "society of the old" that derive from involvement in community level activities, telephone networks, and dyadic relationships in which one person networks with another. The networks of the elderly include younger persons. Rowles adds that for those who have aged in place, there is an attachment to place which adds a distinct emotional dimension.

Many experts say that service delivery models should supplement rather than supplant the diversity of existing sociospatial support systems and should harness the local people in caretaker roles and as facilitators. Ethnographic studies of communities should be included in the research methodology to reveal the subtleties of rural life and aid in an understanding of the behavior (as well as the needs) of the rural elderly. In-depth studies of the elderly such as anthropological (qualitative) methodology would add depth to the broad coverage provided by the statistical analysis that gerontologists generally provide. Qualitative research would also help to explain the paradox between the low social indicators and the general satisfaction rural elderly express with their lives.

Shenk's (1987) study of rural elderly women in central Minnesota emphasizes the desirability of making use of the social support systems and local networks available to these women in providing care. Her methodology included participant observation, collection of life histories, interviews, and network analysis to provide comprehensive data that are a vital complement to an earlier central Minnesota needs assessment.

Schweitzer's qualitative study of rural Anglo elderly in north central Oklahoma focused on how aging is affected by and reflects a particular historical and cultural context. Descendants of land-rush pioneers, these elders reflect the pioneer and frontier heritage of their ancestors. The same values and attributes of independence, self-reliance, positive attitudes, hard work, and resourcefulness that ensured survival for their ancestors in extremely difficult times are the same ones that support them in their aging years. The challenges of growing old are met with optimism and determination within the framework of the independence and self-reliance that have been an intrinsic part of their lives and heritage.

CONCLUSIONS

Research strategies that combine qualitative methods with broad survey data acquired from large-scale questionnaires and statistical analyses have the potential for adding a necessary dimension to the study of rural elderly. Using a variety of methods can enhance understanding and appreciation of the behavior and the needs of aging people, and better inform those whose role it is to provide services for the rural Anglo elderly.

References

Coward, R.T., and G.R. Lee, eds. 1985. *The Elderly in Rural Society.* Springer Series on Adulthood and Aging. New York: Springer.

Krout, J.A. 1986. *The Aged in Rural America.* Contributions to the Study of Aging, No. 5. Westport, Conn.: Greenwood Press.

Rowles, G.D. 1983. Geographical dimensions of social support in rural Appalachia. In *Aging and Milieu,* edited by G.D. Rowles and R.J. Ohta. New York: Academic Press, 111–30.

Schweitzer, M.M. 1983. *On Golden Cimarron: Aging in a Rural Community.* Paper presented at the annual meeting of the American Anthropological Association, Chicago.

Shenk, D. 1987. *Someone to Lend a Helping Hand: the Lives of Rural Older Women in Central Minnesota.* St. Cloud, Minn.: Central MN Council on Aging.

Van Willigen, J. 1989. *Gettin' Some Age on Me—Social Organization of Older People in a Rural American Community.* Lexington, Ky.: University of Kentucky Press.

Youmans, E.G., ed. 1967. *Older Rural Americans: A Sociological Perspective.* Lexington, Ky.: University of Kentucky Press.

Marjorie M. Schweitzer

S

Skin Care

Skin changes that take place as we age are the result of the aging process itself as well as the cumulative effects of environmental damage, for example, the chronic exposure to sunlight. The skin becomes less efficient, more fragile and more vulnerable to infection, tears, wounds and bruises.

PRESSURE ULCERS

The problem of pressure ulcers is of major concern because of the high cost of medical and nursing care, the high risk for complications such as sepsis which increases mortality, and the added stress placed upon the patient and family. Those most vulnerable are bed- or chairbound elderly who cannot reposition themselves. The prevalence of pressure ulcers among persons residing in institutional facilities has been studied; its prevalence in home care settings is not fully known, as research on this subject has been limited.

Definition

A pressure ulcer, also referred to as decubitus ulcer or bedsore, is damage to the skin and underlying tissue caused by unrelieved pressure. When pressure on the skin occurs, particularly over bony prominences, and is exerted without relief, the area becomes ischemic and starved of vital nutrients and oxygen.

Stages of Skin Breakdown

The severity of the skin/tissue breakdown is described by a staging system and serves as the basis for treatment protocols. According to the Clinical Practice Guidelines developed by the Agency for Health Care Policy and Research (ACHPR), U.S. Public Health Service, staging is as follows:

Stage I: Nonblanchable erythema of intact skin; the heralding lesion of skin ulceration.

Stage II: Partial thickness skin loss. The ulcer is superficial and presents clinically as an abrasion, blister or shallow crater.

Stage III: Full thickness skin loss. The ulcer presents clinically as a deep crater with or without undermining of adjacent tissue.

Stage IV: Full thickness skin loss with extensive tissue destruction or damage to muscle, bone, or supporting structures (for example, tendon or joint capsule).

Risk Factors

Risk factors that contribute to skin breakdown and development of pressure ulcers include immobility, incontinence, impaired nutritional status, and altered level of consciousness. Because these factors are frequently observed with the aging population, it becomes essential that patients admitted to a home care program be assessed and reassessed at periodic intervals. Validated assessment tools exist such as the Braden Scale and Norton Scale, and their use ensures systematic evaluation of individual risk factors, thereby assuring the basis for a care plan to preserve and maintain the patient's skin integrity.

Pressure factors. The greatest threat to skin breakdown is when the patient is unable to move independently. Conditions such as stroke, arthritis, multiple sclerosis, depression, and confusion contribute to immobility. When tissues are externally compressed the blood supply is reduced. Common pressure points susceptible to pressure ulcers are bony prominences such as the hip, ankles, heels, and vertebrae. Other sites include elbows, ribs, ears, and back of head. It should be noted that for those who sit for prolonged periods or are wheelchair-bound are extremely susceptible to this kind of breakdown at the ischial (pelvic bones) pressure point.

Physical factors. (1) Friction caused by dragging or pulling the patient across a sheet results in damage to the skin, (2) shearing which occurs when two or more layers slide on each other, and stretch and kink the blood vessels, (3) maceration caused by moisture, due to perspiration or fecal and urinary incontinence, which softens the skin and reduces its resistance.

Other factors. Malnutrition is known to interfere with wound healing and tissue repair, particularly when protein deficiency is known to exist. Medical conditions such as altered mental status, anemia, infections, peripheral vascular disease, edema, diabetes mellitus, and cancer predispose to pressure ulcer formation. Low body weight, smoking, and steroid use are also contributing factors.

Prevention

The goal for the prevention of pressure ulcers is two-fold: maintaining and improving tolerance to pressure to prevent injury, and protecting against the adverse effects of mechanical forces of pressure, friction and shear.

The skin should be regularly inspected for signs of redness; in a dark-skinned person the redness appears as a purplish hue. Redness at a pressure point is usually the first sign of a developing ulcer and warrants immediate attention.

The skin should be kept clean and dry. Hot water should be avoided and a mild soap should be used to minimize irritation. After cleansing, a moisturizing lotion is recommended, particularly if the skin is dry. Massaging over bony prominences should be avoided as this may be harmful. If moisture due to bladder or bowel incontinence cannot be controlled, underpads or briefs made of materials that absorb moisture and present a quick-drying surface to the skin should be used.

For individuals confined to bed, the body position should be changed at least every two hours with correct body alignment. Positioning devices such as pillows or foam wedges should be used to keep the bony prominences of the knees, ankles and heels from direct contact with each other or the mattress. Avoid friction forces such as dragging and pulling. Use instead proper positioning, turning and transferring techniques, involving at least two, and perhaps three or four caregivers to move the patient as efficiently as possible. Lifting devices such as a trapeze or a pull sheet are helpful in moving the patient during repositioning. Avoid elevating the head of the bed more than 30 degrees to reduce the shearing force upon the sacrum. Pressure-reducing devices such as foam, air, sheepskin and gel are available and help to prevent further injury to the skin.

Nutritional requirements must be met to insure that the intake provides the necessary nutrients, calories, and trace elements for healthy skin and wound healing. Hydration must also be maintained.

Treatment

Local treatment for pressure ulcers is essential for Stage I through IV, the goals of which are as follows:

Stage I: To prevent further skin breakdown and allow the blood supply to replenish the tissues for recovery.

Stage II: To prevent further damage and allow the top layer of the skin to recover.

Stage III: To prevent or treat infection by removing all dead tissue and allowing the tissue to granulate (fill in with new tissue).

Stage IV: To reduce and remove dead tissue to obtain a base with a good blood supply to allow tissue to granulate.

All four stages require wound cleansing and dressing. A variety of solutions and coverings are available to promote healing. A careful assessment of the patient and the condition and location of the ulcer is necessary before prescribing treatment. Application of protective ointments or sprays promote healing by lubricating the affected area and increasing the blood supply. Application of a moisture-vapor permeable occlusive dressing or a hydroactive dressing protects the area from friction and further damage, and promotes healing. Wounds with debris need more aggressive treatment by use of enzymatic agents or occlusive dressings. Surgical debridement is the quickest way to remove dead tissue and the only effective method to remove eschar (dead slough).

Measuring and recording the size of the wound once a week is recommended. If the size of the ulcer increases and there is no sign of healing, a change in the treatment plan is indicated. Along with these specific treatment protocols, all preventive measures should be observed. Positioning on the involved area should be avoided if possible. For Stage III and IV ulcers, the use of an air therapy mattress may be indicated to relieve pressure to a maximum degree.

Pressure ulcer prediction, prevention, and treatment depend on the coordinated efforts of the health care team, family, and patient. Each group needs essential information through educational programs that focus on primary, secondary and tertiary prevention. By reducing the risk of developing pressure ulcers and preventing their progression from mild to severe, a higher quality of care and cost savings can be achieved.

References

Allman, R.M. 1992. Pressure ulcers in the elderly. In *Textbook of Internal Medicine*, 2d ed. Edited by W.N. Kelley. Philadelphia: Lippincott, 2425–28.

Maklebust, J. 1987. Pressure ulcers: etiology and prevention. *Nurs Clin North Amer* 22(2):359–77.

Pajk, M. 1990. Pressure sores. *The Merck Manual of Geriatrics*. Rahway, N.J.: Merck Co., Inc., 140–50.

Panel on the Prediction and Prevention of Pressure Ulcers in Adults. 1992. *Pressure Ulcers in Adults: Prediction and Prevention*. AHCPR Pub. No. 92–0050. Rockville, Md.: Agency for Health Care Policy and Research, U.S. Public Health Service, U.S. Department of Health and Human Services.

Jennifer Boondas

Stroke

INTRODUCTION

A cerebrovascular accident (CVA or stroke) is the abrupt onset of a neurological deficit resulting from disease of one or more of the blood vessels that supply the brain, causing impaired blood supply to the brain. A stroke occurs as a result of a number of pathological processes, but the event of stroke is the same—a lack of blood (and therefore oxygen) to the brain. Manifestations of stroke are variable, and can be slight or severe, temporary or permanent, depending on the locations in the brain that have suffered damage.

The National Institute of Neurological Disorders and Stroke has developed a classification of cerebrovascular diseases. (1) Transient ischemic attack (TIA) is a brief episode of neurological deficit lasting from less than 30 minutes to 24 hours, that passes without apparent residual effects. It is estimated that of all people who have a TIA, one-third will have only the one episode, one-third will have other TIAs but will not have a completed stroke, and one-third will eventually have a completed stroke. (2) Reversible ischemic neurological deficit is characterized by a neurological deficit that remains after 24 hours but leaves no residual signs or symptoms after days or weeks. Some experts consider this to be a completed stroke with minimal to no residual effects. (3) Stroke in evolution is a progressing stroke that develops over a period of hours or days. The clinical picture is most characteristic of an enlarging intra-arterial thrombus (blood clot). Usually, an evolving stroke will continue to completion. (4) Completed stroke is one in which the neurological deficits are unchanged over a period of 2 to 3 days. An embolic stroke may have this characteristic from onset. Other than a completed stroke due to a ruptured aneurysm, a completed stroke signals readiness for more aggressive rehabilitative treatment. In the case of an aneurysm, activity may be restricted for up to four weeks to prevent further hemorrhage.

PREVALENCE AND INCIDENCE

Stroke is the third most frequent cause of death in the United States. Currently, heart disease and cancer are the first two most frequent causes. On the positive side, a 30 percent decrease in the incidence of stroke has occurred since the early 1970s, probably because of a decrease in the number of cigarette smokers, and an increase in the amount and kind of exercise performed by people of all ages. Sixty to 70 percent of strokes occur in those over 65 years of age. The incidence of first-time strokes is 500,000 per year, with one-half to one-third of these fatal. Of those who survive a first stroke, about 40 percent have moderate to severe disability and require assistance with activities of daily living (ADLs).

Stroke therefore has a significant economic impact on patients, families, and the total society. The estimated cost per year, both direct and indirect, is $14 billion. Considering the effects of stroke, prevention and control of risk factors are particularly important.

RISK FACTORS

Research findings suggest that the risk factors associated with stroke can be divided into two categories: (1) nonreversible, and (2) potentially reversible. The risk increases concomitantly with the number of risk factors in individuals. Nonreversible risk factors include gender, age, race, and heredity. Currently, men are more at risk for stroke than women, older more than younger persons, and Blacks more than Whites. There appears to be a genetic factor in terms of stroke, but the precise relationship and its relative significance have not yet been determined.

Reversible risk factors include hypertension, cardiac disease, diabetes, high serum cholesterol and hyperlipidemia, and life-style patterns. The most recent research findings indicate that the control of hypertension is the major area of prevention that can effectively decrease the incidence of stroke. Cigarette smoking and high blood cholesterol have also been shown to be major risk factors in stroke. In women, the use of oral contraceptives appears to be a risk factor.

CLASSIFICATION OF STROKES

Strokes are generally classified under two types: ischemic or hemorrhagic, as determined by the underlying pathology occurring at the time of the stroke.

Ischemic Strokes: Thrombus or Embolus

Ischemic strokes are a result of decreased blood flow to the brain because of partial or complete occlusion of an artery supplying the brain. Ischemic strokes are much more common than hemorrhagic strokes. This type of stroke can be further classified as either thrombotic or embolic. Both are a result of blood clots or plaques in the cerebral circulation. A thrombus is a blood clot or co-agulum that occurs generally as a result of hypertension or diabetes, resulting in narrowing of the lumen of the artery. Both hypertension and diabetes can cause atherosclerosis, a buildup of plaques inside the blood vessels. High cholesterol levels also cause the buildup of fatty plaques. Again, a genetic factor may play an important role in the development of atherosclerosis. Because the risk factors of hypertension, diabetes, diet, and exercise can be altered, it is important for older persons to be monitored for these health problems, to diminish the risk of stroke.

Thrombotic strokes may be heralded by particular transitory neurological symptoms such as paresthesias (abnormal sensations), paresis (decreased strength and mobility of an extremity), or aphasia (disturbance of speech/language functions). Because these symptoms are transitory, they are referred to as TIAs—transient ischemic attacks, indicating that temporary episodes of decreased blood/oxygen to the brain are occurring, but not sufficiently severe to result in a full-blown stroke. Often thrombotic strokes occur following sleep, that is, early in the morning. There is an erratic progression of signs and symptoms, based on the severity of the oxygen lack, and how quickly the brain is affected in terms of swelling. Generally, signs and symptoms reach their peak in 72 hours, when the maximum damage becomes apparent. As the swelling subsides over a period of days and weeks, improvement is noted in the patient's neurological status. With appropriate therapy and rehabilitation, maximum improvement usually occurs within 12 to 24 weeks, but additional improvement can occur up to two years post-stroke.

An embolus is a thrombus that breaks away from its primary location, usually the inside layer of the heart, and travels through the circulation. The embolus reaches a narrow point of an artery and obstructs the passage of blood (embolism), thus causing ischemic infarction. In general, diseases of the heart such as chronic atrial fibrillation, valvular disease or replacement, rheumatic heart disease, bacterial endocarditis, and atherosclerotic plaques in the arteries leading to the brain can cause emboli. Emboli are increasingly being implicated in TIAs.

Signs and symptoms of an embolic stroke are more variable than those caused by a thrombus, and often occur in younger people, if the underlying cause is rheumatic heart disease. Herald signs are not as common as in thrombotic strokes. The prognosis following embolic stroke is also more variable, and can be relatively favorable to poor, depending on the size of the embolus, where it lodges, and what areas of the brain are affected. If, for example, the embolus lodges in the main stem of the middle cerebral artery, most of the lateral cerebral hemisphere suffers damage and the prognosis is poor.

Hemorrhagic Strokes

Atherosclerosis or hypertension can result in intracranial (within the brain) bleeding, when degenerative changes that have occurred as the result of disease processes within the walls of arteries result in rupture of the wall of the artery and hemorrhage at the point of tear. The severity of the hemorrhage determines the prognosis, since the escaping blood forms a mass which then displaces the brain. When a large hemorrhage occurs, herniation of brain tissue can occur, usually resulting in coma and death. The outcome for hemorrhagic strokes is generally worse than for ischemic strokes. Modern diagnostic computerized tomography (CT) and imaging (MRI) techniques can precisely locate the area of the hemorrhage and make definitive (sometimes surgical) intervention more successful.

A subarachnoid (beneath the second and between the second and third membranes covering the brain—dura mater, arachnoid, and pia mater) hemorrhage can occur as the result of an intracranial aneurysm (ballooning defect or weakness in the wall of a vessel that may, eventually, break, allowing hemorrhage into the surrounding tissue). About a third of this type of hemorrhage occurs during sleep. Unlike other types of stroke, a massive subarachnoid hemorrhage can cause sudden death.

CONCLUSION

Strokes occur as a result of vascular problems within the brain. While the problem occurs in the brain, the cause of the problem may originate outside the brain, but always within the circulatory system. Neurological deficits that may remain following survival of stroke include both physical and mental deficits. Physical problems may involve the musculoskeletal system, the genitourinary system, and the gastrointestinal system. Mental deficits can occur in such areas as communication, sensory/perception, and emotional/psychological. Mood swings are common in stroke survivors, partly because of damage to areas in the brain and due partly to the emotional and psychological traumas that occur to individuals who suddenly find themselves dependent on others for the simplest tasks of living. Stroke, based on its suddenness and severity, can change the entire world of the individual and the family. Prevention may not eliminate the occurrence of all strokes, but it can help to decrease the current incidence.

References

Boss, B.J., J. Heath, and P.M. Sunderland. 1990. Alterations of neurologic function. In *Pathophysiology*, edited by K.L. McClance and S.E. Huether. St. Louis: Mosby Year Book.

Dawson, T. 1987. *Be Stroke Smart*. Denver, Colo.: National Stroke Association.

Kuller, L.H. 1989. Incidence of strokes in the eighties: the end of the decline of stroke? *Stroke* 20:841–43.

Lewis, S.M., and I.C. Collier. 1992. *Medical-Surgical Nursing: Assessment and Management of Clinical Problems*, 3rd ed. St. Louis: Mosby.

Toole, J.F. 1984. *Cerebrovascular Disorders*, 3rd ed. New York: Raven Press.

Whisant, J.P. 1990. Classification of cerebrovascular diseases, III. *Stroke* 21:637–76.

Ada Romaine-Davis

Suicide in the Elderly

EPIDEMIOLOGY

Although the tragedy of suicide in youth and young adults has garnered much attention in the lay and professional press, it is the elderly who are at greater risk for suicide than any other age group. There are about 12 suicides per 100,000 individuals in the United States each year. However, rates rise with age throughout the life course to a high of 28/100,000 in 80–84 year olds. Males are at higher risk than females, and whites are at higher risk than non-whites at all ages. The group at highest risk is white males 80–84 years of age, whose rate of approximately 72/100,000 is six times the nation's age adjusted rate.

Epidemiological studies have shown that cohort effects exert a powerful influence on suicide rates. For example, the age cohort born in the post-war "baby boom" has carried with it throughout life higher suicide rates than did earlier cohorts. As "baby boomers" enter late life, some experts speculate that their risk may rise further, well above the rates of our current elderly cohort. In addition, the size of the aged population will continue to expand rapidly through the first half of the twenty-first century. These factors in combination may lead to a sharp increase in the absolute number of elderly suicides in coming decades.

Suicide is a complex and multi-determined behavior, the understanding of which requires consideration of social, psychological, and biological dimensions. Although little research has been conducted to define suicide risk factors specific to later life, prospective follow-up of psychiatric patients at risk and retrospective studies of completed suicides in the general population (the psychological autopsy), provide some indications:

Social Isolation

Studies of completed suicide have shown that a higher proportion of older people who commit suicide live alone at the time of death than do younger suicide victims or community-dwelling elderly controls. Living alone contributes to suicide risk through a complex combination of social, psychological, and environmental processes. For example, living alone may increase the lethality of suicidal behavior (e.g., one who lives alone is less likely to be rescued following a self-destructive act). Among the negative psychological responses that living alone may evoke in some vulnerable older people are feelings of loneliness and fear of dependence or abandonment. Alternately, both suicidal behavior and social isolation may arise independently from a common risk factor. Chronic alcoholism, for example, both increases suicide risk and has a destructive impact on one's social network. More research is needed to clarify the role played by social and cultural factors in determining suicide risk.

Stressful Life Events

The elderly frequently face loss and life change. Research has demonstrated that older psychiatric patients experienced more stress prior to their suicide attempts than did nonsuicidal controls, whereas no such difference was evident between younger attempters and controls. The loss of spouse, other family, and friends are common events in late life, and bereavement is a significant risk factor for suicide at all ages. While elderly widowers may be at relatively lower risk than widowers in younger cohorts, the frequency of the loss of significant others in later life makes it a pressing issue for future research. Retirement and the threatened loss of autonomy (such as functional disability or impending nursing home placement) are other losses associated with late life suicide. The most commonly cited precipitant, however, is physical ill-health, which studies estimate contributed to suicide in up to 70 percent of victims aged 60 years and over. It is important to note, however, that among completed suicides, only two to four percent had a terminal physical illness, and that among people with such serious medical conditions, suicidal intent is rare in the absence of a concurrent clinical depression. In all likelihood, the association between physical illness and suicide is mediated by affective disorder, as a psychological and/or biological process.

Neurobiological Correlates

An active search is under way to identify biological markers of suicide risk, with a substantial literature demonstrating that, in mixed age samples of suicide attempters and completers, central serotonin (5HT) functioning may be altered. Replicated findings include an inverse correlation between cerebrospinal fluid (CSF) levels of the 5HT metabolite 5HIAA and aggressive, impulsive behavior in suicide attempters with depression and other diagnoses; low central nervous system concentrations of 5HT and 5HIAA in suicide victims as seen in post mortems, increased postsynaptic 5HT receptor binding, and decreased presynaptic imipramine binding. Abnormalities in other neurochemical systems, including catecholamines, opiates, and the hypothalamic-pituitary-adrenal axis have been postulated, but less rigorously studied. Only one study to date has looked specifically at the neurochemistry of suicidal elderly, finding lower CSF levels of 5HIAA in those subjects who had attempted suicide than in either nonsuicidal patients or normal age matched controls.

History of Suicide Attempts

Epidemiological data demonstrate that community based elderly have a far lower prevalence of lifetime suicide attempts than younger populations. The ratio of completed to attempted suicides rises dramatically with increasing age from as much as 1:200 in young adult women to 1:4 in the elderly. The few studies that consider the phenomenology of completed suicide across the life course have made the same observations—elderly suicides are significantly less likely than younger victims to have had a past history of suicidal behavior. Although the relative frailty and isolation from rescue of older suicidal people may in part account for these observations, it has also been demonstrated that with increasing age, suicide victims acted with greater lethality of intent. Suicidal behavior in the elderly, therefore, appears to be more malignant than in younger people.

Psychiatric Illness

No single factor can be said to "cause" suicide. Nonetheless, the findings from numerous carefully conducted, community-based psychological autopsy studies indicating that diagnosable psychopathology was present in 90–100 percent of victims suggest that psychiatric illness may be a necessary, if not sufficient, predisposing factor. These studies show affective disorder to have been present in 30–80 percent of cases, substance use disorders in up to 60 percent of cases, and schizophrenia in 2–15 percent of suicide victims. The wide range in prevalence of diagnoses is accounted for by variations in diagnostic criteria, and the use of hierarchical diagnostic strategies in some studies while others allowed more than one diagnosis per subject.

Those few studies that compared diagnosis and phenomenology as a function of age show interesting distinctions between older and younger suicide victims. Whereas substance use disorders, primary psychoses, and comorbid conditions are most common in young adulthood, alcoholism, affective disorder, and their comorbidity are characteristics of middle age suicide. In elderly suicide victims, substance abuse is less prevalent than in younger cohorts. Nonetheless, it remains a major contributor to suicidal behavior. Older persons who commit suicide frequently have abused alcohol, or prescription sedatives and painkillers. Psychotic illness and comorbid conditions are less common in young adulthood and middle age, while uncomplicated unipolar major depression is the most frequent diagnosis in late life suicide.

TREATMENT CONSIDERATIONS

Once identified as being at risk, the suicidal person should be evaluated professionally. Hotlines, emergency rooms, community mental health centers, and the private offices of mental health professionals are important resources. However, older people make disproportionately few visits for psychiatric care; less than 25 percent of elderly suicide victims had any past history of mental health contacts. On the other hand, 70 percent or more had seen their primary care provider in the last month of life. Over one-third had visited their doctor within the last week. Therefore, while elders at risk for suicide are uncommonly in psychiatric treatment, the great majority are actively receiving primary medical care.

That the elderly at highest risk for suicide have ready access to health care is reason for optimism. Major depression, the psychiatric illness with which a large majority of elderly suicide victims died, is considered a good prognostic disorder. When treated with psychotherapy and antidepressant drugs or electroconvulsive therapy, clinical depression in late life resolves in more than 75 percent of cases. As the depressive disorder remits, the suicidal crisis passes.

Education of the general public as well as primary care physicians about the symptomatic presentation and effective treatment of depression in late life may reduce the number of completed suicides in that population. Improved access of older people to mental health care will likely lead to lower rates, as will the development of biological markers of suicide risk and the more refined definition of social and psychological factors predisposing elders to take their own lives.

References

Blazer, D.G., J.R. Bachar, and K.G. Manton. 1986. Suicide in late life—review and commentary. *Journal of the American Geriatrics Society* 34:519–25.

Conwell, Y. 1993. Suicide in the elderly. In *Diagnosis and Treatment of Depression in Late-Life*, edited by L.S. Schneider, C.F. Reynolds III, B.D. Lebowitz, and A.J. Friedhoff. Washington, D.C.: American Psychiatric Press, Inc.

Kreitman, N. 1988. Suicide, age, and marital status. *Psychological Medicine* 18:121–28.

Moscicki, E.K., P. O'Carroll, D.S. Rae, B.Z. Locke, A. Roy, and D.A. Reiger. 1988. Suicide attempts in the epidemiologic catchment area study. *The Yale Journal of Biology and Medicine* 61:259–68.

National Center for Health Statistics. 1991. *Vital Statistics of the United States, 1988, Volume II, Mortality, Part A*. Washington, D.C.: Public Health Service.

Stanley, M., and B. Stanley. 1989. Biochemical studies in suicide victims. *Suicide and Life-Threatening Behavior* 19:30–42.

Yeates Conwell

T

Technology (High) in the Home

Home care is one of the fastest growing segments of the U.S. health care delivery system. This is due, in part, to the emergence and rapid growth of "high-tech" home health care: the provision in the patient's domicile of services previously reserved for the hospital. The growth in high-tech home care was a response to three main initiatives: pressure from third-party payers to decrease, or at least contain, costs; the availability of technology that could be utilized in the home; and the desire of many patients to be treated in their own homes. The increasing numbers of elderly in the population will further contribute to the increase in utilization of high-tech care in the home.

Home hemodialysis began in the early 1960s and was the first high-tech procedure used in the home. The first home infusion therapies for parenteral nutrition were used in the late 1960s. Ventilators began being used in the home in the 1970s. Despite a quarter of a century of high technology use in the home, there are still many issues to be resolved. Precise counts of the number of elderly individuals using high-tech are not available, primarily because of the different types of payment mechanisms; complete data cannot readily be compiled from all the sources. Important questions related to policy, financial, ethical, and quality issues must be addressed.

The term "high-technology" is often used without a clear definition other than a listing of services. Liebig (1988) notes that the high technology most related to health care in the home includes dialysis, ventilation, infusion, enteral and total parenteral nutrition, cardiac monitoring and defibrillation, and intravenous therapy. The problem with definitions such as this is that they do not address what we know is true of technology—it is dynamic and changing rapidly. A more generic definition, therefore, is required. Jennett (1985) operationalized high technology as being "that which is complex, expensive, restricted in availability, and for which some form of explicit rationing is required." However, as commonly used technology becomes less complex, more available, and less expensive, this definition becomes less useful. High-technology in the home is generally considered less expensive than its hospital counterpart. Fox et al. (1987) define high-tech as "intensive and complex services" with the commonality that "until recently they were available only in a hospital." High-technology home care is usually a substitute for hospital care. It most often allows for early discharge, but may occur to prevent hospitalization or following an outpatient procedure.

Perhaps a better start to defining high-tech is to look at a definition of technology. The definition must include not only the drugs, devices, and procedures used in medical and surgical care, but also the organizational and support systems in which they are provided. It is the latter part of the definition—the organizational and support systems—that are critical to the discussion of high-tech home care.

Home care can be conceptualized as a model with three components: the home, the clinical service, and the supply service. High-tech home care requires a team effort on the part of those three components: the home environment, including the patient and the caregivers; the clinical service, which provides the nurses, therapists, and other home health aides to care for the patient; and the supply service, which provides the equipment and staff. On the continuum from no technology to high technology, it is difficult to determine exactly where high tech begins. From the supply service, high-technology care involves a demand not only for equipment and supplies, but for personnel to provide the required training and maintenance. From the clinical service, the knowledge and skills of professionals are needed, in addition to the care provided by paraprofessionals. From the home side, there must be willingness and ability to learn skills that are not inherent to the layman. The definition, however, includes more than just the components noted above. There is also a certain amount of risk, largely due to the fact that most of the procedures are invasive and the patient has a higher acuity level. To be at the high technology end of the continuum, a mix of all these components is needed.

Several factors must be considered in determining whether or not high-technology home care is appropriate.

1. *The Patient.* First, is the patient stable enough to be treated in the home environment? Does the patient want to be home? Does the elderly patient have cognitive disabilities in addition to needing complex care? Is custodial care also needed?

2. *Home Environment.* Does the home have adequate facilities to provide for the necessary equipment? This includes space, electricity, refrigeration, running water, or other physical aspects. It may also refer to sanitation or cleanliness within the home.

3. *Caregivers.* A common problem in high-technology home care of the elderly is that the caregivers themselves are elderly. High technology adds to the caregiver burden. Leader and Liebig (1988) note that "extended periods of high-tech caregiving can lead to permanent physical and mental health problems for caregivers." Stiller (1988) found that the abilities and problems of the family caregivers were more important in determining the success of home care than the specific high-tech procedure that was required. Various questions must be asked: Are there one or more persons with the interest, skill, and knowledge to provide care for the patient? Can these persons be available on a 24-hour basis? What other demands are placed on their time? This assessment must be made not just initially, but if high-tech care progresses over time, must be repeated to assure continuing availability of appropriate caregivers.

4. *Supply Service.* Is there a supplier in the area who provides the needed technology? Does the supplier have adequate staff to provide teaching and follow-up? What provisions have been made for emergencies? How will the high-tech equipment be maintained?

5. *Clinical Service.* Does the clinical agency have adequate professional and nonprofessional staff to meet the needs of the patient? Is there a relationship between the supplier and the clinical service? How available are the personnel from the agency? Does the staff have the advanced knowledge and skills to work safely with the technology?

6. *Payment Mechanism.* The technology to provide for home care has developed faster than the payment mechanisms to provide for it. Is the patient eligible for Medicare or Medicaid? Is there any private insurance? What services will be covered? Fox et al. (1987) suggest that we will not see the projected growth in high-tech home care until payment mechanisms are in place to support that growth.

7. *Quality.* Will the care provided in the home be of higher or lower quality than could be provided in an institutional setting? Responsibility for the home care patient tends to be very fragmented. The standards that do exist tend to stress process and structure, but not outcomes. The payers and the prospective and current users of high-tech home care need answers to quality concerns.

8. *Liability.* Issues of liability are of concern to physicians, health care professionals, clinical agencies, and suppliers. Providers can decrease their risk of liability by carefully assessing their overall involvement in high-tech home care, as well as the particular challenges related to each patient. Are there caregivers who can support the high-tech care? Is the home environment acceptable? What will happen in emergency situations, for example, electric outage? Do the home care agency and supplier have adequate resources? The supplier may be held liable for problems with the equipment, inadequate support regarding its usage,

staffing problems, or problems with set-up, maintenance, or emergency back-up of the equipment. Both the clinical service and the supply service need adequate numbers of appropriately prepared staff.

9. *Ethics*. High technology home care requires large amounts of capital and labor. Should everyone be eligible to receive high-tech care? More specifically, in an era of limited resources and continuing focus on cost containment, should the elderly be entitled to have high-tech home care? Who should decide: the patient, the payer, the family, or someone else? Do patients and their families have enough information on high-tech care to make the right decisions for them?

THE FUTURE

Speaking from an international perspective and referring to both high and low technology, van Beekum and Banta (1989) note that "the immediate problem is the lack of planned, coherent, integrated home care systems capable of incorporating new technology and assuring its wise use." Suppliers, and not just home health agencies, need to be covered by federal Medicare regulations. Data that give accurate numbers of high-tech home care users must be collected so that payment issues can be addressed and future costs can be predicted. Finally, standards of quality care must be established for both the clinical and supply services. All of these issues must be resolved before high-tech home care can move forward.

References

Fox, D.M., K.S. Andersen, A.E. Benjamin, and L.J. Dunatov. 1987. Intensive home health care in the United States: financing as technology. *International Journal of Technology Assessment in Health Care* 3:561–73.

Jennett, B. 1985. High technology medicine: how defined and how regarded. *Milbank Memorial Fund Quarterly/Health and Society* 63(1):141–73.

Leader, S., and P. Liebig. 1988. High-tech home care: a reexamination. *Caring* 7(9): 5–7.

Liebig, P.S. 1988. The use of high technology for health care at home: issues and implications. *Medical Instrumentation* 22(5):222–25.

Stiller, S.B. 1988. Success and difficulty in high-tech home care. *Public Health Nursing* 5(2):68–75.

van Beekum, T., and H.D. Banta. 1989. Possibilities and problems in the development of home care technology. *Health Policy* 12:301–7.

Judith A. Feustle

Technology (Low) in the Home

"Low-technology" home care is an interesting concept, and one that had virtually no meaning before the presence of "high technology" in home care. Low technology is a term that undergoes continuous changes in meaning, and it is difficult to fix the definition at a certain point in time. Jennett (1985) says that "today's high technology may be tomorrow's low technology." Even currently, some technology which is considered to be "low tech" in the hospital environment, for example, infusion pumps, is considered to be "high tech" in the home environment.

HISTORY OF LOW TECHNOLOGY

Knollmueller (1985), in providing an overview of the use of technology, notes that "until the 1960s, nurses rendering care in the home assumed that a piece of equipment or certain supplies required for treatment procedures were to be improvised or invented by the nurse rather than to be purchased or rented commercially." She describes home-made equipment, home-prepared solutions, and home sterilization as examples. In 1965 when Medicare was started, a rental benefit for durable medical equipment (DME) was included. Spiegel (1987) summarized the Health Care Financing Administration's definition of DME as "equipment that can withstand repeated use, is primarily and customarily medical in nature, is generally not useful to a person who does not have an illness or injury, and is appropriate for use in the home." The vendor or supplier of DME becomes an added member of the home health care team.

Low technology home care involves the use of durable medical equipment. Common examples are hospital beds, commodes, walkers, wheelchairs, and canes. The equipment is not considered to be complex, and its use is easily mastered. Durable medical equipment is often used to assist the patient with activities of daily living and may be either rented or purchased, depending on the supplier, the payer, and the needs of the user.

Like high technology, low technology is a term that undergoes continuous change in meaning and is therefore difficult to define. One way to define low technology home care is by considering what it is not. Clearly, it is not the opposite of high-technology home care. A few examples will clarify this. Cost of equipment does not differentiate between high and low technology home care. A hospital bed, which is considered to be low technology, costs far more than an infusion pump, which is considered to be high technology in home use. Nor can it be said that "low-tech" care places less stress on the family or is less time-consuming. Caring for the patient with Alzheimer's disease does not require high technology, yet the "36-hour day" experienced by the family caregivers of those patients is a reflection of both the amount of time spent and the amount of stress. Low technology care could be thought of as palliative, used to keep the patient comfortable, while high technology care is thought of as more aggressive. Yet hospice patients, whose care could be defined as palliative, may use either high or low technology, depending on the situation.

When considering home care, there are three basic components: the home environment, including the patient and the caregivers; the clinical service, which may provide nurses or other home health aides to care for the patient; and the supply service, which may provide equipment and/or staff. In low technology home care, the supply service provides the DME, but usually does not need to provide any personnel support. The clinical service may provide care by para-professionals, or may not be involved at all. Liebig (1988) feels that low technology care at home is within the control of the family in its natural environment. Low technology care is seen as causing less risk for the patient than high technology care.

While low technology may be seen on a continuum with no technology at one end and high technology at the other, it is possible to picture the same patient using both low and high technology. Kohrman (1991) actually uses the term "low technology" in describing the care needed by high-tech patients. Although referring to children, the parallel to the elderly is clear. Kohrman says: "The stabilized technology-dependent child, for example, one totally or partially ventilator-dependent, needs low-technology services and care—education, the reassurances of family and familiars, sympathy and encouragement—all essential for adaptation to living and growing with a disability."

Liebig (1988) notes that the home is traditionally regarded as a low technology environment. Orleans and Orleans (1985) present an interesting view in which they consider the physical structures of the house itself to be the low technology. They suggest, for instance, that architects concern themselves with overall functional abilities, instead of architectural revisions for specific groups of disabled individuals. Thus, functional difficulties such as loss of balance, decreased vision and/or hearing that may occur with various neurological disorders also occur with normal aging. Changes such as replacing doorknobs with lever-type hardware make sense not only for the "disabled," but for the increasing elderly population in the United States. The authors suggest that these and other similar changes, perhaps built into the initial design of houses and other buildings, would benefit many people.

As long as payment mechanisms provide for durable medical equipment, and as long as DME primarily supports activities of daily living, the use of low technology home care for the elderly will continue to grow. The increasing elderly population and ongoing pressures to decrease length of stay in hospitals will further ensure that this trend persists.

References

Jennett, B. 1985. High technology medicine: how defined and how regarded. *Milbank Memorial Fund Quarterly/Health and Society* 63(1):141–73.

Knollmueller, R.N. 1985. The growth and development of home care: from no-tech to high-tech. *Caring* 4(1):3–8.

Kohrman, A.F. 1991. Psychological issues. In *Delivering High Technology Home Care*, edited by M.J. Mehlman and S.J. Younger. New York: Springer Publishing Company, 160–78.

Liebig, P.S. 1988. The use of high technology for health care at home: issues and implications. *Medical Instrumentation* 22(5):222–25.

Orleans, M., and P. Orleans. 1985. High and low technology: sustaining life at home. *International Journal of Technology Assessment in Health Care* 1:353–63.

Spiegel, A.D. 1987. *Home Health Care*, 2d ed. Owings Mills, Md.: National Health Publishing, 80.

Judith A. Feustle

Temporal Arteritis

Temporal arteritis (inflammation of the arteries), a systemic inflammatory vasculitis (inflammation of the blood vessels), is also known as giant cell, cranial, or granulomatous arteritis.

The inflammatory process involves primarily the arteries that branch from the upper aorta, especially the ones that supply the extracranial (outside the skull) structures of the head. The most commonly affected are the temporal arteries, hence the name of the syndrome. However, almost any artery in the body, as well as veins, can become involved in the vasculitic process. Temporal arteritis occurs almost exclusively in people over the age of 50. The average age at onset is about 70 years. Women are affected more than men. The syndrome is also more common in persons of European origin and is rare in blacks and Asians.

Neither the etiology (cause) of the syndrome nor its pathogenesis (how it happens) have been clearly elucidated. Patients who suffer from temporal arteritis frequently complain of headaches, scalp tenderness, visual problems, including double vision or blindness, and jaw or tongue pain when chewing. Overall (systemic) symptoms can include anorexia (poor appetite), weight loss, fatigue, and fever. The onset of symptoms may be gradual or abrupt, but in the majority of individuals the symptoms, especially the systemic ones, have been present for weeks or months before the diagnosis is made.

A separate group of musculo-skeletal symptoms, present in about 50 percent of those with temporal arteritis, is referred to as polymyalgia rheumatica. These symptoms include pain of an aching quality and morning stiffness, usually gradual in onset, involving shoulders, upper arms, hips, thighs, neck, and torso. The symmetry and proximal location of the pain are characteristic of polymyalgia rheumatica, as is the severity of subjective (felt by the patient) symptoms when compared to usually minor, if any, objective findings seen on physical examination. About 50 percent of patients with temporal arteritis also have symptoms of polymyalgia rheumatica while only about 15 percent of patients with polymyalgia rheumatica are found to have evidence of arteritis.

Headache is the most common symptom of temporal arteritis and is present in two-thirds of patients. It is frequently the initial symptom. Headaches of temporal arteritis are usually, but not always, severe and boring in nature, and are often present in the temporal regions. The scalp tenderness, another symptom of temporal arteritis, is also most commonly felt in the temporal areas, but may be diffuse. Visual disturbances are usually sudden in onset and may be transient or permanent. Visual loss (blindness) is the most severe form of visual involvement in patients with the syndrome.

Typical findings on physical examination of these patients include tenderness and erythema (redness) over the temporal areas, with or without palpable nodules. There may or may not be an associated decrease in temporal artery pulsations, and absence of peripheral pulses if the distal arteries are also affected. Patients with temporal arteritis may appear ill or wasted, and they may be pale or febrile. Persons with accompanying polymyalgia rheumatica may have significant immobility because of pain and stiffness.

The majority of patients with temporal arteritis have abnormal results of several blood tests. Erythrocyte (red blood cell) sedimentation rate is classically, but not universally, elevated. In about 1 to 2 percent of patients, the sedimentation rate is normal or only slightly elevated. Frequently, the sedimentation rate seems to be disproportionately high for the clinical findings. The higher the sedimentation rate, the more likely the diagnosis of temporal arteritis. Anemia is also common among these patients. Although its presence is not specific for temporal arteritis, anemia, when present, usually correlates well with the degree of systemic inflammation.

The definitive test for temporal arteritis is a temporal artery biopsy (surgical resection of a portion of one or both temporal arteries), with microscopic examination of the tissue performed by a pathologist. The presence of granulomas with or without giant cells (a positive biopsy) is diagnostic of the syndrome. A positive biopsy is very helpful, since it firmly establishes the diagnosis and justifies the initiation of a fairly toxic therapy with large doses of steroids for up to a year. Unfortunately, a positive yield for temporal arteritis in unilateral temporal artery biopsy is only about 60 percent. Performing a contralateral biopsy may allow the physician to make a diagnosis in an additional 15 percent. Some investigators recommend performing simultaneous bilateral biopsies in all cases of suspected temporal arteritis.

Overall, a histologic (microscopic) confirmation of the syndrome is possible in only up to 80 percent of patients, which implies that a negative biopsy does not rule out the disease. Thus, one may still consider instituting empiric therapy with high dose corticosteroids in selected patients with negative biopsies whose presentation strongly suggests temporal arteritis. Favorable response to this therapy may confirm the diagnosis in these more questionable cases. Steroids used in temporal arteritis eliminate the underlying pathology (vasculitis) and, in addition to relieving the symptoms, prevents the irreversible vascular complications such as stroke and blindness.

The usual dose of prednisone used to treat temporal arteritis is 60 to 80 mg in a single morning dose. This regimen is continued for several weeks (usually a month), at which point the patient is re-evaluated clinically and with laboratory studies. By this time all abnormalities should have resolved and, in fact, the majority of patients experience a clinical remission within 10 to 14 days of initiation of treatment. When the disease is clinically inactive, prednisone is gradually tapered over several months until the drug may be stopped completely, usually within one year.

The prognosis for patients with temporal arteritis is generally very good. The recovery rate is almost always complete and long-term sequelae are rare. The main concern in treated patients is the long-term toxicity of the steroid preparations, so that follow-up is mandatory over months or even years.

References

Bleecker, M.L., and C.J. Meyd. 1993. Temporal arteritis. In *Principles of Ambulatory Medicine*, 3rd ed. Edited by L.R. Barker, J.R. Burton, and P.D. Zieve. Baltimore: Williams & Wilkins, 1083.

Kelley, W.N., ed. 1992. *Textbook of Internal Medicine*, 2d ed. Philadelphia: Lippincott, 960.

Norris, T.E. 1994. Temporal arteritis. In *Family Medicine: Principles and Practice*, 4th ed. Edited by R.B. Taylor. New York: Springer-Verlag, 907.

Anna M. Plichta

Thyroid Gland Diseases

Perhaps one of the most misunderstood glands in the body is the thyroid. Weighing between 15 and 25 grams, this H-shaped organ overlies the windpipe and is responsible for much of the way the body feels, looks, and acts. Working under stimulation from TSH (thyroid stimulating hormone), a hormone produced by the pituitary gland, a master gland lying at the base of the brain, the thyroid produces two major forms of hormone necessary for one's well-being: thyroxine, otherwise known as T_4, and triiodothyronine, or T_3. The "4" and "3" refer to the number of iodine molecules attached to the hormone's structure. T_3 is also produced as T_4 circulates throughout the body and loses one iodine as enzymes located in muscles, the liver, and other organs work to keep a carefully controlled balance. Since T_3 is 3 to 5 times more potent than T_4, the body is constantly deciding how to balance these hormones in relation to need.

TOO LITTLE OR TOO MUCH

When something goes wrong and the thyroid fails to produce sufficient quantities of thyroid hormone, hypothyroidism results. Hyperthyroidism, on the other hand, occurs when too much thyroid hormone is produced.

LABORATORY TESTS

The best way to know whether the thyroid is functioning normally is to measure circulating levels of thyroid hormone by means of a simple blood test. In general, the serum TSH test is the best way to see if the thyroid is producing sufficient amounts of hormone. TSH is elevated whenever the body senses that not enough thyroid hormone is present. Hyperthyroidism is best determined by directly measuring circulating levels of T_4. In rare cases, circulating levels of T_3 will be elevated despite normal T_4 values, and a direct measure of T_3 will confirm the suspicion of hyperthyroidism.

Because abnormalities of the thyroid gland may masquerade as other problems and thus are commonly overlooked until late, it has been recommended that thyroid tests be included as part of any complete physical examination for persons over the age of 50 or at any time that the health care provider suspects that a problem with the thyroid gland may exist. People should feel free to discuss with the health care professional whether any problem they may be having might be due to a thyroid abnormality.

HYPOTHYROIDISM

Hypothyroidism may manifest itself in a number of ways. Many persons complain of a general lack of energy, not being able to do things they were previously accustomed to do easily. Skin may feel dry; nails may become brittle; and hair may become more sparse and coarse. The voice may sound raspy. Frequently, a weight gain may be noted and constipation is a common occurrence. As the thyroid continues to produce insufficient quantities of thyroid hormone, more serious problems may result, such as heart failure, memory loss, and even coma. Because so many of the symptoms of hypothyroidism resemble those of other diseases or of the aging process itself, this condition unfortunately is often under-reported and misdiagnosed. Once hypothyroidism has been diagnosed, treatment is simple. A daily oral replacement dose of thyroid hormone (thyroxine; T_4) is all that is needed to restore one's usual health.

One of the oldest therapies for persons who needed to take thyroid hormone was an extract of ground-up thyroid glands from animals, most commonly the cow and pig. Because of variations among various batches of this medication and because this medication contains all of the thyroid's hormones, some of which are viewed as being potentially problematic, a synthetic version of thyroid hormone, L-thyroxine (T_4), has been developed. L-thyroxine is currently recommended by the American Thyroid Association as the treatment of choice for persons with hypothyroidism. This medication is available in many dosages and provides a constant blood level if taken as prescribed. It should be taken once daily and only under the direction of a physician. Dosages are individually adjusted and will require laboratory monitoring (blood test) to confirm that the correct dose is being prescribed. Although USP Thyroid can continue to meet specific needs, it is not viewed as being as reliable or as safe in the long run as L-thyroxine. As with any specific treatment, however, a frank discussion with the health care provider should take place to discuss all treatment options and their inherent benefits and risks.

HYPERTHYROIDISM

Excessive production of thyroid hormone, or hyperthyroidism, is an abnormal state that occurs most commonly in women during their 20s, 30s, and 40s. Despite this, it may occur at any age and men are not immune. In fact, elderly men and women appear to be affected equally as often. The most common cause of hyperthyroidism is Graves' disease. This is associated with a diffusely enlarged thyroid gland and is thought to result from an abnormality within one's own immune system. While Graves' disease may spontaneously remit in some people, more commonly medical treatment will be required. Hyperthyroidism may also result from an abnormal nodule, or growth, within the thyroid gland that continues to produce excessive amounts of thyroid hormone regardless of how high the circulating levels may be. This is a more common finding in elderly persons, and treatment will be required in almost all cases.

Hyperthyroidism may present in any number of ways. In general, persons feel irritable, nervous, and anxious. A significant weight loss may be noted despite an increase in one's daily food consumption. Frequent bowel movements, the presence of a tremor, and smooth skin, particularly over the elbows, are often tips that something is not right. The eyes may feel sandy or gritty, and tearing is common. A protuberance of the eyeball itself may also occur. A rapid pulse, the feeling of palpitations, and trouble paying attention are also common signs and symptoms.

With age, these symptoms become less reliable and in fact hyperthyroidism is a great masquerader for other problems in the elderly. Elderly persons who are hyperthyroid frequently look depressed. Significant weight loss is common in association with a poor appetite. A worsening of pre-existing heart problems may alert the physician that the thyroid may be producing too much hormone, but more frequently symptoms are dismissed as being due to "old age."

Treatment of hyperthyroidism should begin as soon as the diagnosis has been confirmed. In most cases, medication will be prescribed to be taken by mouth. This will return the excessively high level of circulating thyroid hormone to normal within a few weeks. Depending on the cause of the hyperthyroidism, treatment may also include the administration of radioactive iodine by mouth, or surgery. In all cases, treatment must be individualized and performed under the guidance of a skilled physician.

SUMMARY

In cases of thyroid problems, although diagnosis is often delayed, relatively simple treatments are available that can alleviate troublesome symptoms and allow the older person to live much more comfortably. Elderly persons and caregivers should persist in delineating signs and symptoms that affect the individual, which may result in earlier diagnosis and treatment of an underlying thyroid problem.

References

Berg, D., L. Cantwell, G. Heudebert, and J.L. Sebastian, eds. 1993. *Handbook of Primary Care Medicine*. Philadelphia: Lippincott, 541–56.

Gregerman, R.I. 1991. Thyroid disorders. In *Principles of Ambulatory Medicine*, 3d ed. Edited by L.R. Barker, J.R. Burton, and P.D. Zieve. Baltimore: Williams & Wilkins, 952–77.

Harper, M.B., and E.J. Mayeaux Jr. 1994. Thyroid disease. In *Family Medicine: Principles and Practice*, 4th ed. Edited by R.B. Taylor. New York: Springer-Verlag.

Solomon, D.H. 1992. Thyroid disorders in the elderly. In *Textbook of Internal Medicine*, 2d ed. Edited by W.N. Kelley. Philadelphia: Lippincott, 2366–69.

Steven R. Gambert

U

Urinary Incontinence

Urinary incontinence (involuntary urine loss) is a major clinical problem that affects all age groups, but is particularly common among older adults. As many as one in three community-dwelling elderly have some degree of urinary incontinence (UI). Involuntary urine loss is twice as prevalent among women as among men. Among homebound individuals, prevalence rates as high as 53 percent have been reported and this condition often contributes to the decision to place homebound individuals in long-term care facilities.

The economic cost of UI is staggering. In the community, more than $10 billion a year are spent on direct costs related to urinary incontinence. Unfortunately, less that 0.5 percent of this money is spent on evaluation and treatment of the problem. This is true despite the fact that in the majority of cases, urinary incontinence can be cured or significantly improved. Data on home health care agencies indicate that from 1974 to 1986, urinary incontinence was among the ten leading principal diagnoses of people receiving home care, and fourth in total home care Medicare charges.

Despite numerous articles written by nurses and others describing the evaluation and management of UI in outpatient and long-term care, little of this knowledge has been applied to the home setting. Typically, home nursing care for incontinence has focused on skin protection, advice about pads/undergarments, catheters, and encouragement of toileting rather than on systematic assessment and treatment. However, the methods are available and preliminary work has begun. One early study described the successful implementation of behavioral treatments in homebound patients by nurses utilizing habit training, pelvic muscle exercises, and biofeedback. Currently, the authors are conducting a study funded by the National Institute for Nursing Research from 1992–1997 to evaluate the use of behavioral therapies in the treatment of UI in homebound older adults. This study focuses on men and women 60 years of age and older who are homebound. The behavioral treatments include the use of biofeedback, assisted pelvic muscle exercises for persons who are able to learn new skills, and prompted voiding for subjects who have memory problems. The preliminary findings are very encouraging for the successful use of these treatment strategies in the home.

TYPES OF INCONTINENCE

Acute Incontinence

Urinary incontinence is generally classified as either acute (transient) or chronic (persistent). It is estimated that one-third of the cases of incontinence seen among community-dwelling older adults are acute, while the remaining two-thirds are chronic. Acute incontinence has a sudden onset, is generally associated with some medical or surgical problem, and generally resolves when the underlying cause is corrected.

Chronic Incontinence

Persistent incontinence is not related to an acute illness. It continues over time, often becoming worse. Major types of persistent incontinence include stress, urge, overflow, and functional incontinence. These types of incontinence can occur in combination, causing mixed incontinence.

Stress incontinence. In stress incontinence involuntary loss of urine occurs as the result of a sudden increase in intra-abdominal pressure. Individuals with stress incontinence leak urine with physical exertion such as coughing, sneezing, laughing, lifting, exercise, and changing position.

Urge incontinence. Urge incontinence typically causes involuntary urine loss following a sudden urge to void. Urgency and involuntary urine loss can be precipitated by the sound of running water, cold weather, or the sight of a toilet.

Overflow incontinence. Urine leakage occurs from a chronically full bladder.

Functional incontinence. In functional incontinence, involuntary urine loss occurs as a result of inability or unwillingness to toilet appropriately. It can be the result of physical, mental, psychological, or environmental factors.

TREATMENT OF URINARY INCONTINENCE

There are a variety of treatment measures available for urinary incontinence including behavioral interventions, medications, and surgery. The choice of therapy depends on the type of incontinence and patient characteristics.

Behavioral Interventions

In 1988 the National Institutes of Health held a consensus conference to review the current status of knowledge on urinary incontinence. They stated that generally the least invasive or dangerous procedures should be tried first and that for many forms of incontinence, this means behavioral techniques. These techniques are especially well suited for the homebound patient. For many of these patients, co-existing medical conditions preclude the use of other interventions or increase the risk of adverse effects. Behavioral interventions are free of side effects and are effective for patients with stress, urge, or functional incontinence. The most appropriate behavioral intervention depends on the type of incontinence and the patient's cognitive status.

Cognitively Intact

Behavioral interventions used in cognitively intact patients include bladder retraining and pelvic floor muscle exercises. These interventions may be used alone or in combination. Bladder retraining consists of gradual expansion of intervals between voids. Patients are asked to postpone voiding until the scheduled time, voiding by the clock rather than each time they get an urge. This procedure is most useful for patients with urge incontinence and frequent urination.

Pelvic floor muscle exercises consist of alternating contraction and relaxation of the muscles of the pelvic floor. Diminished pelvic floor muscle strength is often related to urinary incontinence. Correctly performed pelvic floor muscle exercises will strengthen the muscles, allowing the patient to voluntarily use them to prevent urinary accidents.

Clinicians often use verbal feedback during digital examination of the rectum or vagina to help patients identify their pelvic floor muscles. Many patients are not able to identify the appropriate pelvic floor muscles and need additional help in identifying and learning to use them. These patients will often benefit from pelvic floor muscle feedback.

Biofeedback is not a treatment in itself, but is a technique used to help patients identify and use their pelvic floor muscles to prevent involuntary urine loss. During biofeedback, the patient is given immediate auditory and/or visual feedback of pelvic floor muscle contractions.

After training with biofeedback or verbal feedback, the patient must practice the pelvic floor muscle exercises at home. Once patients master the exercises, they are taught strategies to prevent involuntary urine loss.

Cognitively Impaired

The techniques described previously (bladder retraining, pelvic floor muscle exercises, and biofeedback) require active patient involvement. Treating urinary incontinence in individuals with cognitive impairment requires the use of other behavioral techniques that are caregiver, rather than patient, dependent. These include techniques such as habit training, patterned urge response therapy, and prompted voiding. The success of these techniques is in large part dependent on the availability and motivation of the caregiver.

In habit training, the patient is toileted on a regular, pre-set schedule. Patterned urge response training (PURT) uses an individualized toileting schedule based on an intense baseline assessment of the patient's normal voiding pattern. Once the patient's normal voiding pattern is established, he/she is toileted at these times. Although still a caregiver-dependent therapy, in prompted voiding there is more active patient involvement. The goal is to increase patient awareness of the need to toilet and, it is hoped, to increase the frequency of self-initiated toileting. The patient is approached on a regular schedule, asked if he/she is wet or dry, and then prompted to toilet.

PHARMACOLOGIC THERAPY

Although urinary incontinence generally responds well to behavioral interventions, and are considered the safest initial therapy, in some cases pharmacological treatment is indicated. The type of medications used will depend on the type of incontinence. Drugs with anticholinergic or bladder smooth muscle relaxant properties can be used to treat incontinence. These drugs can produce bothersome anticholinergic side effects (e.g., dry mouth and constipation), and can precipitate urinary retention in some patients.

Drugs that increase urethral resistance are sometimes used in the treatment of stress incontinence. Research findings on the effectiveness of these drugs are mixed, with some studies reporting good results and some reporting only modest benefits.

SURGICAL TREATMENT

Surgical treatment is indicated if evaluation demonstrates that an anatomic obstruction such as prostatic hypertrophy or pelvic prolapse is causing the incontinence, or if behavioral interventions are ineffective.

HOLISTIC APPROACH

Successful treatment of UI requires a holistic approach that includes attention to adequate fluid intake, elimination of caffeine, prevention of constipation, and good skin care. For short-term use in conjunction with other treatment measures, pads or garments provide convenience and comfort. They are, however, expensive for long-term use and can be associated with skin rashes and breakdown if not changed frequently. They should not be used as a substitute for the evaluation and treatment of incontinence.

CONCLUSION

Urinary incontinence is a prevalent problem among homebound older adults, but preliminary research indicates that most of these individuals can be successfully treated utilizing low-risk behavioral interventions.

References

Agency for Health Care Policy and Research. 1992. *Clinical Practice Guidelines, Urinary Incontinence in Adults*. Washington, D.C.: U.S. Department of Health and Human Services.

Hu, T. 1990. Impact of urinary incontinence on health care costs. *J Amer Geriatric Society* 38:292–95.

McDowell, B.J., and K.L. Burgio. 1992. Urinary elimination. In *Gerontologic Nursing: Care of the Frail Elderly*, edited by M.M. Burke and M.B. Walsh. St. Louis: Mosby Year Book.

McDowell, B.J., Burgio, K.L., Dombrowski, M., Locher, J.L., and E. Rodriguez. 1992. An interdisciplinary approach to the assessment and behavioral treatment of urinary incontinence in geriatric outpatients. *J Amer Geriatric Soc* 38:265–72.

Ouslander, J.G. 1992. Incontinence in the elderly. In *Textbook of Internal Medicine*, 2d ed. Edited by W.N. Kelley. Philadelphia: Lippincott, 2404–7.

Rose, M.A., Smith, J.B., Smith, D., and D. Newman. 1990. Behavioral management of urinary incontinence in homebound older adults. *Home Health Care Nurse* 8(5): 10–15.

Joan McDowell and Sandra Engberg

V

Vision Impairment

THE PROBLEM

The ability to see is usually taken for granted until vision loss begins to disrupt everyday living. Elderly people with vision loss can become functionally impaired. They become dependent on others in the performance of daily activities such as preparing meals, doing housework, taking medication, getting around outdoors, driving, or using public transportation. Their participation in hobbies or leisure time activities such as reading, watching TV, painting, and needlework is reduced or discontinued. Inability to function independently has a detrimental effect on self-esteem and personal pleasure. Vision loss in one or both eyes is often attributed to eye diseases that occur more frequently with advancing age. Cataracts, glaucoma, diabetic retinopathy, and macular degeneration are the primary causes of vision loss. They are progressive disorders, but early diagnosis and treatment can prevent or slow the deterioration.

Vision involves two components—the eye and the brain. The eye is a complex structure that has the capacity to form an image on the retina. This image is converted into electrical impulses that are transmitted along the optic nerve to the area of the brain which is concerned with vision. Vision impairment occurs when the normal vision process is disrupted.

CATARACTS

A cataract is the loss of transparency of the lens behind the iris (the colored portion of the eye). It develops gradually without pain or discomfort. As the lens transparency diminishes, the clarity of vision is progressively lost. If only slightly cloudy, the lens can still function with little or no difficulty, but if the opacity is large in size and density, vision becomes blurred. As less light reaches the retina, the individual will complain that light is never bright enough for reading or close work. Night driving becomes a problem because the opacity in the lens causes scattering of light rays from oncoming headlights, causing "halos" around lights. Also, prescription glasses are not much help in overcoming the problem.

Once a cataract develops, there is no way to restore the transparency of the lens. Nor is there a way to prevent the formation of cataracts. Cataracts in the elderly are so common that it is often viewed as a normal process of aging. For persons over 65, there is some degree of opacity, usually minor and confined to the edge of the lens. By age 75, the opacities progress and vision deterioration is noticed. If the cataract is allowed to grow in size and density, vision will be reduced to the point where only light and motion are perceived. Ultimately vision is lost completely. To restore refracting power of the eye, the lens must be surgically removed. There are three options available to the individual: (1) an intraocular lens may be inserted in the eye, (2) the person may use prescribed cataract glasses, or (3) contact lenses. With new developments in microsurgery, the surgical procedure is safe and almost always successful, and the trauma of surgery is significantly reduced. Lens implant is the option of choice. Although it provides excellent distant vision, most people will need reading or bifocal lenses for close vision following the surgery.

GLAUCOMA

Normally, minimal pressure from fluid (aqueous humor), which bathes and nourishes the lens and cornea in the front of the eye, is required to maintain the shape of the eyeball. When the intraocular pressure rises, tiny nerve fibers that make up the optic nerve are destroyed. Prolonged pressure deteriorates the field of vision and, if not halted in time, leads to tunnel vision and blindness. This is the nature of glaucoma. Vision loss is permanent and in no way can it be restored.

The most common form of glaucoma is chronic open-angle, which rarely occurs before age 40. It develops slowly over a period of time. Symptoms are not apparent until late in the disease when the affected person becomes aware of vision loss. Fortunately, chronic glaucoma can be detected by regular routine eye examinations that include (1) applanation tonometry by which eye pressure is measured, (2) examination of the retina from optic nerve abnormalities, and (3) visual field testing for subtle changes in peripheral vision.

Although the underlying cause for chronic glaucoma is not fully understood, it can be effectively controlled with prescribed eye drops and oral medication that reduce the pressure within the eye. In some cases, laser treatment or surgery may be indicated. Loss of vision can be prevented most of the time provided the condition is detected and treated early, before damage to the optic nerve occurs.

MACULAR DEGENERATION

A major cause of central vision loss is macular degeneration. The condition affects the tiny critical part of the retina, the macula, which is responsible for the sharp central vision that is needed for reading, for performing fine close-up tasks such as sewing, and for recognizing faces. When this area of the retina undergoes deterioration, gradual blurring or distortion of vision occurs which is most noticeable when reading.

Macular degeneration is divided into two types: dry and wet. The dry form, the most common type, is caused by a slow breakdown or thinning of the macula. In the early stage, good vision is maintained for many years. In the wet form, vision changes occur quickly. Straight lines become crooked and vision is distorted and blurred. This is the result of abnormal blood vessels that grow under the retina and fluid leakage or bleeding occurs. Nerve tissue is destroyed and is replaced by scar tissue. Unfortunately, the dry type can progress to the more severe wet type. Also, if one eye is affected by this condition, at a later time, visual problems are likely to occur in the other eye.

Macular degeneration does not cause total blindness because side or peripheral vision is not affected. The condition can be detected early if periodic eye examinations are performed by an ophthalmologist. Early diagnosis and treatment make it possible to seal off any leakage with a laser beam and thus prevent further damage and further vision loss.

DIABETIC RETINOPATHY

Diabetes mellitus, a metabolic disorder, can affect the eyes and cause visual impairment. This complication, known as retinopathy, begins with the deterioration of the small vessels in the retina which may balloon, and leak fluid or blood. This causes swelling of the retina or deposits of exudates. Sometimes, the leakage collects in the macula. This condition may be mild and never cause visual problems. For some, the continued leakage with fluid build-up in the macula, the critical area of the retina, causes blurred vision. In more severe cases, fragile new vessels rupture and bleed into the center of the eye (vitreous) causing blockage of the light rays and image distortion. The formation of scar tissue may pull on the retina and detach it from the back of the eye, which may result in severe vision loss or permanent blindness.

For this reason, a comprehensive eye examination by an ophthalmologist is the best prevention. Early detection of diabetic retinopathy guards against progression of this condition. Laser treatment aimed at sealing the leaking blood vessels may be indicated to reduce the risk of blindness or severe vision loss, and stop the retinopathy from progressing. Unfortunately, laser treatment cannot restore sight that has been already lost due to retinal damage.

LIVING WITH VISUAL LOSS

Acceptance of visual loss as a consequence of aging is no longer acceptable. The eye disorders that occur more frequently in old age do not mean inevitable impairment with a significant reduction in the quality of life. Protecting eyes and conserving sight require individual action in the area of health promotion. Regular health check-ups are important to detect and treat conditions such as diabetes at an early stage. Complete periodic eye examinations should be made by an ophthalmologist and should include refraction and eyeglass prescription, if indicated. Eye pressure checks, as well as an internal and external eye examination to detect existing or potential eye problems, should be part of the routine examination. Signs of vision loss or other eye problems require immediate attention. Those with a history of diabetes or a family history of eye disease require frequent monitoring.

Low vision optical aids are available for those who still have partial vision. These devices, like closed-circuit television, can magnify writing or the printed word many times the actual size. This makes it possible to read and write letters, to read books, newspapers, and magazines, and pursue hobbies. There are many aids to choose from, so advantages and disadvantages of each product should be understood and weighed before selecting the one best suited to an individual's needs.

Nonoptical aids such as large-print books and magazines are also available, as well as large-print telephone dials, needle threaders, playing cards, and calculators. To maximize their use, increased lighting is essential. Tinted lenses to reduce glare from bright sunlight are helpful.

Resources should be explored and tapped to assist individuals and their families to benefit from services available, such as counseling, visual training, and low-vision aids. These services could enable individuals to overcome frustration and resume a normal life within their limitations. Participation in a self-help group provides not only fellowship, but also support, encouragement, and sharing of experiences and information. An outstanding resource that provides information on specific diseases affecting the eye and learning to live with impaired sight is the National Society to Prevent Blindness, 79 Madison Avenue, New York, N.Y. 10016.

References

Abrams, W.P., and R. Berkow, eds. 1990. *The Merck Manual of Geriatrics*. Rahway, N.J.: Merck & Co, Inc., 1055.

Agency for Health Care Policy and Research. 1993. *Cataract in Adults: Management of Functional Impairment.* (DHHS Publication No. 93-0542). Rockville, Md.: U.S. Public Health Service.

The American Medical Association. 1989. *Encyclopedia of Medicine.* New York: Random House.

The National Institute on Aging. 1991. *Age Page: Aging and Your Eyes.* Bethesda, Md.: U.S. Public Health Service.

Jennifer Boondas

Visually Impaired Older Adults: Social Services

INTRODUCTION

There is a growing awareness of the association between old age and vision loss, and of the need to understand the barriers to adequate provision of services to visually impaired older adults. Demographic changes influencing the prevalence of vision impairment in older persons have occurred for several reasons. Medical developments have reduced the prevalence of blindness in children while there has simultaneously been an increase in the proportion of the population that is elderly. Not only is there a larger number of older adults, but the proportion of the population aged 85 and over is growing at a faster rate. Over 50 percent of the people in the United States who are blind are elderly, and the population of persons who are age 65 and over has the highest incidence of new blindness.

The collaborative project of Union Settlement and the Lighthouse National Center on Vision and Aging (NCVA) is a model for service provision to elderly visually impaired persons.

HISTORICAL BACKGROUND

The network of agencies providing services to older Americans and the service network assisting blind and visually impaired persons have traditionally operated separately. Biegel and his colleagues (1989) suggested that agencies serving the elderly have historically used a prevention model and have assisted the well elderly, but have inadequately assisted persons such as the visually impaired elderly who need specialized services. They also suggested that agencies providing services to the visually impaired population have generally addressed needs resulting from blindness or visual impairment and not due to age.

PROBLEMS CONFRONTED BY THE ELDERLY VISUALLY IMPAIRED POPULATION

Vision loss is experienced in different ways in old age, but the consequences tend to be loss, isolation, and increased dependency. Usually, blindness is a new and often terrifying experience for older persons. It occurs as one of many losses in old age, making adjustment to the vision impairment even more difficult. Goodman (1985) has described the impact of vision problems as they intersect with older persons' physical, social, and economic losses. Wainapel (1991) addresses the fact that older persons are at increased risk of medical as well as visual disabilities. According to Orr (1991), the accompanying conditions that occur most frequently and which affect physical mobility are arthritis, heart disease, hypertension, and post-stroke syndrome.

Many visually impaired older adults need home care services, since, as Cherry and her colleagues (1991) noted, there is an age-related increase in need for assistance with activities of daily living (ADL). Vision impairment affects older persons' capacity for self-care and maintenance, as well as their potential for social interaction and enrichment. The elderly's ability to cope with changes such as vision loss affects their ability to live in the community. Because of the often severe limitations brought about by vision impairment, a high proportion of these older persons live in institutions.

INTEGRATED PROGRAM FOR SIGHTED AND VISUALLY IMPAIRED ELDERLY

This collaborative program, the Integrated Program for Sighted and Visually Impaired Elderly (IP), continued from May 1987 through June 1988 as an effort to overcome some of the traditional barriers in service provision to visually impaired older persons and to meet the expected needs of this population in East Harlem. The IP, founded in 1985, was established to provide consultation, training, and public education. Union Settlement is the largest settlement house in New York City, serving more than 8,000 people of all ages with programs in education, health, job training, counseling, economic development, and recreation. The IP worked closely with two of Union Settlement's programs and received consultation and training services from the NCVA. One of the agency programs with which this project was most involved was Settlement Home Care, a program providing Medicaid-reimbursable home care services for 460 homebound frail elderly and handicapped individuals. Service is provided for home care clients from four to twenty-four hours a day.

The second program with which the project was involved was the East Harlem Coalition of Senior Centers, which includes four congregate nutrition programs and a meals-on-wheels program funded by the New York City Department for the Aging. The nutrition sites, located in public housing projects, also provide recreational, medical, and social services. In addition, the Senior Home Companion Program provides friendly visiting.

The Integrated Program provided outreach, senior center and home care staff training, medical examinations and follow-up, environmental modification in senior centers, recreational activities that integrated sighted persons and persons who were visually impaired, a gardening project, and supportive services that included friendly visiting and referrals for counseling and other practical services. Through outreach, information was gathered through telephone or in-person interviews, from 443 individuals, most of whom were at least 60 years of age. Fifty-nine were found to be visually impaired.

The most relevant aspects of the project regarding home care were outreach and training. Eight of the 59 visually impaired persons were referred by Settlement Home Care. As the referrals originated from many different sources, this was a relatively large number of referrals from a single source. The referrals were made late in the project year, although the Settlement Home Care supervisory staff and 120 home attendants received training on site through NCVA.

Of these 59 individuals, 24 were attending senior centers, while 35 were not. Only three persons indicated that lack of vision alone prevented them from participating in a senior center. In four individuals, vision was one of the difficulties that appeared to impede participation. Numerous nonphysical reasons were given for lack of participation in a senior center but, most relevant to home care services, visually impaired persons gave many physical reasons for lack of participation in centers: difficulty walking, bedfast due to stroke, physical pain, recent surgery, wheelchair bound, fear of falling if they left their apartment, appointments for dialysis, and difficulty breathing.

Considering this information, and that the professional literature also documents the existence of multiple physical problems in the visually impaired elderly, training is essential for staff who provide home care services to visually impaired elderly. Because specialized information about vision impairment is not generally available in the aging network agencies, a program model like the Integrated Program could be helpful in providing this needed information. Having a contact person available in any of the aging networks who could accept referrals regarding visually impaired individuals needing help in their homes would be a necessary link in the network. Delays in making referrals can impede an individual's ability to receive timely services, sometimes making their condition worse. Many visually impaired individuals require specialized services beyond the usual services provided by home care agencies.

CONCLUSION

It was apparent to those working in the Integrated Project that the needs of visually impaired elderly are not being adequately met. Barriers to an individual's receiving assistance include lack of coordination among agencies, and lack of knowledge by home care providers and others that visually impaired individuals require specialized services that can enhance their ability to be self-sufficient. However, home care providers are in a unique position to adequately assess the needs of the elderly, particularly those elderly who are experiencing loss of vision, and to communicate to other agencies that specialized services are needed for these individuals.

References

Biegel, D.E., M.K. Petchers, A. Snyder, and B. Beisgen. 1989. Unmet needs and barriers to service delivery for the blind and visually impaired elderly. *The Gerontologist* 29:86–91.

Cherry, K.E., M.J. Keller, and W.N. Dudley. 1991. A needs assessment of persons with vision impairments: implications for older adults and service providers. *J Gerontological Social Work* 17:99–124.

Goodman, H. 1985. Serving the elderly blind: a generic approach. *J Gerontological Social Work* 8:153–68.

Orr, A. 1991. The psychosocial aspects of aging and vision loss. *J Gerontological Social Work* 17:1–14.

Stuen, C. 1991. Awareness of resources for visually impaired older adults among the aging network. *J Gerontological Social Work* 17:165–79.

Wainapel, S.F. 1991. A tale of two cultures: cross disciplinary perspectives in the care of older adults with combined visual and medical disabilities. *J Gerontological Social Work* 17:77–84.

Patricia J. Kolb

Appendix A:
Public and Private Organizations
Related to Home Care

Except where specific authors are cited, the information in this section is derived from National Institute on Aging. 1993. *Resource Directory for Older People*. Washington, D.C.: U.S. Department of Health and Human Services, Public Health Service, National Institutes of Health.

ACTION: VOLUNTEERS IN SERVICE TO AMERICA

ACTION is an agency within the U.S. Government that sponsors many volunteer programs that are conducted by older adults who contribute their time to providing assistance and services to their peers.

Examples of volunteer programs include the Foster Grandparent Program which offers the opportunity for older adults to develop close relationships with children who have special needs—those children who have physical, psychological, or mental disabilities. These children are in public and private institutional or home settings. The Retired Senior Volunteer Program (RSVP) members work in courts, day care centers, hospitals, libraries, schools, and other similar settings. They assist education and health professionals by providing individual attention and care to those children most in need of services.

The Senior Companion Program participants provide support services to older persons with special education, health, and social needs. These services are provided in many settings: community health agencies, home health care agencies, hospitals, and social work agencies. These services allow older people to remain in their own homes, and avoiding institutionalization.

ACTION provides many valuable free publications such as *Foster Grandparent Program: Where Love Grows*, *RSVP: The Retired Senior Volunteer Program*, *The Senior Companion Program: Serving With Compassion*, *Caring as Friends*, *ACTION: Volunteers Meeting the Needs of the Community*, and others.

The national office of ACTION is located at 1100 Vermont Avenue, N.W., Washington, D.C. 20525, telephone (202) 606-4855. The toll free telephone for Volunteers in Service to America is 1-800-424-8867.

These groups of volunteers willingly offer information, education, and services to many home-bound and community elderly and their families.

Many large cities have regional ACTION offices.

ALZHEIMER'S ASSOCIATION

The Alzheimer's Association is a voluntary organization that provides public education programs and supportive services to patients and families who are coping with Alzheimer's disease (AD).

The Association has a 24-hour toll-free hotline that offers information about Alzheimer's disease and links families with those chapters close to the caller's home. These local chapters are familiar with the available community resources, and can offer practical suggestions for daily living and special problems and needs of both patients and families.

The Association also funds research aimed at finding a cure for Alzheimer's disease.

A publication of the Association is the *A.D. Newsletter* that is distributed quarterly to all Association members and those interested in Alzheimer's disease. Educational materials are also available in both English and Spanish.

The Alzheimer's Association is located in Suite 1000, 919 North Michigan Avenue, Chicago, IL. 60611, telephone (312) 335-8700. Information and referral services can be obtained through the toll-free number 1-800-272-3900. The hearing impaired can call (312) 335–8882.

AMERICAN ASSOCIATION OF RETIRED PERSONS (AARP)

The mission of the American Association of Retired Persons (AARP), a nonprofit organization, is to help older Americans achieve lives of independence, dignity, and purpose.

In carrying out this mission, the AARP provides many services:

- Local AARP chapters, listed in telephone directories, sponsor educational programs on crime prevention, consumer protection, defensive driving, and income tax preparation.

- The Health Care Campaign works to contain health care costs for older people and to make health care more responsive to consumer needs.

- The Minority Affairs Program seeks to focus greater public awareness of the needs of older members of minority groups.

- Members of AARP have the opportunity to participate in group health insurance programs, automobile and home insurance programs, an investment program, and travel services.

- The Women's Initiative Program provides information about the special needs and concerns of older women.

- The Worker Equity Program seeks to protect the rights of older workers through public education and legislation.

- The AARP mail-order pharmacy service offers members discounts on prescription medications. Regional offices are located in California, Connecticut, Florida, Indiana, Missouri, Nevada, New York, Oregon, Pennsylvania, Virginia, and Washington, D.C.

- AgeLine, a computerized bibliographic database, provides information about journal articles, books, government documents, reports, and research projects dealing with middle age and aging. Topics covered include economics, family relationships, health care services, and population studies. The database is available through BRS Information Technologies, a commercial database vendor.

- The AARP makes available to its members several publications. The *AARP News Bulletin* is distributed each month, and *Modern Maturity* is published bimonthly. Other publications are available on exercise, health, housing, leisure, money management, retirement planning, travel, and other helpful topics.

The national headquarters of AARP are located at 601 E. Street, N.W., Washington, D.C. 20049, telephone (202) 434-2277.

AMERICAN OCCUPATIONAL THERAPY ASSOCIATION, INC.

The American Occupational Therapy Association is an organization whose members are professionals who help people with functional problems caused by injury or illness, and other disabilities of any nature.

Occupational therapists (OTs) assist patients to maintain, increase, or restore their ability to perform daily living skills such as cooking, eating, bathing, dressing, and other similar activities.

The Association's services include continuing education programs for both occupational therapists and occupational therapy assistants. Information is available to the public about the role of occupational therapy in promoting functional independence, preventing disability, and maintaining wellness.

Publications of the Association include *OT Week*, published weekly, and the *American Journal of Occupational Therapy*, published monthly. Several publications and posters are available to health professionals. A catalog listing available publications can be requested.

The offices of the Association are at P.O. Box 1725, 1383 Piccard Drive, Rockville, MD. 20849-1725, telephone (301) 948-9626.

AMERICAN SOCIETY ON AGING

The American Society on Aging is a nonprofit, membership organization that informs the public and health professionals about issues that affect the quality of life for older persons and promotes innovative approaches to meeting the needs of the elderly.

The American Society on Aging sponsors professional education opportunities each year, and publishes *Generations* quarterly and *Aging Today* bimonthly for members and subscribers.

The offices of the Society are located in Suite 512, 833 Market Street, San Francisco, CA. 94103, telephone (415) 882-2910.

ASSOCIATION FOR ANTHROPOLOGY AND GERONTOLOGY

Introduction

The Association for Anthropology and Gerontology (AAGE) was organized in the mid-1970s by anthropologists who shared an interest in applying the methods and perspectives of anthropology to the study of aging. It is well known that anthropologists often interviewed elderly people to learn about disappearing cultural lifeways, but it was not until the late 1960s and early 1970s that they turned to the study of aging and the aged as a specific focus of research.

In 1979 AAGE was officially incorporated as an educational nonprofit organization with the intent of focusing on the study of aging and the elderly from a cross-cultural perspective, with an emphasis on anthropological (qualitative) methodology. The cross-cultural perspective promised to broaden the understanding of aging by looking at the cultural influences on aging and at the similarities and variations of aging in different cultures.

Although AAGE began as an organization to bring together anthropologists who were interested in the aging process, it has expanded far beyond the boundaries of the discipline to include scholars, educators, and practitioners from many diverse fields.

Statement of Purpose

Article II of the Bylaws of AAGE contains the following as the statement of purpose of the organization:

> Aging is a universal part of the human experience, whose processes and consequences are conditioned by the diversity of human culture. The goal of AAGE is to understand the universal through exploration of diversity. AAGE intends to broaden research on age with the cross-cultural, holistic, and empiric perspectives of anthropology, and in turn to enrich the empirical and theoretical resources of our discipline. A further aim of AAGE is to make knowledge available to those who are involved in the practical resolution of difficulties facing people of all ages. (By-Laws of the Association for Anthropology and Gerontology 1979:1)

Organizational Structure and By-Laws

Each year, the membership of AAGE elects an Executive Board by mail ballot. The Board is composed of a President, President-Elect, Recording Secretary, and Corresponding Secretary who each serve a one-year term and a Treasurer who serves a two-year term. The Board is assisted by a Steering Committee composed of the Chairpersons of each of six Standing Committees. Ad hoc committees are appointed as the need arises.

Membership is open to anyone who subscribes to the purpose of the organization and pays the annual dues as proposed by the Executive Council (composed of the Executive Board and the Steering Committee) and voted on by the general membership.

The annual meeting of AAGE is held in conjunction with the annual meeting of the American Anthropological Association.

Research Interests

The members of AAGE are interested in a wide variety of topics. These topics cover all of the categories in anthropology from social structure to evolution, from language to politics, and from kin groups to voluntary associations as they relate to aging and the aged. Research ranges from caregiving as a cultural system to the medicalizations of old age, from biological theories of aging to the study of long-lived Abkhasians, from elderly women's special roles in African culture to the cultural aspects of menopause for the women of India, from the cultural dimensions of aging in China to the role of ethnicity for American Indian elders.

Activities

AAGE sponsors symposia at the annual meetings of the American Anthropological Association, the Gerontology Society of America, the Association for Gerontology in Higher Education, the Canadian Association for Gerontology, the International Congress of Gerontology, and the International Congress of Anthropological and Ethnological Sciences.

One of the prime benefits of membership in AAGE is the international network which exists among people from different disciplines. Serving on committees, planning symposia, and meeting at different regional and national conferences foster collaboration between scholars on research and writing projects and the continued sharing of information and experiences. Not the least of the benefits of active membership in AAGE are the lasting friendships that are formed.

Publications

Association for Anthropology and Gerontology Newsletter. AAGE publishes a quarterly Newsletter which is sent to all members of AAGE. The Newsletter is the means by which AAGE transmits information about the Association (e.g., elections of officers, announcements about the annual meeting), dates of other meetings on aging, new publications on aging, and short reports of research on various aspects of aging (e.g., U.S. Population-based Studies of Hip Fracture Risk Factors Among Persons Aged 65 and Over by Toni P. Miles. Vol. 13, No. 1, 1992).

Directory of Anthropologists and Anthropological Research in Aging. The 11th Edition of the Directory was published in 1992 and lists the members of AAGE, their addresses, and their research and/or teaching interests. With a 1992 membership of over 360, the disciplines represented include nursing, gerontology, medicine, sociology, anthropology (including medical, biological, cultural, and linguistic anthropology as well as archeology), social work, geriatrics, higher education, caregiving, policymaking, demography, psychology, and public health.

Teaching About Aging: Interdisciplinary and Cross-Cultural Perspectives. Edited by Doris Francis, Dena Shenk and Jay Sokolovsky, Association for Anthropology and Gerontology, 1990. Part I contains thirty course outlines/syllabi that focus on various aspects of aging. Courses deal with topics such as aging and culture, aging from a cross-cultural perspective, aging and anthropology, and aging and the environment. While the content of each of the courses would add understanding of the various dimensions involved in home care, readers of this volume would find of special interest the courses that deal directly with caregiving: "Cross-National Perspectives in Long Term Care: Policies and Practices," and "Aging and Caregiving—Family, Community, and Societal Perspectives." Each course description includes reading selections and a list of books and other resources where students can find additional material. Part II, Teaching Resources, includes chapters on how to teach the topic of gerontology, techniques for obtaining oral histories from the elderly, a bibliography, and a list of films about aging.

Anthropology and Aging—Comprehensive Reviews. Edited by Robert L. Rubenstein. Boston, MA.: Kluwer Academic Publishers, 1990. Conceived and prepared as a project of the Association for Anthropology and Gerontology. In the first of what is planned as a continuing series, *Anthropology and Aging* presents a current accounting of critical issues and areas of interest in the anthropology of aging. This volume contains reviews of three major topics: Biological and Health Issues, Cultural Issues, and Area Studies. The authors of each chapter provide critical analyses and reviews that range from biological anthropology, nursing and aging, and health and aging, to more culturally oriented questions dealing with the life course in comparative perspective, and gender and aging. The area studies provide a precise focus on aging in Japan and China.

Anthropology of Aging: A Partially Annotated Bibliography. Edited by Marjorie M. Schweitzer. Bibliographies and Indexes in Gerontology, Number 13. Westport, Conn.: Greenwood Press, 1991. Prepared under the auspices of the Association for Anthropology and Gerontology. The bibliography is organized according to (1) subject topics such as Health and Social Services, and (2) regional/cultural groups such as China/Black Americans. Important citations are annotated. The Anthropology of Aging Bibliography is a source appropriate for use by teachers of courses on aging, by researchers, and by practitioners. Those who provide care, as well as those who make policies and produce programs specifically for the elderly, can find much of interest in the resources listed here.

Marjorie M. Schweitzer

THE ASSOCIATION FOR GERONTOLOGY IN HIGHER EDUCATION

The Association for Gerontology in Higher Education (AGHE) was established in 1974 to advance gerontology as a field of study in institutions of higher education. Its members are committed to education, training, research, and service programs in the field of aging. AGHE provides a network to assist faculty and administrators in developing and improving the quality of gerontology programs at colleges and universities.

Currently AGHE has more than 300 institutional members throughout the United States, Canada, and abroad. The gerontology programs at member schools range from developing programs offering only a few courses to major research centers in aging. Individual memberships are not available, but persons can subscribe to AGHE's mailing list for $25 per year ($30 international) and receive publications and annual meeting information.

AGHE carries out its purposes through a number of services and programs:

Meetings

Through the annual meeting, information and ideas are shared on curriculum and program development, faculty training, and other issues related to gerontological education and service provision. The Annual Meeting is held in late February or early March each year in a major city. Both members and nonmembers are welcome to attend.

Publications and Technical Assistance

The Association publishes a quarterly newsletter called the *AGHExchange* which provides information about educational developments, opportunities, innovative programs, public policy issues, resources, and research activities. AGHE publishes the *National Directory of Educational Programs in Gerontology and Geriatrics* which describes the programs and activities in aging at colleges and universities. Ordering information for the current edition can be obtained from the AGHE office.

AGHE has developed an important resource to assist faculty members and others in the field of gerontology in selecting the best materials to use in courses they are structuring. The *Brief Bibliography* series initiated in 1985 by AGHE's Technical Assistance Committee now contains over twenty different subject areas related to gerontological instruction. One of these is *Home Health Care*, with co-compilers Dr. Ada Romaine-Davis, Johns Hopkins University School of Nursing, and Dr. Dorothea Zito, Syracuse University (1989 edition). This was updated in 1993 by Dr. Romaine-Davis and Dr. Patricia A. Burns, State University of New York at Buffalo. The references cited cover the major issues and problems in home health care, as well as provide an overview of the present state of these services. Textbooks that provide a general view of the major issues confronting home health care professionals are included, as well as items on financial and policy issues, management, and model programs.

These brief annotated bibliographies were compiled by persons nominated by their peers as "experts" in their area and list, in their judgment, the best quality education and training materials for each subject area. The full list of titles and prices is available from AGHE.

AGHE has published *Standards and Guidelines for Gerontology Programs* which makes recommendations for the development of educational programs in gerontology from the associate to the doctoral level.

AGHE also maintains the Database on Gerontology in Higher Education. This computerized database allows for customized searches to be made to locate programs in aging of particular interest to an individual. Using one of three different report formats, for example, all schools in a particular state or region that offer gerontology instruction or programs in a specific discipline at the associate, undergraduate, or graduate level could be listed. The moderate cost for these customized searches allows students and others to access the information inexpensively. Search forms are available from AGHE.

Advocacy

A major service of AGHE is the role of monitoring and advocating the interests of gerontological education, training, and research among national leaders, government officials, and the private sector.

AGHE worked with other aging organizations for the reauthorization of the Older Americans Act in 1992 and advocates regularly for increased federal appropriations in aging training and research for a number of federal offices of the U.S. Public Health Service, including the Administration on Aging, the Bureau of Health Professions, the National Institute on Aging, and the National Institute of Mental Health.

Research

The focus of research being conducted by AGHE is in the area of manpower needs and gerontology program development in the field of aging. There is continuing need to demonstrate the extent of present and future personnel required to work in the field of aging. The information from these studies should provide important feedback on the quality of gerontology training now going on and the training and personnel needs for the future.

AGHE is a nonprofit association; resources for carrying out these activities are derived from members' annual dues, annual meeting income, sales of publications, and occasional grants. The association has its offices at 1001 Connecticut Avenue, N.W., Suite 410, Washington, D.C. 20036-5504. The Executive Director is Elizabeth B. Douglass. For further information, please contact Joy Lobenstine, Associate Director for Membership and Information, at (202) 429-9277.

Joy Lobenstine

FEDERAL COUNCIL ON THE AGING

The Federal Council on Aging is an advisory group authorized by the Older Americans Act of 1965. Members of the group are selected by the President and the Congress. The 15 members represent a cross-section of rural and urban older Americans, national organizations with an interest in aging, labor, and the general public. The Council reviews and evaluates Federal policies, programs, and activities that affect the lives of older Americans and makes recommendations to the President, the Secretary of the Department of Health and Human Services, the Commissioner on Aging, and the Congress.

The services that the Federal Council on the Aging provides are related to its stated purpose:

- The FCOA informs the public about the problems and needs of older Americans, collects and distributes information on aging, conducts or commissions aging research, and publishes the results of its studies on aging.

- The FCOA convenes public forums to discuss and publicize the problems and needs of older people.

The Council publishes an annual report that is submitted to the President.

For additional information, the offices of the Council are located in Room 4280 HHS-N, 330 Independence Avenue, S.W., Washington, D.C. 20201, telephone (202) 619-2451.

GERONTOLOGICAL SOCIETY OF AMERICA

The Gerontological Society of America (GSA) is a professional organization that promotes the scientific study of aging in the biological and social sciences.

The GSA provides services in various ways, related to its purpose:

- Works to improve the well-being of older people by promoting the study of the aging process.

- Encourages the exchange of scientific information about aging through sponsoring conferences and informational programs, and distributing professional education materials.

- The GSA Information Service is a computerized database that identifies experts and sources of information on aging, and other aging-related databases.

The GSA publishes *The Gerontologist* and the *Journal of Gerontology*, both bimonthly. The *Gerontology News* is a monthly newsletter. A special biannual supplement to the newsletter is the conference calendar, which lists notices of aging-related conferences, meetings, and courses.

The address of the GSA is Suite 350, 1275 K Street, N.W., Washington, D.C. 20005-4006, telephone (202) 842-1275.

HOSPICE HOME CARE ASSOCIATION

The goal of the organization is to promote the concept of hospice care and to provide information to those seeking assistance with hospice care by referring inquiries to individuals or groups that give personal hospice services.

In providing hospice care to terminally ill patients, a hospice team of professional and support staff work with patients and their families to keep patients at home and as comfortable as possible throughout the final months of life, and to maintain the dignity of the individual during this stressful period. One of the major emphases in hospice care is to give appropriate medications to relieve pain.

Hospice care is comprehensive in that physical, emotional, spiritual, and financial needs are addressed. Families are involved in the care as much as is feasible.

The Hospice Home Care Association also provides information about financial sources to pay for the specialized care provided. Generally, these services are reimbursed through Medicare.

For additional information, The Hospice Home Care Association is located at 519 C Street, N.E., Washington, D.C. 20002. Please call (202) 547-7424.

LEGAL SERVICES FOR THE ELDERLY

Legal Services for the Elderly is an advisory center for lawyers who specialize in the legal problems of older persons.

The services of the Legal Services for the Elderly are not provided directly to clients.

Lawyers on the staff offer advice, prepare memoranda of laws, and develop briefs for other lawyers who service older citizens.

Issues of interest to Legal Services for the Elderly include, but are not limited to, Medicaid, Medicare, Social Security, supplemental security income, unemployment insurance, disability, voluntary and involuntary commitment, involuntary committee appointment, conservatorship, intestacy, age discrimination, pensions, elderly rent increase exemptions, rent control/housing, and nursing home care.

The Legal Services for the Elderly organization has a number of publications available to the general public, including *A Survey of the Legal Problems of the Elderly*, *Mandatory Retirement*, *Cost Crisis of Senior Travelers*, and *Savings for Seniors*. A list of materials and publications is available on request.

The office of the Legal Services for the Elderly are: 17th Floor, 130 West 42nd Street, New York, N.Y. 10036, telephone (212) 391-0120.

NATIONAL AGING RESOURCE CENTER ON ELDER ABUSE

The National Aging Resource Center on Elder Abuse (NARCEA) is a joint project operated by the American Public Welfare Association, the National Association of State Units on Aging, and the University of Delaware.

The purpose of NARCEA is to develop and provide information, data, and expertise to states, communities, professionals, and the public to help them effectively combat the problems of elder abuse.

Services that the NARCEA provides include an information clearinghouse through which it disseminates resources and information to both professionals and the public; training and technical assistance to professionals in the field of gerontology and aging; and conducts and publishes research in the field of elder abuse and neglect.

Publications of NARCEA include *Elder Abuse: Questions and Answers—An Information Guide for Professionals and Concerned Citizens* and *Elder Abuse in the United States: An Issue Paper*.

For additional information, write or call NARCEA, c/o American Public Welfare Association, Suite 500, 810 First Street, N.E., Washington, D.C. 20002-4205, telephone (202) 682-2470.

NATIONAL ASSOCIATION OF AREA AGENCIES ON AGING

The National Association of Area Agencies on Aging (NAAAA) represents the interests of Area Agencies on Aging across the country. These local agencies are listed in telephone directories.

The services provided by the Area Agencies on Aging include direct services such as transportation, legal aid, nutrition programs, housekeeping, senior center activities, shopping assistance, employment counseling, preretirement advising, and information and referral programs.

The NAAAA provides the communication, training, and technical assistance necessary to enable America's aging network to serve and represent older persons in an efficient and effective manner.

Toward these goals, the NAAAA annually sponsors a training conference and exposition that showcases innovative program developments in services to older persons.

Publications of the NAAAA include the *Network News*, a monthly newsletter, and *The Directory of State and Area Agencies on Aging*, published annually.

The address and telephone number are: Suite 100, 1112 16th Street, N.W., Washington, D.C. 20036, telephone (202) 296-8130.

NATIONAL ASSOCIATION FOR HISPANIC ELDERLY/ ASOCIACION NACIONAL PRO PERSONAS MAYORES

The National Association for Hispanic Elderly works to ensure that older Hispanic citizens are included in all social service programs for older Americans.

Toward this goal, the Association provides the following services:

- Studies the needs of older Hispanics.

- The Senior Community Service Employment Program, funded by the Department of Labor and administered by the Association, employs low-income people 55 years of age and older in ten States.

- Regional offices throughout the country provide information about the needs and capabilities of older Hispanics and other low-income older people in both private and public agencies. These regional offices are located in Chicago, Detroit, Kansas City, Laredo, Los Angeles, Miami, New Orleans, Philadelphia, San Antonio, and Washington, D.C.

The Association also publishes the *Legislative Bulletin* quarterly, both English and Spanish articles, brochures, and audiovisual materials, which covers topics such as Social Security, Medicare, health-related issues, and how to start volunteer groups to serve low-income older people. In addition, research reports regarding older people, including Hispanics, are available.

The main headquarters of the Association is in Suite 800, 3325 Wilshire Boulevard, Los Angeles, CA. 90010-1724, telephone (213) 487-1922.

NATIONAL ASSOCIATION FOR HOME CARE

The National Association for Home Care (NAHC) is a professional organization that represents a variety of agencies that provide home care services, including home health agencies, hospice programs, and homemaker/home health aid agencies.

Services provided by the NAHC include (1) helping to develop appropriate professional standards for agencies that offer home care services; (2) providing continuing education programs for staff members of home health agencies; (3) monitoring Federal and State legislation that affects the delivery of home care services; and (4) informing the general public about how to select a home care agency.

The NAHC publications include *Caring Magazine*, *Home Care News*, and *NAHC Reports* that are published monthly for members. Other publications about home care are distributed and are listed in a directory of publications, available on request.

The location of the NAHC offices is 519 C Street, N.E., Washington, D.C. 20002, telephone (202) 547-7424.

NATIONAL ASSOCIATION OF MEAL PROGRAMS

The National Association of Meal Programs (NAMP) is a group of professionals and volunteers who provide congregate and home-delivered meals to people who are frail, disabled, or homebound.

The services related to this goal are (1) to offer training and technical assistance to those who plan and conduct congregate and home-delivered meal programs; (2) to offer national and regional workshops about fundraising, program management, recruitment of volunteers, nutrition, and a wide range of related topics; (3) to offer program insurance to its members; and 4) to conduct member surveys to collect statistical data and to analyze trends.

Materials that the Association publishes are a membership directory that is distributed annually, and a bimonthly newsletter, *Between the Lines*.

The NAMP is located at 206 E Street, N.E., Washington, D.C. 20002, telephone (202) 547-6157.

NATIONAL CAUCUS AND CENTER ON BLACK AGED, INC.

The National Caucus and Center on Black Aged is a nonprofit organization that works to improve the quality of life for older black Americans.

The services that the organization provides are aimed at achieving the stated goal, and include (1) strengthening existing national and community-based organizations that provide services to older blacks; (2) sponsoring employment, housing, and transportation programs; (3) advising community groups and conducting seminars on subjects of interest to blacks; (4) promoting intergenerational dialogue between older and younger blacks through the Living Legacy Program; and (5) encouraging older black volunteers to work on behalf of members of the black community.

The COBAs *Newsletter* and *Golden Age* are published quarterly.

The COBAs offices are in Suite 500, 1424 K Street, N.W., Washington, D.C. 20005, telephone (202) 637-8400.

NATIONAL COUNCIL ON THE AGING

The National Council on the Aging (NCOA) is a nonprofit membership organization for professionals and volunteers which serves as a national resource for information, technical assistance, training, and research relating to the field of aging.

The NCOA is made up of the Health Promotion Institute, the Senior Community Service Employment Project, Retirement Planning Program, National Institute of Senior Centers, National Institute of Adult Daycare, National Center on Rural Aging, and the National Institute of Senior Housing.

The services available through the NCOA include the following:

- The NCOA advocates on behalf of older Americans and develops innovative methods of meeting the needs of older people.

- The Council provides a national information and consultation center, offers conferences, conducts research, supports demonstration programs, and maintains a comprehensive library of materials on aging, with emphasis on the psychological, economic, and social aspects of aging.

- The NCOA provides information regarding training programs for older workers, services available to frail older persons living in their own homes, ensures access to health and social services, and promotes increased participation by older people in artistic and cultural programs.
- Geriatric fellowships are awarded to medical students through the Traveler's Insurance Company.

The NCOA is located in Suite 200, 409 Third Street, S.W., Washington, D.C. 20025, telephone (202) 479-1200.

NATIONAL HISPANIC COUNCIL ON AGING

The National Hispanic Council on Aging is a private, nonprofit organization that works to promote the well-being of older Hispanics.

The services provided through the Council are many.

- The Council represents the interests of older Hispanics to the government and to the private sector.
- The Council's demonstration projects evaluate innovative programs that provide needed health care and social services to older Hispanics.
- The NHCOA develops and publishes educational materials that are culturally and linguistically appropriate for older Hispanics.
- The NHCOA sponsors training institutes, workshops, and conferences for people who work with older Hispanics.
- The Council provides enrichment programs for undergraduate and graduate Latino students who are either planning to enter the field of gerontology or are in the process of selecting a future career.

Publications of the Council include the quarterly newsletter *Noticias, Prevention and the Latino Elderly, Access and Utilization of Services by the Latino Elderly, Long-Term Care: Hispanic Elderly, The Hispanic Older Woman, Dialogue on Health Concerns for Hispanics,* and *Mature Driving: Edicion en Espanol.* A listing of publications is available on request.

The address of the NHCOA is 2713 Ontario Road, N.W., Washington, D.C. 20009, telephone (202) 265-1288.

NATIONAL INDIAN COUNCIL ON AGING

The National Indian Council on Aging is a nonprofit organization funded by the Administration on Aging, a federal agency of the Department of Health and Human Services. The NICOA works to ensure that older Indians and Alaskan Native Americans have equal access to quality, comprehensive health care, legal assistance, and social services.

The services provided by the Council are the following:

- The Council works with agencies and programs that serve the older Indian population.

- The NICOA provides technical assistance and training to the staffs of Indian tribal organizations.

- The Council conducts surveys to identify specific needs of older Native Americans and serves as a clearinghouse of information about issues of special concern to this population.

The Council publishes *Elder Voices* each month. Monographs on topics related to aging within the Native American population, and other topics, are available. A complete listing of publications is available through the NICOA offices, located at City Center, Suite 510W, 6400 Uptown Boulevard, N.E., Albuquerque, N.M. 87110, telephone (505) 888-3302.

NATIONAL INSTITUTE ON AGING

The National Institute on Aging (NIA), part of the National Institutes of Health, is the Federal Government's principal agency for conducting and supporting biomedical, social, and behavioral research related to aging processes, and the diseases and special problems of older people.

Services provided by the NIA include the following:

- The Baltimore Longitudinal Study of Aging, in which the same people are followed over a long period of time, is providing researchers valuable information about health and illness in the older population.

- Researchers at NIA-supported centers around the country are studying new methods for diagnosing and treating Alzheimer's disease.

- The NIA funds research to learn more about the genetic mechanisms of aging, intellectual changes that occur with aging, and age-related changes that develop in the heart, brain, nervous system, and other organs.

- Studies are under way to find better ways to diagnose and treat urinary and fecal incontinence, to discover how the health and well-being of older people are affected by personal and environmental factors, and to learn how nutritional needs change throughout the life span.

The NIA address and telephone number are: Public Information Office, 9000 Rockville Pike, Building 31—Room 5C27, Bethesda, MD. 20892, telephone (301) 496-1752. For information about publications, the toll-free number is: 1-800-222-2225.

NATIONAL INSTITUTE OF ARTHRITIS AND MUSCULOSKELETAL AND SKIN DISEASES

The National Institute of Arthritis and Musculoskeletal and Skin Diseases (NIAMS), part of the National Institutes of Health, is the Federal Government's principal agency for research on a number of chronic, disabling diseases, such as osteoarthritis, rheumatoid arthritis, muscle diseases, osteoporosis, Paget's disease, back disorders, gout, psoriasis, icthyosis, and vitiligo.

The services of the NIAMS are the following:

- Researchers at NIAMS-funded arthritis and musculoskeletal disease centers around the country develop and carry out programs in basic and clinical research, professional and patient education, and research in epidemiology and health services for patients with these conditions.

- Researchers at NIAMS-funded specialized centers of research study basic and clinical aspects of rheumatoid arthritis, osteoarthritis, and osteoporosis.

- In-depth research on the diagnosis and treatment of various rheumatic conditions is conducted by members of the Cooperative System Studies Program in Rheumatic Diseases at 11 centers in the United States.

- The NIAMS also supports research on joint replacement methods and materials, bullous skin diseases, eczema, and other skin disorders.

The address and telephone number of the NIAMS is: Information Office, Building 31—Room 4C05, 9000 Rockville Pike, Bethesda, MD. 20892, telephone (301) 496-8188.

NATIONAL INSTITUTE OF MENTAL HEALTH

The National Institute of Mental Health (NIMH) is part of the Federal Government's Alcohol, Drug Abuse, and Mental Health Administration. The NIMH conducts and supports research to learn more about the causes, prevention, and treatment of mental and emotional illnesses.

Services provided by the NIMH include the following:

- NIMH-supported researchers in hospitals, universities, and mental health centers around the country are studying biological, genetic, psychological, social, and environmental factors related to mental health and mental illness.

- The Mental Disorders of the Aging Program specializes in research to learn how the aging process affects mental health and mental illness.

- The NIMH collects and distributes scientific and technical information related to mental illness, as well as educational materials for the general public.

Publications of the NIMH include *Useful Information on Alzheimer's Disease, Plain Talk About Aging, Plain Talk About Handling Stress*, and *If You're Over 65 and Feeling Depressed: Treatment Brings New Hope*. A complete list of publications is available on request from the NIMH, Information Resources and Inquiries Branch, Room 15C–05, 5600 Fishers Lane, Rockville, MD. 20857, telephone (301) 443-4513.

NATIONAL INSTITUTE OF NEUROLOGICAL DISORDERS AND STROKE

The National Institute of Neurological Disorders and Stroke (NINDS) is part of the National Institutes of Health and is the Federal Government's principal agency for research on the causes, prevention, detection, and treatment of neurological diseases and stroke.

Services provided by the NINDS include the following:

- NINDS-supported researchers in Bethesda, Maryland, and at medical centers around the country are studying stroke, head and spinal cord injuries, tumors of the central nervous system, and effective treatments for chronic headache and back pain.
- NINDS is investigating new methods of diagnosing and treating epilepsy.
- NINDS studies a number of neurological diseases, such as Alzheimer's disease, Parkinson's disease, Huntington's disease, multiple sclerosis, and amyotrophic lateral sclerosis (Lou Gehrig's disease).

Information on neurologic diseases and stroke is available to the general public and to health professionals. Free publications include *Medicine for the Layman: Brain in Aging and Dementia* and *Fact Sheet: Smell and Taste Disorders*. The *Hope Through Research* series includes publications on stroke, Parkinson's disease, hearing loss, the dementias, chronic pain, dizziness, shingles, headache, brain tumors, multiple sclerosis, and amyotrophic lateral sclerosis. A complete listing of publications is available on request.

The address and telephone number are: Information Office, Building 31—Room 8A06, 9000 Rockville Pike, Bethesda, MD. 20892, telephone (301) 496-5751.

NATIONAL PACIFIC/ASIAN RESOURCE CENTER ON AGING

The National Pacific/Asian Resource Center on Aging is a private organization that works to improve the delivery of health care and social services to older members of the Pacific/Asian community across the country.

To meet this goal, the NP/ARCOA provides the following services:

- Provides technical assistance to local Pacific/Asian community groups to enhance their ability to meet the needs of older people in this population.
- Conducts training programs and workshops for health care providers and social service professionals.
- Collects and distributes information about family and community support groups.
- Compiles statistics on the Pacific/Asian population.

Information is provided through publications: *Update* is published bimonthly. *The National Community Service Directory: Pacific/Asian Elderly* and other publications are available. A list of publications can be requested from the organization at: Melbourne Tower, Suite 914, 1511 Third Avenue, Seattle, WA. 98101, telephone (206) 624-1221.

ORGANIZATION OF CHINESE AMERICANS

The Organization of Chinese Americans (OCA) works to ensure equal opportunities for Americans of Chinese ancestry.

The services provided by the OCA include the following:

- The OCA encourages Chinese Americans to participate in civic affairs and works to foster positive images of Chinese and Asian Americans.
- The OCA advocates for Chinese and Asian groups at both state and federal levels, to ensure equal opportunities for this population in education and employment.
- The OCA sponsors community health fairs and supports housing programs for Chinese/Asian older people.

The OCA publishes the *OCA Image* quarterly. Additional information can be obtained through the OCA offices in Room 707, 1001 Connecticut Avenue, N.W., Washington, D.C. 20036, telephone (202) 223-5500.

PRIDE LONG-TERM HOME HEALTH CARE INSTITUTE

The Pride Institute is a private organization that works to coordinate research and policy development in the field of long-term home health care for older persons.

Services that are available through the Institute include the following:

- Technical assistance and training services are offered to organizations in the process of developing long-term home health care programs.
- The Institute develops policies and programs for agencies that provide long-term home health care services to older home-bound people.
- The Institute sponsors a number of conferences and exhibits on home health care issues.

Publications include the *Journal of Long-Term Home Health Care*, which is published quarterly.

The Institute's offices are located at 153 West 11th Street, New York, N.Y. 10011, telephone (212) 790-8864.

SELF-HELP FOR HARD OF HEARING PEOPLE, INC.

The Self-Help for Hard of Hearing People (SHHH) is a nonprofit, educational organization devoted to the welfare and interests of those who have hearing impairments.

Services provided by the SHHH include the following:

- Local SHHH groups offer people with hearing impairments support and encouragement, as well as information about community resources.

- Information is available about prevention of hearing loss and on the detection and treatment of hearing problems.

- Special programs for older people offer information about coping with hearing problems, hearing aids, and ways to communicate effectively.

- Professional education and workshops are available to those who provide health care to older people with hearing impairments. Conventions are held annually.

The SHHH publishes *SHHH, A Journal About Hearing Loss* six times a year. Other publications are available on speech reading, coping with hearing loss, and assertiveness training. A list of publications can be requested.

The offices of SHHH are located at 7800 Wisconsin Avenue, Bethesda, MD. 20814, telephone (301) 657-2248 (Voice), and (301) 657-2249 (TDD).

VISITING NURSE ASSOCIATIONS OF AMERICA

Visiting Nurse Associations (VNAs) are community-based and supported nonprofit home health care providers, governed by voluntary boards of directors. The mission of the Visiting Nurse Associations is to provide quality care to all people, regardless of their ability to pay.

The services available through VNAs include the following:

- Provide home health care to patients of all ages in both rural areas and major cities.

- Offer personal care; physical, speech, and occupational therapy; social services; and nutritional counseling.

- Operate adult day care centers, wellness clinics, hospices, and meals-on-wheels programs.

A fact sheet about the Visiting Nurse Associations is available on request.

The headquarters are located in Suite 900, 3801 East Florida, Denver, CO. 80218, telephone (303) 753-0218. A toll-free information service number is: 1-800-426-2547.

VOLUNTEERS OF AMERICA

The Volunteers of America (VOA) is a nonprofit organization that offers programs and services to meet the specific needs of a local community. Social services are provided to young people, older persons, families, persons with disabilities, alcoholics, and others.

The services provided by VOA include the following:

- Provides child care centers, adolescent group homes, senior centers, rehabilitation centers for alcoholics, community-based support groups for people with disabilities, and apartments for older people.

- Offers programs specifically for older people such as home repair services, homemaker assistance, meals-on-wheels, and transportation services.
- Sponsors foster grandparent and senior volunteer programs, and offers adult day care, group homes for older people, and nursing home care.

The VOA publishes the *Volunteers Gazette* quarterly.

For additional information, contact the VOA offices at 3813 North Causeway Boulevard, Metairie, LA. 70002, telephone (504) 837-2652.

Appendix B:
Entry List by Topic

Abuse
Abuse of the Elderly: Kinds of Abuse
Abuse of the Elderly: Mistreatment, Assessment, and Intervention

Access to Care
African-Americans and Health Care
Home Health Care: Supportive Services
Minority Issues: A Social Work Perspective

Accidents
Accidents: Environmental Hazards
Emergency Medical Care
Preventive Care and Health Maintenance

Addiction
Alcohol and Drugs: Misuse and Dependence
Pain Control: Drug Regimens in Cancer

ADLs
Assessment (Functional)
Assistive Technology
Assistive Technology Devices

Administration
Administration of Home Care Services
Classification of Patients and the Prospective Payment System
Classification Systems of Patient

Adult Day Care
Alzheimer's Disease: Diagnosis and Care

African-Americans
African-Americans and Health Care
Minority Issues: A Social Work Perspective

AIDS
AIDS and the Elderly

Alcohol
Alcohol and Drugs: Misuse and Dependence
Medication History Intake

Allergy
Medication History Intake

Alzheimer's Disease
Alzheimer's Disease: Diagnosis and Care
Alzheimer's Disease: Eating Behaviors
Alzheimer's Disease: Social Work Intervention
Alzheimer's Disease: Wandering Behaviors

American Indians
American Indians

Amputation
Amputee Rehabilitation

Anticoagulation
Anticoagulation Therapy (Oral) and Monitoring
Stroke

Arthritis
Arthritis

Assessment
Alcohol and Drugs: Misuse and Dependence
Assessment (Functional)
Dementia and Urinary Incontinence
Discharge Planning
Gynecologic Problems
Hope in the Elderly: Clinical Assessment
Medication History Intake
Parkinson's Disease
Physical Therapy and Physical Agents in the Home
Preventive Care and Health Maintenance
Psychological and Psychiatric Disorders and the Elderly

Stroke
Suicide in the Elderly
Technology (High) in the Home

Assistive Technology
Assistive Technology
Assistive Technology Devices

Bereavement
Depression and Late-Life Bereavement
Suicide in the Elderly

Cancer
Cancer Patient Care
Gastrointestinal Problems
Pain Control: Drug Regimens in Cancer
Preventive Care and Health Maintenance

Cardiac Disease
Cardiac Patient Care

Care Coordination
Care Coordination: Case Management
Care Coordination: Social Work Perspective
Home Health Care: Supportive Services

Caregivers, Caregiving
Alzheimer's Disease: Diagnosis and Care
Alzheimer's Disease: Social Work Intervention
Caregivers (Family)
Caregiving (Informal)
Caregiving (Informal): Financing Issues
Caregiving: Obtaining Meaning Through
Cognitively Impaired Elders and Family Care
Dementia and Behavioral Management
Dementia and Urinary Incontinence
Hispanic Informal Support Systems
Hispanic Informal Support Systems: A Research Study
Hospice Care
Living at Home/Block Nurse Program
Technology (High) in the Home
Technology (Low) in the Home

Case Management
Care Coordination: Case Management

Cholesterol
Cholesterol Management

Classification Systems
Classification of Patients Systems
Classification of Patients Systems and the Prospective Payment System
Home Health Care: Public Policy Issues

Cognition
Cognitively Impaired Elders and Family Care
Dementia and Behavioral Management

Communication
Alzheimer's Disease: Social Work Intervention
Communicating With the Elderly

Community
Ethnicity and Variations in Family Support and Caregiving
Living at Home/Block Nurse Program

Compliance
Anticoagulation Therapy (Oral) and Monitoring
Prescriptions and Frail Elderly in the Home

Computers
Computers and Home Health Care

Cost
Administration of Home Care Services
Caregiving (Informal): Financing Issues
Diabetes Mellitus
Health Services Utilization Among the Elderly

Crime
Abuse of the Elderly: Kinds of Abuse
Abuse of the Elderly: Mistreatment, Assessment, and Intervention

Cross-Cultural
American Indians
Ethnicity and Home Care
Ethnicity and Variations in Family Support and Caregiving
Hispanic Informal Support Systems
Minority Issues: A Social Work Perspective
Rural Anglo-Americans

Dementia
AIDS and the Elderly
Alzheimer's Disease: Social Work Intervention
Alzheimer's Disease: Wandering Behaviors
Dementia and Behavioral Management
Dementia and Urinary Incontinence

Dental
Gastrointestinal Problems
Preventive Care and Health Maintenance

Dependency
Alcohol and Drugs: Misuse and Dependence
Family Relationships in Later Life

Depression
Depression and Late-Life Bereavement
Gastrointestinal Problems
Psychological and Psychiatric Disorders and the Elderly
Suicide in the Elderly

Diabetes Mellitus
Diabetes Mellitus
Diabetic Foot Problems: Prevention and Care
Prescriptions and Frail Elderly in the Home

Diagnosis Related Groups
Administration of Home Care Services

Diet
Anticoagulation Therapy (Oral) and Monitoring
Cholesterol Management
Diabetes Mellitus
Preventive Care and Health Maintenance

Disability
Amputee Rehabilitation
Arthritis
Cognitively Impaired Elders and Family Care

Discharge Planning
Discharge Planning

Drug Abuse
Alcohol and Drugs: Misuse and Dependence

Drug Interaction
Alcohol and Drugs: Misuse and Dependence
Medication History Intake
Prescriptions and the Frail Elderly in the Home
Preventive Care and Health Maintenance

Eating Disorders
Alzheimer's Disease: Eating Behaviors

Education
Cardiac Patient Care

Emergency Care
Emergency Medical Care

Entitlement
Home Care Policy
Home Health Care: Public Policy Issues
Medicare, Medicaid, Other Federal Programs

Environment
Accidents: Environmental Hazards
Alzheimer's Disease: Wandering Behaviors
Dementia and Urinary Incontinence
Emergency Medical Care
Technology (High) in the Home

Ethics
Ethics in Health Care

Ethnicity
Ethnicity and Home Care
Ethnicity as a Policy Issue
Ethnicity and Variations in Family Support and Caregiving
Minority Issues: A Social Work Perspective

Euthanasia
Ethics in Health Care

Exercise
Cholesterol Management
Preventive Care and Health Maintenance

Falls
Accidents: Environmental Hazards
Emergency Medical Care

Family
Caregivers (Family)
Caregivers (Family): Economic Supports
Caregiving (Informal): Financing Issues
Cognitively Impaired Elders and Family Care
Ethnicity and Home Care
Ethnicity and Variations in Family Support and Caregiving
Family Relationships in Later Life
Hispanic Informal Support Systems

Hospice Care
Nursing Home Placement
Retirement Attitudes and Adaptation

Federal Expenditures
Home Care Policy
Medicare, Medicaid, and Other Federal Programs

Financial Planning
Expenditure Patterns of the Elderly

Financing
Alzheimer's Disease: Diagnosis and Care
Caregiving (Informal): Financing Issues
Classification Systems of Patients
Health Services Utilization Among the Elderly
Home Care Policy
Home Care Use: Predictors
Home Health Care: Supportive Services
Living at Home/Block Nurse Program
Pet Therapy
Technology (High) in the Home

Frail Elderly
Emergency Medical Care
Prescriptions and the Frail Elderly in the Home

Functional Status
Assessment (Functional)
Dementia and Urinary Incontinence
Preventive Care and Health Maintenance

Gastrointestinal
Gastrointestinal Problems

Gender
Ethnicity and Home Care
Ethnicity and Variations in Family Support and Caregiving
Family Relationships in Later Life
Gender Issues in Health Care
Hispanic Informal Support Systems

Gynecology
Gynecologic Problems

Health Care
Home Health Care: National Trends

Health Care Providers
Administration of Home Care Services
Gerontological Nurse Practitioners

Health Maintenance
Preventive Care and Health Maintenance

Health Problems
Cancer Patient Care
Cardiac Patient Care
Cholesterol Management
Diabetes Mellitus
Diabetic Foot Problems: Prevention and Care
Gastrointestinal Problems
Gynecologic Problems
Osteoporosis
Parkinson's Disease
Polymyalgia Rheumatica
Stroke
Temporal Arteritis
Thyroid Gland Problems

Health Promotion
Cardiac Patient Care
Preventive Care and Health Maintenance

Hearing Impairment
Hearing Impairment

Hispanics
Hispanic Informal Support Systems
Hispanic Informal Support Systems: A Research Study

Homemaker Services
Administration of Home Care Services

Home Health Aides
Administration of Home Care Services

Hope
Hope in the Elderly: Clinical Assessment

Hospice
Administration of Home Care Services
Cancer Patient Care
Hospice Care

Measurement
Health Services Utilization Among the Elderly
Home Care Use: Predictors
Home Health Care: National Trends

Medicaid
Administration of Home Care Services
Home Care Policy
Medicare, Medicaid, and Other Federal Programs

Medicare
Administration of Home Care Services
Home Care Policy
Medicare, Medicaid, and Other Federal Programs

Medication History
Medication History Intake

Medications
Pain Control: Drug Regimens in Cancer
Prescriptions and the Frail Elderly in the Home

Mental Health
AIDS and the Elderly
Amputee Rehabilitation
Dementia and Behavioral Management
Gastrointestinal Problems
Hope in the Elderly: Clinical Assessment
Psychological and Psychiatric Disorders and the Elderly
Retirement Attitudes and Adaptation
Suicide in the Elderly

Metabolic Problems
Diabetes Mellitus
Thyroid Gland Problems

Minority Issues
African-Americans and Health Care
Minority Issues: A Social Work Perspective

Models of Care
Classification of Patients Systems
Classification of Patients Systems and Prospective Payment System
Home Health Care: Supportive Services
Living at Home/Block Nurse Program

Models of Use
Health Services Utilization Among the Elderly

Medication History Intake
Prescriptions and the Frail Elderly in the Home

Predictors
Health Services Utilization Among the Elderly
Predictors of Home Care Use

Prejudice
African-Americans and Health Care
Minority Issues: A Social Work Perspective

Prevention
Cardiac Patient Care
Preventive Care and Health Maintenance
Skin Care

Prospective Payment System
Classification of Patient Systems and Prospective Payment System

Public Policy
Home Care Policy
Home Health Care: Public Policy Issues
Home Health Care: Supportive Services
Minority Issues: A Social Work Perspective

Quality Assurance
Administration of Home Care Services
Classification Systems of Patients
Home Health Care: Public Policy Issues
Technology (High) in the Home

Quality of Life
Diabetes Mellitus
Hospice Care
Living at Home/Block Nurse Program
Retirement Attitudes and Adaptation

Rehabilitation
Amputee Rehabilitation
Stroke

Reimbursement
Administration of Home Care Services
Caregiving (Informal): Financing Issues
Home Health Care: Public Policy Issues

Relationships
Family Relationships in Later Life

Research
American Indians
Caregivers (Family)
Cognitively Impaired Elders and Family Care
Expenditure Patterns of the Elderly
Hispanic Informal Support Systems: A Research Study
Nursing Home Placement
Rural Anglo-Americans

Resources
Caregivers (Family): Economic Supports
Caregiving (Informal): Financing Issues
Hispanic Informal Support Systems

Retirement
Retirement Attitudes and Adaptation

Rural Elderly
Rural Anglo-Americans

Skin Care
Diabetic Foot Disease: Prevention and Care
Skin Care

Sleep Patterns
Alzheimer's Disease: Wandering Behaviors

Smoking
Alcohol and Drugs: Misuse and Dependence

Social Work
Alzheimer's Disease: Social Work Intervention
Care Coordination: A Social Work Perspective
Visually Impaired Older Adults: Social Services

Socioeconomic Status
African-Americans and Health Care
Family Relationships in Later Life
Retirement Attitudes and Adaptation

Standards
Administration of Home Care Services
Gerontological Nurse Practitioners
Home Health Care: Public Policy Issues

Stress
Caregiving (Informal)
Hope in the Elderly: Clinical Assessment

Stroke
Anticoagulation Therapy (Oral) and Monitoring
Emergency Medical Care
Stroke

Substance Abuse
Alcohol and Drugs: Misuse and Dependence

Suicide
Suicide in the Elderly

Support Systems—Formal
Administration of Home Care Services
Home Health Care: Supportive Services

Support Systems—Informal
Alzheimer's Disease: Diagnosis and Care
Caregivers (Family)
Caregivers (Family): Economic Support
Caregiving (Informal)
Caregiving (Informal): Financing Issues
Ethnicity and Variations in Family Support and Caregiving
Hispanic Informal Support Systems

Technology
Assistive Technology
Assistive Technology Devices
Computers and Home Health Care
Technology (High) in the Home
Technology (Low) in the Home

Temporal Arteritis
Temporal Arteritis

Terminal Illness
Administration of Home Care Services
Cancer Patient Care
Hospice Care
Pain Control: Drug Regimens in Cancer

Therapists
Administration of Health Care Services
Assistive Technology
Physical Therapy and Physical Agents in the Home

Thyroid Problems
Thyroid Gland Diseases

Urinary Incontinence
Dementia and Urinary Incontinence
Urinary Incontinence

Utilization
Ethnicity and Variations in Family Support and Caregiving
Health Services Utilization Among the Elderly
Home Care Use: Predictors
Home Health Care: National Trends

Victimization
(see **Abuse**)

Vision
Vision Impairment
Visually Impaired Older Adults: Social Services

Volunteers
Living at Home/Block Nurse Program
Parish Nurse

Wandering
Alzheimer's Disease: Wandering Behaviors

Widowhood
Depression and Late-Life Bereavement
Suicide in the Elderly

Women
Caregiving (Informal)
Dementia and Behavioral Management
Ethnicity and Variations in Family Support and Caregiving
Gender Issues in Health Care

Index

414

About the Contributors

ERIC G. ANDERSON, MD is a charter diplomate of the American Board of Family Practice. He is a senior contributing editor at *Physicians Management*, a contributing writer at *Postgraduate Medicine*, and a columnist at *Geriatrics*. Semi-retired and now working part-time for a large medical group in San Diego, he writes regularly for a national medical press on socioeconomics.

SUSAN E. APPLING, MS, RN, CRNP has, for the last 10 years, been a full-time faculty member at the Johns Hopkins University School of Nursing and currently practices as an adult nurse practitioner in the Breast Lesion Evaluation Program. She is Chairperson of the Legislative Committee of the Nurse Practitioner Association of Maryland, Inc., and has received a national publishing award for co-authoring a series of physical assessment articles for a major nursing journal.

DAVID E. BIEGEL, PhD is the Henry L. Zucker Professor of Social Work Practice and Professor of Sociology, Mandel School of Applied Social Sciences, Case Western Reserve University. Currently, he also serves as Co-Director of the Center for Practice Innovations and the Cuyahoga County Community Mental Health Research Institute at the Mandel School. Dr. Biegel's books include: *Family Caregiving Across the Lifespan*, *Family Caregiving in Chronic Illness: Alzheimer's Disease, Cancer, Heart Disease, Mental Illness and Stroke*, *Family Preservation Services: Research and Evaluation*, and *Aging and Caregiving: Theory, Research, and Policy*.

SUSAN BLUMENFIELD, DSW is Director of the Department of Social Work Services at Mount Sinai Medical Center, Associate Director in Clinical Operations in the Mount Sinai Hospital, and Associate Professor in Community Medicine in the Mount Sinai School of Medicine.

LYNN BORGATTA, MD, MPH is the Medical Director of Planned Parenthood of

Westchester/Rockland, Inc. and Associate Professor of Clinical Obstetrics and Gynecology, New York Medical College.

LAURENCE G. BRANCH, PhD is Director of Long-term Care Research for Abt Associates Inc. in Cambridge, Mass., holds a professorial appointment at Boston University School of Medicine, and is Director of the Massachusetts Health Care Panel Study. Dr. Branch contributes regularly to health policy journals and has authored over 100 articles in peer-reviewed journals and over 40 chapters and monographs. He is currently co-editor of the *Journal of Aging and Health* and is on the editorial board of *The Gerontologist*. Dr. Branch is also responsible for the evaluation of the On Lok replications.

CLAUDIA BROWN, OTR, MS is an Occupational Therapy Rehabilitation member of the Rehabilitation Medicine Service, Vancouver Division, Veterans Affairs Medical Center in Portland, Oreg.

PAMELA C. BUNCHER, RN, FNP has worked as a hospice home care nurse and hospice clinical specialist. Her research focuses on topics pertaining to ambulatory care and health maintenance activities.

ROBERT N. BUTLER, MD has been Brookdale Professor and Chairman of the Department of Geriatrics and Adult Development of Mount Sinai Medical Center in New York City since 1982. A prolific writer, he won the Pulitzer Prize in 1976 for his book *Why Survive? Being Old in America.* He is a member of the Institute of Medicine of the National Academy of Sciences, a founding Fellow of the American Geriatrics Society, and has served as a consultant to the United States Senate Special Committee on Aging, the National Institute of Mental Health, Commonwealth Fund, and numerous other organizations. He is editor-in-chief of the journal *Geriatrics.*

KAM-FONG MONIT CHEUNG, MA, MSW, PhD is Associate Professor and Chairperson of the Children and Families Concentration at the Graduate School of Social Work at the University of Houston, Texas. She has published extensively in gerontology and social work journals.

YEATES CONWELL, MD is Associate Professor of Psychology and Oncology at the University of Rochester School of Medicine. As Director of the Department of Psychiatry's Laboratory of Suicide Studies, he coordinates multidisciplinary research.

DONNA M. COX, PhD is currently Project Coordinator for The Long-Term Care Project, jointly conducted by faculty from the University of Maryland at Baltimore and the Johns Hopkins University.

NEAL E. CUTLER, PhD directs the Boettner Institute's multidisciplinary research program in Financial Gerontology, University of Pennsylvania. He is a Fellow of the Gerontological Society of America (GSA), a member of the GSA Finance Committee, and a member of the GSA Economics of Aging Special Interest Group. He serves on the Board of Directors of the American Society on Aging, the National Institute of Financial Services for the Elderly, and SeniorNet. He is also a member of the Editorial Boards of *Aging and Health, Aging Today,* and *American Journal of Alzheimer's Care and Research.*

EMILIE M. DEADY, MSN, RN has served as the CEO of the Visiting Nurse Association of Northern Virginia since 1978. In 1984 she was named President of the newly established parent corporation, Visiting Nurse Home Care. She is also CEO of two other subsidiary corporations, Alpha Home Care and VNA Community Hospice. Ms. Deady is a member of many community health organizations in Arlington, Alexandria, and Fairfax, Va., including the Executive Committee of the Hospital Council of National Capital Area, National Association for Home Care, Visiting Nurse Associations of America, the American Public Health Association and is past president and board member of the Virginia Association of Home Care. She was named Washington's Woman of the Year and is listed in *Who's Who in American Nursing*. She has published widely in the area of community-based and home care nursing, including a chapter "Changes in Medicare Reporting: Its Impact on a Home Health Agency" in *Nursing Administration in Complex Organizations*.

ANNE MARIE DJUPE, MA, RNC serves as Director of Parish Nursing Services at Lutheran General HealthSystem [sic]. She has been a consultant to the development of parish nursing since its inception. The Parish Nursing Services is funded by a W.K. Kellogg Foundation grant, of which she is Project Director. She is co-editor and contributing author of *Parish Nursing: The Developing Practice*, co-author of *Reaching Out: Parish Nursing Services, Looking Back: The Parish Nurse Experience* and a white paper, "Expanding Our Understanding of Health and Well-Being: The Parish Nurse Program."

SANDRA ENGBERG, PhD, CRNP is a faculty member at the University of Pittsburgh School of Nursing, teaches in the family nurse practitioner program, and maintains clinical practice at the Continence Clinic of the Benedum Geriatric Center. She is currently the Co-Principal Investigator on a federally funded study examining the treatment of urinary incontinence in homebound, older adults.

JEFFREY E. ESCHER, MD is Associate Professor of Clinical Medicine at the New York Medical College and Westchester County Medical Center, where he is Director of Outpatient Geriatric Assessment, Director of Clinics within the Division of Geriatrics, and Director of the Geriatrics Consultation Service. Dr. Escher also serves as Track Director of the Programs in Gerontology of the Graduate School of Health Sciences of New York Medical College. He is Fellow of the Gerontological Society of America and currently serves as Chair of the Special Committee on geriatrics of the New York County Medical Society and Vice-President of the NY-Metropolitan Area Geriatrics Society.

CAROL J. FARRAN, DNSc is Associate Professor, Department of Psychiatric Nursing, Rush Alzheimer's Disease Center and Center for Research on Health and Aging at Rush-Presbyterian-St. Luke's Medical Center, Chicago. She has published research in *The Gerontologist, American Journal of Alzheimer's Care and Research, Western Journal of Nursing Research, Archives of Psychiatric Nursing, Journal of Psychosocial Nursing, Issues in Mental Health Nursing*, and *Clinical Nursing Research*, and she is a co-author of *Hope and Hopelessness*.

JOHN FEATHER, PhD is Clinical Associate Professor in the Department of Medicine and Executive Director of the Primary Care Resource Center in the SUNY Buffalo School of Medicine and Biomedical Sciences. He is also Director of the Western New York Geriatric Education Center, SUNY Buffalo.

JUDITH A. FEUSTLE, ScD, RN is currently Director of Nursing Education at the Union Memorial Hospital and Chairperson of the Nursing Division at Villa Julie College in Baltimore, Md.

DOROTHY J. FISHMAN, EdD, RN, FAAN is currently on the editorial board of *Computers in Nursing*, Project Manager of the Physician Office Network, Clinical Instructor in Patient Care Information Systems, Baystate Health Systems, and a consultant to health care institutions in the area of informatics. Her book, *Nursing in the 1990s*, is a best seller. Dr. Fishman is also the author of three interactive videodisc programs on nursing education that was funded under a Special Projects grant and numerous articles on journals such as *Computers in Nursing*.

WALTER B. FORMAN, MD, FACP is currently the Associate Chief of Staff for Geriatrics and Extended Care at the Albuquerque Veterans Medical Center and Associate Professor in the geriatric division at the University of New Mexico. He has been in private practice in Oncology and an active member of several cancer cooperative treatment groups.

TERRY FULMER, PhD, RN, FAAN is the Anna C. Maxwell Professor in Clinical Research and Associate Dean for Research at the Columbia University School of Nursing. She co-authored *Inadequate Care of the Elderly: Health Care Perspective on Abuse and Neglect*, which received the American Journal Nursing Book of the Year Award in 1987 and recently co-authored *Critical Care Nursing of the Elderly*. Dr. Fulmer is a Fellow of the American Academy of Nursing, Fellow of the Gerontological Society of America, and Distinguished Practitioner of the National Academies of Practice.

STEVEN R. GAMBERT, MD is Professor of Medicine and Acting Chairman of the Department of Medicine at New York Medical College where he is also Associate Dean for Academic Programs. He was elected President of the American Aging Association; Chairman, Geriatrics Section, New York Academy of Medicine; Chairman and Secretary, Clinical Medicine Section, Gerontological Society of America; and is a Fellow of the American Geriatrics Society, Gerontological Society of America, and American College of Physicians. He has authored and co-authored over 300 journal articles, book chapters, and research reports.

DONALD E. GELFAND, PhD is a Professor at the Institute of Gerontology and Department of Sociology at Wayne State University.

MINDY S. GELLIN, BSN, RNC is Past Coordinator of Animal-Assisted Therapy Program for Mid-Community Services, Inc. Currently, she is a full-time homemaker and mother of two young sons.

MARION ZUCKER GOLDSTEIN, MD is Clinical Associate Professor, SUNY Buffalo School of Medicine and Biomedical Sciences, Department of Psychiatry; Director, Division of Geriatric Psychiatry; and Unit Chief, Geriatric Psychiatry, Erie County Medical Center. Currently, she is the Principal Investigator of a National Institute of Mental Health grant, "Neuropsychiatric Disorders in the Elderly Undergoing Surgery." She is Guest Editor of *Practical Geriatrics in Psychiatric Services* and Assistant Editor of the *American Journal of Geriatric Psychiatry*. She is Chair of the Task Force on Models of Practice in Geriatric Psychiatry.

KRISHAN L. GUPTA, MD, FACP is currently Professor of Clinical Medicine at New York Medical College and Chief of Medical Services at Ruth Taylor Geriatric and Rehabilitation Institute, Westchester County Medical Center. He is the author or co-author of over 15 books and book chapters and contributes papers regularly to medical and scientific journals. He is a Fellow of the New York Academy of Medicine, the American College of Physicians, and the Royal College of Physicians (Ed.).

ROBERT W. HAMILL, MD is Professor and Chair of Neurology at the University of Vermont College of Medicine, and Chief of Neurology at the Medical Center Hospital of Vermont in Burlington.

JANE HARLEY, MSN, RN, CFNP is a certified diabetes educator and is employed in women's health.

MARILYN D. HARRIS, MSN, RN, CNAA, FAAN currently is Executive Director of the Visiting Nurse Association of Eastern Montgomery County/Department of Abington Memorial Hospital, Willow Grove, Pa. She also is Adjunct Lecturer at the University of Pennsylvania School of Nursing. Her articles have appeared in *Nursing & Health Care*, *Journal of Maternal-Child Nursing*, *Home HealthCare Nurse* [sic], *Caring*, and *Journal of Nursing Administration*. She has been editor of three books: *Home Health Administration*, *Home Health Agency Policy Manual*, and *Handbook of Home Health Care Administration*.

LAURIE RUSSELL HATCH, PhD is Associate Professor in the Department of Sociology and a Faculty Associate with the Sanders-Brown Center on Aging at the University of Kentucky. She currently is writing a book on gender and aging.

MARJORIE K. JAMIESON, MS, RN, FAAN, a nurse executive, was among six women in her community who designed and implemented the Block Nurse Program, now merged with the Living at Home/Block Nurse Program for her neighbors. She volunteered as Director of Services and was the first Chairperson of the Board.

EILEEN M. JOHNSON, MS, RN, CS is a research nurse for the Rochester Alzheimer's Disease Center, a project funded by the National Institute on Aging, and a nurse clinician for the Geriatric Neurology and Psychiatry Clinic at Monroe Community Hospital in Rochester, N.Y.

CAROL L. JOSEPH, MD is currently the Director of Extended Care Services, Gerontology Section, and Medical Director of the Adult Day Health Care and the Geriatric Substance Abuse Programs at the Portland Veterans Affairs Medical Center. She also is Assistant Professor of Medicine, Oregon Health Sciences University in Portland.

KATHERINE K. KATSOYANNIS, MD is the Medical Director of the New Rochelle Nursing Home and is a member of the Attending Faculty at New Rochelle Hospital Medical Center.

PATRICIA J. KOLB, PhD is currently Housing and Education Coordinator in the Social Service Department at Jewish Home and Hospital for Aged in New York City; Adjunct Instructor of Sociology at College of Mount St. Vincent, Bronx; and Adjunct Assistant Professor at Columbia University School of Social Work. She is also a Fellow at the Hunter College Brookdale Center on Aging.

KARL KOSLOSKI, PhD is Associate Professor of Gerontology at the University of Nebraska, Omaha.

JOY C. LOBENSTINE is the Associate Director for Membership and Information of the Association for Gerontology in Higher Education. She is the editor of the *National Di-*

rectory of Educational Programs in Gerontology and Geriatrics, 6th ed., Project Director for an AARP Andrus Foundation grant, and the operator of the National Database on Gerontology in Higher Education. Her other publications include *Sources of Information about Fellowships in Gerontology and Geriatrics*.

DIRK LUCAS, PharmD is Assistant Professor of Pharmacy Practice in the College of Pharmacy, University of Houston. He is developing the Center for Pharmaceutical Care for the Elderly at the University of Houston.

MARY E. MCCARTHY, MS, RN is the director of Adult Day Health Care at St. Ann's Home and an adjunct faculty member at St. John Fisher College in Rochester, NY. She is currently an Alzheimer's Association family support group facilitator, and a member of its Family Education and Providers' Network committees. She also is a member of Sigma Theta Tau National Nursing Honor Society.

ROSE MCCLEARY, ASCW, BCSW is currently in the ABD phase of her doctoral studies on Social Work and is Research Assistant at the Tulane School of Social Work, with the Tulane Center for Aging, Research, and Education.

PHILIP W. MCCLURE, MS, PT, OCS is currently a doctoral candidate in Biomedical Science and Assistant Professor, Department of Orthopedic Surgery & Rehabilitation at Hahnemann University, Philadelphia.

B. JOAN MCDOWELL, PhD, CRNP, FAAN is Associate Professor of Nursing at the University of Pittsburgh. Currently she is the principal investigator for a National Institute of Nursing Research funded study of "Behavioral Treatment of Urinary Incontinence in Homebound Elderly." Dr. McDowell is also the director of the Continence Program at the Benedum Geriatric Center, University of Pittsburgh School of Medicine. She has recently published articles in the *Journal of the American Geriatrics Society*.

MARY LYNN MCPHERSON, PharmD, BCPS, CDE is Assistant Professor at the University of Maryland School of Pharmacy. Dr. McPherson maintains a practice in home health care, hospice, home infusion therapy, and ambulatory care. She is author of several books, book chapters, and numerous articles.

IRENE MOORE, ACSW, LISW is Assistant Professor in the Department of Family Medicine at the University of Cincinnati where she is Director of the Geriatric Evaluation Center, Director of the Memory Assessment Center, and Associate Administrator for the Geriatric Medicine Fellowship Program. She was recently appointed a panel member for the Agency for Health Care Policy and Research, and a member of the Panel on Recognition and Initial Assessment of Alzheimer's and Related Dementia.

MADELINE A. NAEGLE, PhD, RN, FAAN is Associate Professor, Division of Nursing, School of Education, New York University. Dr. Naegle is widely known for her writing on substance abuse education.

MARGUERITE CONRAD NICKEL, BSN is a facilitator for an Alzheimer's support group and lectures to professionals and community groups about caregiver stress and managing difficult behavior.

SUE E. NICKOLEY, MS, RN is a Clinical Nurse Specialist in Gerontology at Monroe Community Hospital in Rochester, N.Y.

MARCIA G. ORY, PhD, MPH is Chief, Social Science Research on Aging, Behavioral and Social Research Program, National Institute on Aging, National Institutes of Health, Bethesda, Md. Dr. Ory is active in professional organizations and serves on several national task forces and advisory boards dealing with aging and health issues.

RONALD J. OZMINKOWSKI, PhD is a Senior Health Economist at Abt Associates Inc.

JOAN A. PANCHAL, RN, PhD is Assistant Professor of Nursing at Pennsylvania State University, University Park, Pa.

MARY A. PATERSON, PhD, RN is Assistant Professor of Health Care Administration at the University of Nevada, Las Vegas. She has published in such journals as *Family and Community Health*, *Cambridge Quarterly of Health Care Ethics*, and *Journal of Allied Health*.

ANNE GRISWOLD PEIRCE, RN, PhD is the Director of Doctoral Studies in the School of Nursing at Columbia University, New York City.

GRETCHEN PENA, BA received her undergraduate education in Religious Studies and is currently a Ministerial candidate at the Unity School of Religious Studies Ministerial Education Program.

ANNA MARIA PLICHTA, MD is currently Assistant Professor of Medicine at New York Medical College (NYMC) and Medical Director of the Ruth Taylor Geriatric and Rehabilitation Institute (RTI), affiliated with NYMC and part of the Westchester County Medical Center.

LINDA J. REDFORD, PhD, RN is Director of the National Resource Center on Rural Long-Term Care and a Senior Research Associate with the Center on Aging at the University of Kansas Medical Center (KUMC). She is Adjunct Professor in the School of Nursing at KUMC and recently completed a National Kellogg Fellowship. She serves as a consultant to several state agencies and federal grant programs involved in health and long-term care projects.

THOMAS A. REINER, PhD is Professor of Regional Science and City & Regional Planning at the University of Pennsylvania.

KAREN L. RICE, MA is Chair of the Research Committee for Alzheimer's Disease and Caregiver Stress, the American Sociological Association, and Convener of Alzheimer's Disease Research, the Gerontological Society of America.

BARBARA E. RILEY, BS, MST is a Kinesiotherapist at the Nursing Home Care Unit, Department of Veterans Affairs Medical Center in Portland, Oreg. She has been an instructor in Kinesiology and Adapted Physical Education for the Department of Health Studies at Portland State University since 1982 and lectures on geriatric topics at the Oregon Geriatric Education Center's Summer Institute and the Oregon Health Sciences University Allied Health Geriatric Education Project.

RICHARD J. ROCHE, MD is Assistant Professor in the Department of Internal Medicine, Division of Gerontology, at the University of New Mexico and serves as Director of the Geriatric Evaluation and Management Unit at the New Mexico Regional Federal Medical Center.

JOAN C. ROGERS, PhD, OTR is Professor of Occupational Therapy in the School of Health and Rehabilitation Sciences and Assistant Professor of Psychiatry in the School of Medicine, University of Pittsburgh. She provides clinical, educational, and research occupational therapy services for the Geriatric Psychiatry Module of Western Psychiatric Institute and Clinic. Dr. Rogers is a Fellow of the American Occupational Therapy Association/Foundation, a charter member of the Academy of Research, and an Eleanor Clarke Slagle Lecturer.

KENNETH M. SAKAUYE, MD is Professor of Clinical Psychiatry at Louisiana State University Medical School in New Orleans and Director of Geriatric Psychiatry for the Woldenberg Center for Gerontological Studies. He currently chairs the American Psychiatric Association's Committee on Minority Elderly that published *Ethnic Minority Elderly: A Task Force Report of the American Psychiatric Association.*

CARMEN D. SÁNCHEZ is Associate Professor at the Graduate School of Social Work, University of Puerto Rico. She has published two books in Social Work about the aged and several articles on American, European and Latin-American Journals and is a Fellow of the Brookdale Center on Aging and President of the Puerto Rican Gerontological Society.

BARRY M. SCHULTZ, MD, MS, FACP is Chief of the Division of Gerontology and Geriatric Medicine at The Long Island College Hospital in Brooklyn, New York, Assistant Professor of Medicine at the State University of New York Health Science Center at Brooklyn, research Fellow at the Wagner School's Health Research program, and the Principal Investigator of a study funded by the Robert Wood Johnson Foundation evaluating a new system of Medicaid long-term care reimbursement in New York state.

MARJORIE M. SCHWEITZER, PhD is Professor Emeritus in the Department of Sociology at Oklahoma State University. She is a charter member of the Association for Anthropology and Gerontology and was editor of the book *Anthropology of Aging: A Partially Annotated Bibliography* (Greenwood, 1991).

VIRGINIA L. SMERGLIA, MA is an Instructor in the Department of Sociology and the Honors College, and a Fellow of the Institute for Life-Span Development and Gerontology at the University of Akron.

ROBYN STONE, DrPH is currently Deputy Assistant Secretary for Disability, Aging and Long-Term Care Policy, Office of the Assistant Secretary for Planning and Evaluation, U.S. Department of Health and Human Services (DHHS). Dr. Stone was Chair of the White House Task Force on Health Care Reform's long-term care workgroup which developed the long-term care component of the Clinton Health Care Proposal.

MARK A. STRATTON, PharmD is Professor and Chair, Department of Clinical Science and Administration, College of Pharmacy, University of Houston. He is currently establishing a Center for Pharmaceutical Care of the Elderly at the University of Houston.

GAIL W. STUART, PhD, RN, CS, FAAN is Administrator of the Institute of Psychiatry at the Medical University of South Carolina where she is a Professor in the graduate program of the College of Nursing and an Associate Professor in the Department of

Psychiatry and Behavioral Sciences in the College of Medicine. In addition to her administrative activities, she developed the master's program in psychiatric nursing at the Medical University and is active in clinical practice and research activities in the Department of Psychiatry. She serves on national boards and represents nursing on a number of panels sponsored by the National Institute of Mental Health Care Policy and Research. Her numerous publications include *Principles and Practice of Psychiatric Nursing*.

DONALD E. STULL, PhD is Associate Professor of Sociology at the University of Akron. Dr. Stull is on the editorial board of *Research on Aging* and he is co-editor and contributing author of *Ethnic Elderly and Long-Term Care*.

JANE SWINTON, CSW is currently with the Family Outreach Program, Monroe Community Hospital, Rochester, N.Y. She has 13 years' experience in home health care, primarily in the area of Alzheimer's disease and hospice care.

DAVID R. THOMAS, MD, FACP is Associate Professor of Internal Medicine in the Division of Gerontology/Geriatric Medicine at the University of Alabama at Birmingham, and Scientist at the UAB Center for Aging in Birmingham. He is Medical Director of the Hospital-based Home Care Program in Birmingham and Attending Physician in the Kirklin Geriatric Assessment Clinic. He serves on the regional Long-term Care Task Force and the Jefferson County Omsbudman Committee and has been active in advocacy for older adults at the state level in North Carolina and Alabama. He is a member of the American Geriatrics Society, the Gerontological Society of America, the Alabama Gerontological Society, and a Fellow of the American College of Physicians.

KRISTIN VON NIEDA, PT, MEd is Assistant Professor and Academic Coordinator of Clinical Education, Programs in Physical Therapy, at the Hahnemann University in Philadelphia. She is Director of Rehabilitation Services at Thomas Jefferson University Hospital, and Consultant for Independence for Blue Cross. She practices as a physical therapist in the home care setting and at the Germantown Hospital and Medical Center. Currently, she teaches a course on the therapeutic use of heat, cold, compression, light, and water in rehabilitation.

MARK T. WAGNER, PhD is Assistant Professor at the Medical University of South Carolina and holds a dual appointment in the Department of Psychiatry and Behavioral Sciences, and the Department of Neurology. He is on the teaching faculty for the PhD psychology internship and post-doctoral training programs, the psychiatry residency training program, is a Research Preceptor for medical students and post-doctoral fellows, and is Director of Neuropsychological Services at the MUSC's Memory Disorders Clinic. He has written a number of peer-reviewed articles and book chapters focusing on neurocognitive and psychological aspects of neurologic diseases that afflict the elderly.

LORE K. WRIGHT, PhD, RN, CS is Associate Clinical Director of Geriatric Psychiatry at the Medical University of South Carolina, with joint appointments in the College of Medicine and the College of Nursing. For her work on Alzheimer's disease and marriage, Dr. Wright received the Outstanding New Investigator Award from the American Nurses' Association, Council of Nurse Researchers, and the D. Jean Wood Award for Nursing Scholarship from the Southern Nursing Research Society. She has published numerous articles in the field of aging and mental health and a book *Alzheimer's Disease and Marriage: An Intimate Account*.

SIDNEY ZISOOK, MD is Professor of Psychiatry at the University of California, San Diego School of Medicine and Director of Research and Training at the University of California, San Diego, Outpatient Psychiatric Clinic. Dr. Zisook is also a Fellow of the American Psychiatric Association and President of the West Coast College of Biological Psychiatry.